"Jonathan Hoglund's [...] with Scripture, respectful o[...] [...]ons and sensitive to the doctrine's complexities. [...] treatment of the effectual call's content is particularly insightful. This book calls each of us to hear again the Word of the triune God by the Spirit, that Jesus is our saving Lord."
Daniel J. Treier, Blanchard Professor of Theology, Wheaton College Graduate School

"Here are the new ground rules for how to think well about God's effectual call. The deep structure of conversion may remain a holy mystery, but this book rescues it from being a theological muddle or the source of needless conflict. Hoglund's approach to the triune God's rhetoric of salvation is exegetically clarifying, ecumenically helpful, and evangelistically useful. This is a deeply persuasive book about the deepest kind of persuasion."
Fred Sanders, Torrey Honors Institute, Biola University

"Evangelism and conversion are topics of perennial concern, perhaps especially in a post-Christian society. Given the significant contributions of anthropology and sociology to such areas of study in recent years, we need solid help in developing a robust theological account of spiritual change—one that is rooted in careful reading of God's Word. To that end, Jonathan Hoglund helps us listen carefully—patiently, attentively, and with the communion of saints—to what Holy Scripture might say regarding God's action in summoning us into his saving lordship. This volume models dogmatic thinking on the effectual call that is attentive to the shape of doctrinal debate through the centuries and around the globe and, for just that reason, is resolutely exegetical in its orientation to the questions at hand. Much wisdom can be found and much gain can be had in going to school with Hoglund."
Michael Allen, associate professor of systematic and historical theology, Reformed Theological Seminary, Orlando

"Jonathan Hoglund presents an exegetically rigorous and historically informed case for refining the church's understanding of the doctrine of effectual calling. He meticulously explores the various biblical metaphors that reveal the manner by which the triune God calls sinners to salvation. One need not agree with every conclusion in order to benefit from this provocative study. Anyone who seeks a deeper understanding of this wonderful doctrine should definitely consult this book with great profit."

J. V. Fesko, academic dean and professor of systematic and historical theology, Westminster Seminary California

"Hoglund's work on the divine call is an elegant and richly informed study of the doctrine. He mines biblical exegesis, historical theology, and systematics in this profound work. At the same time, he construes God's call in terms of divine rhetoric. Hoglund's work represents an excellent example of theological interpretation that marries biblical exegesis and systematic reflection."

Thomas R. Schreiner, James Buchanan Harrison Professor of New Testament Interpretation, associate dean, The Southern Baptist Theological Seminary, Louisville, Kentucky

"How does God work on human hearts to convert what is initially darkened, hard, and implacably resistant to the truth of the gospel into something that rejoices in and welcomes it? If being born again is less an impersonal causal effect than an effectual personal call, how are we to understand the latter? Hoglund here provides what is to date the best response to these important and long-standing questions, making fresh proposals about the agent and content of the call as well as its peculiar efficacy. I especially appreciated the combination of serious exegetical analysis coupled with rigorous dogmatic reflection. This is theological interpretation of Scripture at its best."

Kevin J. Vanhoozer, research professor of systematic theology, Trinity Evangelical Divinity School

"Jonathan Hoglund's book on effectual calling is very welcome for three reasons. First, it tackles a theological issue that has been relatively neglected in recent study. Second, it is a model of theological method, combining effectively careful exegesis of the Scriptures, insights from the history of discussion, and doctrinal considerations. Finally, the focus on divine speech provides a way to affirm God's initiative in the call to salvation without obscuring the personal relationships between Creator and created."

Douglas J. Moo, Wessner Chair of Biblical Studies, Wheaton College, chair, Committee on Bible Translation

CALLED *by* TRIUNE GRACE

Divine Rhetoric and the Effectual Call

◆◆◆◆◆◆◆◆◆◆◆◆◆◆◆◆◆◆◆◆◆◆◆

Jonathan Hoglund

An imprint of InterVarsity Press
Downers Grove, Illinois

InterVarsity Press
P.O. Box 1400, Downers Grove, IL 60515-1426
ivpress.com
email@ivpress.com

©2016 by Jonathan Hoglund

All rights reserved. No part of this book may be reproduced in any form without written permission from InterVarsity Press.

InterVarsity Press® is the book-publishing division of InterVarsity Christian Fellowship/USA®, a movement of students and faculty active on campus at hundreds of universities, colleges and schools of nursing in the United States of America, and a member movement of the International Fellowship of Evangelical Students. For information about local and regional activities, visit intervarsity.org.

Scripture quotations, unless otherwise noted, are from The Holy Bible, English Standard Version, copyright © 2001 by Crossway Bibles, a division of Good News Publishers. Used by permission. All rights reserved.

Cover design: Cindy Kiple
Interior design: Beth McGill
Images: Interpretation of Rublev's Icon of the Trinity, 1995 by Sophie Hacker (Contemporary Artist)/Private Collection/Bridgeman Images

ISBN 978-0-8308-4881-2 (print)
ISBN 978-0-8308-9154-2 (digital)

Printed in the United States of America ∞

As a member of the Green Press Initiative, InterVarsity Press is committed to protecting the environment and to the responsible use of natural resources. To learn more, visit greenpressinitiative.org.

Library of Congress Cataloging-in-Publication Data
A catalog record for this book is available from the Library of Congress.

| P | 23 | 22 | 21 | 20 | 19 | 18 | 17 | 16 | 15 | 14 | 13 | 12 | 11 | 10 | 9 | 8 | 7 | 6 | 5 | 4 | 3 | 2 | 1 |
| Y | 36 | 35 | 34 | 33 | 32 | 31 | 30 | 29 | 28 | 27 | 26 | 25 | 24 | 23 | 22 | 21 | 20 | 19 | 18 | 17 | 16 |

The Word of God, powerful in all things,
and not defective with regard to His own justice,
did righteously turn against that apostasy, and redeem from it
His own property, not by violent means, . . . but by means of persuasion,
as became a God of counsel, who does not use violent means
to obtain what He desires; so that neither should justice
be infringed upon, nor the ancient handiwork
of God go to destruction.

Irenaeus of Lyons,
***Against Heresies* 5.1.1 (*ANF* 1:527)**

Contents

Acknowledgments ... ix

List of Abbreviations ... xi

1 The Call to Salvation ... 1
   An Evangelical Call: Common Ground ... 2
   A Definition of Effectual Calling ... 4
   The History of the Term ... 6
   Conversion and Converting Change ... 16
   Dogmatic Questions for an Effectual Call ... 21

2 God's Call as Speech ... 23
   Affirming Dort: Regeneration Occurs Before
      or Within Effectual Calling ... 23
   The Communicative Call ... 31
   The Dialogical Effectual Call ... 38

3 Calling in Paul: A Sovereign Summons ... 41
   An Argument for Divine Calling ... 42
   Calling in the Thessalonian Letters ... 45
   Calling and Creation ... 50
   Objections to a Divine Summons ... 52
   A Summary of Pauline Usage ... 58

4 The Content of the Call ... 61
   Oswald Bayer and the *Verbum Efficax* ... 63
   Word Incarnate: The Finnish Luther and
      Christ Present in Faith ... 67
   Hyper-Calvinism: "You Are Already Mine" ... 68
   Michael Horton: "Let There Be Righteousness!" ... 71
   Calling and "Our" Gospel ... 73

5 Divine Light and Conversion	79
Divine Light in New Testament Texts	82
Saving Illumination in 2 Corinthians 4:6	87
Summary	91
6 Illumination and Testimony	93
John Owen and Illumination	94
Claude Pajon and Intellectual Illumination	101
Friedrich Schleiermacher and Christ's Illuminating Presence	110
Illumination and Testimony	117
Conclusion: Illumination and Effectual Calling	120
7 New Birth and Resurrection	123
Birth from Above, Resurrection and Regeneration	127
Raised with Christ: Ephesians 2 and Colossians 2	139
Spiritual Resurrection and Its Limits	145
8 Resurrection as Culmination of the Call	149
Edwards and Biblical Images for Converting Change	150
Communicative Theism and Regeneration	158
Calling and Regeneration	165
9 Triune Rhetoric and Converting Change	169
Rhetoric in Contemporary Theology	170
Divine Rhetoric: Persuasion and Accommodation	175
Triune Rhetoric: Trinitarian Theology and Rhetoric	189
Lydia and Divine Rhetoric	205
Divine Rhetoric and Effectual Calling	209
10 God's Call and the Church	213
The Effectual Call in Practice	216
Effectual Calling and the Church	225
Bibliography	229
General Index	253
Scripture Index	261

Acknowledgments

A PROJECT THAT POSITIONS GOD'S ACTION as communicative and dialogical must acknowledge how the same process was at work in its creation. I note below with Augustine that when Christ promises to speak through those "handed over" to martyrdom he also promises to do the same for those who "hand over" God's Word to his people. That passing on comes about in various ways, not all of which are intended or planned. Nevertheless, I give thanks to God for the support, encouragement and influence of many people who "handed over" an appropriate word in the dialogical process of this book.

Kevin Vanhoozer provided the initial stimulus for this project in response to my study of the quote by Irenaeus above. He graciously continued as my supervisor despite his move away from Wheaton College. In addition to his invaluable contribution to this project at every stage, he has shown me what it means to have an insatiable interest in the world and in other people. For his careful input and consistent example I am very grateful. Daniel Treier has been an example to me as an instructor and scholar. His probing questions to me and to others have been a great stimulus toward rigorous thought. His diligence and thoughtfulness about all aspects of education continue to influence my ideals.

I am indebted to numerous scholars for interaction with versions of several chapters, including Albert Gootjes, Doug Moo, Nicholas Perrin and Kevin Hector. I was given new questions and directions through conversations with Eric Johnson, David Morlan, Henk van den Belt, Doug Sweeney, Matthew Barrett, Beth Jones and J. V. Fesko. I especially appreciate the feedback of the editorial board for the Studies in Christian Doctrine and Scripture series, who helped focus the revised version.

The book took form as a PhD dissertation at Wheaton College. In addition to class seminars and colloquia together, I am thankful to colleagues who read and discussed various stages of this project, including Dan Brendsel, Robbie Crouse, James Gordon, Matthew Patton and Ashish Varma. Jordan Barrett, Jeremy Treat and Hank Voss helped to fine tune my research proposal at its outset. Offhand comments from Drew Burlingame and Carmen Imes served as catalysts for further refinement.

Finally, I thank my wife, Andrea, who has been the biggest supporter of this project while also offering some of its most poignant criticisms. Her sacrifice of time and energy to free me for this task is invaluable. That we can work together for the sake of our union, for our family and for Christ's kingdom is the greatest joy of my life.

List of Abbreviations

AB	Anchor Bible
ANF	*The Ante-Nicene Fathers*. Edited by A. Roberts and J. Donaldson. Buffalo, 1885–1896. Reprint, Grand Rapids: Eerdmans, 1975.
BCCT	Brill's Companions to the Christian Tradition
BECNT	Baker Exegetical Commentary on the New Testament
BETL	Bibliotheca ephemeridum theologicarum lovaniensium
BSCH	Brill's Series in Church History
CC	*Calvin's Commentaries*. 44 vols. Edinburgh: Calvin Translation Society, 1844–1856. Reprinted in 22 vols. Grand Rapids: Baker, 1999.
CD	Barth, Karl. *The Church Dogmatics*. 4 vols. in 12 parts (I/1–IV/4). Edited by Geoffrey W. Bromiley and T. F. Torrance. Translated by Geoffrey W. Bromiley. Edinburgh: T&T Clark, 1956–1975.
CH	*Church History*
ChJA	Christianity and Judaism in Antiquity
CHRC	*Church History and Religious Culture*
CNTUOT	Beale, G. K., and D. A. Carson, eds. *Commentary on the New Testament Use of the Old Testament*. Grand Rapids: Baker Academic, 2007.
CR	Corpus Reformatorum. Edited by Guilielmus Baum, Eduardus Cunitz and Eduardus Reuss. Halle, 1834–1900. Reprint, New York: Johnson Reprint, 1964.
CSCD	Cambridge Studies in Christian Doctrine
CSRT	Columbia Series in Reformed Theology
CTJ	*Calvin Theological Journal*
DTIB	Vanhoozer, Kevin J., Craig G. Bartholomew, and Daniel J. Treier, eds. *Dictionary for Theological Interpretation of the Bible*. Grand Rapids: Baker Academic, 2005.
EDNT	*Exegetical Dictionary of the New Testament*. Edited by Horst Balz and Gerhard Schneider. ET. Grand Rapids, 1990–1993.

ESV	English Standard Version
HeyJ	*Heythrop Journal*
ICC	International Critical Commentary
IJST	*International Journal of Systematic Theology*
Int	*Interpretation*
IVPNTC	The IVP New Testament Commentary Series
JEH	*Journal of Ecclesiastical History*
JETS	*Journal of the Evangelical Theological Society*
JP	*Journal of Pragmatics*
JPT	*Journal of Pentecostal Theology*
JR	*Journal of Religion*
JRT	*Journal of Reformed Theology*
KGA	Schleiermacher, Friedrich Daniel Ernst. *Kritische Gesamtausgabe*. Berlin: de Gruyter, 1980–.
LCC	Library of Christian Classics
LCL	Loeb Classical Library
LNTS	Library of New Testament Studies
LSJ	Liddell, Henry George, Robert Scott, and Henry Stuart Jones. *A Greek-English Lexicon*. 9th ed. with revised supplement. Oxford: Clarendon, 1996.
LW	*Luther's Works*. Edited by Jaroslav Pelikan and Helmut T. Lehmann. 56 vols. St. Louis: Concordia; Philadelphia: Fortress, 1955–1986.
MJT	*Mid-America Journal of Theology*
ModTheo	*Modern Theology*
NETS	*A New English Translation of the Septuagint: And the Other Greek Translations Traditionally Included Under That Title*. Edited by Albert Pietersma and Benjamin G. Wright. Oxford: Oxford University Press, 2007.
NICNT	New International Commentary on the New Testament
NIDNTT	*New International Dictionary of New Testament Theology*. Edited by Colin Brown. 4 vols. Grand Rapids, 1975–1985.
NIGTC	New International Greek Testament Commentary

NIVAC	NIV Application Commentary
NovTSup	Novum Testamentum Supplements
NPNF¹	*Nicene and Post-Nicene Fathers*, Series 1. Edited by Philip Schaff. 1886–1890. Reprint, Peabody, MA: Hendrickson, 1994.
NPNF²	*Nicene and Post-Nicene Fathers*, Series 2. Edited by Philip Schaff and Henry Wace. 1890. Reprint, Peabody, MA: Hendrickson, 1994.
NTOA	Novum Testamentum et Orbis Antiquus
NV	*Nova et Vetera*
OG	Old Greek
PG	Patrologia Graeca [= Patrologiae cursus completus: Series graeca]. Edited by J.-P. Migne. 162 vols. Paris: Migne, 1857–1866.
PiNTC	Pillar New Testament Commentary
PL	Patrologia Latina [= Patrologiae cursus completus: Series Latina]. Edited by J.-P. Migne. 221 vols. Paris: Migne, 1844–1891.
ProEccl	*Pro Ecclesia*
PRRD	Muller, Richard A. *Post-Reformation Reformed Dogmatics: The Rise and Development of Reformed Orthodoxy, ca. 1520 to ca. 1725*. 4 vols. Grand Rapids: Baker Academic, 2003.
PTMS	Princeton Theological Monograph Series
RelS	*Religious Studies*
SBET	*Scottish Bulletin of Evangelical Theology*
SCJ	*Sixteenth Century Journal*
SMRT	Studies in Medieval and Reformation Traditions
SP	*Sacra Pagina*
SP	*Studia Patristica*
SST	T&T Clark Studies in Systematic Theology
ST	Thomas Aquinas, *Summa Theologiae*. 61 vols. New York: McGraw-Hill, 1964–1981.
TDNT	*Theological Dictionary of the New Testament*. Edited by Gerhard Kittel and Gerhard Friedrich. Translated by Geoffrey W. Bromiley. 10 vols. Grand Rapids: Eerdmans, 1964–1976.
Them	*Themelios*

TJ	*Trinity Journal*
TS	*Theological Studies*
TSRPrT	Texts and Studies in Reformation and Post-Reformation Thought
WA	*Luthers Werke: Kritische Gesamtausgabe.* 97 vols. In 112 parts. Weimar: Böhlau, 1883–1985.
WBC	Word Biblical Commentary
WCF	*The Westminster Confession of Faith, 1647.* In *Creeds and Confessions of Faith in the Christian Tradition,* edited by Jaroslav Pelikan and Valerie Hotchkiss, 2:601-49. New Haven, CT: Yale University Press, 2003.
WJE	*The Works of Jonathan Edwards.* 26 vols. New Haven, CT: Yale University Press, 1957–2008.
WJEO	Works of Jonathan Edwards Online. Vols. 27-73. Jonathan Edwards Center, Yale University, 2008. http://edwards.yale.edu/.
WLC	The Orthodox Presbyterian Church. *The Larger Catechism.* In *The Westminster Confession of Faith and Catechisms,* 153-353. Lawrenceville, GA: Christian Education & Publications, 2007. http://www.pcaac.org/resources/wcf/.
WSA	Works of Saint Augustine. A Translation for the 21st Century. Edited by John E. Rotelle and Boniface Ramsey. Hyde Park, NY: New City, 1990–.
WSC	The Westminster Shorter Catechism, 1648. In *Creeds and Confessions of Faith in the Christian Tradition,* edited by Jaroslav Pelikan and Valerie Hotchkiss, 2:652-62. New Haven, CT: Yale University Press, 2003.
WTJ	*Westminster Theological Journal*
WUNT	Wissenschaftliche Untersuchungen zum Neuen Testament
ZKG	*Zeitschrift für Kirchengeschichte*

ONE

The Call to Salvation

> *It is so powerful that it cannot be overcome, and at the same time it is so lovely that it excludes every form of compulsion. Its power is so excellent that the depraved nature is renewed by it, and, at the same time, so friendly and winsome that it fully respects a person's rational and moral nature.*
>
> HERMAN BAVINCK

CHRISTIANS RECOGNIZE THAT GOD *calls* his people to salvation. This conviction arises from Scripture, particularly from the Pauline epistles that use the verb "to call" as a description of God's action in individual conversion. Despite various conclusions about the results of God's work in applying salvation to individuals, Christians cannot avoid the task of integrating "calling" into a theology of salvation.

I set forth here a dogmatic account of the *call* to salvation. That is, I ask after the relation of God's call to other loci in the doctrine of salvation and offer a constructive account based on the scriptural descriptions of God's action in conversion. A dogmatic account, following John Webster's use of the term, seeks to understand what it means when the church confesses that God calls, primarily in language drawn from "the triune God's saving and revelatory action."[1] A dogmatic account employs doctrinal language in an effort to clarify the church's witness to God's work in Christ.

---

[1] John Webster, *Holy Scripture: A Dogmatic Sketch* (Cambridge: Cambridge University Press, 2003), 1. For dogmatics as testing of ecclesial witness according to the gospel, see R. Michael Allen, *The Christ's Faith: A Dogmatic Account*, SST (London: T&T Clark, 2009), 3.

Specifically, I engage the Christian tradition that utilizes the vocabulary of *effectual* calling. While earlier theologians such as Augustine[2] and Thomas Aquinas[3] understood *calling* as a way to describe God's operative grace, only in the Protestant Reformed tradition did the addition of *effectual* clarify the certain results of the call. Although the Remonstrants[4] and later Arminian traditions refer to God's action as *calling*, they distinguish it from the effectual call with other modifying terms in order to deny that God's action is irresistible.[5]

The Reformed term *effectual calling* provides the basis for this study because it best upholds a core biblical insight—that God works salvation on behalf of and within his people. I reappropriate voices from the Reformed tradition because I believe they best follow the grain of the biblical text when asking how God brings about salvation.[6] Such a move from Scripture to theology cannot be separated completely from the apologetic task of answering objections and discrediting alternatives to the doctrine as it has found its home in the Protestant Reformed tradition. Nevertheless, several factors make the effectual call worthy of a second look for evangelicals of all sorts.

An Evangelical Call: Common Ground

Calling as a locus within the doctrine of salvation (as distinguished from "calling" to spheres of life and ministry) addresses two primary concerns of

---

[2]Augustine, *Miscellany of Questions in Response to Simplician* 1.2.13, trans. Boniface Ramsey, *Responses to Miscellaneous Questions*, ed. Raymond Canning, WSA I/12 (Hyde Park, NY: New City, 2008), 195. "But the person on whom he has mercy he calls in such a way as he knows is appropriate for him, so that he may not reject him who calls."
[3]Aquinas, *ST* 1-2.113.1 ad 3.
[4]Jacob Arminius presided over a disputation on calling in his final public appearance before his death in 1609. See Henk van den Belt, "The *Vocatio* in the Leiden Disputations (1597–1631): The Influence of the Arminian Controversy on the Concept of the Divine Call to Salvation," *CHRC* 92 (2012): 542.
[5]H. Orton Wiley, *Christian Theology* (Kansas City, MO: Beacon Hill, 1952), 340-42; Kenneth Keathley, *Salvation and Sovereignty: A Molinist Approach* (Nashville: Broadman & Holman, 2010), 116-19.
[6]By "Reformed," I mean theological traditions stemming from the sixteenth-century Reformers and codified, representatively, in either the Westminster Standards or the Three Forms of Unity (Belgic Confession, Heidelberg Catechism and Synod of Dort). This tradition has been variously referred to as "reformed orthodoxy" or "federal Calvinism." In this study, "broadly Reformed" refers to any theologian or tradition self-identifying with magisterial Protestant traditions, including those who consciously revise elements of Reformed orthodoxy (e.g., Karl Barth, Friedrich Schleiermacher).

non-Reformed Protestants.[7] First, Wesleyan authors in particular emphasize God's personal address to individuals in the call to faith. They speak of God as a lover wooing his beloved.[8] God displays his radical love for the beloved by the use of means that are meant to produce repentance and faith. There is no one-size-fits-all divine call. I present a doctrine of effectual calling that agrees with this emphasis. As will be shown, the quest of Reformed theologians to generalize about God's work in calling does not militate against the individualized nature of God's action. God addresses us in dialogue, through our thinking and processing capacities, and this process is unique to each individual. A reworked doctrine of calling maintains the Wesleyan emphasis on personal engagement with God.

Second, non-Reformed theologians seek to avoid imagining God's work as mechanistic.[9] If God's call is *effective*, this may imply that God treats human beings as machines. In such a conception, the proper input is given to a person—namely, the regenerative motion of the Holy Spirit—and this inevitably leads to the output of repentance and faith. If God works on human beings as a person works on machines, Christian theology not only cheapens human value but also makes the process of salvation much less interesting. There is a qualitative difference between talking to one's car while changing the oil and speaking with a friend as a way to provide counsel. It is precisely this difficulty that *calling* probes. Wesleyans are right to ask whether conversion has become mechanized. Calling, a word that indicates a type of discourse, invites Christians to examine how individual salvation is more than a physical process of repair.

As we will see, the Reformed tradition on converting change (usually called regeneration) may be open to these criticisms *unless* it remembers the nature of God's work as a call. As rearticulated here, the effectual call

---

[7] I am speaking here to contemporary evangelicals who self-identify within the Arminian and Wesleyan traditions. E.g., Kenneth J. Collins, *The Scripture Way of Salvation: The Heart of John Wesley's Theology* (Nashville: Abingdon, 1997), and the authors in Kenneth Collins and John H. Tyson, eds., *Conversion in the Wesleyan Tradition* (Nashville: Abingdon, 2001).

[8] John Wesley, "The Scripture-Way of Salvation: A Sermon on Ephes. ii. 8," in *Sermons, II, 34-70*, vol. 2 of *The Works of John Wesley*, ed. Albert C. Outler (Nashville: Abingdon, 1985), 156.

[9] John Miley, *Systematic Theology* (New York: Hunt & Eaton, 1892), 273. The charge of mechanism is leveled at the Thomistic tradition by David Bentley Hart, "Providence and Causality: On Divine Innocence," in *The Providence of God: Deus Habet Consilium*, ed. Francesca Aran Murphy and Philip G. Ziegler (London: T&T Clark, 2009), 34-56.

satisfies Wesleyan concerns that God's action be seen as personal and non-mechanical. That God calls people into "the fellowship of his Son, Jesus Christ" (1 Cor 1:9) "through our gospel" (2 Thess 2:14) is an evangelical doctrine that displays common ground among evangelical Protestants.

A Definition of Effectual Calling

The results of this study are twofold: a definition of effectual calling that highlights it as an instance of God's speech, and a statement on how effectual calling relates to regeneration, the primary alternative term used within the Reformed tradition to describe God's action in converting change.

First, a definition:

> The *effectual call* is an act of triune rhetoric in which God the Father appropriates human witness to Christ the Son in order to convince and transform a particular person by ministering, through the presence of God the Spirit, understanding and love of Christ.

For the purpose of this study the use of *calling* in the Synod of Dort and in the Westminster Standards will serve as a basis for discussion. Question 31 of the Westminster Shorter Catechism asks: "What is effectual calling?" It answers:

> Effectual calling is the work of God's Spirit, whereby, convincing us of our sin and misery, enlightening our minds in the knowledge of Christ, and renewing our wills, he doth persuade and enable us to embrace Jesus Christ, freely offered to us in the gospel.[10]

My definition intends to be in continuity with previous definitions such as this while making explicit the personal and communicative dimensions of calling. First, my definition associates human proclamation of the gospel closely with divine action. This aims to clarify that calling is not a distinct inner voice, but rather the transforming power of a personal, dialogical encounter that occurs within speech. I further maintain that the effectual call is a description of God's *literal*, though analogical, speech. I criticize some Reformed views for making the call purely *metaphorical*. In such a conception, the term *calling* marks an action of God so distinct from speaking

---

[10]Cf. *WCF* 10.1-4; *WLC* Q. 66-68. Effectual calling also occurs in discussion of God's eternal decree (*WCF* 3.6, 8) and is repeated as a necessary condition for justification (*WCF* 11.1), sanctification (*WCF* 13.1) and perseverance (*WCF* 17.1).

and hearing that it is difficult to discern what if any elements of a "call" are appropriate to God.[11] Second, I specify how the call can be an act of the entire Trinity. The Shorter Catechism assigns primary agency for the call to God's Spirit. This reflects a common Christian judgment that the Spirit is especially responsible for bringing about the ends or perfections of God's creatures.[12] By assigning the primary role in calling to the Spirit, however, the Shorter Catechism might portray God's call as purely metaphorical, since the mode of the Spirit's agency is often untraceable (Jn 3:8). But the diversity among the three documents associated with the Westminster Assembly suggests that the choice of the Spirit here is not definitive.[13] In order to make plain that the *ad extra* works of the Trinity are indivisible, it may be helpful to assign to the Spirit the power behind the call's efficacy, as do the two other Westminster documents when they state that God works "by his Spirit." My own definition assigns the origination of the call to the Father,[14] both because of the traditional designation "from the Father, through the Son, by the Spirit," and because the New Testament consistently refers to "God" as the one who calls distinct from Jesus Christ.[15] Finally, the proposed definition confesses the effectual call as a divine communicative act in which God, in a way only analogous to creatures, literally speaks so as to transform human affections and elicit faith in Christ. I call this *triune rhetoric* to emphasize that God's unique persuasion takes place within human discourse and understanding.

A second dogmatic question for the effectual call is the relationship between calling and regeneration. I argue that some Reformed accounts overemphasized the latter to such an extent that the former was not given

---

[11]This typically happens when the term *calling* is defined using the metaphor of resurrection or regeneration. The error here is a focus on the result of God's call to the exclusion of its means.

[12]Colin Gunton, *The One, the Three, and the Many: God, Creation, and the Culture of Modernity* (Cambridge: Cambridge University Press, 1993), 189. "The Spirit's peculiar office is to realize the true being of each created thing by bringing it, through Christ, into saving relation with God the Father." Cf. John Owen, ΠΝΕΥΜΑΤΟΛΟΓΙΑ *[Pneumatologia], or, a Discourse Concerning the Holy Spirit*, vol. 3 of *The Works of John Owen*, ed. William Goold (London: Johnstone & Hunter, 1852; repr., Carlisle, PA: Banner of Truth Trust, 1966), 94.

[13]*WLC* (Q. 67) assigns the call to "God's almighty power and grace." *WCF* 10.1 assigns the call simply to "God."

[14]For this argument, see John Murray, *Redemption, Accomplished and Applied* (Grand Rapids: Eerdmans, 1955), 110-11.

[15]E.g., Rom 8:30; 1 Cor 1:9; Gal 1:15; Eph 1:17-18. For interaction with Karl Barth's argument that Christ calls, see chap. 9.

appropriate place in descriptions of converting change. Regeneration, understood as the instantaneous creation of a distinct form of spiritual life in a person, highlights a discontinuity between the individual's life before and after converting change. Emil Brunner criticized this view of regeneration because it imports "causal" categories where "personal" categories are more fitting for the interrelation between God and humans.[16] The continued presence of *calling* as a dogmatic locus in the Reformed tradition, however, indicates that theologians felt compelled to describe God's action as personal. I emphasize this aspect by drawing on voices from within the tradition. Thus I propose, in relation to the "narrow" definition of regeneration,

> *Effectual calling* is the means by which God gives his people *new life* (new birth or regeneration). This new life refers to a reordering of a person's affections, so that the person whom God calls now sees Christ and his gospel as excellent.

Spiritual resurrection, then, is a reordering of affections or loves. In what follows, I outline the history of effectual calling and its relation to regeneration in order to motivate a fresh study of the doctrine. I then set the parameters of this study before evaluating contemporary options in the following chapter.

THE HISTORY OF THE TERM

While Augustine referred to the call as "effective" in bringing about a good will,[17] the Protestant Reformers picked up the use of "calling" in the Augustinian tradition and made the *effectual call* a technical term. Throughout the sixteenth and seventeenth centuries, Reformed theologians sought to emphasize the effectiveness of God's work in applying salvation alongside a desire to do justice to God's use of words in bringing about faith. At times these accounts portrayed God's work in ways that could be seen as impersonal or mechanistic. "Calling" served as a reminder that God deals with his people as speaking and hearing persons.

In his *Institutes*, John Calvin refers to the "special" or "internal" call in his discussion of converting grace,[18] but he uses the phrase "effectual call" (*vocatio*

---

[16]Emil Brunner, *The Christian Doctrine of God*, trans. Olive Wyon, vol. 1 of *Dogmatics* (Philadelphia: Westminster, 1949), 315-16.
[17]Augustine, *Simplician* 1.2.13.
[18]John Calvin, *Institutio Christianae religionis* [1559] 3.24.1-2, in *Ioannis Calvini Opera quae supersunt omnia*, ed. Guilielmus Baum, Eduardus Cunitz and Eduardus Reuss, CR 30 (Halle:

efficax) in several other documents. First, in his *Antidote to the Council of Trent* (1547), Calvin cites Augustine against the council to the effect that God finds no goodwill in a person before his gift of grace. As scriptural evidence he notes, "When Luke speaks of effectual calling, he tells us that not those who were disposed of themselves, but those who were pre-ordained to eternal life, believed (Acts 13:48)."[19] Effectual calling is the effect of God's ordaining some to eternal life and comes about through a response to gospel proclamation. Second, in a commentary on 1 Corinthians 1:9 from the following year (1548), Calvin relates effectual calling to perseverance. Believers should conclude that Christ has adopted them because of their conversion, "For effectual calling ought to be to believers an evidence of divine adoption; yet in the meantime we must all walk *with fear and trembling*."[20] Here, Calvin understands Paul's reassurance to the Corinthians, that they "were called into the fellowship of his [God's] Son," as a reference to their experience of coming into the "knowledge of Christ." Already in these early uses by Calvin one may observe the points at which others have challenged the effectual call theologically and practically. Theologically, the effectual call is a result of divine election and so implies a broadly Augustinian doctrine of predestination. Practically, Calvin believes that individual Christians can rely on their calling for a sense of personal assurance. The implication that a subjective analysis of one's faith helps ground assurance has received criticism as leading to excessive introspection.[21]

Schwetschke, 1864), 711-14; trans. Ford Lewis Battles, under the title *Institutes of the Christian Religion*, ed. John T. McNeill, LCC 20-21 (Philadelphia: Westminster, 1960), 964-67 (hereafter *Institutes*, with page numbers to this edition following the citation of the work). "Effectual calling" is not a technical term for Calvin here. For instance, he says that God "withdraws the effectual working of his Spirit from them [the wicked]" (*Institutes* 3.24.2, 967), implying that there are gradations of the Spirit's "effectual" work.

[19]John Calvin, *Antidote to the Council of Trent*, in *Calvin's Tracts*, trans. Henry Beveridge (Edinburgh: Calvin Translation Society, 1851), 3:121. He is discussing *Council of Trent*, session 6, chap. 7, which says the Spirit works to justify "in view of each one's dispositions and cooperation" (Jaroslav Pelikan and Valerie Hotchkiss, eds., *Creeds and Confessions of Faith in the Christian Tradition* [New Haven, CT: Yale University Press, 2003], 2:830). For recent exegetical arguments in favor of this interpretation of Acts 13:48, see Christoph Stenschke, *Luke's Portrait of the Gentiles Prior to Their Coming to Faith* (Tübingen: Mohr Siebeck, 1999), 283-88.

[20]John Calvin, *Comm. 1 Cor. 1:9* (CC 20:60). Cf. Calvin, *Comm. 1 Pet. 1:1-2* (CC 22:25).

[21]E.g., Phillip Cary, "Why Luther Is Not Quite Protestant: The Logic of Faith in a Sacramental Promise," *ProEccl* 14 (2005): 447-86. For a defense of Calvin and criticism of the Reformed tradition, see Randall C. Zachman, *The Assurance of Faith: Conscience in the Theology of Martin Luther and John Calvin* (Minneapolis: Fortress, 1993), 244-46.

Following Calvin's use of "effectual calling" as a technical term, Reformed theologians in the next generation made it a significant locus in their theology. Theodore Beza (d. 1605) placed *vocatio efficax* in his 1570 chart outlining the divine decrees.[22] Scottish theologian Robert Rollock (d. 1599) titled his exposition of Christian theology *A Treatise of God's Effectual Calling* (1597), highlighting the central place of calling.

> God's Effectual Calling is that whereby God calleth out of darkness into his admirable light, from the power of Satan unto God, in Christ Jesus, those whom he knew from eternity, and predestinated unto life, of his mere favour, by the promulgation of the covenant of grace, or preaching of the gospel.[23]

While Rollock affirms the proclaimed gospel as the means by which God's call comes to an individual, he emphasizes human passivity when he describes the inner element of calling:

> In this first grace of God, which we call a new creation of divine qualities in the soul, man standeth mere passively before God, and as the material cause of God's work.... Yet we say not that man in this new birth is no more than a trunk or dead tree: for that there is in man (that so I may speak) a passive power to receive that divine grace and life of God, as also the use of reason, which dead trees have not.[24]

Rollock gives two sides to his answer. He wishes to attribute efficacy to God's action, yet he recognizes that fallen humans possess a "passive power to receive" God's grace and the "use of reason." Examples such as Rollock's could be repeated,[25] but this tension comes out most clearly in the decisions of the Synod of Dort.

Regeneration as an infusion of new qualities. At the Synod of Dort (1618–1619), the Reformed churches of the Netherlands decided against theses put forward by a group of theologians known as the Remonstrants, who were inspired by Jacob Arminius (d. 1609). Among these theses, the

---

[22] A reproduction of Beza's chart can be found in Richard A. Muller, "Perkins' *A Golden Chaine*: Predestinarian System or Schematized *Ordo Salutis*?," *SCJ* 9 (1978): 71-72.

[23] Robert Rollock, *A Treatise of God's Effectual Calling*, trans. Henry Holland, vol. 1 of *Select Works of Robert Rollock* (London: Kyngston, 1603; repr., Edinburgh: Wodrow Society, 1849), 29.

[24] Ibid., 31-32.

[25] See examples in Heinrich Heppe, *Reformed Dogmatics*, ed. Ernst Bizer, trans. G. Thomson (Grand Rapids: Baker, 1978), 518.

synod opposed the Remonstrant argument that God's action in converting change is ultimately resistible.[26] In its response, the Synod of Dort alludes to both calling and regeneration. First, in reference to God's decision in election, God "calls" his chosen ones into fellowship: "He decided to give the chosen ones to Christ to be saved, and to call and draw them effectively into Christ's fellowship through his word and Spirit."[27] The canons clarify that calling takes place in time as a result of a prior choice on God's part: "Just as from eternity he chose his own in Christ, so within time he effectively calls [*efficaciter vocat*] them, grants them faith and repentance, and, having rescued them from the dominion of darkness, brings them into the kingdom of his Son."[28] In its use of calling vocabulary, Dort recognizes that everyone who hears the proclaimed gospel is "called seriously"[29] by God according to his revealed will, but the synod does not entirely define what distinguishes the effectual call from the general call. The authors point to the results of an effectual call, namely, that Christ's elect ones enter into fellowship with him.

Immediately following this explanation of God's work, the synod adds the term *regeneration* to specify God's action in converting change.

> [God] not only sees to it that the gospel is proclaimed to them outwardly, and enlightens their minds powerfully by the Holy Spirit so that they may rightly understand and discern the things of the Spirit of God, but, by the effective operation of the same regenerating Spirit, he also penetrates into the inmost being of man, opens the closed heart, softens the hard heart, and circumcises the heart that is uncircumcised. He infuses new qualities into the will, making the dead will alive . . . so that, like a good tree, it may be enabled to produce the fruits of good deeds.[30]

The Holy Spirit here does more than make the words of the gospel effective. The Spirit also "infuses new qualities into the will" (*voluntati novas qualitates infundit*).[31] This whole work is "the regeneration, the new creation,

---

[26] *The Remonstrance*, article 4; Pelikan and Hotchkiss, *Creeds*, 2:549.
[27] *The Canons of the Synod of Dort* 1.7, in Philip Schaff, ed., *The Creeds of Christendom: With a History and Critical Notes*, 6th ed. (Harper & Row, 1931; repr., Grand Rapids: Baker, 1983), 3:553; trans. Pelikan and Hotchkiss, *Creeds*, 2:572. (References to Schaff are to the Latin text, and those to Pelikan and Hotchkiss are to the English translation.)
[28] *Dort* 3/4.10 (Schaff, *Creeds of Christendom*, 3:586); Pelikan and Hotchkiss, *Creeds*, 2:585.
[29] *Dort* 3/4.8; Pelikan and Hotchkiss, *Creeds*, 2:585.
[30] *Dort* 3/4.11; Pelikan and Hotchkiss, *Creeds*, 2:586.
[31] *Dort* 3/4.11 (Schaff, *Creeds of Christendom*, 3:566).

the raising from the dead, and the making alive so clearly proclaimed in the Scriptures, which God works in us without our help."[32] The authors wish to distinguish their view from the Remonstrants, for whom "it still remains in the power of man to be regenerated or not." This led to a strong distinction between regeneration as the Spirit's work, and conversion as the human response. The Spirit works first to open the heart or make the will alive, and then "the will, now renewed, is not only activated and motivated by God but in being activated by God is also itself active."[33] The canons of Dort thus marked off *regeneration* as the crucial renewal of the human person that precedes an expression of faith. Among several descriptions, they called the Spirit's action "infusing new qualities" into the will.

G. C. Berkouwer, who interprets Dort sympathetically, acknowledges that for many, "it seemed to them that the Canons had capitulated to the Catholic view of a mystical intrusion of a higher order of being."[34] It would seem that with this phrase the Dortian divines followed the Thomistic/Dominican tradition. Aquinas had defined *calling* as preparation for justifying faith: "Vocation or calling is to be referred to the assistance of God moving and stirring the soul from within to withdraw from sin. This motion from God is not the forgiveness of sin itself but its cause."[35] "Moving and stirring the soul" sounds similar to Dort's terms, that God "activates and strengthens the will."[36] Two articles later, Thomas attributes the movement of the free will in justification to God's "infused" gift: "With all who are capable of being so moved [by free will, that is, all except infants], God infuses the gift of justifying grace in such wise that he also moves the free will to accept it."[37] This is causal language at its finest, and Dort's choice of the same term, *infused*, seems to indicate that grace becomes a habit resident in the person so converted.

---

[32]*Dort* 3/4.12; Pelikan and Hotchkiss, *Creeds*, 2:586. In the sixteenth century, "regeneration" typically referred to the entire process of sanctification. E.g., Calvin defines regeneration as "repentance" (Calvin, *Institutes* 3.3.9, 601), as the "beginning of sanctification" (*Institutes* 2.3.6, 298), and as the whole life of renewal (*Institutes* 3.3.9, 601).
[33]*Dort* 3/4.12; Pelikan and Hotchkiss, *Creeds*, 2:586.
[34]G. C. Berkouwer, *Faith and Sanctification*, Studies in Dogmatics (Grand Rapids: Eerdmans, 1952), 79.
[35]Aquinas, *ST* 1-2.113.1 ad 3.
[36]*Dort* 3/4.11; Pelikan and Hotchkiss, *Creeds*, 2:586.
[37]Aquinas, *ST* 1-2.113.3 reply.

Significantly, in this article Thomas discusses how God "moves all things according to the mode proper to each." Dort has the same interest. The Remonstrants had charged that the Reformed separated the key regenerative moment from the ministry of the word.[38] God's central action in conversion seems to occur apart from means when considered as a sovereign act of the Spirit. The authors of Dort therefore clarify, "The aforementioned supernatural work of God by which he regenerates us in no way rules out or cancels the use of the gospel, which God in his great wisdom has appointed to be the seed of regeneration." Grace is even "bestowed through admonitions, and the more readily we perform our duty [to preach], the more lustrous the benefit of God working in us usually is and the better his work advances."[39] One may ask then, by what mode does God give his grace "through admonitions"? Dort juxtaposes God's action through the proclaimed word and God's action by the Spirit in regeneration. This represents a consistent tension in Reformed theology to integrate the preached word into a theology of converting change.

Good trees and blocks of wood.

> Either make the tree good and its fruit good, or make the tree bad and its fruit bad, for the tree is known by its fruit. (Mt 12:33)[40]

The Synod of Dort codified two terms, *calling* and *regeneration*, as God's actions in converting change. When discussing these two terms, Reformed theologians after Dort desired to affirm both human passivity and also human dignity as those addressed by God in speech. They used arboreal metaphors for both concepts, and these illustrate a continuing tension.

Good trees and good fruit. The Synod of Dort proclaimed that God's Spirit brings the disobedient human will to life so "that, like a good tree, it may be enabled to produce the fruits of good deeds."[41] Among Reformed theologians, Matthew 12:33 warranted this separation of God's regenerating act (making the tree good) from the resulting human act of faith. For Francis

---

[38]See summary in Herman Bavinck, *Saved by Grace: The Holy Spirit's Work in Calling and Regeneration*, ed. J. Mark Beach, trans. Nelson D. Kloosterman (Grand Rapids: Reformation Heritage, 2008), 42.
[39]*Dort* 3/4.17; Pelikan and Hotchkiss, *Creeds*, 2:588.
[40]Scripture quotations are from the ESV unless otherwise noted.
[41]*Dort* 3/4.11; Pelikan and Hotchkiss, *Creeds*, 2:586.

Turretin (d. 1687), "a thing ought to exist before it can work." A fallen human cannot "understand and will in the sphere of morals unless renewed by supernatural dispositions and habits. An evil tree cannot bring forth good fruit, unless from an evil it is first made a good tree."[42]

The bad tree / good tree description is one of many in Scripture. Turretin cites other analogous changes.

> Just as in restoring sight to the blind, Christ did two things: he first opened their eyes and so restored the power of seeing; then he caused the man to see at the same moment. So in the resurrection of Lazarus, the soul was first restored to the body, then he elicited vital actions. Thus God by his omnipotent acting produces in the man (or in the will) new qualities; then he excites those faculties to action.[43]

In Turretin, then, there is a logical separation between the Spirit's work to give life to the human will and the subsequent opportunity for that life to become manifest when one hears the gospel. Turretin uses Matthew 12:33 to say that there can be no good fruit (i.e., faith) until the tree is made good by the Spirit's supernatural act. On its own, this is uncontroversial among Reformed or broadly Augustinian traditions. God's gracious action must precede and bring about the human response of faith in order to protect God's grace as unearned and unmerited. The distinctive contribution of *regeneration* in Turretin's examples, however, is that the Spirit implants a new spiritual disposition or orientation in a passive (i.e., spiritually dead) person in an unmediated way. The Spirit's work possesses its own unique form of causality, akin to raising the dead or changing the "nature" of a tree.

Logs and stones. While affirming this direct operation of the Spirit, Reformed theologians were also aware of an objection. By describing conversion in the miraculous terms of transforming a tree from bad to good, it appeared that God's action on humanity did not differ from physical action

---

[42]Francis Turretin, *Institutes of Elenctic Theology*, ed. James T. Dennison Jr., trans. George Musgrave Giger (Phillipsburg, NJ: P&R, 1992), 15.4.13, 2:522-23; cf. George Carleton et al., "The Collegiate Suffrage of the British Divines," in *The British Delegation and the Synod of Dort (1618–1619)*, ed. Anthony Milton, Church of England Record Society 13 (Woodbridge: Boydell, 2005), 258; Thomas Hooker, *The Application of Redemption* (London: Peter Cole, 1657; repr., New York: Arno, 1972), 150.

[43]Turretin, *Institutes* 15.4.14, 2:523; Herman Bavinck, *Reformed Dogmatics*, ed. John Bolt, trans. John Vriend (Grand Rapids: Baker Academic, 2003), 4:47.

on a stone or a log.⁴⁴ They answered this objection by appealing to God's use of the external call.

The very existence of an external call, or the public announcement of the gospel, gives proper space for human personhood. God chose to use "the voice of the gospel and the preaching of the word" as means for conversion, because "nothing fitter and better adapted to a rational creature could be given in order that man who is gifted with speech [λογικός] might harmonize with the word [λόγῳ]."⁴⁵ For Turretin, the human ability to speak is significant for understanding how God acts. The external call, or public proclamation of the gospel, is sufficient to show that God respects the nature of humanity in conversion. The external call, though ineffective without the Spirit's work, still addresses humans as rational creatures. Thus God is not treating people as "stocks or brutes."

The means of arboreal transformation. These authors are sensitive to the question of how humanity can be like a tree in need of radical transformation and yet not be treated as a mindless tree in the call to salvation. They display a tension between the need for radical transformation and the desire to protect human integrity. What then could be the means of arboreal transformation?

Reformed theologians appealed to the Spirit's work as mysterious. The Spirit "glides most sweetly into the soul" and infuses "supernatural habits by which it [the soul] is freed little by little from its innate depravity."⁴⁶ An appeal to the Spirit's mysterious or ineffable agency may, however, problematize the part played by gospel proclamation. While the Reformed sought to integrate proclamation as a means of grace in contrast to opponents whom

---

⁴⁴Bavinck, *Dogmatics*, 3:573. "Blocks and stones" or "stocks and brutes" language appears throughout the confessional tradition. E.g., Dort 3/4.16; Pelikan and Hotchkiss, *Creeds*, 2:587. Martin Luther had said that humans were less capable of accomplishing salvation than a block of wood. Cited in the *Solid Declaration of the Formula of Concord* 2.20-21; Robert Kolb and Timothy J. Wengert, eds., *The Book of Concord: The Confessions of the Evangelical Lutheran Church* (Minneapolis: Fortress, 2000), 548-49. Calvin (*Institutes* 2.5.14, 334) asks, "For who is such a fool as to assert that God moves man just as we throw a stone?"

⁴⁵Turretin, *Institutes* 15.1.4, 2:501-2, in *Institutio theologiae elencticae, in qua status controversiae perspicuè exponitur, praecipua orthodoxorum argumenta proponuntur & vindicantur, & fontes solutionum aperiuntur* (Geneva: Apud Samuelem De Tournes, 1688), 2:546. Cf. William Ames, *The Marrow of Theology*, trans. John Dykstra Eusden (Boston: Pilgrim, 1968; repr., Grand Rapids: Baker, 1997), 1.9.6, 107.

⁴⁶Turretin, *Institutes* 15.4.14, 2:524.

they perceived as overemphasizing the Spirit, it is often unclear what role proclamation itself plays in the process other than providing an occasion for the Spirit's regenerating work. While Reformed theologians agreed that the proclaimed word is God's instrumental means, the Spirit's simultaneous or even preceding work was determinative for creating the ability to respond.

To explain how this comes about, John Owen (d. 1683) distinguishes between moral agency and physical agency. Although the external call is an instrument of God's calling, it possesses insufficient power for regeneration. The external call appropriates arguments, reasons, considerations and other logical means to persuade, but these are ineffective without the Holy Spirit. Owen concludes negatively about God's external call, "Hence his operation is herein moral, and so metaphorical, not real, proper, and physical."[47] Moral operation is "metaphorical," as opposed to the "real" physical work of regeneration. Moral agency is inadequate because it leaves the person's will undetermined and does not give "real supernatural strength" to the soul.[48] Rather, Scripture drives one to explain regeneration in terms that evoke radical change. Owen then calls this work a "physical, immediate operation of the Spirit."[49] The Spirit's work occurs directly on the soul, without the mediation of arguments or persuasion.

Within the sixteenth-century context, "physical" refers technically to the Spirit's efficacy without regard to the mode of this efficacy. For instance, Johannes Maccovius (d. 1644) explains that theologians "call *physical* that which really produces an effect, whether that be spirit or body, God or creature, and whether it be produced by omnipotent power or by finite or limited power. They call *moral* that which is the cause of a thing by urging, warning, admonishing."[50] This sense of *physical* shows the tension more clearly. If used in Maccovius's sense as efficacious, it seems to exclude the possibility that a cause may be morally effective.[51]

---

[47]Owen, *Pneumatologia*, 307. Turretin (*Institutes* 15.4.23, 2:526) calls it a "hyperphysical operation" to emphasize the supernatural work of the Spirit.
[48]Owen, *Pneumatologia*, 308-12.
[49]Ibid., 317.
[50]Cited in D. Sinnema, "Reformed Scholasticism and the Synod of Dort (1618–19)," in *John Calvin's Institutes: His Opus Magnum*, ed. B. J. van der Walt (Potchefstroom: Institute for Reformational Studies, 1986), 490. Cf. Bavinck, *Dogmatics*, 4:84; Henri A. Krop, "Philosophy and the Synod of Dordt: Aristotelianism, Humanism, and the Case against Arminianism," in *Revisiting the Synod of Dordt (1618–1619)*, ed. Aza Goudriaan and F. A. van Lieburg, BSCH 49 (Leiden: Brill, 2011), 49-79.
[51]Peter van Mastricht, *A Treatise on Regeneration* (1699; Morgan, PA: Soli Deo Gloria, 2002), 37-

One can observe the same difficulty in John Calvin. Calvin struggles, for instance, to find a nonphysical mode of explaining divine causality. He summarizes God's action on the "godly":

> When the Lord establishes his Kingdom in them, he *restrains* their will by his Spirit that it may not according to its natural inclination be dragged to and fro by wandering lusts. That the will may be disposed to holiness and righteousness, He *bends, shapes, forms,* and *directs*, it to the rule of his righteousness. That it may not totter and fall, he *steadies* and *strengthens* it by the power of his Spirit.[52]

With the possible exceptions of "directs" and "strengthens," these are all physical motions. When pushed to explain divine agency, then, the Reformed recognized the Spirit's work as mysterious, but appropriated physical analogies. This may well be a Christian theologian's only recourse in light of Scripture, but the persistent tensions make it possible to explore fresh ways to describe the Spirit's agency.

Thus, in Reformed orthodoxy of the sixteenth and seventeenth centuries, *regeneration* and *effectual calling* are technical terms for divine action in converting change. In accounts roughly before the Synod of Dort (e.g., Robert Rollock), *calling* was understood to include both the circumstances in which the gospel is proclaimed and the power of the Spirit awakening or creating faith. But while the sixteenth-century Reformers used *regeneration* to refer broadly to God's work of sanctification following conversion, this term took on a narrower sense in the seventeenth century.[53] Regeneration came to refer to the supernatural, unmediated infusion of new qualities into the soul.[54] These theologians

---

38, uses *physical* with a sense more closely approaching mechanical. The Spirit works in regeneration by "a mere, absolute, physical agency," just as God's power "in raising Christ from the dead was not moral, but physical in the highest sense."

[52] Calvin, *Institutes*, 2.5.14, 334 (emphasis added).

[53] E.g., Owen, *Pneumatologia*, 329. Late seventeenth-century sources are quite clear in this regard. See Herman Witsius, *The Economy of the Covenants Between God and Man: Comprehending A Complete Body of Divinity*, trans. William Crookshank (1693; Edinburgh: Thomas Turnbull, 1803), 361; van Mastricht, *Regeneration*, 7-8.

[54] Charles Hodge, *Systematic Theology* (New York: Scribner, 1871; repr., Grand Rapids: Eerdmans, 1940), 3:5, gives a consensus definition: "The word regeneration is now used to designate, not the whole work of sanctification, nor the first stages of that work comprehended in conversion, much less justification or any mere external change of state, but the instantaneous change from spiritual death to spiritual life."

struggled between affirming God's omnipotent action in conversion and maintaining that God acts in ways appropriate to human creatures. The tension is most clearly seen when these theologians describe what sort of agency God uses in conversion. While wishing to affirm the importance of the gospel content, the vocabulary of regeneration in the narrow sense tends toward a physical or mechanical agency. Ultimately, a new heart can be implanted only by open-heart surgery. No amount of persuasion, even divine persuasion, can effect the needed change.

Given the challenges above, a contemporary doctrine of calling needs to describe the relationship between calling and regeneration. In addition, it asks what form of causality may be implicit in each way of referring to God's action. Reformed orthodox theologians believed that the scriptural witness demanded radical analogies of creation and bringing-to-life in order to make sense of God's action. I argue that "calling" modifies this drive by pointing to God's use of words. Since both terms, *calling* (Rom 8:28-30) and *regeneration* (Tit 3:5), are drawn explicitly from biblical texts, a contemporary account of calling must also address how the doctrine accords with recent exegesis.

Conversion and Converting Change

This book addresses how Scripture ought to inform the doctrine of effectual calling specifically in conversation with the Reformed tradition. I follow this theological tradition because I believe it has most faithfully explored the biblical text in this regard. Despite the concerns I raise about how some advocates of the effectual call have shed any connection with a spoken "call," this tradition asks crucial questions that flow from New Testament usage of the term. The benefit of this approach may be contrasted with an exclusive focus on the human experience of conversion as recorded in the New Testament.

Studies of conversion in the New Testament often appropriate definitions from the philosophy of religions.[55] Scot McKnight defines conversion as "the

---

[55]Conversion may be generalized as a "reorientation of the soul of an individual, his deliberate turning from indifference or from an earlier form of piety to another, a turning which implies a consciousness that a great change is involved, that the old way was wrong and the new is right" (Arthur D. Nock, *Conversion: The Old and the New in Religion from Alexander the Great to Augustine of Hippo* [Oxford: Clarendon, 1933], 7). For this genre, see Beverly Gaventa, *From Darkness to Light: Aspects of Conversion in the New Testament*, Overtures to Biblical Theology 20 (Philadelphia:

formation of self-identity in accordance with the central features of a faith."[56] He appeals to sociology for the vocabulary of conversion in the hope that this will enlighten New Testament conversion stories.[57] He concludes that one cannot systematize a conversion experience. Jesus' call to discipleship was individualized, particular and comprehensive.[58] McKnight does not ask about divine action in conversion or about theological descriptions of conversion in the Gospels and Epistles. He primarily points out the dangers of a focus on uniformity among conversion experiences through the example of the apostle Peter. This may be a helpful side road, but a dogmatic account of effectual calling describes God's action specifically.

The object of this study, then, is not the experience of conversion, but a description of God's action in the change that results in conversion. I understand conversion as an individual's public and social change of identification. A dogmatic account of effectual calling analyzes the divine causes of such change, and so I refer to this book as a study of *converting change*. This use of "converting change" is unprecedented, but it reflects the need to bring together various accounts of God's action, if possible, into a coherent statement.[59]

Preserving diversity in converting change. McKnight worries that a schematized conversion experience causes the church to devalue a "person's integrity, individuality, and identity."[60] Given such a danger, it may be asked how a doctrine of calling can claim that there is a describable, universal work of God in converting change, and yet preserve a form of diversity and individualized

---

Fortress, 1986); Richard Peace, *Conversion in the New Testament: Paul and the Twelve* (Grand Rapids: Eerdmans, 1999); Scot McKnight, *Turning to Jesus: The Sociology of Conversion in the Gospels* (Louisville, KY: Westminster John Knox, 2002); Stephen J. Chester, *Conversion at Corinth: Perspectives on Conversion in Paul's Theology and the Corinthian Church*, Studies of the New Testament and Its World (London: T&T Clark, 2003); Joel Green, "Conversion in Luke-Acts: God's Prevenience, Human Embodiment," in *The Unrelenting God: God's Action in Scripture*, ed. David J. Downs and Matthew L. Skinner (Grand Rapids: Eerdmans, 2013), 15-41.
[56]McKnight, *Turning to Jesus*, 1.
[57]Ibid., 48. McKnight draws on James Fowler, *Stages of Faith: The Psychology of Human Development and the Quest for Meaning* (San Francisco: Harper & Row, 1981), 252, and Lewis Rambo, *Understanding Religious Conversion* (New Haven, CT: Yale University Press, 1993).
[58]McKnight, *Turning to Jesus*, 177.
[59]Brenda B. Colijn, *Images of Salvation in the New Testament* (Downers Grove, IL: IVP Academic, 2010), explores similar evidence in the New Testament, but without explicit discussion of this evidence in a theology of conversion.
[60]McKnight, *Turning to Jesus*, 182.

experience. In other words, is it in any sense proper to speak about a common work of God underlying the experience of St. Augustine, the preaching of Bernard of Clairvaux and a conversion from animistic practices to Pentecostal Christianity in a modern missionary context? Or, how can Jonathan Edwards claim that God's work in conversion is a "divine and supernatural light immediately imparted to the soul" without marginalizing the nearly innumerable variety of Christian conversion experiences?[61] Kenneth Keathley asks if such a "light switch" definition of converting change does justice to the ebb and flow of human response, especially as recorded in Scripture.[62]

Amid the variety of personal histories, however, biblical authors describe universal Christian experience. One must be "born from above" (Jn 3:3). God "shone in our hearts" (2 Cor 4:6). "He called you through our gospel" (2 Thess 2:14). And he "made us alive together with Christ" (Eph 2:5). It may be debated how these apply to converting change, but in each case the author makes reference to an experience of divine action applicable beyond an isolated individual.[63] Matthias Wenk worries that if one defines unifying characteristics in converting change, one destroys the celebration of individual conversion experiences.[64] But it seems that the New Testament comfortably does both. I maintain that the New Testament accounts not only record a variety of conversion experiences but also interpret these experiences as instances of divine action.

James Dunn illustrates the challenges of balancing unity and diversity, particularly in Paul's theology. He notes the variety of metaphors for the "beginning of salvation" and concludes, "It would be a mistake to take any one of Paul's metaphors and to exalt it into some primary or normative status so that all the others must be fitted into its mould."[65] This is not an idle question given that the effectual call appropriates one of Paul's metaphors (calling) as a universal description of God's action in converting change. He concludes,

---

[61]Taken from the title of Edwards's 1733 sermon. Jonathan Edwards, "A Divine and Supernatural Light," in *Sermons and Discourses, 1730–1733*, ed. Mark Valeri, *WJE* 17 (New Haven, CT: Yale University Press, 1999), 405-26.
[62]Keathley, *Salvation and Sovereignty*, 133.
[63]I address each of these texts in the following chapters.
[64]Matthias Wenk, "Conversion and Initiation: A Pentecostal View of Biblical and Patristic Perspectives," *JPT* 17 (2000): 80.
[65]James D. G. Dunn, *The Theology of Paul the Apostle* (Grand Rapids: Eerdmans, 1998), 332. Cf. a similar concern in Colijn, *Images of Salvation*, 14-16.

however, that the numerous metaphors for the beginning of salvation together point to a unified experience of converting change.

> A particularly striking feature of Paul's letters is the frequency with which he refers his audiences back to their beginnings, to the decisive hearing, the act of commitment, the initial experience of grace. Paul's aorists again and again recall his readers to that initial stage and to its character as determinative for their ongoing discipleship.[66]

This seems to be a fair summary of the importance of conversion in Paul's theology. Dunn feels that Paul's words compel him to offer a unifying account of what occurs in converting change.[67]

I aim to respect the diversity of biblical descriptions of conversion while striving for a statement of how God acts based on these descriptions. As an analogy, in a theology of the atonement one may argue that several biblical metaphors (sacrificial, victory, judicial, example) provide perspectives on God's multifaceted work of bringing about fellowship with humanity.[68] It may be necessary to relate them as means to end or in other ways, but one assumes that the presence of biblical metaphors funding each model warrants their inclusion in a comprehensive description of how "in Christ God was reconciling the world to himself" (2 Cor 5:19). The same may be said about a theology of divine action in converting change. God's action can be described as calling (or causing to hear), shining (or causing to see) and giving new life. Each of these models describes God's action in general while also presenting distinct emphases.

Biblical reasoning and theology. The doctrine of effectual calling appeals to the Bible for the term *calling*. In addition, exponents of the effectual call have appealed to a variety of texts that explain or describe God's action in converting change. As an exposition of a theological concept drawn from biblical terms, this practice is an instance of "biblical reasoning." It attempts to reason along the grain of Scripture for the sake of clarity and coherence in the church's witness. In John Webster's terms, "biblical reasoning is the analytical

---

[66]Dunn, *Theology of Paul*, 324.

[67]Beverly Gaventa (*Darkness to Light*) attempts to divide conversion stories into alternations, transformations and conversions. Such an attempt is artificial, however, and leaves contemporary Christians unsure about the category of God's action in their lives.

[68]E.g., Alan Spence, *The Promise of Peace: A Unified Theory of Atonement* (London: T&T Clark, 2006).

and schematic presentation of the Christian gospel as it is announced in Holy Scripture."[69] For a doctrine of salvation in particular, Webster emphasizes that since salvation is God's work on behalf of humanity, human reason must consciously submit itself to God's self-presentation as Lord of salvation in Scripture. The New Testament consistently affirms that God has achieved salvation for humans in Christ, and apart from this witness we would have no knowledge of God's work on our behalf. Soteriology, then, seeks to account for how in Christ God was reconciling the world to himself according to God's revelation of that work. To this point members of non-Reformed Protestant traditions would likely agree. There is a common desire among Christian theologies to honor God's work in bringing about human redemption. But Webster infers further that soteriology also "traces the work of salvation back into the will of God, and forward into the life of the many, who by it are made righteous."[70] Biblical reasoning then, leads to and is informed by theological conclusions. This may be contrasted with a project to catalog and juxtapose images of salvation in the New Testament.[71] Such an approach isolates the various images without offering conclusions about how they work together. Biblical reasoning as a way of doing systematic theology argues that tracing the connections of doctrines and images and relating these to the trinitarian work of salvation is inescapable. To read Scripture and not ask, what is God doing? is to miss God's purposes in these texts.

Webster's "biblical reasoning" gives the Christian confidence to confess what God has done in Christ by probing the presuppositions and implications of Scripture's testimony. Biblical reasoning assumes that God works through human thought and reason, and so offers opportunity for believers to form, in Kevin Vanhoozer's terms, "the same judgments about God (e.g., doctrines) in terms of present-day conceptualities as those expressed in Scripture in terms of conceptualities that may no longer be extant."[72] Hence biblical reasoning depicts the theological

---

[69] John Webster, "'It Was the Will of the Lord to Bruise Him': Soteriology and the Doctrine of God," in *God of Salvation: Soteriology in Theological Perspective*, ed. Ivor Davidson and Murray Rae (Burlington, VT: Ashgate, 2011), 16.
[70] Ibid., 15.
[71] Colijn, *Images of Salvation*, 36-39.
[72] Kevin J. Vanhoozer, *Remythologizing Theology: Divine Action, Passion, and Authorship*, CSCD (Cambridge: Cambridge University Press, 2010), 188.

task as responding to God's revelation in Scripture through the use of created and sanctified human reason.

Vanhoozer does something similar with his "remythologizing" approach. Remythologizing seeks to avoid the twin errors of either conceiving God as an idolatrous extension of humanity ("mythologizing") or of conceiving God in universal terms apart from a particular history ("demythologizing"). One ought rather to give full credit to the biblical *mythos* (i.e., story) as divine discourse from which one may draw conclusions about God's being and action. Vanhoozer asks, "What must God be like if he is actually the speaking and acting agent depicted in the Bible?"[73] This question is fundamental to confessing the effectual call because the call points to a communicative and personal form of agency.

Biblical reasoning thus provides the formal structure of this project. Because God has revealed himself in a written witness that invites human reasoning and discernment, Christians will confess how God has acted in Christ through the use of a variety of terms and concepts accountable to the judgments standing behind biblical testimony. My account of effectual calling seeks to do this by testing and refining one of the church's affirmations of God's action in Christ through the various biblical descriptions of converting change.

Dogmatic Questions for an Effectual Call

When the church names God's action in converting change as an effectual call, it characterizes God's action both as accomplishing its purpose (effectual) and as analogous to a call. Given the use of the term "call" in broadly Augustinian and Reformed traditions and given its close tie to biblical language, the effectual call deserves attention and exposition. I propose three dogmatic questions that get at the nature of calling:

1. Who calls?

2. What is the content of the call?

3. What change occurs in the person called?

---

[73]Ibid., 23.

Motivating this study is an assumption that Scripture's use of the speaking verb *call* gives specificity to theological reflection on God's action in converting change. Although calling is not the exclusive description of God's action, Scripture repeatedly affirms that God speaks to people in bringing about converting change. In chapter two I will note how contemporary Reformed treatments have sought to reemphasize this dynamic of call and response in the work of redemption, especially through the doctrine of effectual calling.

To answer these three dogmatic questions, I then examine three sets of biblical images for converting change and their use in theological descriptions. I begin with *calling* (chapter three) in the New Testament and what this concept implies about God's work through human hearing and speaking. I evaluate proposals for the content of the effectual call as God's speech (chapter four) including the Lutheran theologian Oswald Bayer and the Reformed theologian Michael Horton. I then ask how the images of light and illumination depict further aspects of God's action in converting change (chapter five). I interact with John Owen, Claude Pajon and Friedrich Schleiermacher (chapter six) in order to show that the divine light in calling is a personal encounter with the authority of God displayed in Christ. Regeneration and coming-to-life metaphors typically dominate Reformed expositions of converting change. I probe the exegetical foundations of this move (chapter seven) and examine the theology of Jonathan Edwards in conversation with Kevin Vanhoozer (chapter eight). This is the heart of a communicative account of the effectual call. I appropriate Edwards and Vanhoozer to show that the Spirit's ineffable, "immediate" work nevertheless takes place in a "medium," that is, within the process of human understanding.

After establishing the plausibility of the effectual call from the various metaphors in the New Testament for converting change, I propose that the call may be analogously understood as an instance of triune rhetoric (chapter nine). Calling is a form of persuasion, but unique because it is an action of the triune God. In the conclusion (chapter ten), I locate the effectual call in its relations to other doctrines and propose how it might contribute broadly to an evangelical doctrine of salvation. I discuss the effectual call in an order of salvation and its potential contribution to a theology of infant salvation.

TWO

God's Call as Speech

God by his Spirit engraves on human hearts
what he speaks through his mouth to their ears,
not before or after but at the same time.

JOHN CALVIN

THE PREVIOUS CHAPTER NOTED a tension in earlier accounts of calling between the effectiveness of God's action and respect for created human capacities such as speech. While conservative Reformed theologians have consistently affirmed Dort's definition of regeneration as an unmediated work of God to change a person's disposition and prepare them to receive the gospel, some have sought to incorporate this work within the effectual call. Herman Bavinck and John Murray present such approaches. While acknowledging this consensus, I examine a constructive proposal through the work of Kevin Vanhoozer and Michael Horton. I suggest that Vanhoozer and Horton address the twin concerns of an effectual call best by preserving divine sovereignty in the application of redemption (the *effective* side) and highlighting human dialogical nature (the *call*) as the crucial way forward for explaining elements of the Spirit's mysterious work.

AFFIRMING DORT: REGENERATION OCCURS BEFORE OR WITHIN EFFECTUAL CALLING

Theologians have described God's action in converting change as both calling and regeneration. What relationship, if any, is there between these two terms? In the consensus codified at the Synod of Dort, they correspond roughly to

God's action externally through the proclamation of the gospel and internally through the work of the Spirit.[1] God's Spirit makes people able and active so that they bring forth the good fruit of faith. God's action in regeneration is *immediate* or unmediated because its efficacy is not dependent on the proclaimed gospel. In some expositions of a doctrine of salvation, calling and regeneration occupy different sections or chapters.[2] Further, in John Owen and others, *regeneration* is practically the exclusive term for God's action in converting change.[3] I suggest that there is a danger in privileging this unmediated transformation effected by the Spirit at the expense of *calling* because this minimizes the time-bound application of redemption. As I discuss below, Abraham Kuyper (d. 1920) does just this. He separates regeneration and calling as distinct events often occurring at different times. The more dominant view understands the terms to describe the same phenomenon. God's effectual or internal call carries the power of regeneration.

Abraham Kuyper: Regeneration occurs before calling. Abraham Kuyper so separates regeneration from calling that the call is directed at already-regenerate people. In regeneration, the Spirit secretly plants a seed within a person, a new "faith-faculty." This seed bears the fruit of faith when God calls. Kuyper explains, "In the first stage of regeneration, that of quickening, God works *without means*; in the second stage, that of conversion, He *employs means*, viz., the preaching of the Word."[4] The call, here understood as the proclaimed gospel, "serves to make manifest those who are regenerated, both unto themselves and unto others."[5]

Kuyper goes further and describes how God adds to a person's constitution. "In regeneration something is planted in man which by nature he

---

[1] See "God works in his elect in two ways: within, through his Spirit; without, through his Word" (Calvin, *Institutes* 2.5.5, 322) (for full citation information for Calvin's *Institutes*, see chap. 1, n. 18).
[2] Louis Berkhof, *Systematic Theology* (Grand Rapids: Eerdmans, 1941), 454-79; John Murray, *Redemption, Accomplished and Applied* (Grand Rapids: Eerdmans, 1955), 88-105.
[3] William Shedd, *Dogmatic Theology* (Edinburgh: T&T Clark, 1889; repr., Grand Rapids: Zondervan, 1953), 490-91, acknowledges "calling" on the first page but never returns to it in the following chapter on regeneration.
[4] Abraham Kuyper, *The Work of the Holy Spirit*, trans. Henri De Vries (London: Funk & Wagnalls, 1900; repr., Grand Rapids: Eerdmans, 1946), 318-19.
[5] Herman Bavinck, *Saved by Grace: The Holy Spirit's Work in Calling and Regeneration*, ed. J. Mark Beach, trans. Nelson D. Kloosterman (Grand Rapids: Reformation Heritage, 2008), 8. Bavinck ultimately criticizes Kuyper's position.

lacks."[6] If before regeneration a person's nature was entirely sinful, after regeneration it is holy.[7] Kuyper seeks to avoid saying that a metaphysical change occurs in conversion, but postulating a "seed of regeneration" other than the word seems to push in that direction. As Berkouwer points out, "This construction would seem to eclipse the good pleasure of God in justifying the wicked"[8] since one's inner nature is already holy through a prior regeneration.

In the background of Kuyper's exposition is his understanding of "presumptive regeneration" as the warrant for baptizing the infant children of Christian parents.[9] In his view, the church presupposes that a child of Christian parents is already regenerate and so deserves baptism, even though the church expects a period of time to elapse before conversion. Hence Kuyper sees a temporal separation between regeneration and calling, a period of new but dormant spiritual life.[10] When God chooses, the gospel "addresses itself not to the deaf but to the hearing, not to the dead but to the living, although still slumbering." Kuyper's bedrock principle is "first life, and then the activity of life."[11] While agreeing with this principle, few of the Reformed are willing to make a temporal separation between regeneration and calling the rule.[12] Kuyper's separation of regeneration from calling emphasizes God's freedom in bestowing salvation but does this at the cost of denigrating the place of the proclaimed gospel in conversion. The Spirit's real work of applying the benefits of Christ happens without the knowledge

---

[6] Kuyper, *Holy Spirit*, 311.

[7] Ibid., 311-12. Berkouwer defends Kuyper, "Regeneration . . . is an act of God by which the direction—not the substance—of human life is changed" (G. C. Berkouwer, *Faith and Sanctification*, Studies in Dogmatics [Grand Rapids: Eerdmans, 1952], 90).

[8] Berkouwer, *Faith and Sanctification*, 89.

[9] Herman Bavinck subtly criticizes this view and presents an alternative, that infant baptism is the sign of introducing the children of Christian parents into the new covenant community (Bavinck, *Saved by Grace*, 66-93).

[10] Like most of the Reformed, Kuyper affirms that regeneration may occur at any time (Kuyper, *Holy Spirit*, 317), but functionally it is important to him that regeneration and calling are distinct actions of God. Cf. Bavinck, *Saved by Grace*, 89.

[11] Kuyper, *Holy Spirit*, 298.

[12] Both Louis Berkhof (*Systematic Theology*, 470-72) and William Shedd (*Dogmatics*, 490-528) echo Kuyper's order by listing regeneration before calling. But they are less radical in separating regeneration and calling temporally. While Kuyper claims the heritage of Dort, he cites mainly two authors, Gisbertus Voetius (d. 1676) and Johannes Maccovius. For criticism of his use of sources, see William Young, "Historic Calvinism and Neo-Calvinism. Part 1 & 2," *WTJ* 36 (1973): 48-64, 156-73.

of believers. Their own subjective change becomes the manifestation of an already-realized truth rather than a genuine change of status.

John Murray: Calling contains the power of regeneration. Another stream of Reformed thought holds that the internal call is the Spirit's act to produce the change of regeneration.[13] The effectual call (understood as the internal or special call) is the creation of new life. The internal call just is regeneration. John Murray's exposition is representative.[14] "God's call is an efficacious summons and therefore carries with it, carries as it were in its bosom, the grace that ensures the requisite response on the part of the subject."[15]

Murray defends his choice to place calling before regeneration from Scripture. Calling is the "act of God by which we are *actually* united to Christ (1 Cor 1:9)."[16] Romans 8:30 lists *calling* as the first stage in the application of salvation. Calling is consistently listed as the first action of God that accords with his eternal purpose to save individual humans (2 Tim 1:9).[17] God's call "carries with it the operative grace whereby the person called is enabled to answer the call and to embrace Jesus Christ as he is freely offered in the gospel."[18]

But Murray also distinguishes calling from regeneration. Calling is an objective declaration, while regeneration is a subjective change.[19] Because of the "utter incongruity between the condition of the called and the calling," the Spirit must renew a person's disposition or *habitus*.[20] Although regeneration logically follows calling and is hypothetically contained in the call, it is ultimately not brought about through the proclaimed gospel. Rather, the word in question is God's effective command, his "immediate act of creative

---

[13]See Heinrich Heppe, *Reformed Dogmatics*, ed. Ernst Bizer, trans. G. Thomson (Grand Rapids: Baker, 1978), 518; Paul Helm, *The Beginnings: Word and Spirit in Conversion* (Carlisle, PA: Banner of Truth, 1986); A. A. Hodge, *Outlines of Theology* (New York: Armstrong, 1897), 448; Anthony Hoekema, *Saved by Grace* (Grand Rapids: Eerdmans, 1989), 80-112; Augustus Hopkins Strong, *Systematic Theology: A Compendium and Commonplace-Book Designed for the Use of Theological Students* (Philadelphia: Judson, 1907), 809-25.
[14]Murray, *Redemption*, 109-15; Murray, *Collected Writings of John Murray* (Carlisle, PA: Banner of Truth, 1977), 2:161-99.
[15]Murray, *Collected Writings*, 2:172.
[16]Murray, *Redemption*, 114.
[17]Ibid., 115.
[18]Ibid., 96.
[19]Murray, *Collected Writings*, 2:165.
[20]Ibid., 2:170.

power."[21] But here emerges a tension. While wanting to affirm the importance of the proclaimed word, Murray posits two words—that preached externally and the divine fiat operating internally. While there is a literal "call," the announcement of the gospel, the effectual call is a metaphorical call. It marks an action of God distinct from speaking. The relationship of external call to internal call comes out ambiguously: "Regenerative grace is carried to us in the bosom of the effectual call, and since the latter is by the Word we must never think of regeneration even in the restricted sense as wrought outside of a context that has reality and meaning only as a result of the Word."[22] This is a constructive attempt to link calling and regeneration. The challenge is to maintain the link between what God is doing with the words of the call and the result of regeneration. When Jesus cursed the fig tree (Mk 11:14) or when he announced, "Be still!" to the wind (Mk 4:39), he was doing more than uttering syllables. But there was still a connection between the locutions he used and the results.

Murray makes a significant contribution to integrate the divine word into calling and regeneration. He still struggles, however, to describe the agency of the word. What part does the proclaimed gospel play in regeneration? We are left without an answer. Murray affirms that regeneration occurs within "a context that has reality and meaning only as a result of the Word." But this leaves the "Word" ambiguous. Is it the divine fiat or the gospel proclaimed, or some combination of the two?

Kuyper and Murray display two alternative readings within the Reformed tradition. For Kuyper, regeneration is not connected to the external call. In fact regeneration must precede any saving calling. Murray insists that calling and regeneration are temporally concurrent, because the call carries the power of regeneration by the Spirit. While the Spirit's work is still unmediated, Murray maintains that the Spirit's work is integrally connected to the word, even if this connection is ineffable.

Herman Bavinck: *The word as instrument*. Herman Bavinck provides the most recent detailed study of how the two terms *regeneration* and *effectual calling* relate in the Reformed tradition. He published a series of articles in 1902 and 1903 in the midst of a controversy in the Dutch Reformed Church

---

[21] Ibid., 2:196.
[22] Ibid., 2:197-98.

over eternal justification and presumed regeneration.[23] He also treated the issue later in his *Reformed Dogmatics*.[24] Bavinck delves deeper than Murray to explain the gospel as instrument in calling. But he still leaves the effectual call as a metaphorical description for God's work of regeneration.

Bavinck argues that the Reformed tradition consistently listed *calling* as logically antecedent to *regeneration*. He affirms both that regeneration "presupposes the use of means," and that a dimension of the Holy Spirit's work is *immediate* or unmediated.[25] He must then answer the question, If the work of the Spirit is unmediated, why does it logically follow the preaching of the gospel, and not precede it?

He argues that unless calling precedes regeneration there is no connection between Christology and soteriology. One "might draw the obvious conclusion that actually Christ's person and work are not necessary to salvation, and that God may equally well regenerate the sinner aside from Christ by the Holy Spirit alone."[26] If the word about Christ does not logically precede the Spirit's work, then there is no visible continuity of Christ's work in the past to an individual's salvation today. Christ and the Spirit, in this case, would work on "two separate parallel tracks."[27]

Second, Bavinck affirms the logical priority of calling because God's speech is unique. "The word by which regeneration is effected ... is not after all the word of God in general, not his word in creation and providence, but his word in re-creation, that is, the word that in Christ he speaks in our hearts by his Spirit."[28] He distinguishes this word from God's power considered on its own. In 1 Peter 1:23-25, for instance, Christians are born again through the word of God, the same word that was preached to them. Bavinck points to the call itself as the means by which God changes human hearts. God's work is "one" divine call that is both "effectual and moral":

---

[23]Bavinck, *Saved by Grace*. The Dutch original is titled "Calling and Regeneration" (Bavinck, *Roeping en Wedergeboorte* [Kampen: G. Ph. Zalsman, 1903]), pointing out the crux of the question. "Eternal justification" states that the elect are already justified eternally in God's counsel.

[24]Herman Bavinck, *Reformed Dogmatics*, ed. John Bolt, trans. John Vriend (Grand Rapids: Baker Academic, 2003), 4:29-94. This second edition of Bavinck's *Dogmatics* was published between 1906 and 1911. See Henk van den Belt, "Herman Bavinck and His Reformed Sources on the Call to Grace: A Shift in Emphasis Towards the Internal Work of the Spirit," *SBET* 29 (2011): 51-52.

[25]Van den Belt, "Call to Grace," 54; Bavinck, *Saved by Grace*, 17.

[26]Bavinck, *Dogmatics*, 4:79.

[27]Ibid., 4:80.

[28]Ibid., 4:79.

It is so powerful that it cannot be overcome, and at the same time it is so lovely that it excludes every form of compulsion. Its power is so excellent that the depraved nature is renewed by it, and, at the same time, so friendly and winsome that it fully respects a person's rational and moral nature.[29]

God's call is "lovely" and "friendly," but also infinitely "powerful." Here it seems that God's call, uniting God's word with the power of God's Spirit, produces the change needed to draw a person to saving faith.

But what might it mean that Christians are born again *through* the living word of God? For Bavinck, the proclaimed gospel supplies the "object and content" for the response of faith. The word

> is a genuine means, a moral instrument, but nonetheless a means in the proper sense, effectuating and working that for which it is equipped and designed. It bestows upon faith its object and content, just as language supplies a child with ideas for which that child is suited in terms of the child's capacities for thought and speech.[30]

The analogy with a child is instructive. Bavinck uses the example to show that a child has the capacity for language, and that this capacity finds a path to actualization in the spoken language it hears. A goat kid, by contrast, does not grow into a speaking creature by hearing human language precisely because it lacks this capacity. The analogy then applies to a type of faith capacity. Preaching provides the occasion for faith, but it affects only those who have received the capacity to express it. This ability must come by another mode of action, by the supernatural infusion of qualities in regeneration.

Bavinck seeks to avoid reducing regeneration to purely natural or created means. He wishes to preserve God as the efficient cause of faith and as the agent of calling and regeneration. But his illustration of the proclaimed gospel as the words that develop a child's ability to speak is perhaps misplaced. If the ability to speak is analogous to the ability to have faith, it is difficult to see how he could maintain that the human sinful condition is a moral inability. As noted above, Reformed sources cite the

---

[29]Bavinck, *Saved by Grace*, 154. Bavinck echoes the Synod of Dort. Regeneration "is an entirely supernatural work, one that is at the same time most powerful and most pleasing." *The Canons of the Synod of Dort* 3/4.12; Jaroslav Pelikan and Valerie Hotchkiss, eds., *Creeds and Confessions of Faith in the Christian Tradition* (New Haven, CT: Yale University Press, 2003), 2:586.
[30]Bavinck, *Saved by Grace*, 151.

human ability to speak as significant for the way in which God interacts in redemption. Bavinck himself affirms that God's action in regeneration is eminently personal.

> The application of salvation is and remains a work of the Spirit . . . and is therefore never coercive and violent but always spiritual, lovely, and gentle, treating humans not as blocks of wood but as rational beings, illuminating, persuading, drawing, and bending them. The Spirit causes their darkness to yield to the light and replaces their spiritual powerlessness with spiritual power.[31]

Bavinck evokes the consistent language of Reformed orthodoxy that God interacts with human persons in a way that conforms to their nature as living and thinking creatures. The work of regeneration is not "simply natural," as when one throws a stone, and yet it is not "simply ethical," since God's work does not leave the human person undetermined. "It is therefore in a class of its own, simultaneously ethical and natural (supernatural), powerful and most pleasing."[32] In one sense this is entirely satisfactory. But by so closely associating regeneration with the internal call, the call for Bavinck threatens to lose its literal referent. The internal call is so unlike speech that it requires its own ineffable apparatus for explaining its effectiveness. Bavinck maintains throughout, however, that the proclaimed gospel functions as the call of God. There is only one effectual call for Bavinck with external and internal poles. I suggest that despite its strengths, Bavinck's presentation could develop more clearly the idea that when the Spirit works, the humanly proclaimed gospel is no longer a mere word, but the speech of the creator God.

Summarizing the Reformed consensus. Kuyper's view above separates regeneration from calling so much that there is little room for affirming God's use of means in converting change. Bavinck and Murray bring forward the Dortian position best. They recognize the importance of the gospel word in conversion, but ultimately equivocate on the place of the word in regeneration. Murray hints at a way forward by assigning instrumentality to calling and referring to regeneration as the result.

---

[31]Bavinck, *Dogmatics*, 3:573.
[32]Ibid., 4:84.

THE COMMUNICATIVE CALL

The presence of "calling" in Scripture and in the tradition forces one to ask about the type of agency God employs in bringing about salvation. It is too simple to name it only as either infusion or influence. Among contemporary theologians, Kevin Vanhoozer gives the effectual call a primary place and attempts to understand God's action in communicative terms.[33] Michael Horton incorporates Vanhoozer's proposal into his own program for understanding the order of salvation as the result of God's declarative speech act of justification.[34] These two presentations offer the most significant development in the exposition of effectual calling and are seminal for what follows in this book.

Michael Horton: A covenantal order without infusion. Horton argues that the traditional Reformed doctrine of regeneration sails too close to physical causality.[35] He admits that Reformed theologians "never conceived of the effectual call in anything other than personal terms and regarded it as the work of the Spirit *within*, not merely *upon*, the believer, winning consent and not coercing compliance."[36] But he asks, "Can the vocabulary of cause-and-effect make the point well?"[37] In other words, the earlier Reformed expositions lacked a conception of causality appropriate to the task of describing interpersonal relationships. Although they affirm the personal nature of calling, Reformed theologians subsequently remove the personal interaction when describing regeneration. The early modern classical theist is at least tempted to think of God's action as a form of mechanical causality. One may encounter God as a speaker in classical theism, but this God is, as a contemporary critic declares, pure "efficient supremacy."[38] Horton seeks to reinvest God's action with its properly personal dimension.

---

[33] Kevin J. Vanhoozer, *Remythologizing Theology: Divine Action, Passion, and Authorship*, CSCD (Cambridge: Cambridge University Press, 2010), 297-386.

[34] Horton brings up the question of the "content" of the call in ways that resemble confessional Lutheranism. I address this in chap. 4.

[35] Michael S. Horton, *Covenant and Salvation: Union with Christ* (Louisville, KY: Westminster John Knox, 2007), 221.

[36] Ibid., 222.

[37] Ibid., 221.

[38] David Bentley Hart, "Providence and Causality: On Divine Innocence," in *The Providence of God: Deus Habet Consilium*, ed. Francesca Aran Murphy and Philip G. Ziegler (London: T&T Clark, 2009), 42.

Horton points to the language of "habits" as problematic:

> The question is whether we can articulate an *ordo* (i.e., the application of redemption) without *any* appeal to infused habits. In other words, does God's Word, rendered effectual by the Spirit, have the illocutionary and perlocutionary force to bring about the world of which it speaks? Yes.[39]

God's speech, as spoken from the Father in the Son and by the Spirit, creates the reality it calls into being without the seemingly mechanical language of infusion. The instrument of calling just is God's speech. God speaks the word of justification to one, and this same word produces in one willing assent, trust and faith.[40] Horton thus interprets calling as the paradigmatic covenantal encounter.[41]

But keeping the language of calling and regeneration entirely on the level of speech and interpersonal relationships is no easy task. Horton explains the efficacy of the call: "The Father preaches, the Son is preached, and the Spirit is the 'inner preacher' who illumines the understanding and inclines the will to receive him."[42] And this preaching, or speaking, is effective whenever God the Spirit chooses to make the words effective. Horton does not want to posit an infusion of new qualities prior to God's call, and so, like Murray, he locates the power in the call itself. Calling is the "Spirit's sovereign work of raising those who are spiritually dead to life in Christ through the announcement of the gospel."[43]

Horton describes the Spirit's invisible work using categories from speech-act theory. God speaks a word, the content of which is the "announcement of the justification of the sinner."[44] When the Spirit accompanies this

---

[39] Michael S. Horton, *The Christian Faith: A Systematic Theology for Pilgrims on the Way* (Grand Rapids: Zondervan, 2011), 610. For a study of *habitus* in John Owen that illustrates Horton's point, see Christopher Cleveland, *Thomism in John Owen* (Farnham, UK: Ashgate, 2013), 69-89.

[40] Cf. Bruce L. McCormack, "What's at Stake in Current Debates over Justification? The Crisis of Protestantism in the West," in *Justification: What's at Stake in the Current Debates*, ed. Mark Husbands and Daniel Treier (Downers Grove, IL: IVP Academic, 2004), 115-16.

[41] His *covenantal ontology* centers on God's decision to meet and speak with humans. Michael S. Horton, *Lord and Servant: A Covenant Christology* (Louisville, KY: Westminster John Knox, 2005), 10-16; Horton, *Covenant and Salvation*, 166. Cf. John Frame, *Systematic Theology: An Introduction to Christian Belief* (Phillipsburg, NJ: P&R, 2013), 528: "God accomplishes all his mighty acts by speech."

[42] Horton, *The Christian Faith*, 567; Horton, *Covenant and Salvation*, 218.

[43] Horton, *The Christian Faith*, 572.

[44] Horton, *Covenant and Salvation*, 203. I analyze this proposition in chap. 3.

announcement, it carries with it a perlocutionary effect—the awakening of faith and repentance in those called. Horton appeals to *creatio ex nihilo* for an analogy. God created the world by speaking, and so God also creates the new world of the new creation by speaking. Thus calling consists in both a divine creative word focused on right standing before God—"Let there be justification!"—and the Spirit's presence creating an appropriate human response—"Let them bring forth faith!"[45]

In a slightly different mode, effectual calling is the casting call for a theater production.

> Effectual calling does not mean mere influence or coaxing, but a thoroughly effective speech-act. It is particularly when God is the dramatist, in command of both the plot (redemption) and the casting (effectual calling), that we can conclude that in this case at least, the "new creation" is simultaneously effective and uncoerced.[46]

God speaks a drama into existence and places cast members in it. But what sort of call is a casting call? For Horton, creation and resurrection ultimately judge the vocabulary for calling: "'Persuasion' is too weak a term to express this analogical connection. God did not *persuade* creation into being or lure Christ from the dead, but summoned, and it was so, despite all the odds. At the same time, one can hardly think of these acts of creation and resurrection as *coerced*."[47] While true enough to these examples, this seems to run against Horton's own objection to the traditional Reformed position that regeneration consists in the unmediated infusion of new qualities.

Horton has deepened the mystery by proposing that God's words, ministered by the Spirit, effect faith and repentance. The call to faith is God's "vocal, lively, and active speech."[48] But we need to ask, what sort of speech is it? When Horton points to the creation word (Gen 1:3; Rom 4:17) as the closest analogue, he risks leaving the mode of God's communication undefined or confined to a single utterance. The *creatio ex nihilo* analogy leaves little room for God's use of means and use of a medium over time. Horton

---

[45]Horton uses the phrases "Let there be . . ." and "Let them bring forth . . ." to bring out the difference between primary and secondary causality (inter alia, Horton, *The Christian Faith*, 347). I have added the objects.
[46]Horton, *Covenant and Salvation*, 225.
[47]Ibid.
[48]Horton, *The Christian Faith*, 573.

elucidates a continuing challenge: Can one describe God's call without simply asserting that God speaks words while he acts?

Kevin Vanhoozer: Communicative theism and dialogue. Kevin Vanhoozer seeks to think "of the God-world relation in terms of communicative rather than causal agency."[49] Without denying God's ability as Creator to manipulate the physical universe, Vanhoozer suggests that all God's action in the world is framed by speech. He further asserts that the primary drama of the world involves God's dialogical interaction with human persons.[50]

The argument here is inductive. Christian theology observes God speaking in Scripture, both in the economy of redemption and within the Trinity. The drama of redemption shows that the God who exists in perfect communicative communion (as Trinity) decides to extend this communion to include humanity. "The God of the Christian gospel is the Father, Son, and Spirit working in perfect communion for an even greater communion."[51]

This greater communion of God with his creatures, he maintains, comes about through communicative acts. The classic focus on God as causal agent in Aquinas and the Reformed orthodox is liable to the criticism that God's redemption is impersonal. Vanhoozer answers that a personal relationship exists if we consider God's action as analogous to that of an author.

The authorial analogy. Vanhoozer appeals to authorship as an analogical description of God's action in the world.[52] *Dialogical* is the key term for this communicative approach to providence and redemption. Following Mikhail Bakhtin's interpretation of Dostoevsky's novels, Vanhoozer notes that a dialogical author such as Dostoevsky, while still preserving his right as author to create characters, allows them to develop themselves freely through dialogue. Bakhtin observed that Dostoevsky uses dialogue exclusively (whether interpersonal or as monologue)[53] to bring about a character's realization (e.g., Ivan and Aloysha's conversations, Raskolnikov's running dialogue with himself). By analogy, God authors the world in such a way that he is

---

[49]Kevin J. Vanhoozer, "Effectual Call or Causal Effect? Summons, Sovereignty and Supervenient Grace," in *First Theology: God, Scripture and Hermeneutics* (Downers Grove, IL: InterVarsity Press, 2002), 117.
[50]Vanhoozer, *Remythologizing*, 337.
[51]Ibid., 259.
[52]Ibid., 298-99.
[53]For Bakhtin there is no monologue proper. All self-reflection is a pretended viewing of oneself from outside.

transcendent—he bestows the final say-so on his characters—and still cultivates an appropriate freedom in his creatures. "The dialogical author is 'the paradigm of a new kind of agency,' one suited neither to examining dead things nor to manipulating objects but rather to engaging the living consciousnesses of human heroes."[54]

The "new kind of agency" is the main point. Thus conceived along Bakhtinian lines, "God as Author is not a coercive cause pushing against our freedom in a manner that interferes with (or intervenes in) our heroic integrity. On the contrary, the divine Author is an interlocutor who interrogates and tests our freedom, consummating our existence in the process."[55] But if this is the case, how can God work redemption? An interlocutor stands outside us and speaks to us. At first glance it is difficult to see how Vanhoozer moves beyond what Dort calls mere "moral suasion" or the giving of advice.[56] In other words, is God's interjection really different from human influence?

Vanhoozer points to the incarnation. God chooses to communicate himself through dialogical means, that is, through the actions and words of Christ.[57] Scripture too participates in this as God "uses the variety of human authorial voices and points of view to communicate the meaning of the Word made flesh."[58] But God's speech must be understood, and here enters the work of the Spirit. For Vanhoozer, God's call typifies the primacy of God's dialogical interaction with human creatures. "The effectual call is the Spirit's ministering the word in such a way that hearers freely and willingly answer God by responding with faith."[59] "In such a way" is still ambiguous and leaves open the possibility that the call is simply fitting—*congruous* in the terms of the Roman Catholic Robert Bellarmine (d. 1621)—to a person who possesses libertarian freedom. But Vanhoozer wishes to preserve both the Spirit's necessity and sufficiency. When and where he wills, God the Spirit ensures both understanding (necessary but not sufficient) and

---

[54]Vanhoozer, *Remythologizing*, 333. The "new kind of agency" comes from Alexandar Mihailovic, *Corporeal Words: Mikhail Bakhtin's Theology of Discourse* (Evanston, IL: Northwestern University Press, 1997), 219.
[55]Vanhoozer, *Remythologizing*, 336.
[56]*Dort* 3/4. Rejection of Errors 7; Pelikan and Hotchkiss, *Creeds*, 2:590.
[57]Vanhoozer, *Remythologizing*, 357.
[58]Ibid., 365.
[59]Ibid., 374-75.

persuasion.[60] Vanhoozer summarizes Acts 16:14 and the opening of Lydia's heart: "God's calling is his restoring and reorienting those spiritual and cognitive capacities taken captive to an unclean spiritual and cognitive environment."[61] Perhaps Vanhoozer is approaching the traditional Reformed view. Restoring capacities sounds like the unmediated work of infused qualities. It would seem that Vanhoozer is near Murray's position that the call carries the power of regeneration "in its bosom."

But Vanhoozer's claim is more pervasive. He proposes that God's action with humanity as portrayed in Scripture is ultimately interpersonal.

> The Bible's depiction of divine action locates it on the interpersonal level. This is only fitting, for the conflict in the drama of redemption concerns the hearts and minds of men and women, and it is largely at this level that their fate, and that of the whole world as well, will be decided.[62]

The above quotation shows both the continuity of a communicative view with the Reformed orthodox tradition and its innovation. According to Bakhtin's view of the polyphonic author, interpersonal action means that God primarily shapes his people through dialogue or a sequence of call and response. We have observed that a stream of Reformed theology insists on the necessity of the proclaimed word in converting change. The term *effectual calling* points strongly in this direction. But because the Spirit's unmediated work is ultimately decisive, the call often becomes only the occasion for the Spirit's work. Vanhoozer makes explicit that the Spirit is sovereign and effective specifically in giving the proclaimed word its proper results. In this, God works through a process of dialogical interaction.

Objections to a dialogical call. Vanhoozer deals primarily with objections against classical theism and against God's effective (or irresistible) work in redemption. Thus his interlocutors are primarily contemporary theologians who have taken a broadly panentheistic or process theology turn. For these theologians, God gives up his independence when he chooses to create. For a doctrine of effectual calling, however, a stronger objection may be raised from theologians who view a dialogical call as unnecessarily weak on divine

---

[60] Ibid., 375.
[61] Ibid.
[62] Ibid., 368.

action. I present two objections that occur within the history of Reformed theology and have been suggested recently by Paul Helm.

First, one might object that although communicative theism brings out aspects of God's immanent and economic life, this cannot describe God's radical action against fallen human wills. Helm criticizes Vanhoozer for concluding that God only interacts with humans on the level of spoken dialogue. Such "cannot do justice to the passivity of the soul in regeneration."[63] According to Helm, a communicative approach to effectual calling fails to grapple with the depths of sin described in Scripture and so does not affirm the passivity of the converted person in the first moment of converting change. For Helm, dialogue cannot account for a change in will. Until the tree is made good, it cannot produce good fruit.

Reformed theologians affirm that there must be a change in sinful people before these can exercise faith, but the crucial question here concerns the means of producing this change. Horton and Vanhoozer agree that God's calling is effective, but "the communicative movement of word and Spirit is irresistible . . . *not because it bypasses our hearts and minds but precisely because it opens and illumines them.*"[64] A dialogical effectual call thus affirms human helplessness, but also recognizes that Scripture portrays human change coming about through divine discourse. God forms his people by communicating with them, and even in dialogue with them.

A second objection to a dialogical effectual call is its doctrine of providence. According to Bakhtin, an author such as Dostoevsky exercises control of a story and its characters through a form of providence. Dostoevsky develops his hero dialogically by introducing additional characters or voices that confront and interrogate the hero, showing the hero's true colors or developing the hero's character. Writing against French Calvinist Claude Pajon, Francis Turretin challenges that God's providential ordering of events and people is not a sufficient reason to attribute converting change to God's action. "Now if the providence of God (which is concerned about evil by the arrangement of objects and circumstances) did not make him

---

[63]Paul Helm, "Vanhoozer IV—The Personal and the Mechanical," *Helm's Deep*, August 1, 2010, http://paulhelmsdeep.blogspot.com/2010/08/vanhoozer-iv-personal-and-mechanical.html. Cf. Helm, *Faith, Form, and Fashion: Classical Reformed Theology and Its Postmodern Critics* (Eugene, OR: Cascade, 2014).

[64]Vanhoozer, *Remythologizing*, 383 (emphasis original).

the author of sin, why should the arranging of objects and circumstances which draw us to Christ make him the author of our conversion?"[65] If only circumstances must be changed, then the Spirit's selectivity would seem to be at issue. A dialogical effectual call must distinguish itself here from a Molinist doctrine of God's middle knowledge.[66] According to Bellarmine's *congruent* grace, God arranges circumstances in order to elicit faith from those he knows would exercise faith in those circumstances. God knows this through his "middle knowledge," a supposed knowledge of creaturely possibilities that is independent of God's decision to create just these creatures. I agree that if God chooses to shape his people and bring them to consummation through dialogue, including his own speaking, this inevitably involves his choice to actualize particular circumstances that are appropriate and fitting for persuading them. But the effectual call denies that God does this based on a middle knowledge that exists antecedent to the divine decree. Rather, as will be argued throughout, the effectual call is a special and selective instance of divine speech motivated by God's decision for his elect.

THE DIALOGICAL EFFECTUAL CALL

Reformed orthodox authors recognized the need for a special form of agency to describe the call. In addition to a general dignity of causality given to creatures, the call in Reformed orthodoxy affirmed a dignity of communicative interaction. Turretin points to the human ability to speak and thus communicate as significant for understanding God's work.[67] Twentieth-century authors such as Bavinck and Murray help clarify that the internal or special call of God contains the power to give new life to sinful humans. But regeneration consistently appears to trump all notions of God's acting by means of words. Can one so construe God's action so that God's call

---

[65]Francis Turretin, *Institutes of Elenctic Theology*, ed. James T. Dennison Jr., trans. George Musgrave Giger (Phillipsburg, NJ: P&R, 1992), 15.4.45, 2:539.

[66]For the discussion in Roman Catholic theology, see Réginald Garrigou-Lagrange, *Predestination*, trans. Bede Rose (St. Louis: Herder, 1939), 153-63. In relation to Reformed theology, see Richard A. Muller, *PRRD* 3:422. For a recent discussion, see Terrance Tiessen, "Why Calvinists Should Believe in Divine Middle Knowledge, Although They Reject Molinism," *WTJ* 69 (2006): 345-66; Paul Helm and Terrance Tiessen, "Does Calvinism Have Room for Middle Knowledge? A Conversation," *WTJ* 71 (2009): 437-54.

[67]Turretin, *Institutes* 15.1.4, 2:501-2.

brings about regeneration? Or must one posit a preparatory, unmediated act of God's Spirit to insert new values and inclinations?

Emphasizing communicative categories appears to be the best approach for relieving this tension to the extent possible.[68] Vanhoozer and Horton make explicit that God's call is a personal encounter with the speaking, covenant-enacting triune God. In order to solidify and test their accounts, a doctrine of effectual calling needs to attend to the diversity of metaphors in Scripture for converting change and the ways in which theologians draw from these texts to argue for the call. In addition, I will suggest that each illustrates potential pitfalls. Horton puts so much weight on the announcement of justification that the call loses its character as a summons. This declaration only tells what is already the case if it is understood as the content of the effectual call.[69] On the other hand, converting change in Vanhoozer could become so intellectualized that the noetic effects of sin seem to be lost. His description of the Spirit's work needs to answer how it can preserve the effectiveness of the call.[70] As I will maintain, understanding the effectual call as God's speech through human witnesses to Christ as ministered by the Spirit allows a Reformed soteriology to account for the role of the gospel message in bringing about converting change.

---

[68] Acknowledging that the Spirit's work is ultimately mysterious.
[69] See below, chap. 4.
[70] See below, chap. 8.

Calling in Paul

A Sovereign Summons

> *Therefore a man becomes a Christian, not by
> working but by listening. And so anyone who wants to
> exert himself toward righteousness must first exert
> himself in listening to the Gospel.*
>
> MARTIN LUTHER

ACCORDING TO MARTIN LUTHER, the person justified by faith primarily *hears*. Faith requires a posture that receives what God is saying. If faith is essentially a posture of listening, what does one hear? The claim of this book is that in conversion, God speaks powerfully and we hear. The focus on God's speech emerges primarily from how Paul uses the verb *to call* when he describes God's action. A study of how Paul conceives of calling leads to the conclusion that God's call is selective, gracious and powerful for producing the change of conversion. This is crucial evidence for the *effectual* call, that in bringing about conversion, God appropriates human discourse about Christ to transform human affections and elicit faith.

I present an argument here that is plausible by the standards of contemporary exegesis in an effort to show how the doctrine of effectual calling emerges from Scripture. While theologians are interested in incorporating the full scope of biblical evidence and so feel free to appeal to different texts and authors to argue their point,[1] this style may leave one open to the danger

---

[1]This is especially true for premodern authors. For drawing a doctrine of calling from numerous metaphors, see William Ames, *The Marrow of Theology*, trans. John Dykstra Eusden (Boston:

of proof-texting, that is, appealing to isolated texts without proper respect for genre, context and interpretive distance.[2] Some recent exegetes argue that this occurs when theologians cite Pauline calling texts to support the effectual call.[3] If alternative readings of these texts proved persuasive, a theological account would be forced to use other metaphors for converting change. This would undermine my focus on God's action in converting change as triune rhetoric. A dogmatic account of effectual calling cannot ignore this challenge.

An Argument for Divine Calling

The New Testament never qualifies calling with the favorite Reformed adjectives *internal*, *special* or *effectual*. Both earlier biblical theology studies[4] and more recent attempts[5] to map the semantic domain of καλεῖν and its cognates (κλητός and κλῆσις) have agreed, however, that Paul uses these terms distinctively in comparison with other authors. This reflects a relative consensus that when Paul uses καλεῖν with God as the subject he refers to the process of Christian conversion with an emphasis on divine action.[6] But this is only a first brick in the edifice of the effectual call. Therefore I begin with a sample argument from Pauline usage.

Three representative texts from Paul's letters provide the basis for the effectual call. For Thomas Schreiner, whose argument I present here, "calling"

Pilgrim, 1968; repr., Grand Rapids: Baker, 1997), 1.26.4, 157; Calvin, *Institutes* 3.24.1 (for full citation information for Calvin's *Institutes*, see chap. 1, n. 18).
[2]Daniel J. Treier, "Proof Text," in *DTIB* 622-24. See the proposal of R. Michael Allen and Scott R. Swain, "In Defense of Proof-Texting," *JETS* 54 (2011): 589-606.
[3]Most notably Brian J. Abasciano, *Paul's Use of the Old Testament in Romans 9.1-9*, LNTS 301 (London: T&T Clark, 2005), 207.
[4]Werner Bieder, *Die Berufung im Neuen Testament* (Zürich: Zwingli, 1961); Dietrich Wiederkehr, *Die Theologie der Berufung in den Paulusbriefen*, Studia Friburgensia 36 (Freiburg: Universitätsverlag, 1963); K. L. Schmidt, "Καλέω κτλ," in *TDNT* 3:487-536; L. Coenen, "Call," in *NIDNTT* 1:271-76; J. Eckert, "Καλέω, Κλῆσις, Κλητός," in *EDNT* 2:240-44.
[5]William W. Klein, "Paul's Use of *Kalein*: A Proposal," *JETS* 27 (1984): 53-64; Stephen J. Chester, *Conversion at Corinth: Perspectives on Conversion in Paul's Theology and the Corinthian Church*, Studies of the New Testament and Its World (London: T&T Clark, 2003), 59-112, presents the largest recent treatment of calling in Paul; David S. Morlan, *Conversion in Luke and Paul: An Exegetical and Theological Exploration*, LNTS (Edinburgh: T&T Clark, 2012), chap. 8, explores the dynamic of divine and human agency in Rom 9–10 through God's call and human response.
[6]Schmidt, "Καλέω," 489; Chester, *Conversion at Corinth*, 85. For calling as conversion, see N. T. Wright, *Paul: In Fresh Perspective* (Minneapolis: Fortress, 2005), 122; James D. G. Dunn, *The Theology of Paul the Apostle* (Grand Rapids: Eerdmans, 1998), 324.

in Paul's letters is an "effective initiative in summoning people to salvation."[7] The call is not an invitation that can be refused, but a "performative, in which the call accomplishes what is demanded."[8] This can be seen, first, in Romans 8:30, "Those whom he predestined he also called [ἐκάλεσεν], and those whom he called he also justified."[9] These three groups—those predestined, called and justified—are the same individuals.[10] But given Paul's statements about justification through faith (Rom 5:1), the link between "calling" and "justification" requires an explanation. Since predestined, called and justified people consist of one continuous group, this implies that at some point each member of the group exercises faith and is justified. In the verse, calling precedes justification and so it may be inferred that the divine call "must create faith since all those who are called are also justified."[11]

Second, in 1 Corinthians Paul acknowledges that when he proclaims the gospel, many people reject it as something foolish or scandalous (1 Cor 1:23). Yet others receive the message about Christ as displaying God's power and wisdom (1 Cor 1:24). Paul describes these people as the "called" (τοῖς

---

[7] Thomas R. Schreiner, *Paul, Apostle of God's Glory in Christ: A Pauline Theology* (Downers Grove, IL: InterVarsity Press, 2001), 41. On Rom 8:28-30 in particular, see Douglas J. Moo, *The Epistle to the Romans*, NICNT (Grand Rapids: Eerdmans, 1996), 530; James D. G. Dunn, *Romans 1–8*, WBC 38A (Dallas: Word, 1988), 485.

[8] Schreiner, *Paul*, 240-41.

[9] Schreiner here assumes, with the Reformed tradition, that προγινώσκω in Rom 8:29 does not refer to a simple foreknowledge of future events (i.e., that a given person would accept the free offer of the gospel), but rather that the term echoes its use in Rom 11:2 to indicate God's special concern for his own people. It is significant that the objects of this "knowing" are persons, rather than decisions of certain persons. This challenges the conclusion of Ben Witherington, for whom the phrase "those who love God" refers to Paul's readers exclusively as those who have already accepted the gospel and does not probe the source of this status (Ben Witherington, *The Problem with Evangelical Theology: Testing the Exegetical Foundations of Calvinism, Dispensationalism, and Wesleyanism* [Waco, TX: Baylor University Press, 2005], 73-74).

[10] A standard objection is that Paul here refers to the church corporately, regardless of the actual inclusion or exclusion of any individual. See Brendan Byrne, *Romans*, SP 6 (Collegeville, MN: Liturgical Press, 1996), 272.

[11] Schreiner, *Paul*, 241; Schreiner, "Corporate and Individual Election in Romans 9: A Response to Brian Abasciano," *JETS* 49 (2006): 380. For a similar Reformed theological explanation of Rom 8:28-30, see John Murray, *Redemption, Accomplished and Applied* (Grand Rapids: Eerdmans, 1955), 102-3; John V. Fesko, "Romans 8.29-30 and the Question of the *Ordo Salutis*," *JRT* 8 (2014): 35-60. This reading is contested on the ground that Rom 8:30 may not have a logical order in view. See Dane Ortlund, "Inaugurated Glorification: Revisiting Romans 8:30," *JETS* 57 (2014): 130-31. John Frame, *Systematic Theology: An Introduction to Christian Belief* (Phillipsburg, NJ: P&R, 2013), 936-37, dismisses a chronological order yet retains a special place for calling as bringing about union with Christ. The best argument for an "order" here is that Paul consistently relates God's plan or decision to his later fulfillment of that plan (Rom 9:24; Gal 1:15-16).

κλητοῖς). He further clarifies (1 Cor 1:27-28) that they are included in this group in part because God has chosen those who are lowly in order to display his wisdom. Because those "called" are a specific group among those who hear the gospel, "the call . . . is effective in that it produces the conviction that the gospel is the power and wisdom of God."[12] This conviction about the gospel fills the place of faith between calling and justification in Romans 8:30.

Third, Paul recounts that God called him in Galatians 1:15-16. The same logic that applies in Romans 8:30 and 1 Corinthians 1:24-28 also applies here. There is even Pauline testimony (1 Tim 1:16) that God's mercy to him served as an example for others.[13]

To summarize, Reformed theologians argue from Romans 8:30 that the chain from predestination to calling to justification entails that God's call must elicit or create the faith that receives justification. Thus God's call is effective at eliciting faith. This calling is, however, also selective. God chooses to call certain members from the larger groups of Jews and Gentiles (1 Cor 1:24-28; cf. Rom 9:24) in part to demonstrate his wisdom in contrast to that of the world. The central effect of calling is that the person called now views God's action in Christ as wisdom instead of foolishness, and this in large part denotes Paul's understanding of faith. As with Paul's own conversion or call, this calling is gracious and undeserved (Gal 1:15-16). These three texts (Rom 8:30; 1 Cor 1:24-28; Gal 1:15-16), then, establish the Pauline use of calling as a divine summons that is effective in producing faith, selective in where it acts and gracious to the undeserving.

These three texts present the basic outline for the doctrine of effectual calling. In what follows, I maintain that Paul uses the καλεῖν word group to evoke in his readers the memory of their historic conversion through the proclaimed gospel considered as a selective, gracious and effective divine summons. First, this definition emphasizes God's action in the past. In some places, God's call obligates believers to follow the moral imperatives in the gospel (Gal 5:8; Eph 4:1, 4). But I maintain that even these references are

---

[12]Schreiner, *Paul*, 241. Anthony Hoekema notes that it is difficult to read "called" in 1 Cor 1:24 as a general call. The call distinguishes those for whom Christ is God's wisdom from those who view Christ as foolishness. Anthony Hoekema, *Saved by Grace* (Grand Rapids: Eerdmans, 1989), 83.
[13]Paul links his call with that of other believers several times (Rom 1:1, 6; 1 Cor 1:1-2; Gal 1:6).

grounded contextually in a past experience of divine calling. Second, God calls through human discourse, that is, through intelligible speech. This is a form of "double-agency" discourse, in which God appropriates human proclamation for his saving purposes.[14] Second Thessalonians 2:14 shows this most clearly, in which Paul acknowledges his own preaching as the instrument of God's call.

Calling in the Thessalonian Letters

A summons is a form of communication through words. But to speak of God "calling" someone, one needs to clarify the type of speech involved. My own speech is at best analogous to God's speech, given that God's speech accomplishes much more than my human words. Is the effectual call then metaphoric for something else that God does in producing converting change? Or is it a literal yet analogous description of God's action? The Thessalonian correspondence provides evidence that God's call makes use of the apostle's verbally proclaimed gospel.

The Thessalonian correspondence serves as a useful test case because Paul interprets the recent conversion of former pagans in theological terms. Paul thanks God (1 Thess 1:2-5) that they turned from idols to worship the true God. Both the great change effected in their lives (1 Thess 1:6) and the power with which Paul and his companions announced the message about Christ (1 Thess 1:5) demonstrated that God had chosen these members of the Thessalonian community.[15] If calling can be established in Paul's earliest correspondence as a divine summons eliciting faith and conversion, then it likely informs occurrences in his later letters.[16] God's *call* highlights divine action

---

[14] Nicholas Wolterstorff, "Authorial Discourse Interpretation," in *DTIB* 79-80.

[15] I take ὅτι in 1 Thess 1:5 as causal, describing the reason for Paul's confidence in their election, with Charles A. Wanamaker, *The Epistles to the Thessalonians: A Commentary on the Greek Text*, NIGTC (Grand Rapids: Eerdmans, 1990), 78. Pace Abraham J. Malherbe, *The Letters to the Thessalonians: A New Translation with Introduction and Commentary*, AB 32B (New York: Doubleday, 2000), 110, who notes that the combination *eidenai ti hoti* is never causal elsewhere in the New Testament (Rom 13:11; 1 Thess 2:1), but rather epexegetical. But see Rom 8:27, where the construction is causal. In addition, if the response of the Thessalonians to the gospel just is their election, it is difficult to see how Paul's term parallels the election of Israel, which is the only other context where he uses the noun (Rom 9:11; 11:5, 7, 28).

[16] I assume Pauline authorship of 1 Thessalonians shortly after his initial evangelization there in AD 50–51. I further assume that 2 Thessalonians is Pauline. There is no viable situation in which 2 Thessalonians could function apart from Paul's authorship. See Malherbe, *Thessalonians*, 373-75. Καλεῖν occurs four times: 1 Thess 2:12; 4:7; 5:24; 2 Thess 2:14. Κλῆσις occurs in 2 Thess 1:11.

through human proclamation of the gospel. The clearest reference to a past conversion interpreted as divine action is 2 Thessalonians 2:14.

2 Thessalonians 2:13-14. In 2 Thessalonians 2 Paul contrasts those who have obeyed the gospel and believed the truth with those who have not. He aims to give his readers hope that, although they may face opposition culminating in the "man of lawlessness" (2 Thess 2:3), if they wait patiently they will be vindicated on the day of Christ's revelation. God will bring judgment on those "who did not believe the truth but had pleasure in unrighteousness" (2 Thess 2:12). Paul contrasts these with the believers in Thessalonica:

> But we ought always to give thanks to God for you, brothers beloved by the Lord, because God chose [εἵλατο] you as the firstfruits to be saved, through sanctification by the Spirit and belief in the truth. To this he called [ἐκάλεσεν] you through our gospel [διὰ τοῦ εὐαγγελίου ἡμῶν], so that you may obtain the glory of our Lord Jesus Christ. So then, brothers, stand firm and hold to the traditions that you were taught by us, either by our spoken word or by our letter. (2 Thess 2:13-15)

This is Paul's clearest theological explanation of the Thessalonians' conversion. James Denney calls these verses "a system of theology in miniature."[17] It is significant that Paul thanks God. Divine graciousness is evident both when Paul identifies his readers as "beloved" by God and when he says that God chose them for salvation. Additionally, God "called" them to a participation in Christ's glory, which corresponds to God's choice of them for salvation in the previous verse.

God is the author of the call to the Thessalonians. But Paul includes his own preaching as instrument. Throughout these letters, Paul presupposes that he personally announced the "gospel of God" to the Thessalonians (esp. 1 Thess 2:2, 8, 9; cf. Acts 17:1-9). He uses the same expression, "our gospel," in 1 Thessalonians 1:5 for his initial preaching in Thessalonica. In 2 Thessalonians 2:14, then, "our gospel" is not simply the content of the good news about Christ. It also includes Paul as the particular witness to Christ. In this text, therefore, one can observe the term *call* (1) with a divine subject as the

---

[17]James Denney, "The Epistles to the Thessalonians," in *Ephesians to Revelation*, vol. 6 of *The Expositor's Bible*, ed. W. Robertson Nicoll (New York: Ketcham, 1895), 372; for a reading according to categories of effectual calling, see G. K. Beale, *1-2 Thessalonians*, IVPNTC (Downers Grove, IL: InterVarsity Press, 2003), 228-29.

one calling, (2) referring to a past event of human proclamation and (3) leading people away from humanity awaiting destruction into possession of salvation and participation in the glory of Christ. Paul stresses divine action, and this elicits his praise to God that the Thessalonians have experienced the revelation of Jesus Christ among them.[18]

Thus 2 Thessalonians 2:13-14 presents strong evidence that "calling" includes divine choice, effectiveness and the use of created means. Paul affirms that in and through his own proclamation of the gospel God spoke to certain members of his audience. By means of the Spirit's sanctifying work and their belief in the truth these believers proved to be chosen and called for salvation. The same truth was proclaimed to those under judgment in 2 Thessalonians 2:12, but they did not believe it. The deciding factor in this case was God's choice of these people as firstfruits for salvation.

God calls you. Other instances of "calling" in Thessalonians contribute to the interpretation of 2 Thessalonians 2:14 above. First, Paul reminds his readers how he urged and encouraged them to live "worthy of God" when he was with them. He then characterizes God as the one "who calls [τοῦ καλοῦντος] you into his own kingdom and glory" (1 Thess 2:12). The following verse shows how God appropriated Paul's initial proclamation for his call.

> We also constantly give thanks to God for this, that when you received the word of God that you heard from us, you accepted it not as a human word but as what it really is, God's word, which is also at work in you believers. (1 Thess 2:13 NRSV)

This reference to their initial reception of the gospel shows that God's work in the past was a proclaimed word summoning them into God's kingdom. The present participle cannot be pressed to make God "who calls you" into a simple moral exhortation. God calls you into his kingdom and glory—clear indicators that this is the call to salvation. It has ongoing implications, but God's call has a definite beginning point.

The same dynamic occurs in 1 Thessalonians 4:7. In a section exhorting his readers to moral purity, Paul gives both positive motivation, in that their

---

[18]Contra Gordon Fee, *The First and Second Letters to the Thessalonians*, NICNT (Grand Rapids: Eerdmans, 2009), 303, who so emphasizes the corporate experience of salvation among the Thessalonians that these verses no longer speak about personal appropriation of faith.

behavior ought to differ from those who do not "know God" (1 Thess 4:5), and negative motivation, in that the one who wrongs a neighbor through sexual immortality is in danger of the Lord's vengeance (1 Thess 4:6). He concludes, "For God has not called [ἐκάλεσεν] us for impurity, but in holiness. Therefore whoever disregards this, disregards not man but God, who gives his Holy Spirit to you" (1 Thess 4:7-8).

Paul's exhortation has force with these readers only if they remember their call. God had evidently worked so powerfully in their conversion that they could recognize the time of God's particular call. The reference to *his* (God's own) Holy Spirit may also refer to the rare use of the possessive pronoun with the Spirit in Ezekiel 36:27 and Ezekiel 37:14.[19] If such is the case, God's gift of the Holy Spirit refers to the moral renewal promised in Ezekiel, that those given the Spirit would "follow my decrees" (Ezek 36:27). For a doctrine of calling, this text displays the radical transformation that occurred in the past: the Thessalonians came to know God, they recognized a new direction toward moral holiness, and they experienced the gift of God's Spirit for their moral renewal.[20]

Paul's closing prayer in 1 Thessalonians references God as the one who calls, but here Paul speaks of God's action continuing into the future.

> Now may the God of peace himself sanctify you completely, and may your whole spirit and soul and body be kept blameless at the coming of our Lord Jesus Christ. He who calls [ὁ καλῶν] you is faithful; he will surely do it. (1 Thess 5:23-24)

God is generally the "one who calls," but it may be asked if Paul has a particular call in mind. To see this, one might ask, to what is God faithful in this verse? God's faithfulness has to do with his title as "one who calls" and subsequent promise that he will "do it," that is, complete the work of holiness in the lives of these believers. Faithfulness implies a commitment on God's part to fulfill his promises, and Paul assumes that when God calls someone, he accomplishes his purposes to prepare them for the coming of the Lord. Thus God characteristically "calls," but this

---

[19]Malherbe, *Thessalonians*, 234-35.
[20]David Luckensmeyer, *The Eschatology of First Thessalonians*, NTOA 71 (Göttingen: Vandenhoeck & Ruprecht, 2009), 88n82.

call is a continuation of that call by which God acted in the conversion of the Thessalonians.[21]

Finally, in 2 Thessalonians 1:11 Paul addresses the life of believers. Paul prays "that our God may make you worthy of his calling [τῆς κλήσεως] and may fulfill every resolve for good and every work of faith by his power, so that the name of our Lord Jesus may be glorified in you" (2 Thess 1:11-12a). In the previous verses, Paul warns about God's coming judgment for those who do not obey the gospel (2 Thess 1:8). This judgment will also present a day of exaltation for those who have believed (2 Thess 1:10). It is likely that when Paul prays that God would make them worthy of the calling, he asks that God would conform them to a calling already placed on their lives when they became believers.[22] The shape of this calling becomes clear in the following chapter. Those who will exult in Christ on the last day are those who have moved from disobeying the gospel to marveling at Jesus Christ (2 Thess 1:8-10). The change is one of disposition, in which believers now taste or have a relish for Jesus Christ.

A summary and implications. The Thessalonian correspondence provides insight into the combination of human word and divine word. In his ministry, Paul gives both the "gospel of God" and "our very selves" (1 Thess 2:8). When and where God wills, this proclaimed gospel convinces men and women of its truth (2 Thess 2:14). Believers are those who have believed "our testimony" (2 Thess 1:10; cf. 1 Cor 3:5), that is, Paul's missionary proclamation. Paul's use of calling in Thessalonians leads to the following conclusions:

1. When Paul uses *calling* there is either an explicit (1 Thess 4:7-8) or implied reference to a historical experience of conversion in the lives of his readers. God as the "one who calls" is best understood in light of God's prior call in conversion (1 Thess 2:12; 5:23-24).

2. God's initial call to faith comes through the apostolic preaching (1 Thess 2:12-13; 2 Thess 2:13-14).

---

[21]Fee, *Thessalonians*, 231, sees a reference to past conversion. Malherbe, *Thessalonians*, 339-40, views this exclusively as a continual call to ethical living.

[22]Malherbe, *Thessalonians*, 410. Similar logic would apply to the "upward call" in Phil 3:14.

3. The past calling of believers was a radical transformation both in their appreciation for God's revelation in Christ (2 Thess 1:11-12) and their stance toward moral exhortation (1 Thess 4:7).

I proposed above that calling is God's gracious, selective and effective activity in conversion. The Thessalonian correspondence adds especially the notion that God's calling comes through apostolic preaching. All those who have been called by God in this sense have heard the gospel and responded in faith.

Calling and Creation

God uses human proclamation, but the call receives its power from the divine speaker. In 1–2 Thessalonians, God's call comes through Paul's preached gospel and sets a foundation for the believer's further development in holiness. God appropriates the preacher's human witness but works beyond the possibilities of a human word. If the preceding texts show the close relationship between God's call and the proclaimed gospel, Romans 4:17 distinguishes the divine call from a human summons.

In Romans 4:17, God is one "who gives life to the dead and calls [καλοῦντος] into existence the things that do not exist." This offers an additional perspective on the power at work in the call. Romans 4:17 clarifies that the transforming speech of the call possesses the power of God's creative speech. While Paul speaks in other places about the means God uses in converting change, this text adds that these means are effective only as God speaks.

Creating children of Abraham. Paul sets up a parallel between Abraham's faith in God's promise to give him descendants (Rom 4:3) and the faith of Jewish and Gentile Christians (Rom 4:24). Abraham is a common father to all who follow in his faith (Rom 4:16). In Romans 4:17 Paul quotes God's promise to make Abraham the father of many nations (Gen 17:5) and concludes that this promise was the object of Abraham's faith (Rom 4:18). When Abraham believed God's promise, this included a conviction that God gives life to the dead and calls things into existence.[23]

---

[23]For a summary of the content of Abraham's faith, see Simon J. Gathercole, "Justified by Faith, Justified by His Blood: The Evidence of Romans 3:21–4:25," in *The Paradoxes of Paul*, vol. 2 of *Justification and Variegated Nomism*, ed. D. A. Carson, Peter T. O'Brien and Mark A. Seifrid, WUNT 181 (Grand Rapids: Baker Academic, 2001), 161-63.

Paul's use of "calling" in Romans 4:17 is strikingly similar to Jewish texts in which calling refers to creation. The Greek version of Isaiah describes God's creative word as a call. "My hand laid the foundation of the earth, and my right hand bolstered heaven; I will call them [καλέσω αὐτούς], and they will stand together" (Is 48:13 NETS).[24] In Wisdom 11:25, things that exist have their origin in God's call: "How would anything have endured if you had not willed it? Or how would anything not called [τὸ κληθέν] [into existence] by you have been preserved by you?" (NETS, brackets mine). The LXX already shows the use of καλεῖν to describe God's creation work and this likely informs Romans 4:17.[25]

What does God create with his call? God calls the "many nations" into existence, that is, Abraham's future descendants.[26] Paul thus interprets the "many nations" of Genesis 17:5 as the inclusion of Gentiles into God's family as Abraham's descendants.[27] God's call here is his creative power to produce a worldwide family of Abraham characterized by faith.

Romans 4:17 in a theology of calling. How then does this interpretation inform Paul's overall use of καλεῖν? Timothy Chester concludes that "calling is a premeditated and completely undetermined divine act."[28] This reflects Calvin's conclusion: "The word *call* ought not to be confined to preaching, but it is to be taken, according to the usage of Scripture, for raising up; and it is intended to set forth more fully the power of God, who raises up, as it were by a nod only, whom he wills."[29]

"By a nod only" locates the power of the call in the creative divine fiat. Paul here describes God's power to create descendants for Abraham in a situation in which none could be expected by natural means. If taken absolutely, this text would press one to read all of Paul's calling language as creation *ex nihilo*. In this case God's "call" would be metaphorical for another, more fundamental act such as creation. But a purely *ex nihilo* reading of calling will not make

---

[24]Καλεῖν appears fifty-nine times in canonical LXX Isaiah. Divine summons is clear in Is 41:2, 4, 9; 42:6; 43:1; 45:3-4; 46:11; 48:12, 15; 49:1; 51:2. The above reference (Is 48:13) is unique as a creative summons.

[25]See Philo, *The Special Laws* 4.187 (LCL 123). God "calls [ἐκάλεσεν] things not existing into existence."

[26]Thomas R. Schreiner, *Romans*, BECNT (Grand Rapids: Baker, 1998), 237; cf. Moo, *Romans*, 282.

[27]Chester, *Conversion at Corinth*, 78-79; Halvor Moxnes, *Theology in Conflict: Studies in Paul's Understanding of God in Romans*, NovTSup 53 (Leiden: Brill, 1980), 244-49.

[28]Chester, *Conversion at Corinth*, 86.

[29]Calvin, *Comm. Rom. 4:16-17* (*CC* 19:175).

sense of Paul's usage. One cannot simply replace "called" with "made" or "created" in numerous texts (e.g., Rom 8:30; Gal 1:15). In addition, if one reads the creation language as the closest analogical description of calling, this makes the noun "calling" difficult to discern (e.g., 1 Cor 1:24-26; 7:20; Phil 3:14). How does one live worthy of the "creation" God has accomplished? Rather, God's call to salvation is both like and unlike God's action to call creation into existence. Even while Paul discerns the power behind God's action in conversion as the same power that created *ex nihilo*, he gives place for created agency, whether a powerful witness, a powerful message or the dialogical response of the person converted.[30]

Paul identifies God as one who calls things into existence, specifically descendants for Abraham. Paul can describe various activities, including the original creation, God's giving Isaac to Abraham and God's work to bring Christians into fellowship with Christ, as a call. This breadth of reference ensures that a doctrine of effectual calling respects the exclusive creative power of God's words. God's call creates the reality it intends, and ultimately the power behind God's speech is ineffable, just as the power of the word in creation is beyond human understanding. Yet God's call is not exclusively creation from nothing. That God will create descendants for Abraham does not determine precisely how he will accomplish this.

Objections to a Divine Summons

Several key texts point to a Pauline doctrine of calling that includes God's selective decision of whom to call. The Thessalonian correspondence confirms that God's call comes through human discourse. Romans 4:17 clarifies that although God makes use of human discourse, the call is still God's distinct speech.

Yet there are both exegetical and theological objections to calling as a divine summons. Broadly Arminian theologians have interpreted all references to calling as forms of external and indiscriminate gospel proclamation.[31] This view takes Paul's usage in line with the distinction recorded in

---

[30]In this regard, the conversion romance *Joseph and Aseneth* provides a tentative example, although it may be a late Christian text (for this view, see Ross Shepard Kraemer, *When Aseneth Met Joseph: A Late Antique Tale of the Biblical Patriarch and His Egyptian Wife, Reconsidered* [Oxford: Oxford University Press, 1998], 274). See *Joseph and Aseneth* 8.10-11. *Second Clement* 1.8 provides a second-century interpretation of conversion as creation.

[31]"Of a *Vocatio Interna*, as distinguished from the *Vocatio Externa*, there is no trace in Scripture"

Matthew 22:14 between those "called" or invited and those "chosen." Although some texts such as 1 Thessalonians 2:12 may be read this way, it fails to explain all Pauline usage, especially the combination of choosing and calling language in 1 Corinthians 1:26-28.

In particular, however, Brian Abasciano points to texts that he believes provide a better starting point for understanding Pauline usage than does Romans 8:28-30.[32] I. Howard Marshall also argues that the above presentation coupled with a doctrine of perseverance cannot make sense of Paul's exhortations.[33]

Divine naming. The first objection challenges whether calling in Paul is a divine *summons*. What if καλεῖν in Paul refers to God's declaration of a Christian's new name or status? Abasciano argues against "calling" as an effective divine summons from Romans 9. If he can establish a "naming" sense for calling in the five occurrences in that chapter, "the traditional notion of effectual calling would be eliminated, for it is based on the idea of a *summoning* which effectively creates the response of faith and obedience to the call."[34] Abasciano defines calling as God's "act of designating a group as God's elect people," preeminently his designation of the church as God's people on the basis of faith.[35] Calling functions much like the term *justification* does for some New Testament interpreters.[36] In the same way that justification is God's retrospective verdict on who is now a member of God's people, calling for Abasciano means that God states that which is the case for a given person, that is, that such a person has become a Christian.

(William Pope, *A Compendium of Christian Theology: Being Analytical Outlines of a Course of Theological Study, Biblical, Dogmatic, Historical*, 2nd ed. [New York: Hunt & Eaton, 1889], 2:345). "The vocation or call is God's offer of salvation to all men through Christ" (H. Orton Wiley, *Christian Theology* [Kansas City, MO: Beacon Hill, 1952], 2:340).

[32]Abasciano, *Romans 9.1-9*, 196-207; Abasciano, *Paul's Use of the Old Testament in Romans 9.10-18: An Intertextual and Theological Exegesis*, LNTS 317 (London: T&T Clark, 2011), 37-74.

[33]I. Howard Marshall, "Election and Calling to Salvation in 1 and 2 Thessalonians," in *The Thessalonian Correspondence*, ed. Raymond F. Collins, BETL 87 (Leuven: Leuven University Press, 1990), 259-76.

[34]Abasciano, *Romans 9.1-9*, 207. In an earlier article, Klein, "*Kalein*," argues similarly. Klein's study has significant weaknesses. It (1) dismisses several Pauline texts (Rom 4:17; 9:7; 9:24-25), (2) assumes that καλεῖν has a "naming" sense even without a double accusative and (3) concludes that καλεῖν does not specify the means by which someone becomes a Christian while admitting this is the case in a crucial text (2 Thess 2:14)(ibid., 64n29).

[35]Abasciano, *Romans 9.1-9*, 200-201.

[36]E.g., Wright, *Paul*, 121-22.

He reads Romans 9 as Paul's defense of God's right to grant covenant-member status to Gentiles by his own standard apart from the "works of the law," which Abasciano understands as Jewish marks of covenant membership such as circumcision.[37] Paul wants to show that membership in God's family is now a matter of faith rather than dependent on the marks of Jewish identity. Romans 9:8 and 9:12 demonstrate this fundamental distinction between the works of the law and faith. The first text contrasts the "children of the flesh" and the "children of the promise" (Rom 9:8). For Abasciano, one is named a child of the promise because one has become a member of Abraham's family by faith, as in Galatians 3:26-29.[38] That the children of promise are "considered to be offspring" (Rom 9:8) of Abraham is analytic. God does not change anything about these people but recognizes those who have faith as the true seed of Abraham. Once it is clear that faith marks membership in Abraham's family in Romans 9:8, Abasciano argues that the same is the case in the previous verse, in which Paul quotes Genesis 21:12, "Through Isaac your offspring will be *called/named* [κληθήσεται]." Just as God was free to designate or name whom he wished as heirs of Abraham, so he has freely decided that those who are children of promise, that is, those who have exercised faith, will be Abraham's children and heirs regardless of ethnic descent.

Abasciano is correct that one of Paul's primary goals in Romans is to show that those who imitate Abraham's faith are his children (Rom 4:16-17), but calling speaks about God's way of bringing this family about. In Romans 9:11-12, Paul attributes the selection of Jacob over Esau to God's "purpose of election." He describes this purpose as "not because of works but because of him who calls" (Rom 9:11). Abasciano inserts his point about faith into this verse and argues that God's purpose in election is his decision to choose people not on the basis of works, but on the basis of faith.[39] In this reading, Paul distinguishes between a hypothetical God who chooses individuals based on their ethnic lineage and the actual God who chooses on his own sovereign basis, which happens to be an individual's faith.

---

[37] Abasciano, *Romans 9.1-9*, 201.
[38] Ibid., 197.
[39] Abasciano, *Romans 9.10-18*, 55. See argument against this in John Piper, *The Justification of God: An Exegetical and Theological Study of Romans 9:1-23*, 2nd ed. (Grand Rapids: Baker, 1993), 53-55. He notes Rom 11:6, where Paul contrasts works with "grace" in God's electing or choosing purpose.

To do this, Abasciano elevates the "naming" sense in the quotation of Genesis 21:12 as determinative for Paul's use of καλεῖν.[40] He reads Romans 9:7-8 not as evidence for sovereign divine selection (on whatever basis and for whatever purpose), but as a general statement that through a promise—in Genesis, this is Isaac, and in the present, *faith*—God will name some people as members of Abraham's family.[41]

Paul indeed affirms that one's covenant membership comes through faith, but that is not his point in Romans 9:8. Paul's example of a promise in Romans 9:9 demonstrates this. The promise is a miraculous divine word that ensures that Sarah will give birth to a son. Thus although κληθήσεται in Romans 9:7 // Genesis 21:12 is a "naming," this naming is selective and based on God's sovereign word or promise.

Abasciano's reading presents a challenge to the doctrine of effectual calling. His study has not yet reached Romans 9:24-26, but this text provides potential confirmation of his thesis because it includes Paul's own use of calling (Rom 9:24), his insertion of καλεῖν into an LXX quotation (Rom 9:25) and his retaining of καλεῖν in a subsequent citation (Rom 9:26).

> What if God, desiring to show his wrath and to make known his power, has endured with much patience vessels of wrath prepared for destruction, in order to make known the riches of his glory for vessels of mercy, which he has prepared beforehand for glory—even us whom he has called [ἐκάλεσεν], not from the Jews only but also from the Gentiles? As indeed he says in Hosea, "Those who were not my people I will call [καλέσω] 'my people,' and her who was not beloved I will call [verb implied] 'beloved.'" "And in the very place where it was said to them, 'You are not my people,' there they will be called [κληθήσονται] 'sons of the living God.'" (Rom 9:22-26)

It is challenging to balance the different uses of calling in this text. If one privileges the "naming" domain for calling, then Romans 9:24 is difficult. But if one privileges "summoning," then Romans 9:25-26 is difficult, especially in its LXX contexts (Hos 2:25; 2:1 LXX).[42] In Romans 9:24 the

---

[40] For an interpretation that views Rom 9:7 as a creative call/summons, see Moo, *Romans*, 576; Schreiner, *Romans*, 495-96.
[41] Abasciano, *Romans 9.1-9*, 215.
[42] But see Schreiner, *Romans*, 527-28, who maintains that in Rom 9:25-26, καλεῖν is still an effective divine summons.

connection with "preparing beforehand" (προητοίμασεν) strongly pulls in favor of the similar construction in Romans 8:30, where "predestined" and "called" are related in sequence (cf. Gal 1:15). "Summoned" here makes good sense of the dynamic between a prior setting apart and a historical divine address.[43] The absence of a double accusative, which indicates a type of naming, also favors a summons.[44]

But if one accepts a summons sense in Romans 9:24, the following two verses are more difficult. In Romans 9:26, "they will be called 'sons of the living God'" is the declaration of a title rather than a summons. In Romans 9:25, however, Paul replaces the LXX verb "I will say" (ἐρῶ) in Hosea 2:25 with καλέσω: "I will *call* 'not my people,' my people." Paul takes God's declaration that he will restore his rejected people and applies it to Gentile Christians. By using καλεῖν, Paul underscores "the effective character of the Lord's word that makes Not-my-people the Lord's people."[45] Paul has thus modified the Hosea quotation in order to make it an example of "calling" in the sense that he uses the term in Romans 9:24. It is God's gracious action to bring both Jews and Gentiles into his covenant protection.[46]

These texts blur the semantic lines of "summoning" and "designating." But I submit that a divine "summons" can explain the "designation" in a way that the latter cannot explain the former. When Paul inserts καλεῖν into the quotation in Romans 9:25, he connects the two domains. Divine calling is something spoken (ἐρῶ vs. καλέσω) and is effective to create a new status or name.

Abasciano's "naming" domain for calling has difficulty accounting for the references in Romans 9. While some of these texts can be interpreted as a divine naming (Rom 9:7, 25) and while they certainly include a declaratory change of status, to read all Pauline calling texts in this way leaves no place for calling as an event of divine discourse, an element that seems clear in Paul's call (Gal 1:15) and the call of the Thessalonians (2 Thess 2:14). When read primarily as an effective summons, however, texts with a naming range more easily retain their independence. While a naming sense cannot

---

[43]Moo, *Romans*, 611.
[44]Contra Klein, "*Kalein*," 57.
[45]Mark A. Seifrid, "Romans," in *CNTUOT* 647.
[46]Moxnes, *Theology in Conflict*, 253; C. E. B. Cranfield, *A Critical and Exegetical Commentary on the Epistle to the Romans*, ICC (Edinburgh: T&T Clark, 1975), 500.

account for the summons sense, a summons sense includes sufficient room for cases of selective divine naming.

Ineffectual calling: The perseverance objection. A final exegetical objection is that an effectual call cannot account for Paul's admonitions. In other words, calling cannot be sustained in its traditional Reformed sense as an outworking of God's pretemporal election leading ineluctably toward perseverance and glorification.[47] Marshall levels this charge in relation to the use of "calling" and "election" in 1 Thessalonians. He argues that Paul's use of election language in 1 Thessalonians 1:4 includes the possibility that elect believers may turn away.[48] Marshall asks how Paul could refer to the Thessalonian church as elected and called, if some among them would not persevere in their profession of faith. That the Thessalonians are "called" simply recognizes that they have responded to the gospel in conversion.[49]

This touches a perennial question for Reformed theologians regarding the difference between a theological statement that God preserves his elect in faith and one's personal confidence that such is the case for oneself and for others.[50] A proposal that views the warnings as divinely ordained means to preserve the faith of God's elect would answer the general objection.

Specifically in regard to "calling" language, does the term in its New Testament use bear the full weight of the doctrine of perseverance? One cannot discount the evidence of the "golden chain" in Romans 8:28-30, nor Paul's assurance of God's preserving influence begun in a historic call (e.g., 1 Cor 1:7-9; 1 Thess 5:23-24). But a doctrine of perseverance does not rely exclusively either on calling language or on a uniform use of "calling" terms in the New Testament (see Mt 22:14). Calvin has room for an *ineffectual* call—an action of the Holy Spirit that awakens or attracts a person into the sphere

---

[47]See *WCF* 3.8, where the confession declares that people can "be assured of their eternal election" from "the certainty of their effectual vocation."
[48]Marshall, "Election and Calling," 262; cf. Witherington, *Evangelical Theology*, 65.
[49]Witherington, *Evangelical Theology*, 69.
[50]For the warnings as ordained means to preserve the elect, see Thomas R. Schreiner and Ardel B. Caneday, *The Race Set Before Us: A Biblical Theology of Perseverance and Assurance* (Downers Grove, IL: InterVarsity Press, 2001); Judith M. Gundry Volf, *Paul and Perseverance: Staying in and Falling Away*, WUNT 2/37 (Tübingen: J. C. B. Mohr, 1990). It is beyond the scope of this chapter to discuss differences in Augustine's doctrine of perseverance and developments in the Reformed tradition, but see the discussion of Henry M. Knapp, "Augustine and Owen on Perseverance," *WTJ* 62 (2000): 65-87.

of the gospel and yet does not continue.[51] Turretin represents those who posit both an outward and inward form of the covenant so that one may participate in the former (including a form of calling) without the latter.[52]

In analyzing Paul's use of calling I assume that Paul addresses his readers with a charitable judgment that the public evidence of their conversion corresponds with divine action.[53] But I propose that Paul does not presume knowledge of absolute divine reality (Phil 4:3 may be an exception). I submit that the warnings and exhortations can be read consistently as the means by which God preserves his people. "Calling" is eminently fitting for this task, since Paul portrays the life of Christian believers as an ongoing response to their historic conversion or call (Eph 4:1, 4).

A Summary of Pauline Usage

In the Pauline corpus God's call is either a past action or the ongoing implications of that call. Thus when Paul refers to the calling of believers, he reminds them of God's action in their conversion. When Paul uses a finite form of καλεῖν in the aorist, this is the case unambiguously.[54] As we have seen above, Paul also describes God generally as "the one who calls." These texts refer to God as creator (Rom 4:17), God as one who elects (Rom 9:12) or else contain a reference to conversion in context.[55]

The substantives κλητός and κλῆσις are more ambiguous, but still refer to a past divine action. Both the apostle specifically (Rom 1:1; 1 Cor 1:1) and believers generally (Rom 1:6, 7; 1 Cor 1:2) are the "called" (κλητοί), but those who have rejected the gospel are not considered "called" (1 Cor 1:24).[56] One's "calling" can be the time of conversion (1 Cor 1:26; 7:20) or the style of life

---

[51]Calvin, *Institutes* 3.24.8, 974. Calvin preserves the "once enlightened" language of Heb 6:4 for this form of special, yet ineffectual influence: "Yet sometimes [God] also causes those whom he illumines only for a time to partake of it; then he justly forsakes them on account of their ungratefulness and strikes them with even greater blindness."

[52]Francis Turretin, *Institutes of Elenctic Theology*, ed. James T. Dennison Jr., trans. George Musgrave Giger (Phillipsburg, NJ: P&R, 1992), 15.1.6-8, 2:502.

[53]For the "judgment of charity," see Calvin, *Comm. 1 Cor. 1:9* (CC 20:59).

[54]Rom 8:28, 30; 9:24-26; 1 Cor 1:9; 7:15, 17 (perfect indicative), 18, 20-24; Gal 1:6, 15; 5:13; Eph 4:1, 4; Col 3:15; 1 Thess 4:7; 2 Thess 2:14; 1 Tim 6:12; 2 Tim 1:9. Cf. 1 Pet 1:15; 2:9; 2:21; 3:9; 5:10; and 2 Pet 1:3. Hebrews 9:15 may correspond to this category, although the use of καλεῖν in Hebrews is more diverse: God's call is an invitation to Abraham (Heb 11:8, 18), priests are appointed/called (Heb 5:4) and believers possess a heavenly "calling" (Heb 3:1).

[55]1 Thess 2:12; 5:24; Gal 5:8.

[56]That κλητός became a technical term for "believer" can be seen in Rev 17:14 and Jude 1.

arising from that conversion (Eph 4:1, 4; 2 Tim 1:9). This calling is a new vision for life and contains great hope (Eph 1:18), directs one "upward" (Phil 3:14), functions as a standard to which believers aspire (2 Thess 1:11), and as coming from God is dependable and irrevocable (Rom 11:29).

Thus Paul understood God's *call* as God's action in converting change. God's call summons people to himself through the proclamation of the good news about Jesus Christ. This exposition of Paul's use of the term *calling* accords with my definition of the *effectual call* as God's use of human witnesses to Christ in order to convince and transform a particular person so that they value the gospel and respond in faith.

The Content of the Call

> *It has pleased God to impart the Spirit, not without*
> *the Word but through the Word, so as to have us working*
> *in cooperation with him when we sound forth outwardly what*
> *he himself alone breathes inwardly wherever he wills.*
>
> MARTIN LUTHER

GOD'S CALL COMES THROUGH human proclamation of the gospel. In Paul's technical sense, when God calls he ensures that the words of the proclaimer are effective in bringing about the conversion of the hearer. Having established the plausibility of an effective call in Paul, and having pointed to its result in eliciting faith and trust in Christ, I next propose what this content may be. Given that God speaks, what does he say?

I have maintained that the divine call in Paul is a summons and therefore something heard. Throughout Scripture God addresses people with the expectation that this process of response will shape and transform them. "God called you through our gospel" (2 Thess 2:14) means that God has taken up a normative stance in the world of human discourse. God communicates with words, and his words necessitate a response. Thus although God's call is distinct from any human call, especially in its creative power, it still invites analysis as an instance of speech. In this case, the divine interjection is a summons that creates attentiveness to its content. This is exactly what Luke attributes to divine action in Acts 16:14. The Lord opened Lydia's heart "to pay attention to what was said by Paul."

What then does God say in the effectual call? It is not simply a matter of reconstructing what Paul said on a given occasion. The effectual call seeks to describe what unifies all instances of converting change and assumes that God's use of words will differ on each occasion given the variety of human persons and cultures. To probe the content of the call I turn first to the Lutheran tradition because of its emphasis on the proclaimed word. Both contemporary Lutheran Oswald Bayer and the Finnish interpretation of Luther begun by Tuomo Mannermaa offer possible explanations for the gospel as an effective word that brings about the application of redemption, whether referred to as *union with Christ* (Finns) or broadly as *justification* (Bayer). Because Bayer specifies the content of this effective word, he also challenges a Reformed doctrine of calling to clarify what God says. In Bayer's view, the *promissio* is God's direct address announcing to a person, "Your sins are forgiven!" The Finnish interpretation argues that the person of Christ present in the word rather than the content of that word brings about change. In a sense, Christ announces in the call, "I am here within you."

These Lutheran voices help elucidate two Reformed voices: that of Michael Horton and that of the historic movement generally termed "hyper-Calvinism." Horton parallels Bayer's approach of justification *solo verbo*, but I suggest that a similar complication lurks for his understanding of effectual calling. Baptist theologian John Gill (d. 1771) represents an overemphasis on Christ's personal assurance of his presence as in the Finnish interpretation of Luther.[1]

I propose that "Jesus is your saving Lord" fits better as the basic semantic content of calling. This statement reflects elements of apostolic preaching but does not repeat the words spoken in any one specific situation. It comes in the form of a summons in order to maintain conditionality, since the summons could theoretically be refused. But because it is God's speech, the effectual call guarantees the result for which God intends it. The content of the call focuses on Jesus Christ as the goal of God's redemptive plan. He is Lord, but not primarily in the sense of ruler or all-powerful one. He is rather the *saving* Lord. "Saving" clarifies that Christ enters a situation in which rescue is needed. A fuller statement would relate this to sinful human bondage, the history of unfaithfulness in Israel, and the promises in Israel's Scriptures of eschatological

---

[1] I address the dominant Reformed orthodox interpretation in chaps. 7 and 8, on resurrection language. There is surprisingly little discussion of the content of the call in the confessional tradition, although it is typically glossed as the proclaimed gospel or external call. I intend to make this more explicit.

salvation both for Israel and the world. I have added "your" to make explicit that this is a summons. God directs it specifically toward an individual and so sets up a situation in which response is required.

OSWALD BAYER AND THE *VERBUM EFFICAX*

Oswald Bayer draws on Martin Luther and speaks of the proclaimed word as an effective word (*verbum efficax*). A person who hears the gospel in preaching or sacrament undergoes the death and resurrection that Luther associates with faith.[2] Motivating Bayer's project is his thesis that Luther's mature theology arose from a discovery of God's *promissio*, a promise spoken and accomplished by God.[3] *Promissio* covers the characteristic way in which God interacts with the world. For example, Bayer interprets Christ's miracle word "Be opened!" (Mk 7:34) as *promissio*. "*This promise is much more [than a human promise]; it is its own fulfillment; it fulfills itself, and this actually does not take place at a later time, but at the very moment it is uttered; it is* promissio *as a valid promise that takes effect immediately.*"[4] The *promissio* is a creative word, one that summons all of reality to respond appropriately.

The **promissio** *of justification.* For Bayer the application of redemption comes about entirely through hearing the word of the gospel.[5] Luther's term "passive righteousness of faith" is here crucial.[6] Faith is passive in two

---

[2]Bayer's early work, *Promissio: Geschichte der reformatorischen Wende in Luthers Theologie* (Göttingen: Vandenhoeck & Ruprecht, 1971), focuses historically on Luther, but he has maintained a consistent position in his later work. I focus on the following: Oswald Bayer, *Living by Faith: Justification and Sanctification* (Grand Rapids: Eerdmans, 2003); Bayer, *Theology the Lutheran Way*, trans. Jeffrey Silcock and Mark Mattes (Grand Rapids: Eerdmans, 2007); Bayer, *Martin Luther's Theology: A Contemporary Interpretation*, trans. Thomas H. Trapp (Grand Rapids: Eerdmans, 2008). For the movement of "radical" Lutheranism that he represents, see Gerhard O. Forde, *Justification by Faith: A Matter of Death and Life* (Philadelphia: Fortress, 1982), and Robert Kolb, "Contemporary Lutheran Understandings of the Doctrine of Justification: A Selective Glimpse," in *Justification: What's at Stake in the Current Debates*, ed. Mark Husbands and Daniel Treier (Downers Grove, IL: IVP Academic, 2004), 153-76.

[3]Bayer, *Luther's Theology*, 49. Cf. Hans Schaeffer, *Createdness and Ethics: The Doctrine of Creation and Theological Ethics in the Theology of Colin E. Gunton and Oswald Bayer*, Theologische Bibliothek Töpelmann 137 (Berlin: de Gruyter, 2006), 360.

[4]Bayer, *Luther's Theology*, 114 (emphasis original). For illustrations, see Martin Luther, *Lectures on Genesis: Chapters 1-5*, ed. Jaroslav Pelikan, trans. George Schick, LW 1 (St. Louis: Concordia, 1958), 16, 19, 21.

[5]"Justification" for Bayer encompasses several loci surrounding conversion. In relation to a Reformed order of salvation this includes calling, faith and justification.

[6]Luther explains "passive righteousness" in the introduction to his Galatians commentary (*Galatians 1-4*, ed. and trans. Jaroslav Pelikan, LW 26 [St. Louis: Concordia, 1963], 4-5).

senses: first, God works faith in us so that "we experience it in that we suffer it," and second, faith is passive in its content because we acknowledge our helplessness and die "both to justifying thinking and justifying action."[7] Faith for Bayer is something one undergoes. It is a process of dying to oneself and then rising through the divine verdict on one's behalf. God announces his justifying verdict, and this brings about the experience of faith. The "ungodly are pronounced to be righteous and are thereby *made* righteous."[8] The effect here is instantaneous as in the miracle sayings of Jesus. In the event of gospel proclamation the kingdom comes into the world: "As Jesus Christ, as God himself, the gospel, when preached by word of mouth, does more than simply offer us the possibility that I can actualize and make it real by my own decision of faith. The Word itself *is* the power of God, God's kingdom."[9]

"Gospel" is not simply a narration of Jesus' human career (1 Cor 15:1-8). It includes the divine verdict of righteousness spoken to each individual. Luther first grasped this verdict in the statement of absolution during confession, "I absolve you." He concluded that the gospel is both a sign of God's justifying act and the act itself.[10] Bayer thus presents God's action in bringing someone to faith as God's declaration of an effective word. To understand this word in relation to the effectual call, it must be asked what it accomplishes.

For Bayer, the announcement of justification creates the experience of faith. And one hears this saving gospel in baptism.[11] The gospel word spoken in baptism creates an experience of faith in the justifying verdict. The very announcement that one's sins are forgiven in Christ puts one through the experience of faith, that is, through the experience of dying to oneself and living again in God's verdict. The agency involved is a form of God's creative word (as in Rom 4:17) through which he grants faith, even to infants when they are baptized. Bayer thus proposes a form of "effectual" calling. God

---

[7]Bayer, *Living by Faith*, 20, 25.
[8]Ibid., 43. Cf. Reinhard Hütter, *Suffering Divine Things: Theology as Church Practice*, trans. Doug Stott (Grand Rapids: Eerdmans, 2000), 83.
[9]Bayer, *Living by Faith*, 50. Cf. Gerhard Ebeling, *Luther: An Introduction to His Thought*, trans. R. A. Wilson (Philadelphia: Fortress, 1970), 117.
[10]Bayer, *Luther's Theology*, 53. He does not cite Luther at this point.
[11]Ibid., 241. Cf. *Small Catechism* [SC] 2.6; *The Book of Concord: The Confessions of the Evangelical Lutheran Church*, ed. Robert Kolb and Timothy J. Wengert (Minneapolis: Fortress, 2000), 355.

speaks through the sacrament of baptism and creates faith. In short, God announces, "Your sins are forgiven!"

Evaluation. Because the effectual call also emphasizes God's action through words, Bayer's proposal deserves close attention. First, for Bayer, the word is effective at creating only an initial experience of faith. The *verbum efficax* creates faith in the one who hears the proclamation or experiences the sacramental word. But because this effect comes about universally, Bayer must introduce an additional factor to explain why not all who are baptized or hear the gospel have faith.[12] The *Formula of Concord* states that the Holy Spirit's work in this effective word is resistible.[13] This comes from the formula's choice to hold in tension God's efficient agency in creating faith and the universality of God's grace. It appears that Bayer stretches the *Formula* here when he concludes that the *verbum efficax* creates the condition of faith, that is, an experience of dying to self and rising with Christ. Consequently, the battle to preserve faith in a person becomes the deciding factor in salvation. The *promissio* is effective today but remains in doubt for tomorrow.

Second, I suggest that the *promissio* does not account for the conditionality of God's call. The *promissio*, in J. L. Austin's speech-act terms, is a declarative rather than a commissive (a *promise* proper).[14] When God speaks this word, it creates a reality that corresponds with it. "I absolve you" works much like "I now pronounce you husband and wife." The challenge is that one must still ask to what extent this is true. In Bayer's interpretation of Luther one is not forgiven without faith in that declaration. In Luther's words, "Unless faith is present or is conferred in baptism, baptism will profit us nothing."[15] Bayer would add that because it is God's *promissio*, the gospel creates faith as a gift through the sovereign and creative word, as in Romans 4:17. Only a *promissio* preserves the extrinsic element necessary to guard against subjectivism and enthusiasm. As he relates it to forms of

---

[12]The nature of "faith" is also at issue here. Forde, *Justification by Faith*, 22-23, defines faith passively: "Faith is the state of being grasped by the unconditional claim and promise of the God who calls into being that which is from that which is not."

[13]*Solid Declaration of the Formula of Concord* 11.40; Kolb and Wengert, *Book of Concord*, 647.

[14]John Searle, "A Classification of Illocutionary Acts," *Language in Society* 5 (1976): 15n3, notes that there are unique divine declaratives such as "let there be light."

[15]Martin Luther, "The Babylonian Captivity of the Church," in *Word and Sacrament II*, ed. Helmut T. Lehmann, trans. A. T. W. Steinhäuser, LW 36 (Philadelphia: Muhlenberg, 1959), 59.

modern philosophy, the *promissio* is "neither an appeal, nor a statement, nor an expression."[16]

I would object, however, that while *promissio* is a part of the object of faith (Christ *for us*), it is not the exclusive content of the redemptive word. For Bayer, the *promissio* is a word of assurance that Christ and all his benefits apply to the particular person addressed. Certainly for many heirs of the Reformation, faith as *fiducia* consists in an assurance that Christ's death applies to oneself.[17] But even Luther can speak about faith as a confidence in God's conditional promises. In his lecture on Psalm 51:1, "'Have mercy on me, O God, according to Thy steadfast love,'" Luther asks from where David has this confidence in God's steadfast love. He answers that it comes from God's covenantal history with Israel. Luther's anachronistic David cries,

> That I arise and dare to pray, all this I do with trust in Thy Word and promises. I know that Thou art not the god of the Mohammedans or the monks, but the God of our fathers, who hast promised that Thou wilt redeem sinners—not simply sinners but such sinners as know and feel that they are sinners.[18]

Luther has room for faith in a conditional promise. David comes to God in repentance not because he has already heard the word of absolution, but because he has heard the conditional promise of forgiveness for those who "know and feel that they are sinners." I propose that the effective word contains an irreducibly conditional character. The gospel, although an announcement of good news, carries with it an implied condition—accept the judgment of God on your sin and appeal to him for mercy. Bayer's *promissio*, by contrast, is too confined to the word of absolution and would be helped by taking into consideration the New Testament contexts of conversion from paganism. Adults heard the gospel proclaimed before they were baptized. As important as the *promissio* may be for assurance, the *invitatio* is essential for conversion.

---

[16]Bayer, *Theology the Lutheran Way*, 139.
[17]Heinrich Heppe, *Reformed Dogmatics*, ed. Ernst Bizer, trans. G. Thomson (Grand Rapids: Baker, 1978), 532-37, lists both those who held that assurance of mercy is a fruit of faith and those for whom it is constitutive of faith. Cf. Heinrich Schmid, *The Doctrinal Theology of the Evangelical Lutheran Church*, trans. Charles Hay and Henry Eyster Jacobs, 3rd rev. ed. (Philadelphia: Lutheran Publication Society, 1899; repr., Minneapolis: Augsburg, 1961), 411.
[18]Martin Luther, "Psalm 51," in *Selected Psalms: I*, ed. and trans. Jaroslav Pelikan, LW 12 (St. Louis: Concordia, 1955), 319.

Word Incarnate: The Finnish Luther and Christ Present in Faith

Whereas Bayer understands justification as *solo verbo*, Tuomo Mannermaa and his colleagues emphasize that justification comes about *solo Christo*.[19] They propose that God ties himself to his word so closely that in the preaching of the gospel Christ is present. Gospel proclamation (word and sacrament) forms Christ within a person. Christ's indwelling presence in the Christian just is faith, and this presence of Christ is righteousness before God. The "effective word," then, is the effectiveness of the incarnate Word, Jesus Christ. Baptism unites people to Christ not by eliciting a particular experience of death and resurrection known as faith, but because Christ is fully present in his word and so comes to dwell within believers as the new form of their minds. "The presence of Christ's word and the word about Christ in faith are the presence of God himself."[20]

Mannermaa sees in Luther a focus on the transformative element in justification as opposed to the forensic. Christ's *presence* within one just is righteousness. One's righteous status before God comes about because of this ontological union with Christ, rather than through the declaration of Christ's merit imputed to them. The declaration of righteousness (justification) is *analytic*, that is, a recognition that Christ the righteous one is joined with this particular individual.[21] For Bayer, the gospel declaration of absolution is *synthetic*, in that the declaration creates a new status and

---

[19]Tuomo Mannermaa, the founder of the Finnish "research project," first gained notoriety in English through Carl E. Braaten and Robert Jenson, eds., *Union with Christ: The New Finnish Interpretation of Luther* (Grand Rapids: Eerdmans, 1998). This has led to the publication of the work of Mannermaa and his students, Tuomo Mannermaa, *Christ Present in Faith: Luther's View of Justification*, trans. Kirsi Stjerna (Minneapolis: Fortress, 2005); Olli-Pekka Vainio, ed., *Engaging Luther: A (New) Theological Assessment* (Eugene, OR: Cascade, 2010); Vainio, *Justification and Participation in Christ: The Development of the Lutheran Doctrine of Justification from Luther to the Formula of Concord (1580)*, SMRT 130 (Leiden: Brill, 2008).

[20]Tuomo Mannermaa, "Why Is Luther So Fascinating? Modern Finnish Luther Research," in Braaten and Jenson, *Union with Christ*, 12. As with Bayer, it seems that Christ always attends his word. Baptism thus works *ex opere operato* unless resisted.

[21]Michael S. Horton, *Covenant and Salvation: Union with Christ* (Louisville, KY: Westminster John Knox, 2007), 179, criticizes Robert Jenson's definition of "imputation" in Luther as a judgment of fact. Robert Jenson, "Response to Mark Seifrid, Paul Metzger, and Carl Trueman on Finnish Luther Research," *WTJ* 65 (2003): 178, replies, "God judges the sinner righteous because in ontic fact the sinner and Christ make one moral subject, in whom Christ's divine righteousness overwhelms the sinner's unrighteousness." If "ontic" meant "covenantal," Jenson would be very close to a Reformed view of union with Christ.

change in the person. Because justification is a statement of fact for the Finnish interpretation, one's union with Christ comes before this declaration. But in agreement with Bayer, union occurs in baptism.

Baptism "constitutes communion and participation, because all the baptized share in Christ and his goodness."[22] The particular Finnish ontology comes through again here. Baptism is always preceded by the proclamation of the word of God, and this just is the presence of Christ.[23] Christ gives his fullness to the Christian in baptism, and since Christ is the form of faith, the giving of Christ himself to the baptized brings about faith in that person.[24] Baptism, then, impresses Christ on the baptized hearer. After baptism the indwelling of Christ endures like a seal in wax, and believers are taught to rely on it and return to it.

Whether Luther himself would agree with the Finns is far from settled.[25] My interest here is that the Finnish interpretation of Luther offers a constructive proposal for calling and conversion. Like Bayer, the Finnish interpretation views God's speech, understood as the presence of Christ himself, as effective in bringing about a person's right status before God. How might one characterize the content of this word? Although it is not a verbal call, I would submit that for the Finns, Christ says in effect, "I am within you."

HYPER-CALVINISM: "YOU ARE ALREADY MINE"

The above two Lutheran options share a belief that God identifies himself with his words. They differ on how God's words lead a person into a justified relationship with him—whether through a union with Christ that serves as the ground of justification (Mannermaa) or through the declaration of absolution that evokes faith in Christ (Bayer). A similar dichotomy can be discerned in the Reformed tradition. The first tendency, illustrated with so-called hyper-Calvinism, makes one's prior union with Christ the warrant

---

[22]Eeva Martikainen, "Baptism," in Vainio, *Engaging Luther*, 96.
[23]Simo Peura, "Christ as Favor and Gift (*donum*): The Challenge of Luther's Understanding of Justification," in Braaten and Jenson, *Union with Christ*, 53.
[24]Ibid., 54.
[25]For criticism that the Finnish interpretation makes only selective appeal to the early Luther, see Ken Schurb, "The New Finnish School of Luther Research and Philip Melanchthon," *Logia* 12 (2003): 31-36; Carl Trueman, "Is the Finnish Line a New Beginning? A Critical Assessment of the Reading of Luther Offered by the Helsinki Circle," *WTJ* 65 (2003): 231-44. But see the response by Jenson, "Response."

for saving faith today. The other tendency, observed in the contemporary proposal by Michael Horton, makes God's declaration of justification the content of the effectual call.

The label "hyper-Calvinist" has marked out a variety of subgroups in the broadly Reformed tradition, but is here applied loosely to traditions that seek a warrant for faith through knowledge of one's election.[26] John Gill, an eighteenth-century Particular Baptist, denied that exhortations to repent and believe in Scripture applied to everyone who heard them. While everyone who hears is obligated to believe in the general revelation of Christ as Messiah and Son of God, only those given an internal revelation of the gospel have warrant to believe that they may trust in Christ. Gill states:

> The internal revelation of the gospel, and of Christ through it, is by *the Spirit of wisdom and revelation in the knowledge of him*; whereby a soul is made sensible of its lost state and condition, and of its need of a Saviour, is made acquainted with Christ, as the alone Saviour, both able and willing to save to the uttermost, all that come to God by him; whence it is encouraged to venture on him, rely upon him, and believe in him, to the saving of its soul: Now such an one ought to believe, and none but such an one, that Christ died for it.[27]

The internal call is here separated from the external call of the gospel. Or better, the external call addresses already regenerate people differently from

---

[26] "Hyper-Calvinism" here describes seventeenth-century "antinomians" and eighteenth-century "high" Calvinists in contrast to "evangelical" Calvinists. All of these titles are contested, but a stream of theologians and preachers in England and New England can be traced who affirm eternal justification and deny that people in their natural state have a duty to repent and believe the gospel. This latter entails that gospel preaching does not "offer" grace, but "publishes" the good news. For contemporary treatments of the well-meant offer, see Matthew Barrett, *Salvation by Grace: The Case for Effectual Calling and Regeneration* (Phillipsburg, NJ: P&R, 2013), 76-81; Anthony Hoekema, *Saved by Grace* (Grand Rapids: Eerdmans, 1989), 72-78. For hyper-Calvinism generally, see Peter Toon, *The Emergence of Hyper-Calvinism in English Nonconformity, 1689–1765* (London: Olive Tree, 1967); Iain Murray, *Spurgeon v. Hyper-Calvinism: The Battle for Gospel Preaching* (Edinburgh: Banner of Truth, 1995); Barry H. Howson, *Erroneous and Schismatical Opinions: The Question of Orthodoxy Regarding the Theology of Hanserd Knollys (c. 1599–1691)*, Studies in the History of Christian Thought 99 (Leiden: Brill, 2001), 133-93; Clive Jarvis, "The Myth of High-Calvinism?," in *Recycling the Past or Researching History? Studies in Baptist Historiography and Myths*, ed. Philip E. Thompson and Anthony R. Cross, Studies in Baptist History and Thought 11 (Waynesboro, GA: Paternoster, 2005), 231-63. For a defense of John Gill based on the difficulty of defining hyper-Calvinism, see Jonathan Anthony White, "A Theological and Historical Examination of John Gill's Soteriology in Relation to Eighteenth-Century Hyper-Calvinism" (PhD diss., Southern Baptist Theological Seminary, 2010).

[27] John Gill, *The Cause of God and Truth: Being an Examination of the Principal Passages of Scripture Made Use of by the Arminians, in Favour of Their Scheme* (London: Aaron Ward, 1737), 1:151.

the unregenerate. For Gill, "Come to the waters!" (Is 55:1) applies only to the regenerate—those who are already humbled by their sins and who recognize their need. A minister may not announce indiscriminately that anyone may have an interest in Christ by faith. Rather, a minister calls people to the outward means of grace and advises them to wait.[28]

Gill published and annotated the earlier sermons of Tobias Crisp (d. 1643), who, in an effort to help Christians avoid excessive introspection, appealed to the direct testimony of the Spirit for assurance of one's elect status. Crisp interprets Romans 8:16, "The Spirit itself beareth witness," with this sense: "His meaning is, that it is the immediate voice of the Spirit, without any instrument. . . . So the Spirit himself, in his own person comes, and gives this testimony to a man, that he is the child of God."[29] David Parnham explains, "For Crisp, the Spirit revealed to faith that God had already pronounced the wayfarer to be justified."[30] Thus it would seem accurate to describe the content of the effectual call in hyper-Calvinism as a statement of fact, "You are one of my elect." The effectual call is a private invitation with your name stamped on it.

A standard objection to such a view is that the New Testament does not require an assurance of one's eternal election as warrant for faith. Narrative accounts of conversion in the New Testament along with theological explanations of these events (e.g., 1 Thess 1:9-10) emphasize that the focus of an individual's faith is the truth and value of the proclaimed Christ. Gill is forced into considerable difficulties trying to explain how general admonitions toward repentance (e.g., Mt 23:37) apply only to the physical gathering of the people to hear Jesus' message.[31] While the declaration "You are one of my elect" may have a place in the life of the believer, I submit that it is improper as the content of effectual calling.

---

[28]John Gill, *A Body of Divinity* (Grand Rapids: Baker, 1951), 539.

[29]Tobias Crisp, "The Revealing Evidence of the Spirit of Christ," in *Christ Alone Exalted: Being the Compleat Works of Tobias Crisp, D.D.* (London, 1690), 2:470.

[30]David Parnham, "The Humbling of High Presumption: Tobias Crisp Dismantles the Puritan Ordo Salutis," *JEH* 56 (2005): 67-68. Cf. William K. B. Stoever, *"A Faire and Easie Way to Heaven": Covenant Theology and Antinomianism in Early Massachusetts* (Middletown, CT: Wesleyan University Press, 1978), 144.

[31]Gill, *Body of Divinity*, 550. To Gill's credit, in another text he formulates the effectual call as a summons: "In the effectual vocation Christ says 'to the prisoners,' 'Go forth,' opening the prison doors for them; and to them that sit in darkness, in the gloomy cells of the prison, 'show yourselves'; all which is done in virtue of the redemption price paid by Christ for his people" (ibid., 456).

Michael Horton: "Let There Be Righteousness!"

Like Bayer above, Michael Horton appropriates the divine creation word as most closely analogous to the effectual call.[32] Specifically, the announcement of justification creates the effects of individual salvation. "Justification is not simply one doctrine among others; it is the Word that creates a living union between Christ, the believer, and the communion of saints."[33] This comes about in the effectual call:

> In effectual calling, the Spirit grants the faith to receive Christ for justification and for sanctification, but, analogous to God's performative utterance in creation, it is the forensic verdict ("Let there be!") that evokes the inner renewal that yields the fruit of the Spirit ("Let the earth bring forth . . .").[34]

Horton discusses the call within a wider project on union with Christ and the relationship of justification to sanctification. "Union with Christ" is not a distinct element in an order of salvation because the entire order exists to explain how people are united with Christ.[35] Within this broader concept of union, Horton affirms that Christ's benefits are applied to one in time so that one's status before God as justified comes about through faith.[36] The "forensic verdict" of justification elicits the response of faith from the individual called. In the effectual call, then, God declares his verdict: because of the work of Christ on your behalf, you are now justified in Christ. This is a divine *declarative* in that it establishes the situation it announces.

---

[32] Michael S. Horton (*The Christian Faith: A Systematic Theology for Pilgrims on the Way* [Grand Rapids: Zondervan, 2011], 645) cites Bayer, *Living by Faith*, 43.

[33] Horton, *Covenant and Salvation*, 138.

[34] Michael S. Horton, "Calvin's Theology of Union with Christ and the Double Grace: Modern Reception and Contemporary Possibilities," in *Calvin's Theology and Its Reception: Disputes, Developments, and New Possibilities*, ed. J. Todd Billings and I. John Hesselink (Louisville, KY: Westminster John Knox, 2012), 91.

[35] Horton properly criticizes Bruce McCormack ("What's at Stake," 116) for mistakenly equating "union with Christ" with regeneration, rather than viewing regeneration and justification as part of union as the larger whole (Horton, "Union with Christ," 80-83). See the same criticism in Marcus Johnson, "The Highest Degree of Importance: Union with Christ and Soteriology," in *Evangelical Calvinism: Essays Resourcing the Continuing Reformation of the Church*, ed. Myk Habets and Bobby Grow (Eugene, OR: Pickwick, 2012), 241.

[36] Horton, "Union with Christ," 88. For sanctification as the effect of God's justifying declaration, "Your sins are forgiven," pronounced logically *after* one believes, see Eric Johnson, "Rewording the Justification/Sanctification Relation with Some Help from Speech Act Theory," *JETS* 54 (2011): 777.

[Justification] has to do with a Covenant Lord pronouncing a courtroom verdict upon the servant that issues in a completely new ontological, ethical, and eschatological orientation—including the inner life in its sweep.... Thus, the entire reality of the new creation—not only justification but also renewal, and not only the renewal of the individual but also of the cosmos—is constituted by the covenantal speech of the Trinity.[37]

But the sentence, "You are now justified," sounds as if Horton has placed a person's justification prior to the particular union with Christ in calling and faith. Given that he criticizes Bruce McCormack (following Karl Barth) for doing just this, a charitable read will attempt to see it otherwise.[38] I suggest that God's declaration, "You are now justified," articulates what God is doing in the whole order of salvation, namely, uniting a person to Christ for justification and sanctification. Perhaps it is better located in the language of the decree. God decides that this individual will be justified in union with Christ and so decrees, "Let there be righteousness!"[39]

Horton's proposal raises further questions: What does God say? And when does he say it? God most certainly does say, "Let there be justification," in much the same way that God speaks a word that brings about the restoration of Israel after captivity (Is 55:11-13). But I would suggest that this word is enacted through proclamation in the form of an invitation (Is 55:1-3) or exhortation (Is 52:11).[40] I submit that Horton has identified one of God's crucial speech acts, but that this is God's decision or election, rather than the outworking of this election in effectual calling.[41] Is it not conceivable on Horton's terms that the Father announced to the Son, "Let there be justification," in a pretemporal covenant for redemption?

Attention to "calling" texts may help clarify the content of the effectual call. Horton reads the identification of God as the one who "calls that which does not exist as if it does" (Rom 4:17) to refer to the verdict of justification.[42]

---

[37]Horton, *Covenant and Salvation*, 201.
[38]Horton, "Union with Christ," 91.
[39]Horton uses this phrase in *The Christian Faith*, 621.
[40]Horton refers to the call as a "summons" (e.g., Horton, *Covenant and Salvation*, 225) but also names it as the "forensic verdict" (e.g., Horton, "Union with Christ," 91). I view these as two different speech acts.
[41]John Fesko ("John Owen on Union with Christ and Justification," *Them* 37 [2012]: 17-18) interprets Puritan John Owen in just this way.
[42]Horton, *The Christian Faith*, 611, 621, 753.

This speech act is an *ex nihilo* creation. "God creates a new world by speaking the gospel into unbelief."[43] But, as seen in the exegesis of Romans 4:17 above, God creates descendants of Abraham through his call. If so, it is unclear how Romans 4:17 could communicate a point about the verdict of justification. While I agree with Horton that God does call new descendants of Abraham into existence through his sovereign power, it does not seem warranted to say from Romans 4:17 that he does this by announcing their justification in Christ. Unless God's creative word, "Let there be justification," is a proto-logical statement setting forth God's plan for redemption, I do not know how Horton can avoid the conclusion that in effectual calling God informs creatures of the status they have already been given.

Calling and "Our" Gospel

Bayer, Mannermaa and Horton all appeal to an effective word in the application of salvation. Bayer stresses that the word of promise is spoken to us from outside of us. I would challenge Bayer that his focus on *promissio* neglects the New Testament gospel content as *invitatio*. By examining Paul's use of "calling" terms I have urged that the effective word has the character of a summons, thereby preserving its conditional status. This makes possible an explanation that God ensures the result by means of organizing events, circumstances and the developing character of a person, as well as by means of the Spirit's life-giving presence.

The Finnish interpretation stresses the presence of Christ himself with his word. I will seek to make use of the presence of the triune God with his word in chapter nine, but here I agree with numerous critics that the Finnish interpretation, considered as a constructive proposal, does not successfully avoid the criticisms leveled at Andreas Osiander (d. 1552) in the sixteenth century.[44] An ontological union with Christ's divine nature overshadows the New Testament emphasis on Christ's work to obtain the forgiveness of sins. In addition, the Finnish interpretation fails to take into account God's use of created means in working salvation. The proclaimed

---

[43]Paul "also treats justification specifically as a speech act analogous to *ex nihilo* creation itself in Rom 4 (v. 17)" (Horton, *Covenant and Salvation*, 203).

[44]Calvin, *Institutes* 3.11.5-12, 729-43 (for full citation information for Calvin's *Institutes*, see chap. 1, n. 18).

word, which is identical with the presence of Christ, ceases to possess the content of an announcement.

The hyper-Calvinist word illustrates how the effectual call can be divided into two calls, rather than understood as having two aspects. Gill is forced to specify the particular addressee of every biblical exhortation, a process that divides what God announces externally from what he impresses internally. "You are one of my elect" reduces the effectiveness of the effectual call to something purely notional—the called person now knows of her elect status.

For Horton, the effectual call announces the verdict of justification. While "Let there be justification!" fits well with God's decree, it separates the effectual call from the gospel call. God may be doing something called "justification" with the words of the call. As the Westminster standards propose, God unites one to Christ through the effectual call.[45] But if the call is God's speech, and if the call is understandable in light of New Testament evidence, I submit another proposition is needed that accounts for God's call in time.

"Jesus is your saving Lord." I am arguing that the effectual call is God's appropriation of human witness to Christ. In attempting to hold the effectual call as an act of divine rhetoric, it is then appropriate to ask what God says. From interaction with other potential "calls" above and from discussion of calling texts in the New Testament, I distill the following desiderata for the content of the call. It must (1) be expressible orally, (2) have cognitive content, (3) come in the form of a summons, (4) elicit human response and (5) lead to belief or faith. The first three emerge from my interpretation of καλεῖν in the New Testament as a summons rather than as a technical term specifying that God identifies someone as a Christian. Because calling is connected with the awakening of faith, texts that display the cognitive content of belief (Rom 10:17) add support to these first three criteria. The fourth criterion assures one that the call has a conditional character. It demands a response to show its effectiveness. The final criterion points to the goal of calling. Calling unites one to Christ by faith, and so the content of the call will have some connection with faith in Christ. I submit that the announcement "Jesus is your saving Lord!" is an appropriate summary of the content of the effectual call.[46]

---

[45] *WSC* Q. 30.
[46] I am unaware of a treatment of effectual calling that makes a similar claim for the content of

First, "Jesus is your saving Lord" is not an attempt to specify the exact verbal locution. In summarizing God's speech in the effectual call, I mean to explore what God is doing with these words. This presupposes a limitless variety of human utterances. The child's "*Tolle, lege*" near Augustine's garden serves as an example. Augustine understood God's speech in this instance as a summons. Not only, "Take up and read," but also, "Cast off the works of darkness" (Rom 13:12-13). These words came with the authority of God and urged Augustine toward actions embodying a disposition of faith. The effectual call was God's use of human witness to Christ (the child's and Paul's) in order to transform Augustine's affections and perception.[47]

My use of Augustine's "call" may be criticized as special pleading since his mature theology reflects emphases similar to this study. The effectual call, however, is able to account for situations in which God's use of words may not be identical to the human speaker's intended use. One can imagine that someone familiar with Christ, yet uncommitted, may find strength to confess Jesus as saving Lord while listening to a dictator make claims to his or her own lordship. Even in this case, the person's resulting faith is built on human witness to Christ. French Calvinist Paul Testard's gloss for "hearing" the word includes "reading, meditation, and recollection."[48] The effectual call would come through the dialogical formation of memory and recollection.

Second, this sentence has the form of both an announcement and a summons. As many in New Testament studies have emphasized, there is no neutral claim to lordship.[49] Paul shows in 1 Corinthians 8:5-6 that there is

---

the call, although the claim itself is common in literature on Paul. E.g., "When Paul speaks of 'faith' by which we are justified he means essentially acceptance of the gospel which offers God's salvation in Christ and presents Christ as our Lord demanding our obedience to him" (Seyoon Kim, *The Origin of Paul's Gospel* [Grand Rapids: Eerdmans, 1982], 299-300).

[47] Augustine, *The Confessions* 8.12.29, trans. Maria Boulding, WSA I/1 (Hyde Park, NY: New City, 1997), 206-7. For a similar reading of Augustine's conversion, see Nicholas Wolterstorff, *Divine Discourse: Philosophical Reflections on the Claim That God Speaks* (Cambridge: Cambridge University Press, 1995), 1-8.

[48] Quoted in Albert Gootjes, *Claude Pajon (1626–1685) and the Academy of Saumur: The First Controversy over Grace*, BSCH 64 (Leiden: Brill, 2014), 64.

[49] N. T. Wright, *Paul: In Fresh Perspective* (Minneapolis: Fortress, 2005), 59-79, argues for extensive coded rhetoric against the Roman Empire in Paul's letters. But see the criticisms of John M. G. Barclay, "Why the Roman Empire Was Insignificant to Paul," in *Pauline Churches and Diaspora Jews*, WUNT 275 (Tübingen: Mohr Siebeck, 2011), 363-87. They both agree that the claim that Jesus is Lord excludes other similar claims, whether or not the emperor falls in this category.

only one "God" and one "Lord" for the believer. The Thessalonian crowd may have been mistaken to conclude that the Christians proclaimed "another king" (Acts 17:7), but the apostolic proclamation consistently assumes that to name Jesus as Lord means that one opposes certain other powers. For Paul and 1 John, this meant a new allegiance against the structures of the "world" (Gal 6:14-15; 1 Jn 2:15-17). Hence the announcement that Jesus is the saving Lord also functions as a summons to respond. When one understands this announcement, one is given a new view on the plight of the world, of God's covenant people and of oneself.

What then is God doing when he says, "Jesus is your saving Lord"? He is summoning to repentance and faith. The illocutionary act of calling is a divine summons or directive. The locution "Jesus is your saving Lord" is, of course, in the form of an indicative, but it contains an implicit directive. A summons seeks a world-to-word fit, in which the proper response is to conform one's life to the world portrayed in the summons. This is exactly what occurred in Thessalonica, when God called through Paul's proclamation of the gospel and people turned from idols (1 Thess 1:9-10).

"Jesus is your saving Lord" also addresses the concerns raised about other proposals for the content of the call. Unlike the Finnish theologians, it does not rely on an ontological union with Christ's divine nature. Christ is united to the one whom God addresses, but this is through the presence of God the Spirit ministering understanding and faith. For Bayer, God's call is a declaration. I have argued, however, that based on biblical use of the term it is better to preserve the character of a summons in the call. The same is true for Horton's "Let there be justification!" Against the hyper-Calvinist proposal, "Jesus is your saving Lord" has the advantage of preserving the well-meant offer. Preachers may in good conscience announce that Jesus is Lord to everyone they encounter, while trusting that God will impress this gospel truth in such a way that it forms faith and repentance when and where he wills.

Conclusion. From the study of Paul's use of calling vocabulary I have given warrant for the doctrine of effectual calling as making the same judgment as the New Testament texts. This call is selective according to the divine will and effective in bringing about faith. Calling includes cognitive content spoken and heard. God "called" Paul (Gal 1:6, 15) and called Paul's

Thessalonian audience "through our gospel" (2 Thess 2:14). Paul's use of an oral description invites the theologian to further discern God's ways. What type of speech is this? I have proposed that in the effectual call, God appropriates human witness to Christ and summons individuals with the phrase "Jesus is your saving Lord!"

Divine Light and Conversion

> *[The Light] now shines for him in such a way that his closed eyes are
> opened by its shining, or rather his blind eyes are healed by its
> shining and made to see. This is the process of calling. Man
> is called and becomes a Christian as he is illuminated.*
>
> KARL BARTH

IN THE PREVIOUS CHAPTERS, Pauline calling texts served to ground the conclusion that when God brings about converting change he acts and speaks through the words of human witnesses. The effectual call is a literal summons, only properly analogous with human speaking, but speaking nevertheless. As was noted in chapter one, however, a dogmatic account of calling will not be content to extract one lexeme among biblical vocabulary lest the church produce a lopsided confession of God's saving work in Christ. Theology is obliged to account for concepts making the same or similar judgments in other passages of Scripture. I have chosen God as speaking, God as giving light and God as life-giver for this study because these best encapsulate the variety of biblical vocabulary.

In the quote above, Karl Barth does just this. Illumination describes the same phenomenon as does calling. I agree that calling and illumination refer to the same reality or phenomenon, but they do so in different ways. To say that one is illumined or enlightened is to focus on one's renewed abilities to perceive as a result of God's action. In this sense, illumination covers a wider scope of God's work of redemption than does calling. God's call or summons comes with all the power of his address, and it comes tailored for the individual. It may imply God's shaping of the person through dialogue, events and time. But calling is converting change considered primarily from God's side. In the same way, illumination or "shining" may be positioned as God's action. God displays Christ for us in the gospel. Christ shows himself to us in witness of God's glory through his ministry. The Spirit directs our attention to God's glory in Christ. But the metaphor of illumination also includes the resulting subjective human response. As will be observed, Christians are now "light" in the Lord.

In this chapter I examine descriptions of converting change as light or illumination. The following presentation cannot account for all the ways biblical authors utilize light,[1] much less its use in the Christian philosophical and theological tradition for the necessary conditions of knowledge.[2] In relation to converting change, 2 Corinthians 4:6 emerges as the clearest instance of divine action portrayed as illumining or shining.[3] God's light and the resulting enlightenment are realities of the new age or new creation and so encompass the whole saving economy. Whereas illumination has been understood primarily for God's redemption of epistemic capacity in relation to Scripture, a focus on soteriological illumination broadens the scope from a cognitive account so as to include elements of personal interaction.[4] In the effectual call God displays the personal authority of Christ in the gospel through human witnesses. Illumination indicates that the divine light displays a person—Jesus Christ as risen and exalted Lord. This display has the character of a convincing testimony so that illumination is God's action to show a person Christ's glory.

---

[1] I do not deal here with "light" in theology proper. E.g., God dwells in "unapproachable light" (1 Tim 6:16) and "God is light" (1 Jn 1:5).

[2] For a spectrum of uses, see H. Blumenberg, "Light as a Metaphor of Truth," in *Modernity and the Hegemony of Vision*, ed. David Kleinberg-Levin, trans. Joel Anderson (Berkeley: University of California Press, 1993), 30-62. For an account of Augustine's seminal discussion, and the variety of interpretations, see Lydia Schumacher, *Divine Illumination: The History and Future of Augustine's Theory of Knowledge* (Malden, MA: Wiley-Blackwell, 2011), 7-23.

[3] Among New Testament texts, appeal will also be made to 1 Pet 2:9-10; Col 1:12-13; Eph 1:17-19; and Acts 26:18. Hebrews 6:4 and Heb 10:32 may speak of "enlightenment" in a quasi-technical sense for Christian conversion. The Old Testament is rich with language of Torah as light (Ps 19:8; 36:9; 43:3) and of the need for a particular form of vision or capacity to see the worth of Torah (Ps 119:18).

[4] The best contemporary accounts of soteriological illumination are John Webster, "Illumination," *JRT* 5 (2011): 325-40, and Ivor Davidson, "Divine Light: Some Reflections After Barth," in *Trinitarian Theology After Barth*, ed. Myk Habets and Phillip Tolliday, PTMS 148 (Eugene, OR: Pickwick, 2011), 48-69.

In the following chapter I present how John Owen (d. 1683) uses the term *illumination* for both the testimony of the Holy Spirit (*testimonium spiritus sancti*) in the doctrine of Scripture and for converting change. I note that Owen uses illumination primarily for the cognitive side of God's redemptive work and that he views converting change as separable from this illumination.

Friedrich Schleiermacher (d. 1834), in his *Christian Faith*, pushes the Reformed tradition to offer a this-world description of the Spirit's work. For him, Christ's spirit is transmitted through other humans. Whereas Owen uses exclusively theological language for God's action, Schleiermacher portrays converting change as a result of Christ's influence mediated through Christian witness.

While I appreciate the attempt to describe God's action in converting change as a process comparable with other instances of human growth and transformation, ultimately the metaphor of divine light in Scripture pushes the church to recognize God's action as unique. To get at the particular uniqueness of divine illumination, I bring together illumination of Scripture and soteriological illumination. The Holy Spirit's testimony to Scripture may be seen as an instance of soteriological illumination. The Spirit assures us, "Yes! Jesus is your saving Lord," by displaying Christ in the gospel and in human witnesses.

In answer to our dogmatic questions for the effectual call, illumination clarifies the content of the call as a personal encounter with God in the face of Jesus Christ ("face" here means Christ in the gospel). God speaks and shows the crucified and risen Lord as the object of faith. As a testimony, illumination clarifies that this address remains personal. As Owen suggests, for assurance to come about by faith, the form of address must be based on testimony and so be interpersonal or covenantal.[5] In soteriological illumination God shows Christ as the divine light to the convert through human testimony with the conviction that this is God's work. Illumination begins to answer the third question about the change that occurs in the effectual call. Christ in the gospel shines with beauty, authority and persuasion that transform human cognitive capacity so that one concludes inevitably that

---

[5]John Owen, ΠΝΕΥΜΑΤΟΛΟΓΙΑ [*Pneumatologia*], *or, a Discourse Concerning the Holy Spirit*, vol. 3 of *The Works of John Owen*, ed. William Goold (London: Johnstone & Hunter, 1852; repr., Carlisle, PA: Banner of Truth Trust, 1966), 83.

this good news about Christ is true and good. While illumination includes explainable content, its effectiveness arises from a personal encounter with God revealed in Christ by the power of the Spirit.

In evaluating presentations of soteriological illumination I propose (1) that illumination terms are best located in a broader doctrine of salvation rather than narrowly in a doctrine of Scripture, and (2) that enlightenment (the result of illumination) is not merely cognitive, but is a personal transformation that includes a new view of the world or new loves. I begin with New Testament testimony on illumination.

Divine Light in New Testament Texts

Imagery of light and illumination abounds in the New Testament, making it difficult to manage the numerous ways authors use it. At least three loci stand out from texts in which light participates in God's work for salvation.

Light as eschatological epoch. A first group of texts announces the new epoch of God's rule as *light*. In 1 Peter 2:9-10, Christians are identified with titles that belonged to Israel at Mount Sinai—chosen people, holy nation and special possession. Peter focuses primarily on the purpose for which God gave this covenant status—"that you may proclaim the excellencies of him who called you out of darkness into his marvelous light."[6] Consistent with the reading of Paul presented in chapter three, "called" refers to God's action in converting change. Since the following verse (1 Pet 2:10) announces a change of status from not God's people to now a part of God's people, it may be assumed that the change from darkness to light has already occurred. God's marvelous light is the realm or epoch characterized by God's special gift of covenant membership.

The epoch of salvation is also called "light" in Colossians 1:12-13. Here the "inheritance of the saints in light" (Col 1:12) is parallel to the "kingdom of his beloved Son" (Col 1:13). Whereas Colossians 1:12 primarily indicates a future experience of this inheritance, the use of "kingdom" in the following verse for what God has already accomplished shows that a form of already/not yet fulfillment is in view. Believers have already been transferred into this kingdom and so experience its light.

---

[6]Cf. Is 43:21. The "excellencies" are God's works to deliver his people. See Paul J. Achtemeier, *1 Peter*, Hermeneia (Minneapolis: Fortress, 1996), 166.

Jesus Christ brings about this eschatological light. John's prologue identifies Christ the Word as both life and light (Jn 1:4-14). The eschatological moment is such that the "light is already shining" (1 Jn 2:8). And Christ's coming is like the rising of the sun on those in darkness (Lk 1:77-79; 2:30-32).

This is the objective side of light imagery and appears undisputed. New Testament authors identify Christ with light sent from God. The ministry of Christ and the coming of his kingdom are an arrival of light in the world. Believers are said to participate in this light as those who have left darkness and emerged into light.

Enlightenment as reflecting Christ. The epistle to the Ephesians draws on a contrast between light and darkness to show the difference between unbelievers and those in Christ. Paul makes an astounding claim in Ephesians 5:8 that believers once were "darkness," but "now you are light in the Lord." Not only is "light" used for God's revelation in Christ and the arrival of an eschatological epoch, but also believers themselves become this light. The following verses identify the light as an instrument to expose sin and darkness (Eph 5:9-12). In Ephesians 5:13-14, the light then becomes the agent of change. "But when anything is exposed by the light, it becomes visible" (Eph 5:13). This speaks of the light of Christian witness demonstrating the futility of characteristically Gentile forms of sexual sin.[7] But in the next verse Paul turns the phrase around and explains, "for anything that becomes visible is light" (Eph 5:14). Paul implies, according to Peter O'Brien, "that the light not only exposes; it also transforms."[8] Those on whom the light has shined become light, just as Paul stated earlier (Eph 5:8).[9] Ephesians 5:14 indicates that one moves from darkness to light by exposure to God's light, including through the witness of other Christians. The following stanza confirms this soteriological interpretation.

Paul combines imagery from several texts in Isaiah:

Awake, O sleeper,
    and arise from the dead,
and Christ will shine on you. (Eph 5:14)[10]

---

[7]The verb "expose" (ἐλέγχω) in Eph 5:11, 13, shows that the witness of believers is primarily in view.
[8]Peter O'Brien, *The Letter to the Ephesians*, PiNTC (Grand Rapids: Eerdmans, 1999), 372.
[9]Among Pauline texts, 1 Thess 5:1-10 and Rom 13:11-14 refer respectively to Christians as "children of light" and to the "armor of light."
[10]Most commentators plausibly conclude this is a pre-Pauline hymn fragment. But Jonathan Lunde and John A. Dunne argue that Paul composed this stanza as an interpretation of the

Isaiah announced that the dead will rise and awake like those who are asleep (Is 26:19). God also calls for Jerusalem to "awake" and "arise" because judgment is finished (Is 51:17). That Christ will shine on you likely alludes to Isaiah 60:1,

> Arise, shine, for your light has come,
> And the glory of the LORD has risen upon you. (cf. Is 9:1)

All three texts point to a promised deliverance for God's people after a time of suffering. Isaiah 59–60 take on special relevance with a focus on the change from darkness to light.[11] The narrative of Israel's darkness and light parallels that of Paul's readers. Isaiah acknowledges on behalf of Israel that they are "darkness" and like those who are dead (Is 59:9-10; 60:3). God viewed their helplessness, and so "his own arm brought him salvation" (Is 59:16). This salvation is sealed by the gift of God's Spirit (Is 59:21), who represents a covenant with them and will ensure that God's words remain in them. The following paragraph then interprets this redemption as the arrival of light (Is 60:1-3). God's light both shines to enlighten his people and glorifies them by making them attractive to the kingdoms of the world (Israel is "radiant" in Is 60:5). In the same way that God's unilateral act of deliverance for Israel dispelled their gloom and darkness in Isaiah 60, so also through Christ believers experienced a radical change from darkness to light. If the eschatological context of Isaiah 26:19 is in view as well, this light is the beginning fulfillment of the promises of resurrection life for God's people.

Illumination in these texts is the transition away from the realm of darkness, including both noetic (Eph 4:17-18) and ethical dimensions, by the power of Christ's light that exposes evil and transforms individuals. Those who are in Christ participate and reflect this light into the world as witnesses to the coming kingdom.

Isaiah texts ("Paul's Creative and Contextual Use of Isaiah in Ephesians 5:14," *JETS* 55 [2012]: 87-110). A main alternative to my interpretation is Thorsten Moritz, *Profound Mystery: The Use of the Old Testament in Ephesians*, NovTSup 85 (Leiden: Brill, 1996), 97-116, esp. 115. He interprets the stanza as an ethical reminder to Christians to continue exposing themselves to the light of Christ so that they might be an effective witness. Given the allusions to Isaiah, however, the main focus is salvation-historical.

[11] Lunde and Dunne, "Ephesians 5:14," 96. The strong connection with Isaiah is emphasized by O'Brien, *Ephesians*, 376; Markus Barth, *Ephesians*, AB 34 (Garden City, NY: Doubleday, 1974), 2:598-603.

Opened eyes as apostolic mission. By what means, then, does the objective light of Christ's kingdom become resident as subjective light within a person? In one of Paul's accounts of his Damascus road experience, he retells Christ's commission to him. Christ commands,

> Rise and stand upon your feet, for I have appeared to you for this purpose, to appoint you as a servant and witness to the things in which you have seen me and to those in which I will appear to you, delivering you from your people and from the Gentiles—to whom I am sending you to open their eyes, so that they may turn[12] from darkness to light and from the power of Satan to God, that they may receive forgiveness of sins and a place among those who are sanctified by faith in me. (Acts 26:16-18)

The phrases "open their eyes" and "turn from darkness to light" continue illumination imagery from Paul's vision of "a light from heaven, brighter than the sun" (Acts 26:13). Paul's narration of this event evokes the calls of major Old Testament prophets,[13] but the light imagery corresponds most closely with Isaianic servant texts (Is 42:6-7; 49:6). This comes as no surprise since Paul already interpreted his mission as a continuation of Isaiah's servant who brings light to the Gentiles (Acts 13:47).

What is God doing through Paul? It may be that opened eyes are the result of one's personal faith.[14] In some early Lutheran constructions, an order of salvation (*ordo salutis*) describes the journey of a Christian convert.[15] David Hollatz (Hollazius, d. 1713) discerned calling, illumination, conversion, regeneration, justification and union with Christ consecutively in these verses.[16] Among contemporary interpreters, Richard Peace calls

---

[12]Or to "turn them from darkness to light" (NIV, KJV). This is possible (Lk 1:16-17), but given the intransitive sense immediately following in Acts 26:20, people turn themselves as a result of their eyes being now open.

[13]Cf. Ezek 2:1-3; Jer 1:7-8. Robert C. Tannehill, *The Acts of the Apostles*, vol. 2 of *The Narrative Unity of Luke-Acts: A Literary Interpretation* (Minneapolis: Fortress, 1990), 322-23. G. K. Beale, *A New Testament Biblical Theology: The Unfolding of the Old Testament in the New* (Grand Rapids: Baker Academic, 2011), 241-44.

[14]Jaroslav Pelikan, *Acts*, Brazos Theological Commentary on the Bible (Grand Rapids: Brazos, 2005), 272.

[15]See Markus Matthias, "Ordo Salutis—Zur Geschichte eines dogmatischen Begriffs," *ZKG* 115 (2004): 318-46.

[16]Quoted in Heinrich Schmid, *The Doctrinal Theology of the Evangelical Lutheran Church*, trans. Charles Hay and Henry Eyster Jacobs, 3rd rev. ed. (Philadelphia: Lutheran Publication Society,

this text "the essence of Christian conversion"[17] and makes it the foundation for a conversion experience common among Paul and the eleven disciples in Mark's Gospel.

But the focus on human development distracts from the theological question. The clear reference to the Isaianic servant focuses attention on Paul's actions as instrumental for God's actions.[18] The servant has been sent to "open the eyes that are blind" (Is 42:7), but God will "lead the blind" and "will turn the darkness before them into light" (Is 42:16). Joel Green notes that Luke's contribution here is "to ground conversion in the grand narrative of God's ancient and ongoing purpose."[19] But regarding divine action, Green believes the eschatological Spirit in Acts makes repentance morally possible for all people. When Acts calls repentance a gift from God (Acts 5:31; 11:18), Green refers these to the gift of prevenient grace.[20] But the "opening of eyes," Paul's primary goal, does not appear to be a preliminary stage to converting change. Rather, opening eyes and turning from darkness to light both prepare one for receiving the forgiveness of sins.[21] While "turning" (ἐπιστρέφω) is used throughout Luke-Acts for human response, "opening eyes" is dependent on specific divine power. In Luke 24:31, for instance, the disciples' insight into Christ's identity is described as their eyes being "opened."[22]

I suggest, then, that the Lukan narrative portrays Paul's ministry in terms that evoke God's work through the Isaianic servant. Christ sends Paul as a "servant" and "witness" (Acts 26:16) to the in-breaking light of

---

1899; repr., Minneapolis: Augsburg, 1961), 444. Hollatz views the phrase "from the power of Satan to God" as indicating regeneration. He identifies "calling" with Paul's commission ("I will send you"). C. K. Barrett sees *ordo*-construction from this text as flawed, since any of the images could stand in for the whole (*A Critical and Exegetical Commentary on the Acts of the Apostles*, ICC [Edinburgh: T&T Clark, 1998], 2:1162).

[17]Richard Peace, *Conversion in the New Testament: Paul and the Twelve* (Grand Rapids: Eerdmans, 1999), 37. Cf. Joel Green, "'To Turn from Darkness to Light' (Acts 26:18): Conversion in the Narrative of Luke-Acts," in *Conversion in the Wesleyan Tradition*, ed. Kenneth Collins and John H. Tyson (Nashville: Abingdon, 2001), 103-18.

[18]Beale, *Biblical Theology*, 684, calls Paul a "prophetic assistant" to the Isaianic servant.

[19]Green, "To Turn from Darkness to Light," 118.

[20]Ibid., 117.

[21]The two infinitival phrases do not have a grammatical link, leaving the interpreter the task of discerning their relationship.

[22]The verbs are related but different (the unusual διανοίγω in Lk 24:31 vs. ἀνοίγω in Acts 26:18). The close link to Is 42:7 LXX, "to open [ἀνοῖξαι] the eyes of the blind," indicates that the verb is transitive in Acts 26:18.

God's kingdom. The converting change that comes about through Paul's ministry is a turn toward this light and into fellowship with Christ by faith. While Paul certainly participates in opening the eyes of his hearers through his preaching, this result is ultimately attributable to divine action. Acts portrays Paul as the God-appointed means by which God works to bring about converting change.

Light and enlightenment appear in the New Testament in three primary domains. First, there is an objective light understood as the realm of salvific blessing in Christ. Converting change is a movement out of the realm of darkness and into this light. Second, this transition includes a change in disposition in those converted so that they become light. In Ephesians 5, believers are "light in the Lord," that is, they display the light of the eschatological epoch. The parallels with Israel's story in Isaiah 59–60 indicate that this transition comes about by God's decision to work salvation on behalf of his people. Hence there is a third domain—the means by which God brings about this transition. Acts 26:18 points to the human messenger (Paul) as God's instrument to bring about this change. The same movement can be seen in 2 Corinthians 4:6, which represents the clearest appropriation of illumination language for converting change.

Saving Illumination in 2 Corinthians 4:6

Second Corinthians 4:1-6 explains what it means that God's light in Christ becomes resident or reflected in an individual. In the broader context of 2 Corinthians, Paul defends his apostolic ministry and his gospel. This ministry possesses a "far greater glory" (2 Cor 3:8) than that of Moses because it participates in the giving of the eschatological Spirit. The Spirit "not only brings us into the presence of the living God, but does so by removing the veil that otherwise keeps people from beholding God's glory in the face of Christ Jesus."[23] Second Corinthians 4:1-6 presents Paul's reasons for preaching boldly despite both persecution and the ambiguous results of his preaching. He recognizes that his success depends on God's action.

---

[23]Gordon Fee, *God's Empowering Presence: The Holy Spirit in the Letters of Paul* (Peabody, MA: Hendrickson, 1994), 848. In 2 Cor 3:16-17, the veil is primarily hermeneutical, that is, it prohibits one from seeing the true referent of Old Testament texts (2 Cor 3:14). I submit that Paul broadens his discussion in 2 Cor 4:1-6 to universal human inability (Scott J. Hafemann, *2 Corinthians*, NIVAC [Grand Rapids: Zondervan, 2000], 156-59).

> Therefore, having this ministry by the mercy of God, we do not lose heart. But we have renounced disgraceful, underhanded ways. We refuse to practice cunning or to tamper with God's word, but by the open statement of the truth we would commend ourselves to everyone's conscience in the sight of God. And even if our gospel is veiled, it is veiled to those who are perishing. In their case the god of this world has blinded the minds of the unbelievers, to keep them from seeing the light of the gospel of the glory of Christ, who is the image of God. For what we proclaim is not ourselves, but Jesus Christ as Lord, with ourselves as your servants for Jesus' sake. For God, who said, "Let light shine out of darkness," has shone in our hearts to give the light of the knowledge of the glory of God in the face of Jesus Christ. (2 Cor 4:1-6)

The concluding claim that God has "shown in our hearts" is a crucial text for the metaphors of light and illumination as divine action in converting change. If this text is to inform a doctrine of calling, it must be shown to refer to a general form of conversion and to evidence divine action. From this text soteriological illumination is understood as a personal encounter with the authority and transforming glory of the risen and exalted Christ. God shows Christ glorified as the light that overwhelms sinful human darkness.

In chapter three I observed that Paul uses "calling" vocabulary both for himself (Gal 1:15-16) and for his readers (Gal 1:6). I suggest that the same is the case in 2 Corinthians 4:6. Paul testifies to his own enlightenment, likely referring to the Damascus road event, and also views his experience as paradigmatic for Christian converting change.

Paul has confidence to proclaim "Jesus Christ as Lord" (2 Cor 4:5) because God has "shone" in his "heart" (2 Cor 4:6). To ask when God shone in Paul's heart brings up the relation of this passage to the accounts of Paul's Damascus road experience in Acts. The parallels between these two are significant, although not unambiguous. Most prominently, "light" and "shining" appear in all three accounts of Paul's conversion call along with the object of the vision, the exalted Jesus Christ.[24] Paul also testifies that a revelation

---

[24]While Acts has φῶς (light: Acts 9:3; 22:6, 9, 11; 26:13), 2 Cor 4:6 has φωτισμός. In the Acts accounts, the light either "flashed" (Acts 9:3; 22:6) or "blazed" (Acts 26:13). Ananias explains that Paul had "seen" the Righteous One (Acts 22:14). *Pace* Victor Paul Furnish, *II Corinthians*, AB 32A (Garden City, NY: Doubleday, 1984), 250, who contrasts the visible light in Paul's Christophany with the illuminating, internal light here and concludes that Paul speaks only in general about Christian conversion.

of Christ changed him (Gal 1:15-16) and claims to have seen Christ (1 Cor 9:1; 15:8). Thus it is plausible that he is reflecting here on that event.[25]

There is significant debate among New Testament scholars on whether Paul's experience on the road to Damascus is best labeled a *conversion* or a *commissioning*, and whether it resulted in a new *conviction* or a new *direction*.[26] Much of the difficulty involves decisions about the chronological development of Paul's theology that need not detain this discussion of illumination. The similarity of vocabulary and the use of the first-person-plural pronoun in 2 Corinthians 4:6 indicate that Paul is remembering his own experience of recognizing Christ as Lord while also generalizing it as applicable to other believers. In 2 Corinthians 4:4, the "god of this world" has blinded the hearts of unbelievers, while in 2 Corinthians 4:6, God shines in "our" hearts. While Paul certainly gives reasons for his confidence as a minister of the gospel in 2 Corinthians 4:6, and so in this sense God's action is specific to him, the contrast with 2 Corinthians 4:4 and the use of the plural "our" indicate that Paul included believers in general. Since they are not among those who are blinded by the god of this world, believers may have confidence that God has shone in their hearts as well.

This text contributes to the three loci above regarding illumination: the objective light, the subjective results and the means of moving from one to the other. The objective light is the "glory of God in the face of Christ" (2 Cor 4:6), or the "gospel of the glory of Christ, who is the image of God"

---

[25]For an argument against continuity between Paul's letters and Acts, see Beverly Gaventa, *From Darkness to Light: Aspects of Conversion in the New Testament*, Overtures to Biblical Theology 20 (Philadelphia: Fortress, 1986), 17-51. The main argument against reading 2 Cor 4:6 as Paul's recollection of his Damascus road experience is that Paul may be comparing the veiled face of Moses in 2 Cor 3:13 with the brighter face of Christ. So Furnish, *II Corinthians*, 225; James D. G. Dunn, "'A Light to the Gentiles,' or 'The End of the Law'? The Significance of the Damascus Road Christophany for Paul," in *Jesus, Paul, and the Law: Studies in Mark and Galatians* (Louisville, KY: Westminster John Knox, 1990), 95. For a close connection between the two events, see Seyoon Kim, *Paul and the New Perspective: Second Thoughts on the Origin of Paul's Gospel* (Grand Rapids: Eerdmans, 2001), 10; Beale, *Biblical Theology*, 266-79.

[26]Krister Stendahl, "Paul Among Jews and Gentiles," in *Paul Among Jews and Gentiles: And Other Essays* (Philadelphia: Fortress, 1976), 1-77. The debate can be summarized with the positions of James Dunn and Seyoon Kim. James D. G. Dunn, *The New Perspective on Paul*, rev. ed., WUNT 185 (Grand Rapids: Eerdmans, 2008); Dunn, "Paul's Conversion—A Light to Twentieth Century Disputes," in *Evangelium, Schriftauslegung, Kirche: Festschrift für Peter Stuhlmacher zum 65. Geburtstag*, ed. Jostein Adna, Scott J. Hafemann and Otfried Hofius (Göttingen: Vandenhoeck & Ruprecht, 1997), 77-93; Kim, *New Perspective*; Kim, *The Origin of Paul's Gospel* (Grand Rapids: Eerdmans, 1982).

(2 Cor 4:4). The "face" of Christ and the gospel are roughly equivalent. Paul likely refers to his vision of the risen and exalted Christ on the road to Damascus.[27] While for Paul this took place through an overwhelming visionary experience, the parallel between these verses indicates that the proclamation of the gospel is significantly similar to that vision. In 2 Corinthians 4:4, the "glory of Christ" is seen (or in the case of unbelievers, not seen) in the "shining"[28] of the gospel. Paul affirms that the content of his gospel is Jesus Christ *as* Lord in the next verse (2 Cor 4:5; cf. Rom 10:9; 1 Cor 12:3). Paul views his own experience in common with the experiences of his readers. They have all seen God's glory displayed in the gospel of Jesus Christ.

The shining light is Christ revealed in the gospel, but that God causes Christ to shine makes all the difference in its effect. The God who spoke in creation, "Let light shine,"[29] has now also shone in human hearts. The result of God's shining is, roughly, "the shining [φωτισμός] of the knowledge of the glory of God in the face of Christ" (2 Cor 4:6). This may mean that God has shone his light so that believers now possess this same light, understood as knowledge of God's glory.[30] Or it may look forward to Paul's missionary task (2 Cor 4:7), in which case God has caused the knowledge of his glory to shine out from believers in witness.[31] The latter presupposes the former and is more likely here given Paul's purpose in the passage to explain his ministry practice. Thus the revelation of God's glory in the proclaimed gospel is both the content of enlightenment and the instrument by which it is produced. "God creates the Christian believer by showing a person God's glory on Christ's face."[32]

If Paul considers his own illumination to be similar to that of his readers, 2 Corinthians 4:6 grounds a doctrine of soteriological illumination. God

---

[27]Kim, *Origin*, 229-31.
[28]Φωτισμός is difficult to translate, whether "light," "brightness" or even "reflection." See Murray J. Harris, *The Second Epistle to the Corinthians: A Commentary on the Greek Text*, NIGTC (Grand Rapids: Eerdmans, 2005), 330.
[29]Gen 1:3. The exact phrase φῶς λάμψει occurs only in Is 9:2 LXX. This closely blends God's acts of creation and redemption.
[30]Margaret E. Thrall, *A Critical and Exegetical Commentary on the Second Epistle to the Corinthians*, ICC (Edinburgh: T&T Clark, 1994), 318.
[31]Harris, *2 Corinthians*, 337.
[32]Peter Balla, "2 Corinthians," in *CNTUOT* 764.

displayed his glory in Christ, and this effected Paul's transformation. Knowledge of Christ became in Paul a light now displaying Christ in mission. Thus Christian illumination takes place as individuals see "the perfect revelation of God in Christ."[33] The same light that shines becomes reflected light in the person converted.

Summary

In several New Testament texts either light or illumination participates in bringing about salvation. The shining light is the revelation of the new age of God's kingdom. Specifically in 2 Corinthians 4:6, God reveals his glory in Christ in a powerfully persuasive way by presenting Christ as the end and goal of creation.[34] The power behind this presentation is its ability to impress on one that Jesus Christ is the bearer of God's salvation. Christians are enlightened in that they see clearly God's glory in Christ and rejoice in him. As a result, Paul viewed himself and his Christian readers as participants in the spread of light in Christ. His preaching became the means through which God continues to enlighten men and women.

---

[33]Kim, *Origin*, 231.
[34]In chap. 6 I relate this to the "paradigm" or example in classical rhetoric.

Illumination and Testimony

IN TURNING FROM NEW TESTAMENT TEXTS on illumination to the theological tradition, one finds that Christian writers have used illumination in a variety of ways. In later Christian reflection illumination expressed primarily the cognitive aspects of converting change. While God's light includes cognitive content, I argue here that saving illumination is best understood as God's personal testimony to the truth and authority of Christ in the gospel.

This variety of uses makes it difficult to relate a doctrine of illumination to the language of the New Testament.[1] I draw on three figures within the broadly Reformed tradition to show how a saving illumination includes a sense of the personal authority of Christ. John Owen presents illumination as the cognitive side of God's work in conversion, but uses exclusively supernatural language to describe the crucial change of will. Claude Pajon reacts to this Reformed orthodox emphasis in an effort to preserve a place for the proclaimed word. Yet Pajon presents an exclusively intellectualist approach. Friedrich Schleiermacher draws attention to personal influence in conversion, an emphasis other Protestant authors understood in relation to the illumination of Scripture. I draw from each of these to reconstruct a

---

[1]Illumination happened in baptism for many early church figures, specifically as the cognitive understanding of the Trinity. See Justin Martyr, *First Apology* 61 (*ANF* 1:183); Gregory of Nazianzus, *Orations* 39.1-2, 40.8 (*NPNF*² 7:361); Ambrose, *On the Holy Spirit* 1.6.78 (*NPNF*² 10:103). Baptism illumines—or better, God illumines through baptism—by revealing his nature as triune. Augustine uses *light* and *illumination* in several ways. For my purposes, it is sufficient to note the possibility that illumination was the divine enabling of cognitive development. See especially Lydia Schumacher, *Divine Illumination: The History and Future of Augustine's Theory of Knowledge* (Malden, MA: Wiley-Blackwell, 2011).

doctrine of saving illumination with a focus on Christ's personal authority. While illumination is a broader category than calling, they describe different aspects of the same reality. God illumines by displaying the personal authority of Christ in the gospel in an overwhelming fashion.

JOHN OWEN AND ILLUMINATION

John Owen shows the sense among Protestant theologians that illumination had special reference to one's certainty about God's revelation in Scripture. But Owen adds considerable complexity through his discussion of soteriological illumination.[2] Owen's treatises on the Holy Spirit from 1673 to 1680 make up a single work explaining the activity of the Spirit in various areas.[3]

Owen structures his treatment of the Spirit's work in individuals around the term *regeneration*. Calling and regeneration are equivalent, but regeneration emphasizes the supernatural quality of the Spirit's work.[4] With this he primarily opposes those who would reduce the essence of converting change to a reformation of outward morals.

While *regeneration* provides the main locus for his discussion of personal salvation, he uses *illumination* with several different senses. Illumination

---

[2] I treat Owen in this chapter and Jonathan Edwards in chap. 8 as examples of early modern Reformed orthodoxy. Edwards could be substituted here, given the full title of his early manifesto on effectual grace, "A Divine and Supernatural *Light* Immediately Imparted to the Soul . . ." (Jonathan Edwards, "A Divine and Supernatural Light," in *Sermons and Discourses, 1730–1733*, ed. Mark Valeri, WJE 17 [New Haven, CT: Yale University Press, 1999], 405-26). Owen is preferable because he juxtaposes scriptural and soteriological illumination. John Calvin had used "illumination" in similar ways, but I explore Owen here because he does so more explicitly. See Edward A. Dowey Jr., *The Knowledge of God in Calvin's Theology*, exp. ed. (Grand Rapids: Eerdmans, 1994), 172-91.

[3] For John Owen's pneumatology and doctrine of Scripture, see John Webster, "Illumination," *JRT* 5 (2011): 325-40; Maarten Wisse and Hugo Meijer, "Pneumatology: Tradition and Renewal," in *A Companion to Reformed Orthodoxy*, ed. Herman J. Selderhuis, BCCT 40 (Leiden: Brill, 2013), 466-517; Stanley N. Gundry, "John Owen on Authority and Scripture," in *Inerrancy and the Church*, ed. John D. Hannah (Chicago: Moody Press, 1984), 189-222; Kelly M. Kapic, "The Spirit as Gift: Explorations in John Owen's Pneumatology," in *The Ashgate Research Companion to John Owen's Theology*, ed. Kelly M. Kapic and Mark Jones (Burlington, VT: Ashgate, 2012), 113-40; Suzanne McDonald, "Beholding the Glory of God in the Face of Jesus Christ: John Owen and the 'Reforming' of the Beatific Vision," in Kapic and Jones, *John Owen's Theology*, 141-58; Alan Spence, *Incarnation and Inspiration: John Owen and the Coherence of Christology* (London: T&T Clark, 2007).

[4] Owen references effectual calling in an interpretation of 1 Thess 5:23-24 (John Owen, ΠΝΕΥΜΑΤΟΛΟΓΙΑ *[Pneumatologia], or, a Discourse Concerning the Holy Spirit*, in *The Holy Spirit*, vol. 3 of *The Works of John Owen*, ed. William Goold [London: Johnstone & Hunter, 1852; repr., Carlisle, PA: Banner of Truth Trust, 1966], 367).

can be a gloss for all of the Spirit's work in converting change. But it most often refers either to a preparatory stage before regeneration or to the Christian conviction that Scripture is the Word of God, also known as the testimony of the Holy Spirit. Owen shows that illumination refers broadly to several aspects of conversion. This diversity makes it difficult to discern in what mode or manner God illumines his people. Owen hints that God works through personal testimony when he describes the Spirit's testimony to Scripture's truth.

Preparatory illumination. In agreement with other English Puritans, Owen held that some of the Holy Spirit's works are preparatory for regeneration but do not actually constitute regeneration. These activities prepare one for the special work to come in the same way that drying out wood prepares it for fire.[5] Regeneration itself is qualitatively different from this preparation. He cites the creation in which Adam was formed from the dust before he received the breath of life.[6]

The proclaimed gospel often produces the preparatory effects of illumination, conviction and reformation of life.[7] Although these are good and tend toward regeneration, they are incomplete on their own. Owen limits illumination to knowledge about supernatural things without a corresponding disposition to love these things.[8] Nevertheless, illumination and other preparatory graces are God's normal means for leading one to regeneration. Here Owen proposes similarity between preparation and regeneration. "In order of nature [illumination] is *previous* unto a full and real conversion to God, and is materially preparatory and dispositive thereunto; for saving grace enters into the soul by light."[9] But illumination falls short of regeneration. Although the Spirit may work on the human "*mind, conscience, affections, and conversation*," Owen avoids ascribing illuminating change to the *will*.[10]

Preaching illumines through the "moral" operation of explaining and persuading. Owen calls this a "*powerful persuasive efficacy*,"[11] though not an

---

[5]Ibid., 229.
[6]Ibid.
[7]Ibid., 231-34.
[8]Ibid., 231.
[9]Ibid., 233.
[10]Ibid., 238, 643. Illumination is listed among other ambiguous signs of regeneration.
[11]Ibid., 304.

infallible or irresistible efficacy. Although the Spirit uses these moral and persuasive arguments,[12] his work is qualitatively different. In regeneration "there is a real physical work, whereby [the Spirit] infuseth a gracious principle of *spiritual life* into all that are effectually converted and really regenerated."[13] Illumination, in this context, is part of the moral function of proclamation. God's act of illumination is potentially saving, but not infallibly so.[14]

Soteriological illumination. Illumination in the preparatory sense affects only the mind. One is made to understand supernatural truths but is not moved to a full conversion. In regeneration, however, the Spirit restores the three "faculties in our souls" relating to spiritual things: "our understandings, wills, and affections."[15] Nevertheless, Owen can gloss this work as a "saving illumination." A "saving illumination" gives "the mind such a direct intuitive insight and prospect into spiritual things as that, in their own spiritual nature, they suit, please, and satisfy it, so that it is transformed into them, cast into the mould of them, and rests in them."[16] Owen, then, can understand illumination as an element of true converting change.

The agency needed for this transformation involves not just the shining of light into a dark place but also the creation of light within a person. "Spiritual darkness is in and upon all men, until God, by an almighty and effectual work of the Spirit, shine into them, or create light in them."[17] Owen's primary opponent here is an intellectualist explanation of convincing or persuading a person of spiritual truth. To show the qualitative difference of the Spirit's work, Owen cites the allusion to Genesis 1:3 in 2 Corinthians 4:6: "Did God no otherwise work on the minds of men but by an *external, objective proposal* of truth unto them, to what purpose doth the apostle mention the almighty act of creating power which he put forth and exercised in the first production of natural light out of darkness?" Owen concludes that God "conveys light unto them by an act of omnipotent efficiency."[18]

---

[12]"By the reasons, motives, and persuasive arguments which the word affords are our minds affected, and our souls wrought upon in our conversion unto God" (ibid., 307).
[13]Ibid.
[14]Ibid., 303.
[15]Ibid., 493.
[16]Ibid., 238. His citations here all focus on the cognitive content of the gospel or the transformation specifically of the mind: Rom 6:17; 12:2; 1 Cor 2:13-15; 2 Cor 3:18; 4:6.
[17]Ibid., 246, 266.
[18]Ibid., 333.

Light here is not a revealed truth, nor the Holy Spirit, but a new life or new capacity created within a person.

Although Owen indicates that there is a sense in which illumination is necessary in personal salvation, he never views this as a sufficient description of God's act. In sum, the natural mind cannot receive the gospel "so as to have the *sanctifying power* of them [gospel truths] thereby brought into and fixed in the soul, without an internal, especial, immediate, supernatural, effectual, enlightening act of the Holy Ghost."[19] Owen does not settle for a simple definition of illumination in the process of salvation. Illumination or enlightenment indicates the Spirit's act to give the cognitive ability to see and discern spiritual things. This can be considered either as a gloss on the whole process or else as the specifically cognitive change. Given Owen's preference for *regeneration*, while the work of the Spirit in illumination is necessary, it is not sufficient for converting change.

***Scriptural illumination: Owen and the* testimonium.** Illumination is the cognitive element of converting change for Owen, but it is also God's action to show Scripture as his Word. Owen continued his discussion of the Holy Spirit with two treatises on the Spirit and Scripture. In *The Reason of Faith*, he discusses the ground or reason for belief in the divine origin of Scripture. In the second, *Causes, Ways, and Means*, he describes the work of the Spirit to guide believers into a correct understanding of the content of Scripture. *Illumination* is his primary term for the Spirit's action throughout.[20] Owen composed *The Reason of Faith* to address those who claim that an "inward light" exists in all humanity because of the Spirit's universal illumination. This implies a natural human moral ability to submit to God's will.[21] As throughout *Pneumatologia*, Owen confronts the general charge, repeated later by David Strauss, that Protestants are faced with an inevitable choice

---

[19]Ibid., 281-82.

[20]John Owen, *The Reason of Faith*, in *Pneumatologia*, vol. 4 of *The Works of John Owen*, ed. William Goold (London: Johnstone & Hunter, 1852; repr., Carlisle, PA: Banner of Truth Trust, 1967), 7. For similar treatments among Owen's contemporaries, see John V. Fesko, "The Doctrine of Scripture in Reformed Orthodoxy," in *A Companion to Reformed Orthodoxy*, ed. Herman J. Selderhuis, BCCT 40 (Leiden: Brill, 2013), 429-64.

[21]For an interpretation of Owen's interaction with Quakerism, see Joel R. Beeke and Mark Jones, *A Puritan Theology: Doctrine for Life* (Grand Rapids: Reformation Heritage, 2012), 429-39. Owen viewed this controversy as a matter of the authority of Scripture. "We persuade men to take the Scripture as the *only rule*, and the holy promised Spirit of God . . . *for their guide*. They deal with men to turn into themselves, and to attend unto the light within them" (John Owen, *The Causes, Ways, and Means of Understanding the Mind of God*, in *Pneumatologia*, 159).

between rationalism and enthusiasm.[22] In the first volume of *Pneumatologia* he argues against rationalism and for the necessity of the Spirit's work in conversion. In this second volume he argues against enthusiasm and for the Spirit's work as tied to Scripture. The *testimonium* and illumination are crucially not the same as regeneration.[23] Illumination in regard to Scripture is a result of the prior, separable and qualitatively distinct operation of the Holy Spirit in converting change.

Owen defines illumination as a "supernatural knowledge that any man hath or may have of the mind and will of God, as revealed unto him by supernatural means, for the law of his faith, life, and obedience."[24] This refers particularly to Scripture as the "repository of all divine supernatural revelation."[25] Illumination consists in hearing God speaking in Scripture, and for this, one must believe Scripture to be divine revelation and one must understand its content.

The Spirit's testimony, as in Calvin, convinces one of Scripture's truthfulness.[26] For Owen, only God's testimony to Scripture can give one a "faith divine and supernatural, and infallible."[27] By this he means that the affirmation of Scripture's truthfulness is grounded exclusively on the conviction that in it God speaks. A personal human testimony would be insufficient because of the fallibility of the human witness. One's own conviction of the truth of a syllogism or the truth of empirical observation also falls within the broad sweep of that which is fallible. One reaches infallibility, or full assurance, only when one is able to place confidence in God speaking in and through Scripture. "The ground and reason whereon we believe the Scripture to be the word of God are the authority and truth of God evidencing themselves in and by it unto the minds and consciences

---

[22]Cited by Bernard Ramm, *The Witness of the Spirit* (Grand Rapids: Eerdmans, 1960), 105. Strauss called the internal testimony "die Achillesferse [Achilles' heal] des protestantischen Systems" (David Friedrich Strauss, *Die christliche Glaubenslehre in ihrer geschichtlichen Entwicklung und im Kampfe mit der modernen Wissenschaft dargestellt* [Tübingen: C. F. Osiander, 1840], 1:136).

[23]Strictly speaking, for Owen, the *testimonium* is one part of illumination. The other part is the ongoing task of understanding what is written in Scripture.

[24]Owen, *Reason of Faith*, 7.

[25]Ibid., 12.

[26]Ibid., 68. Cf. Calvin, *Institutes* 1.7.3-5 (for full citation information for Calvin's *Institutes*, see chap. 1, n. 18).

[27]Owen, *Reason of Faith*, 15.

of men."[28] When a Christian is asked why she grants Scripture authority, she answers that in and through Scripture she hears and understands the voice of God speaking.

Here Owen separates the *testimonium* from the Spirit's work to bring about such a belief. "The work of the Holy Ghost" to produce divine and supernatural faith "consists in the *saving illumination* of the mind; and the effect of it is a *supernatural light*, whereby the mind is renewed."[29] He cites 2 Corinthians 4:6 for the language of light and glosses, "He irradiates the mind with a spiritual light, whereby it is enabled to discern the glory of spiritual things."[30] This light is not a direct revelation, but rather the power at work allowing one to see clearly. The Spirit's work in this special, saving illumination takes place behind the scenes. In other words, the "saving illumination" fills the space marked out for regeneration earlier in Owen's work. The "saving light which is infused into our minds" has nothing to do with proof for what we believe. The divine light is the power of the Spirit that enables a sure and certain belief.

The *testimonium*, then, is the conviction given to the believer that God is speaking in these Scriptures. But the *testimonium* itself only comes about if the Spirit also gives a saving illumination or regeneration. In other words, the Spirit's saving illumination is "not *the reason* why we believe the Scriptures, but *the power* whereby we are enabled so to do."[31]

Owen recognizes that the semantic content of the gospel message does not transform people on its own. God must work to overcome human sinfulness. But Owen so separates the Spirit's regenerating work from the Spirit's work of testifying that he nearly succeeds in dividing them. The Spirit's *testimonium* of Scripture's truthfulness is dependent on the Spirit's prior work of saving illumination or regeneration. The illumination of Scripture is dependent on the illumination of the person.

Owen on illumination. Owen uses *illumination* in numerous contexts, and his definition remains general enough to include them all. A person's subjective experience of illumination is any "supernatural knowledge . . . of

---

[28]Ibid., 20.
[29]Ibid., 57.
[30]Ibid.
[31]Ibid., 56.

the mind and will of God, as revealed unto him by supernatural means."[32] Illumination may be preparatory to regeneration, may refer primarily to cognitive transformation, may encompass God's work to allow one to understand Scripture or may be a gloss for the whole process of converting change. There is no one moment of illumination or enlightenment.

How might one tie together Owen's diverse thoughts on illumination? He works implicitly with a narrative of illumination. He is aware of the danger of enthusiasm, or new direct revelation bypassing Christ and Scripture. Instead, God's light shines on the definite revelation of Christ and his Word. For Owen, the illumined person responds appropriately to something outside of them so that faith is based neither on personal preference nor on ineffable experience. Owen recognizes, as I observed in relation to the central New Testament passages, that there is both an objective light of God's kingdom revealed in Christ and a subjective reflection of this light in the life of the believer. How the light makes this transition continues to be a challenge. When he affirms that "grace enters the soul by light," the light refers to knowledge about spiritual things.[33] Knowledge is not enough for saving faith, however, and despite his gloss of a "saving illumination," the "real, physical work" of regeneration remains couched in purely supernatural language.

Reformed orthodox polemic for an unmediated work of the Holy Spirit in converting change is meant to oppose theologies that deny that God's grace is irresistible (e.g., Arminianism). But at least one contemporary of John Owen attempted to hold together God's freedom to elicit faith when and where he wills together with a description of converting change that does not appeal to the Spirit's unmediated work separate from the proclaimed word. Claude Pajon challenges theologians such as Owen to describe the part played by human words in this process. Friedrich Schleiermacher then focuses attention on personal presence as the source of power in converting change. I take on board these two sources in order to emphasize the *personal* character of God's action in converting change.

---

[32]Ibid., 7.
[33]Owen, *Pneumatologia*, 231-33.

Claude Pajon and Intellectual Illumination

Claude Pajon was a French Reformed contemporary of John Owen.[34] Because his views were later condemned by provincial synods in France, Pajon's works on conversion were never published.[35] His manuscripts and letters, however, circulated widely and provoked critical response.[36] Pajon maintained that the Spirit's work in conversion is mediated through the proclaimed word. As Albert Gootjes has argued, Pajon's theology attempts to carry on the tradition of French Calvinism influenced by Scotsman John Cameron (d. 1625). Cameron provoked the concerns of continental Reformed theologians when he proposed that the Holy Spirit's illumination of the intellect is sufficient for changing the will. For Cameron, because the will always follows the last dictate of the practical intellect, there is no need for God to infuse new qualities into the will itself. In a discussion of Philippians 2:12-13, Cameron explains how God brings about both willing and doing: "God does all these things by persuading. This movement of God is a persuasion, but most powerful, most vigorous, most efficacious, by which the will is inclined, bent, led and finally seized."[37] The focus on the intellectual

---

[34]The most recent outline of Pajon's theology is Albert Gootjes, *Claude Pajon (1626–1685) and the Academy of Saumur: The First Controversy over Grace*, BSCH 64 (Leiden: Brill, 2014). Additional resources include Gootjes, "Un épisode méconnu de la vie de la communauté réformée au milieu du XVIIe siècle: la première controverse pajoniste sur la grâce," *Bulletin de la Société de l'histoire du protestantisme français* 156 (2010): 211-29; Frans P. van Stam, *The Controversy over the Theology of Saumur, 1635–1650: Disrupting Debates Among the Huguenots in Complicated Circumstances* (Amsterdam: APA-Holland University Press, 1988); Olivier Fatio, "Claude Pajon et les mutations de la théologie réformée à l'époque de la Révocation," in *La Révocation de l'Édict de Nantes et le protestantisme français en 1685*, ed. Roger Zuber (Paris: Sociéte de l'Historie du Protestantisme français, 1986), 209-27; Brian Armstrong, *Calvinism and the Amyraut Heresy: Protestant Scholasticism and Humanism in Seventeenth-Century France* (Madison: University of Wisconsin Press, 1969).

[35]Without access to the archives in Geneva, my research of Pajon comes mainly from the texts included in André E. Mallhet, *La théologie protestante au XVIIe siècle: Claude Pajon. Sa vie, son système religieux, ses controverses d'après des documents entièrement inédits* (Paris: Fischbacher, 1883), 68-146, and the summaries and quotations provided in Gootjes, *Claude Pajon*, and Fatio, "Claude Pajon."

[36]Among Pajon's contemporaries, I appropriate here Pierre Jurieu, *Traitté de la nature et de la grace* (1687; Hildesheim: Georg Olms, 1973), and the discussion of immediate grace largely directed at Pajon's view in Francis Turretin, *Institutes of Elenctic Theology*, ed. James T. Dennison Jr., trans. George Musgrave Giger (Phillipsburg, NJ: P&R, 1992), 15.4.23-57, 2:528-42.

[37]This quotation comes from Cameron's nomination lecture at the Academy of Saumur in 1618. Quoted in Gootjes, *Claude Pajon*, 154. Cf. Armstrong, *Amyraut Heresy*, 66-67. Theologians distinguished between *suasion* and *persuasion*. John Flavel cites Erasmus for the difference. "Suasion is the act of one using endeavours: persuasion the act of an efficient cause. He uses suasion, who gives advice; persuasion is the deed of him who determines a man to what he pleases" (John

side of converting change brings into view the question of this chapter on how to appropriate scriptural vocabulary of light and illumination into a doctrine of calling.

Paul Testard (d. 1650), Pajon's father-in-law and a student of Cameron, pointed to the proclaimed word (understood as the gospel) as God's instrument in conversion. "For the *external* display of the divine light through the *hearing of the Word* (to which *reading, meditation*, and *recollection* are referred) is the *ordinary* means for the internal sending-in, inscription, and faith." He goes further to declare that the Spirit is given to believers "through the Word which is, as we noted already, its *vehicle* as it were."[38] This exclusive focus on the proclaimed gospel is a distinguishing mark of Pajon's teaching.

Pajon's denial of immediate grace. The Saumur Academy appointed Pajon as professor of theology in 1665. He held the office for only ten months before resigning when nearby provinces threatened to withhold financial support from the academy because of Pajon's view on converting grace. In a response to accusations that he was a closet Arminian, Pajon describes his disagreement with his interlocutor, Jacques Guyraut:

> The whole crux of the question is whether Scripture teaches that the Spirit does a certain thing immediately in us in the presence of the word, but to which, however, the word contributes nothing whatsoever and which even precedes in the order of nature the action of the word in us, and which being joined with the action of the word produces faith in our hearts.[39]

This Pajon denies. In Guyraut's conception, the Spirit works "in the presence of the word," but not through and with the word. Pajon argues that this preparing or disposing of the person to hear the word proves either too much or too little. Immediate grace either gives new revelation, which would slide toward "enthusiasm," or else immediate grace only restores a

---

Flavel, *The Method of Grace in the Gospel Redemption*, in *The Works of John Flavel* [1820; repr., Carlisle, PA: Banner of Truth, 1997], 2:74).

[38] Quoted in Gootjes, *Claude Pajon*, 65.

[39] Claude Pajon, "Traité de l'opération de l'Esprit de Dieu en la conversion de l'homme," in Mailhet, *La théologie protestante au XVIIe siècle*, 107. "Tout le noeud de la question est de savoir si l'Ecriture enseigne que l'Esprit fasse quelque chose immédiatement en nous à la présence de la parole, mais à quoy pourtant la parole ne contribue quoy que ce soit et qui précede même dans l'ordre de la nature l'action de la parole en nous, et qui ensuite etant joint avec l'action de la parole produise la foy dans nos coeurs."

person to neutrality, the position his Reformed interlocutors denied against the Remonstrants.[40]

Thus Pajon viewed God's grace in conversion as operating through created means. "The first grace which God does to us is to cause his gospel to be preached to us in a manner so convicting and with the circumstances so effective that it follows necessarily that we are converted."[41] He compares God's work in conversion to swinging an ax. "God, by using the word for the conversion of the elect, accompanies this word with the action of his Spirit, as when someone who cuts a tree with an ax, accompanies the ax with his power."[42] Pajon appeals to Scripture texts that emphasize the word as instrument. Psalm 19:8 affirms that the law of the Lord itself enlightens the eyes. First Peter 1:23 and James 1:18 both affirm the instrumentality of the word in the new birth. For Pajon, illumination takes place through God's word.[43]

Illumination is objective light. Although Pajon wishes to ascribe the agency in converting change to God, he also acknowledges that converting change is a cognitive process. "The Spirit of *illumination* is not immediate grace, but it is the impression of the truth in our understanding and this impression can happen only by means of the ideas that they represent."[44] As in Owen, knowledge of Christ is necessary for converting change. Pajon adds, however, that God works a change within us through this knowledge of Christ.

Given the intellectual bent to Pajon's explanation, his interlocutors ask how God may overcome our "inveterate and invincible malice" for the gospel. Pajon held that "the Spirit uses the Word which contains the truth in order to introduce the knowledge that overcomes human corruption left

---

[40]Ibid., 111.
[41]Ibid., 127. "La première grâce que Dieu nous fait est de nous faire prêcher son Evangile d'une manière si insinuante et avec des circonstances si efficaces qu'il faille necessairement que nous soyons convertis."
[42]Ibid., 114. "Je confesse que Dieu se servant de la parole pour la conversion des élus, accompagne cette parole de l'action de son Esprit, de même que celuy qui abat un arbre à coups de cognée, accompagne la cognee de sa vertu."
[43]Claude Pajon, "Sommaire de la Doctrine de M. Pajon, sur le sujet de la Grâce," in Mailhet, *La théologie protestante au XVIIe siècle*, 76.
[44]Pajon, "Traité," 129. "L'Esprit d'illumination n'est pas la grâce immédiate, mais c'est l'impression de la vérité dans nos entendemens et cette impression ne peut se faire qu'au moyen des idees qui la representent."

by sin."⁴⁵ For Pajon, a type of knowledge overcomes human depravity. Sin has not destroyed human faculties, but has taken them captive to prejudices, ignorance and errors. Here Pajon's faculty psychology comes in to play. Like Cameron, Pajon believed that a person's will always follows the last dictate of the understanding. By nature a person's understanding seeks to know the good. Evil comes about through ignorance of the true good, so that the intellect places an inferior object as the superior. Pajon's doctrine of sin thus affirms that the fallen intellect is capable in principle of apprehending the gospel. But because of sinful prejudice, humans fail to see God's grace in Christ. In order to change the will from love of the world to love of God, the Spirit works to change the understanding so that it perceives God and the gospel as its supreme good. Pajon explains: "The Holy Spirit delivers us from our ignorance and from our errors and removes also the evil dispositions of our souls by the introduction of knowledge in our understanding."⁴⁶ One may say, then, that the Spirit's work is to rescue the understanding from ignorance.

Pajon affirms a form of total depravity. He compares sinful humanity to a sleeping man, but one so deeply asleep that my own shouting cannot awaken him. It is not that he lacks a capacity for hearing (as a deaf man), but that humanly I lack sufficient power to make him hear my call. Pajon proposes that the report from a cannon fired nearby is sufficient to rouse him. The Spirit speaking through the word preached is the divine cannon. And rather than causing deafness, it awakens the enchanted sleeper, so that Christ may shine in him.⁴⁷

To explain how this takes place, Pajon appeals to the "common notions" (*notions communes*) or self-evident truths. In conversion, God presents the gospel to a person and causes these gospel truths to connect with a person's common notions (common sense) in such a way that the gospel truths follow necessarily.⁴⁸ Pajon appeals—significantly—to scientific knowledge, which comes about in the same way. There is no intervening act that makes

---

⁴⁵Gootjes, *Claude Pajon*, 111.
⁴⁶Pajon, "Traité," 108. "Le St-Esprit nous delivre de notre ignoranoe et de nos erreurs et oste ainsi les mauvaises dispositions de nos âmes, par l'introduction de la connaissance en nos entendements."
⁴⁷Ibid., 128.
⁴⁸Ibid., 111. Fatio, "Claude Pajon," 214.

one able to believe that the earth rotates around its own axis. Rather, suitable proofs are presented and a person believes.[49] "Therefore, all the certitude of my faith depends on the certitude of the arguments of the truth which I find in the word."[50] This may be simply an affirmation that Scripture is *autopistic*, or "self-authenticating." Scripture itself provides no external arguments for its own truthfulness.

But it appears that for Pajon, certain arguments presented at a certain time will transform a person. God's action in calling, then, is to tailor circumstances, the words spoken and the perceived ethos of the speaker to the state of a convert to be. The question then arises whether Pajon preserves the gratuity of God's call. While he affirms that the Spirit is the power behind the word when and where he wishes, he also claims to perceive how environmental factors incline a person toward or away from conversion. He notes that someone born in Catholic Spain is far less likely to hear the gospel than in the Protestant parts of France. He tells of a twelve-year-old girl convicted of stealing and concludes that she is deeper in depravity because she had learned this vice from her father, a thief.[51] A Pajonist view, therefore, needs to answer how understanding God's action in converting change primarily as a species of providence allows one to ascribe gratuity to God's call.

Intellectualism. By locating God's work in the understanding faculty, Pajon risks making faith a purely intellectual act. A doctrine of illumination in these terms would view the objective light as a well-argued case for Christ. Turretin argues that without immediate grace God acts in conversion only as a politician or philosopher persuades an audience: "For in both cases there will be a moral and objective action by which the doctrine is proposed and confirmed by various reasons fitted to persuade."[52] Pajon's comparison of conversion to learning scientific knowledge may thus be significant. If the real plane of battle between the gospel and sin becomes not the sinful human will, but also the fallen or malfunctioning understanding,

---

[49]Gootjes, *Claude Pajon*, 113. Gootjes quotes Pajon's earlier dissertation, "De natura gratiae efficacis ad amicum dissertatio" (1660–1662). I have not examined a copy of this work, since it is only in manuscript form.

[50]Pajon, "Traité," 119. "Donc, toute la certitude de ma foy dépend de la certitude des arguments de la verite que je trouve dans la parole."

[51]Ibid., 124.

[52]Turretin, *Institutes* 15.4.44, 2:538.

it would seem that sin is only a result of false information and faith is a matter of cognitive assent. In an ironic reversal, "it is not faith that seeks understanding, but understanding that produces faith."[53] Despite a quotation below that shows his recognition that God's speech differs from our own, the charge that Pajon's system makes God simply a glorified human orator stands largely unanswered.

Implications for a doctrine of providence. Because Pajon affirmed a hypothetical human ability to believe and denied an unmediated work of the Spirit, he viewed God's work in conversion as primarily that of arranging circumstances. God prepares a person through circumstances so that when the gospel is heard, it dispels false ideas by the force of argument. Providential ordering helps explain different responses to the same gospel preaching. But if taken to its metaphysical conclusions, some of his opponents argued it led to a form of causal determinism.

Pierre Jurieu (d. 1713) attacked Pajon on the implications for the Reformed (and Thomistic) affirmation of divine *concursus*.[54] Pajon's view presupposes that a certain organization of circumstances necessarily produces a certain result of the person's free decision (e.g., they believe). In Jurieu's view this succumbs to a mechanistic view of the world. The Thomistic synthesis concretized in the seventeenth century defined *concursus*, the divine accompaniment, as *premotion* or *predetermination*.[55] God must move (or premove)

---

[53] Walter Rex, *Essays on Pierre Bayle and Religious Controversy*, International Archives of the History of Ideas 8 (The Hague: Martinus Nijhoff, 1965), 95.

[54] In the book in question Jurieu attacks disciples of Pajon, but he lists the recently deceased Pajon as "M.P." (Jurieu, *Traitté*, 3). On the relationship between the two men, see Gootjes, *Claude Pajon*, 205-7.

[55] Francis Turretin (*Institutes* 6.5.6-12, 1:506-9) explicitly affirms premotionism as protecting creaturely contingency and liberty of the will. For premotionism and concurrence in seventeenth-century Reformed thought, see W. J. van Asselt, J. Martin Bac and Roelf T. te Velde, eds., *Reformed Thought on Freedom: The Concept of Free Choice in Early Modern Reformed Theology*, TSRPrT (Grand Rapids: Baker Academic, 2010), 145-70; J. A. van Ruler, *The Crisis of Causality: Voetius and Descartes on God, Nature and Change*, Brill's Studies in Intellectual History 66 (Leiden: Brill, 1995), 267-301; van Ruler, "New Philosophy to Old Standards: Voetius' Vindication of Divine Concurrence and Secondary Causality," *Nederlands Archief voor Kerkgeschiedenis* 71 (1991): 58-91. For a recent defense of premotionism, see Steven A. Long, "Providence, Freedom, and Natural Law," *NV* 4 (2006): 557-606. But see criticisms in David Bentley Hart, "Providence and Causality: On Divine Innocence," in *The Providence of God: Deus Habet Consilium*, ed. Francesca Aran Murphy and Philip G. Ziegler (London: T&T Clark, 2009). Among modern treatments of providence and concurrence, see Karl Barth, *CD* III/3:92-118. For criticism of Barth, see Langdon Gilkey, "The Concept of Providence in Contemporary Theology," *JR* 43 (1963): 171. For an affirmation of distinct planes for divine and human action, see Kathryn Tanner, *God and Creation in Christian Theology: Tyranny or Empowerment* (Oxford:

human faculties toward action in every act. A fire burns wood only because God premoves the potential of fire to heat the wood. In a similar way, God premoves or activates the faculties of a free creature in all acts so that these faculties move toward their ends. This ensures that the movement of a free cause (like the will) is never determinable purely on the basis of secondary causes.[56] No matter the preponderance of evidence and persuasion, the will's decision is undetermined apart from the concurrence of divine premotion. One can then distinguish between the *divided* and *combined* senses of necessity. One's decision may be necessary when considered on its own apart from God's decision, or it may be necessary because it is combined with God's decision. Thus a person's decision to believe in Christ may be necessary in the combined sense, meaning that because God has willed it to come to pass, it infallibly will come to pass.[57] But this act is not necessary in the divided sense, meaning that the act of the will itself is not determined by secondary causes.[58] The goal in such a scheme was to preserve contingency for free actions while still acknowledging that God governs and orders all things to their ends.[59] Gisbertus Voetius (d. 1676) views this as entirely positive, since "the predetermination turns the will sweetly and nevertheless strongly to that very end, to which it—certainly being moved and premoved by God—would have turned itself."[60] Divine premotion is determinative, yet the free cause of a human will directs itself at precisely the same end. Premotionism thus sought to affirm what Karl Barth terms the divine "accompanying," that "the free creature does go of itself, but it can and does only go the same way as the free God. It goes its own way, but in fact it always finds itself in a very

---

Blackwell, 1988). For a focus on providence in the economy of salvation, see John Webster, "On the Theology of Providence," in Murphy and Ziegler, *Providence of God*, 158-75; Paul Helm, "Calvin (and Zwingli) on Divine Providence," *CTJ* 29 (1994): 388-405.

[56]Thomas M. Osborne Jr., "Thomist Premotion and Contemporary Philosophy of Religion," *NV* 4 (2006): 624: "The contingent event does not preexist determinately in the secondary cause."

[57]This is the *necessity of the consequence*. The relation between God's will and the resulting action is necessary, but not the resulting action itself. See discussion in van Asselt, Bac and Velde, *Reformed Thought on Freedom*, 35-37.

[58]This is the *necessity of the consequent*.

[59]"A contingent event or thing is a nonnecessary event or thing that either might not exist or could be other than it is" (Richard A. Muller, *Dictionary of Latin and Greek Theological Terms: Drawn Principally from Protestant Scholastic Theology* [Grand Rapids: Baker, 1985], 81).

[60]Van Asselt, Bac and Velde, *Reformed Thought on Freedom*, 151, 167. The text is from a list of theses overseen by Voetius.

definite sense on God's way."[61] For Turretin and Voetius, premotionism functions as an explanation of all events and actions. One may ask then if and how the realm of grace is distinct. If God activates the will in premotion precisely toward the end that the will would otherwise choose, how can this be equated with God's enlivening, immediate act in regeneration?

In the initial controversy Pajon was content to acknowledge a general concurrence of God in all actions. But he denied that concurrence was a sufficient explanation of God's action in converting change.[62] Jurieu argues that this view is inconsistent since converting change is exactly the place in which God's concurrence is most needed. If God's particular concurrence in converting change is not needed, even given human depravity, there is no reason to think that God's concurrence is needed in general.[63] One could argue back, however, that if divine premotion is the focus of God's work in redemption, Jurieu seems to leave little room for arguments and discourse in converting change. Instead it appears that by making converting change a subset of divine concurrence in providence, Jurieu allows a metaphysical scheme to dictate the operation of grace.[64] Without deciding on the specific work of God in each and every act (a form of metaphysics), it may be possible to discuss how God uses created causes to influence and transform a person in converting change. Thus I wish to affirm the possibility of Pajon's early quest to understand God's action in converting change as significantly different from God's general action in providential concurrence.

But Pajon does not give us this opportunity. As Gootjes demonstrates from his correspondence and changes Pajon made in his manuscripts, Pajon eventually denied the general concurrence of God. Jurieu criticizes Pajon and certain of his sympathizers that by denying general concurrence they introduce a mechanical determinism, or determinism of secondary causes. The objection against Pajon is that he denies a metaphysical conclusion about God's interaction with the world at large, leading to a denial ultimately of creaturely contingency.

A doctrine of effectual calling need not be held up at this point. It may be the case that a Reformed doctrine of providence affirms that God concurs

---

[61] Barth, *CD* III/3:92.
[62] I am relying on Gootjes's treatment of Pajon's view (*Claude Pajon*, 120-25, 210-14), since the primary sources were not available.
[63] Jurieu, *Traitté*, 38.
[64] This is Barth's criticism of the classical doctrine of providence (Barth, *CD* III/3:101).

in all creaturely acts to give them true meaning and efficacy.[65] But because the Thomistic tradition also affirms that God ordains the means by which creaturely acts come about as creaturely acts, the two types of causality, uncreated and created, must exist simultaneously and each explain human acts.[66] More fundamentally, scriptural descriptions of converting change impress on one that divine speaking, revealing, shining or raising to life count as God's action in the world. These acts of God are distinct from his general governance of the world.

Pajon's challenge. Pajon denied immediate grace, but not divine involvement in converting change. He opposed a specific notion of immediate grace as the determinative element that precedes human interaction with the proclaimed gospel. God ordains all things that come to pass and in the case of converting change ordains that appropriate created influences encounter a human person and elicit saving faith in the gospel.

Pajon's thought suggests that the language of premotionism may not be properly located in a doctrine of converting change. He argues instead that converting change operates on the level of communication. Pajon recognized that speakers contribute much more than their logical content.

> A man hears gladly and with submission the rebuke of a friend that he would have rejected with furor if it had been made to him by an enemy. . . . The Holy Spirit, who is the mother of events . . . gives all these diverse circumstances with the word in order to make successful the things that God has resolved in his counsel.[67]

These sentences hint at a way forward. Pajon is rightly charged with eliminating much of the distinctiveness of divine speaking. But he recognizes, at least implicitly, that God's speech in converting change is only analogous to

---

[65] Among plausible options, Bavinck utilizes concurrence only to mark out the space between Deism and Pantheism (Herman Bavinck, *Reformed Dogmatics*, ed. John Bolt, trans. John Vriend [Grand Rapids: Baker Academic, 2003], 2:609-15).

[66] Turretin, *Institutes* 6.5.12, 1:509. "Hence these two can at the same time be true: man wills spontaneously, and, with respect to providence or premotion, he cannot help willing. For that premotion of God is such that it takes place in accordance with the nature of things and does not take away from second causes the mode of operation proper to each."

[67] Pajon, "Traité," 112. "Un homme écoute volentiers et avec soumission les remontrances d'un amy qu'il auroit rejetées avec fureur si elles luy avoient eté faites par un ennemy, parce qu'il les conçoit sous une autre idée. Le St-Esprit qui est le maître des évènements, qui souffle où il veut et en la maniere qu'il veut, dispense toutes ces diverses circonstances avec la parole pour faire reussir les choses selon que Dieu l'a résolu dans son conseil."

our own. This broader glance at the circumstances involved in divine and human speaking challenges a doctrine of illumination to answer how God ministers converting change. For Friedrich Schleiermacher, writing more than a century after Owen and Pajon, the Spirit's work in conversion is radically immanent, that is, nearly coterminous with human agency. Whereas Pajon broadly conceived of divine action as arranging circumstances so as to produce an intellectual deduction, Schleiermacher broadens this to include the passing on of Christ's way of being in the world.

Friedrich Schleiermacher and Christ's Illuminating Presence

Friedrich Schleiermacher's *Christian Faith*, although representing a significant modification of traditional Reformed teaching, nevertheless participates carefully in discussions with confessional documents from the seventeenth century. In his doctrine of conversion, Schleiermacher articulates a coherent model for Christ's saving influence, which I understand as a potential complement to Owen's supernatural language for illumination. God's call to us today through human proclamation is identical to the manner by which the first believers (the disciples) were converted. In both cases the words that proclaim the kingdom of God and the summons to repent and believe the good news come through a human agent used by God and empowered by the Spirit. Owen opposed rationalist critics who sought an explanation for faith arising from an intellectual appreciation of the gospel. Pajon shows a potential Reformed appropriation of human means in converting change but flounders on a reductively intellectual epistemology. Schleiermacher goes beyond this and recognizes that God uses the "word in the widest sense" to bring about converting change.[68] The enlightening "word" is not simply the facts of the gospel, but the personal power of the man Jesus Christ communicated through the Spirit's work of witness.

---

[68]"Durch das Wort im weiteren sinn." Friedrich Schleiermacher, *The Christian Faith*, §108.5. *Der christliche Glaube nach den Grundsätzen der evangelischen Kirche im Zusammenhange dargestellt*, ed. Rolf Schäfer, 2nd ed., *KGA* 1:13/1-2 (Berlin: de Gruyter, 2003), 2:184; trans. H. R. Mackintosh and J. S. Stewart, under the title *The Christian Faith* (Edinburgh: T&T Clark, 1928; repr., New York: T&T Clark, 1999), 490. Whenever possible, Mackintosh and Stewart's translation is used. Citations are to proposition and paragraph number and then to page number in *The Christian Faith*. E.g., Schleiermacher, *Christian Faith*, §108.5 (*CF* 490).

One challenge for the inclusion of Schleiermacher is that he does not refer particularly to "illumination." Schleiermacher is an appropriate voice, however, because he is profoundly interested in how one comes to experience the influence of Christ subjectively. This is, I submit, a fundamental question for a doctrine of soteriological illumination. How can one relate the objective light of Christ to the subjective, personal experience of this light? Schleiermacher recognizes the biblical diversity of terms for conversion, but feels free to choose "regeneration" as his primary term, "because regeneration expresses in the most definite way the beginning of a consistent life."[69]

Kevin Hector has appropriated Schleiermacher to describe how Christians "go on in the same way as" Christ himself. Hector outlines a pneumatology based on the transmission of Christ's "normative judgments" through the community of faith within a constructive proposal for a philosophy of language.[70] Hector presents his own theological model for how concepts and norms are passed on in a community and draws this partially from Schleiermacher's understanding of Christ's influence in the world. Hector's interpretation of Schleiermacher provides a way to understand converting change from below, that is, as an analysis of human interaction. While this system presents a fuller account of human interaction than in Pajon, it limits the freedom of God's Spirit to bring about redemption in ways that go beyond our knowledge of the created world.

The word in conversion. For Schleiermacher, regeneration describes the beginning of "living fellowship with Christ."[71] In his discussion of conversion, Schleiermacher details not only the outward manifestation of conversion (repentance and faith) but also the causes that lead to it. In particular he examines the convert's activity and passivity and how the "Word" acts as means for conversion. Schleiermacher's definition of the "Word" is wider than the proposal of truths about Christ. When he refers to the Word, he has in mind the mediated presence of Christ.

Mediated and immediate: Christ's personal presence. Schleiermacher presents conversion both as an unmediated confrontation with Christ and

---

[69]Schleiermacher, *Christian Faith*, §107.2 (*CF* 480).
[70]Kevin Hector, *Theology Without Metaphysics: God, Language, and the Spirit of Recognition*, Current Issues in Theology (Cambridge: Cambridge University Press, 2011), 47-102; Hector, "The Mediation of Christ's Normative Spirit: A Constructive Reading of Schleiermacher's Pneumatology," *ModTheo* 24 (2008): 1-22.
[71]Schleiermacher, *Christian Faith*, §106 (*CF* 476).

as a natural human experience mediated through activities such as preaching.[72] Christ's efficacy consists in the power of his divine presence communicated through human witnesses. In the midst of hearing human discourse and feeling Christ's influence, the convert to be recognizes Christ as present. And this word, a "human communication," is the sum total of Christ's efficacy. "No example can be given of conversion apart from the mediation of the Word."[73]

This raises questions about why Christ's speaking is effective in some situations but not in others. The answer for Schleiermacher, like Pajon, involves a doctrine of providence. Schleiermacher allows that the influence of Christ while on earth continues to ripple out in converting change. In general, God's preservation is seen in the perfect consistency of the natural order,[74] and this natural order corresponds with God's decree for redemption. Divine omnipotence is thus displayed most clearly through the spread of Christ's redeeming and reconciling work by natural means.[75] God's actions are both supernatural, "in so far as they depend upon and actually proceed from the being of God in the Person of Christ," and natural, "in so far as they have a general natural connexion with the historical life of Christ."[76] Thus the divine decree for redemption is instantiated through the miracle of Christ's appearing, a supernatural action. But events leading to conversion are traceable through historical or natural causes.[77]

This natural progress of redemption shows why proclamation is necessary for converting change. The word links one to the historical Christ. If Christ redeems apart from his historically mediated word, then a person is redeemed by "the mere idea of the redeemer, making the actual appearance of Christ superfluous."[78] Therefore a doctrine of conversion that "deprives the Word of its sole place" not only "wipes out all lines of demarcation . . .

---

[72]Ibid., §108.5. See the superior translation of this section by Dawn DeVries, *Jesus Christ in the Preaching of Calvin and Schleiermacher*, CSRT (Louisville, KY: Westminster John Knox, 1996), 64; KGA 1:13/2, 187.
[73]Schleiermacher, *Christian Faith*, §108.5 (*CF* 490-91).
[74]Ibid., §§46-47, 54.
[75]Ibid., §47.1 (*CF* 179). "The most perfect representation of omnipotence would be a view of the world which made no use of such an idea [miracle]."
[76]Ibid., §108.5 (*CF* 492).
[77]"The beginning of the Kingdom of God is a supernatural thing, which, however, becomes natural as soon as it emerges into manifestation" (ibid., §100.4 [*CF* 430]).
[78]Ibid., §108.5 (*CF* 491-92).

but also dissolves all fellowship."[79] The word is necessary in order to preserve a natural and historical connection with the activity of God in Christ.

But what word is it? Schleiermacher concludes his discussion of conversion with the description of the key moment: Christ presents himself both in his "redeeming and reconciling activity," that is, in his prophetic and kingly offices. The "word in the widest sense" is ultimately the presence of Christ in his two roles of redeeming and reconciling, providing the opportunity to imitate Christ's God-consciousness.

Christ's redeeming activity. Christ's redeeming activity is that by which a person comes to share in Christ's perfection, that is, his ceaseless experience of God-consciousness.[80] Redemption, then, is the subjective change in which one is conscious of Christ's activity and life as existing within a person. This comes about as Christ begins to influence a person and Christ's way of living, his "normative judgments," become one's own.[81] For an analogy of Christ's activity, Schleiermacher points to the influence of an attractive teacher. Christ works by evoking a positive response from people, "just as we ascribe an attractive power to everyone to whose educative intellectual influence we gladly submit ourselves."[82] He calls this connection with Christ a *mystical* connection to avoid either a *magical* view (as he observes in the Reformed orthodox) or an *empirical* view in which one's relationship to Christ is a gradual growth toward perfection. The arising of Christ's perfection in a person is neither the result of a pure decision nor a result of an ineffable supernatural activity. Rather, Christ displays a way of being in the world, and this way of living, his "perfection," attracts disciples.[83] Christ announces, "follow me," and this results in conversion primarily because of Christ's personal magnetism.

This display of Christ's perfection and blessedness evokes true repentance, which Schleiermacher glosses as "regret and change of heart."[84] "Christ

---

[79]Ibid., §108.5 (*CF* 492).
[80]Ibid., §100. Christ's "reconciling" role is primarily showing one how to live amid pain and suffering without diminishing one's God-consciousness. One sees this most clearly in Christ's passion, which serves as an example passed on to one (ibid., §101).
[81]Hector, "Mediation," 10; Schleiermacher, *Christian Faith*, §100.2 (*CF* 426).
[82]Schleiermacher, *Christian Faith*, §100.2 (*CF* 427).
[83]Hector's alternative term *attunement* would seem to substitute for "perfection" in this section. See Hector, *Theology Without Metaphysics*, 45 et passim.
[84]The German for "change of heart" is *Sinnesänderung*, "change of mind" (ibid., §108 [*CF* 480-81]; *KGA* 1:13/2, 172).

awakens a wholly perfect regret just in so far as His self-imparting perfection meets us in all its truth, which is what happens at the dawn of faith." As this regret rejects the old life, a desire rises from the "quiescent consciousness" that wishes to receive "the impulses that come from Christ."[85] This moment of change stands between regret and faith. Christ's personal influence, through the proclamation of his perfection and blessedness, awakens the resident but dormant God-consciousness of some who hear it, and these in turn begin to reflect Christ's way of being in the world and so become ministers of his kingdom.

But how is Christ present today in all his perfection to an individual? Kevin Hector develops Schleiermacher to argue that Christ's attunement is present in Christ's people.

Attunement and Christ's normative spirit. Hector proposes that conversion participates in the same dynamic as language learning. When one uses a concept in language, one both receives an "attunement" picked up from other users of the same concept and, as one becomes accepted as a reliable carrier of this concept, also contributes to the normative attunement implicit in that concept. Theological speaking participates in this same dynamic, and this explains the process of Christian discipleship. Disciples of Christ are such because they recognize others as "going on in the same way" as Christ and then attempt to do the same themselves. This "going on in the same way" as Christ is primarily at the level of attunement, or in precognitive, engrained ways of acting and responding in the world, as in Schleiermacher's term *Gefühl*. For Hector, attunement is the precognitive organization of our "manifold," or variety of sensory experience.[86] "Particular ways of being attuned thus circulate through a community and become one's own attunement, in consequence of which one finds oneself with an immediate, non-inferential feel for oneself and one's circumstances."[87] Because Christian discipleship is a process of recognizing how others have gone on

---

[85]Ibid., §108.2 (*CF* 484-85).
[86]*Attunement* is a term from Martin Heidegger, but Hector uses it with his own definition (Hector, *Theology Without Metaphysics*, 53-54). The project of James K. A. Smith is suggestive of similar conclusions, although he has not yet published a doctrine of conversion. See especially *Imagining the Kingdom: How Worship Works*, Cultural Liturgies 2 (Grand Rapids: Baker Academic, 2013), 15-20.
[87]Hector, *Theology Without Metaphysics*, 81.

in the same way as Christ, this can include normative commitments that others have taken, such as confessing "Jesus is Lord." But for the Christian disciple this statement becomes noninferential, that is, one simply lives in a world in which Jesus is Lord.

The Spirit of recognition. If attunement is passed among human persons, what then of the work of the divine Spirit? In Schleiermacher's presentation, the Holy Spirit is resident within Christ's personal influence in the church and so enters into the natural circulation of norms.[88] The Spirit circulates "through a process of inter-subjective recognition in which one links up with (and carries on) a chain of recognition that stretches back to Christ's own recognition of the disciples."[89] One can observe the presence of the Spirit to the extent that a person participates in this chain of recognition.

How then may one attribute agency to the Spirit? Hector addresses how God *attunes* us according to Schleiermacher: "God redeems one by attuning one to Godself, and God does this by incarnating this attunement in Christ and mediating it to one through his Spirit."[90] But Christ is more than an example. Christ's enactment of perfect God-consciousness is contagious and so spreads to the disciples and beyond. The advantage of such an approach is made clear in the way Schleiermacher argues for a "personal" influence of Christ. Gospel preaching does not merely announce information about Christ. Rather, Christ's personal influence is present to a greater or lesser extent in the attunement of Christians and displayed primarily in the record of Christ's attunement in the New Testament. This accords with personal experience that can commonly account for a decision (including faith) by pointing to the influence of various factors including personalities, circumstances and arguments. It also accords with descriptions of converting change in the apostolic record such as Paul's insistence that he shared not only the gospel but also his whole self with the Thessalonians (1 Thess 2:8).

A crucial question for this proposal, however, is how and in what sense the normative judgments of Christ are actually passed on among concrete individuals. The persistent question about why some respond to the preaching of the gospel and others do not is still relevant. If the Spirit's work

---

[88]Ibid., 86.
[89]Ibid., 92.
[90]Ibid., 362.

is entirely circumscribed by the process of intersubjective recognition, is the Spirit imparted to all those who come into contact with the influence of Christ? Hector points to the influence of Christ and of the Spirit: "Christ incarnates perfect faithfulness in human history, thereby supplying the objective possibility of faith, and he imparts his Spirit to one, thereby supplying its subjective possibility."[91] We are left wondering, however, how and when this possibility is actualized. It is unclear in Hector's account whether the Spirit's influence occurs as an automatic result of created causes or whether Christ's attunement mediated by the Spirit affects various individuals according to God's sovereign will. In other words, it would appear that the simple presence of Christ among a group of people would be sufficient to convert those around them. Yet this is not how the New Testament portrays apostolic preaching. Schleiermacher, like Pajon, appeals here to God's governance of times and places. "The difference in [preaching's] efficacy rests on different conditions of susceptibility, and this again depends on the circumstances in which the divine government of the world places different persons."[92] Schleiermacher views redemption as acting naturally in the world, even deterministically according to the fixed order of nature. Christ's incarnation produces a ripple effect that could, in theory, be foreseen based on the causal forces within the world. There is divine governance here, but it is the governance of a divine watchmaker who has let loose a certain amount of redemptive energy that will infallibly run its course.

Two factors limit the utility of Schleiermacher's approach for a doctrine of illumination. First, converting change in Schleiermacher is ultimately an insight into what one has already become. In regeneration one recognizes that Christ is already influencing them, or that one is thinking like Christ in some way. Illumination, we might suppose, is a revelation of what is already the case. But according to 2 Corinthians 4:6, the light of illumination shines on God's objective work in Christ rather than on one's own God-consciousness. Second, when Schleiermacher argues that Christ is mediated through the Spirit resident in his people, he does not leave room for the personality and freedom of the Spirit. If the Spirit is entirely "the vital unity of the Christian fellowship" or "its *common spirit*,"

---

[91]Ibid., 363.
[92]Schleiermacher, *Christian Faith*, §114 (*CF* 531).

despite Schleiermacher's insistence that he is referring to the Holy Spirit, he eliminates the potential for unexpected redemptive action of the Spirit.[93] The preached word is effective in certain people because, given the place, time and their background, they are the sort of people who would be influenced by the whole-life "attunement" encountering them through the Christian community.

These two objections, the inward look of regeneration and the restriction of the Spirit's work to preparing circumstances, limit the usefulness of Schleiermacher's approach. At the same time, he challenges Reformed theology to account for the part played by created, secondary causes in converting change as well as insisting on a living connection between Christ's life on earth and the believer today. A description of converting change as illumination or the shining of divine light will view God's agency as personal rather than mechanistic, as influencing the whole person rather than just the intellect and as directing one's attention outward toward Christ rather than inward.

ILLUMINATION AND TESTIMONY

Illumination language in Scripture often speaks to soteriological change as a whole, and not exclusively to an intellectual component of that change. In 2 Corinthians 4:6, soteriological illumination is a personal encounter with the authority and transforming glory of the risen and exalted Christ. One encounters a person, not simply an argument or a force. The effectiveness of this vision arises from its divine origin. It is fundamental that "men loved darkness rather than the light" (Jn 3:21), but God reserves his special shining, illumination, to fulfill his purposes in salvation. In 2 Corinthians, this revelation of Christ's glory (2 Cor 3:18; 4:6) reaches its climax in Paul's conclusion that in union with Christ, one participates in the "new creation" (2 Cor 5:17).[94] The revelation of Christ's glory inaugurates or brings in the new age or new creation.

As an immanent description of how this comes about, Schleiermacher provides a framework for how norms are passed from one person to another

---

[93]Ibid., §116 (*CF* 535).
[94]I take καινὴ κτίσις as the cosmic, epochal change, although not denying that one's participation in the new creation is real and transformative. The KJV rendering, "new creature," misses the universal eschatological dimension. See Douglas J. Moo, "Creation and New Creation," *Bulletin for Biblical Research* 20 (2010): 39-60.

in communities, specifically through human examples of living and proclaiming Christ. Owen, by contrast, describes the Spirit's work in supernatural terms. That the Spirit "illumines" means that he gives cognitive capacity for knowledge beyond what fallen humans are capable. Owen distinguishes the Spirit's work of illumination, which is generally cognitive, from regeneration, which precedes and makes possible this illumination.[95] Pajon attempts to bridge these two descriptions of converting change: he retains God's freedom to enlighten when and where he wills while attempting to account for the instrumentality of the word or gospel proclamation. Pajon reminds the Reformed tradition that a saving illumination is a work of interpersonal relationship or encounter. Pajon falters, however, when he assumes that gospel proclamation communicates on only one plane, that of discursive reason. He does not sufficiently account for "all the types of communicative action that the use of words makes possible."[96] These theologians affirm together that the objective light becomes subjectively appropriated in conversion and that the root of its explanation lies deeper than a surface description of what a person does or consciously thinks. In John Webster's terms, "We are not simply bathed in light; it does not simply shine over us or upon us. Rather, it illuminates and so creates in creatures an active intelligent relation to itself."[97] How then ought a doctrine of effectual calling respect Scripture's affirmation that in converting change God shines a light into the darkness and enlightens his people?

I propose that the metaphor of illumination for converting change reminds Reformed theology that God engages his people personally through more factors than logical reasoning. If hearing emphasizes the cognitive content of the call, seeing emphasizes the personal presence of God as the one who calls. This can be seen when soteriological illumination is compared with illumination in the doctrine of Scripture. Indeed, illumination finds its home most comfortably in the doctrine of salvation, while what has been called illumination in relation to Scripture is a subset of God's work for human salvation. To say that God shines in our hearts to reveal the glory of

---

[95] As noted above, Owen sometimes speaks of a "saving illumination" as the sum of God's work in converting change.
[96] Kevin J. Vanhoozer, *Remythologizing Theology: Divine Action, Passion, and Authorship*, CSCD (Cambridge: Cambridge University Press, 2010), 265.
[97] Webster, "Illumination," 333.

God in the face of Christ means that the personal presence of God in Christ, in word, actions and "attunement," leads human hearts to reflect back this light in reordered affections, or a reordered stance toward the world. These are indeed "infused habits," since they are not acquired by human effort, but they are infused precisely through the presence of Christ by the Spirit.

The doctrine of the Spirit's testimony, mentioned above, provides a vantage point from which to see both scriptural and soteriological illumination. In both, the Spirit shows us Christ in the gospel. Crucially, the agency at work in the *testimonium* is not a deduction from premises, but a persuasion or conviction based on God's self-attestation in Scripture. As Bernard Ramm explains, "because the *testimonium* is a persuasion, it is a persuasion about something. It is not its own content. The *testimonium* is a revealing action, not a revealed content. It is an illumination, not a communication."[98] Here Ramm draws out the implications of what Owen suggested above, that the Spirit's testimony is not exclusively to the truthfulness of the written Word of God, but to the truthfulness of the gospel proclaimed therein.[99] Ramm argues further that theologically one ought not to separate the Spirit's convincing work that Jesus is the Christ from the conviction that Scripture testifies to God's work in Christ. If one posits two testimonies, one for the authority of Scripture and another for the truthfulness of the gospel applied to oneself, this would create "a work of the Spirit separate from Jesus Christ."[100] These two ought to be held together. As Michael Horton summarizes, "We become convinced of the divine authority of Scripture as we are persuaded by the Spirit of the glory of Christ and his gospel."[101]

The Spirit's testimony, then, is an interpersonal encounter, "just as if we were gazing upon the majesty of God himself."[102] The testimony is the personal witness of God, not as a separate voice assuring one of Scripture's truthfulness, but as the conviction that these words in Scripture are God speaking to one, and so ought to be trusted, valued and acted on as

---

[98]Bernard Ramm, *The Witness of the Spirit* (Grand Rapids: Eerdmans, 1960), 18.
[99]Ibid., 33-34.
[100]Ibid., 103.
[101]Michael S. Horton, *The Christian Faith: A Systematic Theology for Pilgrims on the Way* (Grand Rapids: Zondervan, 2011), 168.
[102]Calvin, *Institutes* 1.7.5, 80.

such.[103] Only persons (as much as this term may be used analogically) testify, and the value of their testimony arises from their personhood (Jn 5:36-38). The Spirit's work consists in giving God's testimony its proper effect in a human heart.

Here Schleiermacher turns inward instead of preserving the external object of the Spirit's testimony. In Schleiermacher, recognition of one's transition into the blessedness of Christ comes about when one discerns within oneself the effects of grace. That I am now going on in the same way as Christ indicates that the crucial change has been accomplished. I have absorbed Christ's way of being in the world and so participate in his reconciliation. I have argued, on the contrary, that the Spirit's testimony is not awareness that one makes reliable judgments about going on in the same way as Christ, but a testimony to something external to the person—that this Jesus has been declared both Lord and Christ.

The Spirit's testimony is thus a summary of soteriological illumination. God displays his redemptive work in Christ through the testimony of Scripture and the living testimony of Christians. The Spirit's work allows one to see this clearly and so rest confidently in it. The Spirit does this through a personal encounter under the form of dialogue and reflection that brings a person to understand, affirm and delight in Christ revealed in the gospel. Scripture's descriptions of soteriological illumination add that these insights or changed dispositions are the marks of God's coming kingdom.

Conclusion: Illumination and Effectual Calling

Are illumination and effectual calling the same thing? As observed above, illumination can refer both to God's action and to its result within a person. Calling focuses more clearly on God's action to summon his people into fellowship with Christ. Yet the two metaphors are combined in several texts. Believers were "called" out of darkness into God's "marvelous light" (1 Pet 2:9). If one may identify this light with the eschatological new creation, or God's kingdom, the same thought may be seen in 1 Thessalonians 2:12, where God "calls you into his kingdom and glory" (cf. 1 Tim 6:12). That Paul likely refers to his Damascus road experience in both

---

[103]Owen, *Reason of Faith*, 4:82-83.

2 Corinthians 4:6 and Galatians 1:15-16 indicates his fluidity with the terms *calling* and *illumination*.

Because of its use in several contexts, illumination describes a wider vista than does calling. But they overlap when speaking about converting change. Calling and illumination refer to the same reality but in different ways. To say that one is enlightened is to focus on one's renewed abilities to perceive as a result of God's action, something not encompassed in "calling" itself. God's call is his summons, which comes with all the power of his address and tailored for the individual. It may imply God's shaping of the person through dialogue, events and time. But it is converting change considered primarily from God's side. The human response is implied, but the "call" itself is God's speech. Illumination or "shining" is similarly God's action. God displays Christ for us in the gospel. Christ speaks to us in witness of God's glory through his ministry. The Spirit directs our attention to God's glory in Christ. But the metaphor of illumination involves both this objective display and the resulting subjective human response.

In Protestant Reformed theology, the traditional home of the "light" metaphor is the doctrine of Scripture, and particularly the doctrine of *illumination*. By attending especially to 2 Corinthians 4:6, it is evident that scriptural illumination and soteriological illumination are parts of a whole—God's light serves as an organizing metaphor for the economy of redemption. Both scriptural and soteriological illumination refer to the Spirit's work to bring about the new creation, understood as the inauguration of the reign of God through Jesus Christ. Christ in the gospel is the objective light that God causes to shine through gospel proclamation. Subjectively, this light becomes the object of vision for the believer. Believers now see God's glory displayed in Christ and so respond in faith. This life of faith reflects Christ, and so believers are now called "light in the Lord." The means by which this objective light transforms a person is ultimately ineffable. But its character as light shows that the Spirit's work gives new vision or perception so that one may understand and see the authority of God revealed in Christ.

Here the Protestant doctrine of the *testimonium* helps elucidate the agency involved in soteriological illumination. The believer's conviction that

Scripture is the Word of God arises from the Spirit's work to persuade one that God is speaking in the gospel as recorded in Scripture. The *testimonium* is a subset of illumination. By the Spirit, the proclamation of the gospel through human witnesses shows one Christ's glory as saving Lord. The light of Christ overwhelms human resistance and transforms human desires so that a person is able to respond in faith and repentance.

New Birth and Resurrection

THE DISCUSSION NOW APPROACHES a third dogmatic question: What change occurs as a result of the effectual call? If it is appropriate to conceive of God's action in converting change as a call or summons that demonstrates the authority of the crucified and exalted Christ in a self-authenticating way administered by the Spirit, what exactly does the call effect?

The answer may be a simple repetition of biblical vocabulary. God called you "out of darkness into his marvelous light" (1 Pet 2:9), "into fellowship with his Son, Jesus Christ" (1 Cor 1:9 NIV), and "into his own kingdom" (1 Thess 2:12). Those called now view the gospel as the wisdom of God (1 Cor 1:26), they are now "saints" (1 Cor 1:2), they are called to "freedom" (Gal 5:13), and they are called to display a variety of lifestyles and thoughts characteristic of God (1 Pet 1:15) or explained as fitting with his calling (Eph 4:1, 4; Phil 3:14; 2 Thess 1:11). The results of the effectual call and explanations of the call as participation in salvation are not difficult to discern. Calling occasions the change from lost to saved status, from alienation to fellowship with Christ, from the kingdom of darkness to the kingdom of light, and even from a form of death to a form of new life. Our question is how to explain the reality of this change. On the level of being, what changes in converting change?[1]

It may be simple enough to answer, "faith." The effectual call makes someone into a believer or elicits from them saving faith in Christ. It may

---

[1] Cf. Herman Bavinck's similar question, "What is it that is effected and brought forth by the regenerative activity of God in the human heart?" *Reformed Dogmatics*, ed. John Bolt, trans. John Vriend (Grand Rapids: Baker Academic, 2003), 4:87.

also be appropriate to answer in the register of the two previous explorations: the result is a saving hearing of the gospel or an illumination of the person. But that would leave a wide swath of biblical language unaccounted for, language that theologians have mined for the ontology of converting change. This chapter examines imagery of believers coming to life or experiencing resurrection as part of their incorporation into God's saving intent. I examine primarily two loci: new birth or new life in John's Gospel (Jn 3:3-5; 5:21-29; 6:63; 11:43-44; cf. 1 Pet 1:23; Jas 1:18) and inaugurated resurrection in Paul (Eph 2:1-10; Col 2:11-14). These two loci provide the clearest potential evidence for death-to-life imagery indicating converting change.[2]

Reformed theologians have summarized death-to-life language with the term *regeneration*. While using a term that indicates new life, Reformed theology has sought to avoid the conclusion that God introduces a new substance to the constitution of humanity.[3] There is also a desire to avoid ascribing regeneration to one particular human faculty, as if either a "resurrected" understanding faculty or willing faculty could be abstracted from the whole person. A new "spirit" in Ezekiel 36:26 is presumed not to imply a pure replacement of whatever may be called the "spirit" of a person.

But Reformed authors have agreed that death-to-life imagery portrays converting change as a radical change from one's prior life, specifically a change in one's orientation or habit. Jonathan Edwards brings into focus this emphasis on radical converting change, while also suggesting a trinitarian framework for this change. In what follows, I place Edwards in conversation with the communicative account of effectual calling offered by Kevin Vanhoozer. Their shared emphasis on God's "communication" of himself propels an exposition of the relationship between calling and regeneration as cause and effect. I propose to understand the relationship as follows:

> *Effectual calling* is the means by which God gives his people *new life* (new birth or regeneration). This new life refers to a reordering of a person's affections, so that the person whom God calls now sees Christ and his gospel as excellent.

---

[2] A fuller study could take account of how the Old Testament uses life as an image for salvation (Ezek 16:6; 37:14; Is 26:19; Dan 12:2). Much of this is presupposed in the Pauline texts.

[3] "In not a single respect does [regeneration] introduce any new substance into the existing creation" (Bavinck, *Dogmatics*, 4:92).

In short, my argument is as follows. Regeneration in the "narrow sense" referred to the "rebirth of mind and will accomplished by the gracious work of the Holy Spirit at the outset of the *ordo salutis*."[4] This is the sense in which, according to the Synod of Dort, the Spirit "infuses new qualities into the soul."[5] Writers appropriated terms such as "hyper-physical" (Turretin) to explain this unique and ineffable operation. The intent was to preserve divine action as distinct from human action, but its use may have depersonalized converting change within the economy of redemption. Edwards agrees with the traditional conclusions about human passivity in the first moment of converting change, yet he uses communicative categories to describe this. For Edwards, God is a "communicative being" first within the immanent Trinity. In redemption God works through the Spirit's communication of himself, that is, through the communication of his holy nature. That the Spirit shares his characteristic attributes defines this work as the Spirit's personal presence. Crucially for Edwards, the gift of the Spirit reorients a person's affections and attention. Thus the Spirit's communication of himself occurs within the hermeneutic process of understanding, rather than before or apart from it. The Spirit's presence providing understanding is the experience of spiritual resurrection. A survey of new-life imagery in the New Testament warrants this interpretation by showing that these texts are compatible with a spiritual resurrection that occurs through God's speaking ministered by the Spirit.

That the New Testament refers to life in Christ as a new life for the person converted is uncontroversial. That this new life is even a participation in Christ's resurrection is not difficult to establish. But to explain what it means to be "made alive" with Christ (Eph 2:5; Col 2:13) raises significant questions regarding the use of the sacraments, the order of salvation and the ontology of converting change.

Three general patterns of reading emerge among interpreters for moving from the scriptural images (new birth, new life) to their theological entailments. The three are not mutually exclusive, but emphasis on one over the

---

[4]Richard A. Muller, *Dictionary of Latin and Greek Theological Terms: Drawn Principally from Protestant Scholastic Theology* (Grand Rapids: Baker, 1985), 259.
[5]*The Canons of the Synod of Dort* 3/4.11; Jaroslav Pelikan and Valerie Hotchkiss, eds., *Creeds and Confessions of Faith in the Christian Tradition* (New Haven, CT: Yale University Press, 2003), 2:586.

others influences a doctrine of conversion. First, one may read "new birth" texts with reference to the experience of new life through sacramental participation, specifically in baptism. Second, one may understand Christian conversion experience as analogical to the experience of resurrection in that one's life and behavior are reoriented around new highest ends or a new social community. Third, one may read the resurrection imagery as portraying a spiritual (i.e., nonphysical) resurrection as an inaugurated fulfillment of the final resurrection of the body confessed by all Christians. Thus new birth and new life may indicate a ritual action, a pattern of changed life and practices, or a participation in Christ's resurrection. Most Christians affirm some place for all three. An emphasis on sacramental efficacy does not preclude a belief that this results in behavioral change and that baptism participates in the eschatological promise of resurrection. An affirmation that "resurrection" terms refer primarily to behavioral change may still incorporate moments of ritual confirmation of this change and the importance of resurrection terms. And an interpretation of new-life imagery as a literal fulfillment of the end-time resurrection promise often assumes that this results in behavioral change and is at least confirmed or sealed in ritual actions such as baptism.

But these emphases have divided confessions. Lutheran and Catholic interpreters read language of new life as fulfilled most directly in the sacrament of baptism.[6] Arminian theologians read this change in relation to changed practices and interpret the terms "new birth" and "resurrection" as metaphorical. Christian conversion is *similar to* a resurrection in this view. But conversion is also, as Steve Lemke argues, similar to giving up one's status as a foreigner (Eph 2:12) or turning away from a path that leads to death (1 Cor 1:18).[7] In the Reformed biblical theology tradition, new-life language refers to an internal change brought about by God the Spirit as a participation in the inaugurated resurrection.[8]

---

[6]*Catechism of the Catholic Church: Revised in Accordance with the Official Latin Text Promulgated by Pope John Paul II*, 2nd ed. (Vatican City: Libreria Editrice Vaticana, 1997), 1215, cites Jn 3:5 and Tit 3:5 for baptism as new birth and regeneration. *Solid Declaration of the Formula of Concord* 2.67; Robert Kolb and Timothy J. Wengert, eds., *The Book of Concord: The Confessions of the Evangelical Lutheran Church* (Minneapolis: Fortress, 2000), 557.
[7]Steve W. Lemke, "A Biblical and Theological Critique of Irresistible Grace," in *Whosoever Will: A Biblical-Theological Critique of Five-Point Calvinism*, ed. David L. Allen and Steve W. Lemke (Nashville: Broadman & Holman Academic, 2010), 130.
[8]Richard Gaffin, *"By Faith, Not by Sight": Paul and the Order of Salvation* (Waynesboro, GA:

All three referents for new-life language intersect in the passages surveyed below. I will focus on how authors within the Reformed tradition have used the biblical language of new birth and resurrection as textual anchors for a doctrine of regeneration. As is well known, the term "regeneration" (παλιγγενεσία) occurs twice in the New Testament. In Matthew 19:28, it references the renewed world in which Jesus' disciples will exercise rule. In Titus 3:5, the "washing of regeneration" indicates an element of personal converting change since it mentions previous sinful behavior (Tit 3:3) and likely refers to the past with the phrase "he saved us." Yet connections with baptism and the eschatological age are debated. The theological term *regeneration*, however, draws on numerous texts that speak of new life, new birth, resurrection and renewal. I examine here two primary loci, new birth in the Gospel of John and being "raised with" Christ in Ephesians 2 and Colossians 2. These texts recur consistently among Reformed theologians when they argue for two theological points about regeneration as the initial renewal of the human person in conversion: (1) human passivity in the first structural moment of conversion, and (2) the instantaneousness of the transition from death to life. Because of human sinfulness, converting change meets no prior willingness in the person who is changed. And because life and death are mutually exclusive, there can be no ambiguous transition from one to the other.

I offer below that the redemptive-historical interpretation of inaugurated resurrection can claim sufficient textual warrant for a theology of converting change. But because of its dependence on biblical vocabulary, this reading leaves a definition of "spiritual resurrection" underdetermined.

Birth from Above, Resurrection and Regeneration

Three primary texts in the Gospel of John warrant a doctrine of regeneration in Reformed theology:

> Jesus answered, "Truly, truly, I say to you, unless one is born of water and the Spirit, [they] cannot enter the kingdom of God." (Jn 3:5)

Paternoster, 2006), 55-73; G. K. Beale, *A New Testament Biblical Theology: The Unfolding of the Old Testament in the New* (Grand Rapids: Baker Academic, 2011), 561-88.

> Truly, truly, I say to you, an hour is coming, and is now here, when the dead will hear the voice of the Son of God, and those who hear will live. (Jn 5:25)
>
> When he had said these things, he cried out with a loud voice, "Lazarus, come out." The man who had died came out, his hands and feet bound with linen strips, and his face wrapped with a cloth. Jesus said to them, "Unbind him, and let him go." (Jn 11:43-44)

John 3:3 and John 3:5 introduce birth "from above" and birth "of water and the Spirit" as prerequisites for participation in the kingdom. These texts have generated significant interpretive traditions regarding entrance into God's saving work. John 5:25 indicates that the voice of the Son of God is powerful to raise the dead. Although reference is made to the final resurrection (Jn 5:28-29), many theologians appeal to this text for a present "spiritual" resurrection. Finally, if Reformed theology has a poster child for regeneration and calling, it is Lazarus, whom Jesus raised from the dead in a dramatic action that included his powerful voice.

The raising of Lazarus and converting change. Protestant Reformed theologians have cited the raising of Lazarus as a paradigmatic example for how God works in conversion. This move from scriptural narrative to theological description, however, is neither transparent nor uncontested. Theologians who appropriate Lazarus for applied soteriology assume that Lazarus's physical resuscitation is analogous to a believer's spiritual regeneration, understood as a participation in the eschatological resurrection or the new creation. Within the Gospel of John, I will argue, these theologians have textual warrant to conclude that Lazarus's coming to life points to the disciples' spiritual coming to life. But these texts alone only begin to answer how a spiritual resurrection is similar to and different from a physical resuscitation.

Lazarus was dead. In the Gospel, there was no doubt that Lazarus was dead. The narrator (Jn 11:17), Jesus (Jn 11:14), Mary (Jn 11:32) and Martha (Jn 11:21) all affirm this fact. Theologians similarly note that the New Testament describes humanity as dead (e.g., Jn 5:25; Eph 2:1) and appeal to Lazarus as the pinnacle illustration. For Jonathan Edwards, Christ's miracles as a whole serve precisely this illustrative function. "Almost all the miracles of Christ that he wrought when on earth were types of his great work of converting sinners." Raising the dead, therefore, "represented his raising dead souls."[9] For Reformed theologians, at least two conclusions flow from the fact that Lazarus was dead.

First, in the same way that Lazarus was passive in his raising, so also the person who receives the grace of regeneration is passive. John Gill gives a stark reading of spiritual deadness. "Men are dead in trespasses and sins; and can no more quicken themselves than a dead man can; as soon might Lazarus have raised himself from the dead, and the dry bones in Ezekiel's vision, have quickened themselves and lived."[10] Peter van Mastricht notes that Lazarus's raising was irresistible. "If you consider that it is God who regenerates and quickens, the subject of regeneration can no more resist God than Lazarus of old could have resisted Christ when He raised him to a natural life."[11] John Owen, writing ten years before van Mastricht, explains spiritual death with an appeal to Lazarus: "So the dead body of Lazarus was quickened and animated again by the introduction of his soul; but in itself it had not the least active disposition nor inclination thereunto."[12] Humanity before regeneration is spiritually dead, unable to respond and therefore passive, just like the body of Lazarus.

Second, the transition from death to life was instantaneous for Lazarus, with no intermediate state between death and life. Jonathan Edwards explains, "There is no medium between being dead and alive; he that is dead has no degree of life in him, he that has the least degree of life in him is alive. When a man is raised from the dead, life is not only in a greater degree in him than it was before, but it is all new."[13] Edwards appeals to John 5:25, which describes a situation "like to the change made in Lazarus when Christ called him from the grave." Here "conversion" is "an immediate and

---

[9] Jonathan Edwards, "Treatise on Grace," in *Writings on the Trinity, Grace, and Faith*, ed. Sang Hyun Lee, WJE 21 (New Haven, CT: Yale University Press, 2002), 162-63. A wider study would consider how theologians before the Reformation appropriated Lazarus. Augustine applies the raising of Lazarus to conversion in *Tractates on the Gospel of John* 49.24 (NPNF[1] 7:277-78).

[10] John Gill, *A Body of Divinity* (Grand Rapids: Baker, 1951), 845.

[11] Peter van Mastricht, *A Treatise on Regeneration* (1699; Morgan, PA: Soli Deo Gloria, 2002), 29.

[12] John Owen, ΠΝΕΥΜΑΤΟΛΟΓΙΑ [Pneumatologia], or, a Discourse Concerning the Holy Spirit, in *The Holy Spirit*, vol. 3 of *The Works of John Owen*, ed. William Goold (London: Johnstone & Hunter, 1852; repr., Carlisle, PA: Banner of Truth Trust, 1966), 295.

[13] Edwards, "Treatise on Grace," 163.

instantaneous work."[14] For van Mastricht, Lazarus specifically counters the possibility of preparation for regeneration. The true "first act or principle of spiritual life" comes instantaneously. There could be no more preparation than "took place in the resurrection of Lazarus to a natural life (Jn 11:43)."[15] In each of these examples, theologians appeal to Jesus' raising of Lazarus as analogous to divine action in conversion. This helped bolster two claims about God's action in conversion: God operates on a passive human subject, and this transformation is instantaneous.

Francis Turretin goes further in theologizing on Lazarus. The elements of a bodily raising become a source for theological reflection. Turretin divides the act of raising Lazarus into two stages to parallel his analysis of converting change as "habitual and actual."

> Just as in restoring sight to the blind, Christ did two things: he first opened their eyes and so restored the power of seeing; then he caused the man to see at the same moment. So in the resurrection of Lazarus, the soul was first restored to the body, then he elicited vital actions. Thus God by his omnipotent acting produces in the man (or in the will) new qualities; then he excites those faculties to action.[16]

Turretin goes further here than the emphases above on passivity and instantaneousness. He breaks down these two miracles into constitutive parts based on a distinction between primary and secondary actualization. The characteristically physical abilities of seeing and living must exist as capacities (*in actu primo*) before the actions corresponding to these abilities take place (*in actu secundo*).[17] He divides the miracle of regeneration along these same lines. God in conversion must create the capacity or ability to believe (faith *in actu primo*) before that faith can be elicited through means such as the proclamation of the gospel. Here the physical miracle of restoring life becomes a strong standard for discerning the attributes of the spiritual miracle of regeneration. Turretin might be challenged for allowing the Thomistic account of infused habits to set the terms for interpreting Christ's

---

[14] Jonathan Edwards, "'Miscellanies,' no. 673," in *The "Miscellanies" (Entry Nos. 501-832)*, ed. Ava Chamberlain, WJE 18 (New Haven, CT: Yale University Press, 2000), 232.
[15] Van Mastricht, *Regeneration*, 28.
[16] Francis Turretin, *Institutes of Elenctic Theology*, ed. James T. Dennison Jr., trans. George Musgrave Giger (Phillipsburg, NJ: P&R, 1992), 15.4.13, 2:522-23.
[17] Muller, *Dictionary*, 150.

miracles and work in regeneration.[18] There is no textual evidence that Christ's words "Come out!" were spoken to an already animated Lazarus. It is just as likely that Christ's speech both restores life and elicits a response in one act. Turretin's deduction of the two stages of a spiritual resurrection appears here to let a philosophical account of action take over the witness of Scripture.

Christ's powerful words. Christ's words at Lazarus's tomb have also drawn attention.[19] Jesus yells, "Lazarus, come out!" (Jn 11:43), and Lazarus emerges from the tomb. In his commentary, Calvin focuses on Christ's voice. By raising Lazarus in this manner, "he exhibited a visible token of his spiritual grace, which we experience every day by the perception of faith, when he shows that his voice gives life."[20] For Calvin, the physical raising of Lazarus signifies the spiritual grace given to us through Christ's voice.

Herman Bavinck wishes to show that the word serves as the necessary instrument in converting change while reserving the Spirit's work through the word as the sufficient condition. He joins the Lazarus miracle with God's life-giving breath in Ezekiel 37:5. God can call dead people "because He calls those things that are not as though they were [Rom 4:17], and particularly by means of this calling He brings them into being."[21] Bavinck argues against his contemporary Abraham Kuyper, who separated calling and regeneration as distinct events. For Bavinck,

---

[18]Claude Pajon rejects the analogy with Lazarus for precisely this point—that we cannot refer to his raising as anything other than a "physical" (as opposed to moral) operation (Claude Pajon, "Traité de l'opération de l'Esprit de Dieu en la conversion de l'homme," in *La théologie protestante au XVIIe siècle: Claude Pajon. Sa vie, son système religieux, ses controverses d'après des documents entièrement inédits*, ed. André E. Mailhet [Paris: Fischbacher, 1883], 123).

[19]For the emphasis on divine speech in the raising of Lazarus among contemporary writers, see Michael S. Horton, *The Christian Faith: A Systematic Theology for Pilgrims on the Way* (Grand Rapids: Zondervan, 2011), 572; Kevin J. Vanhoozer, "Effectual Call or Causal Effect? Summons, Sovereignty and Supervenient Grace," in *First Theology: God, Scripture and Hermeneutics* (Downers Grove, IL: InterVarsity Press, 2002), 118; John Piper, *Finally Alive* (Minneapolis: Desiring God, 2009), 68, 79, 84-85. Karl Barth, *CD* IV/3.2:512, notes Lazarus and the raising of Jairus's daughter (Mk 5:41) as instances in which the awakening to faith is a "call and summons." The raising of Lazarus shows the primary gospel claim that "God confers life to the world through the Word" (Marianne Meye Thompson, "The Raising of Lazarus in John 11: A Theological Reading," in *The Gospel of John and Christian Theology*, ed. Richard Bauckham and Carl Mosser [Grand Rapids: Eerdmans, 2008], 236). See Frederick Dale Bruner, *The Gospel of John: A Commentary* (Grand Rapids: Eerdmans, 2012), 682, 685.

[20]Calvin, *Comm. John 11:43* (CC 17:447).

[21]Herman Bavinck, *Saved by Grace: The Holy Spirit's Work in Calling and Regeneration*, ed. J. Mark Beach, trans. Nelson D. Kloosterman (Grand Rapids: Reformation Heritage, 2008), 99.

deaf persons cannot hear, but under and in connection with the external calling, God can make them to hear. Dead persons cannot rise up, but by means of the Word, God can sow the seed of life in their hearts, so that with the prodigal son they rise up and return to the Father.[22]

Christ's spoken word is indispensible in this process. But Christ's power does not come automatically from the particular combination of sounds (locution) employed. Christ's words are effective precisely because he speaks them as one full of God's Spirit. Stephen Charnock distinguishes the outward word from the Spirit's inward work. "The gospel in itself is like Christ's voice; the gospel with the Spirit is like Christ's power raising Lazarus; other men might have spoken the same words, but the power of rising must come from above."[23] These references show a common Reformed theme: the necessity but not sufficiency of the preached word to effect converting change.[24] Calvin, Charnock and Bavinck illustrate the necessity of the preached word with an appeal to Christ's practice in the raising of Lazarus.

John 5 and spiritual resurrection. Several Reformed authors conclude that Lazarus's raising was not meant merely to restore life to this man, but that it served as an analogy for spiritual resurrection. Charles Hodge offers the connection. "If man is as really spiritually dead . . . as Lazarus was corporeally dead, then is the spiritual resurrection of the one as really a work of divine omnipotence as the bodily resurrection of the other."[25] Hodge appeals to John 5:25 for validation that spiritual regeneration ought to be strongly analogous to bodily resurrection.

In John 5:28-29, Jesus speaks of a general resurrection of judgment and life: "Do not marvel at this, for an hour is coming when all who are in the tombs will hear his voice and come out, those who have done good to the resurrection of life, and those who have done evil to the resurrection of judgment." Whereas this text speaks of an hour that is "coming," John 5:25 speaks of the hour that "is coming and now is." Both refer to life through the

---

[22]Ibid.
[23]Stephen Charnock, *The Doctrine of Regeneration: Selected from the Writings of Stephen Charnock* (Philadelphia: Presbyterian Board of Publication, 1840; repr., Grand Rapids: Baker, 1980), 12-13.
[24]Heinrich Heppe, *Reformed Dogmatics*, ed. Ernst Bizer, trans. G. Thomson (Grand Rapids: Baker, 1978), 517-18.
[25]Charles Hodge, *Systematic Theology* (New York: Scribner, 1871; repr., Grand Rapids: Eerdmans, 1940), 2:705.

voice of Christ, and lexical parallels between these passages and the raising of Lazarus are clearly evident. The "dead" are raised, they emerge from a "tomb" and a powerful "voice" speaks. Yet a string of verbal connections does not prove an intentional connection.

Jesus' teaching here (Jn 5:19-29) draws imagery from the prophecy of Daniel. First, Jesus calls himself the "Son of Man" (Jn 5:27), a distinctive title from Daniel 7.[26] As Stefanos Mihalios argues, the Johannine term "hour" (ὥρα appears in Jn 5:25, 28) refers to the Danielic use of ὥρα in an eschatological sense as the culmination of the prophesied time of deliverance (Dan 12:1).[27] Not coincidentally, Daniel 12:2 is the clearest Old Testament description of a general resurrection: "Many of those who are sleeping in the dust of the earth will be raised, some to eternal life [ζωὴν αἰώνιον], and some to disgrace, and some to eternal degradation and shame" (Dan 12:2 OG). "Eternal life" is distinctive here, since the collocation appears seldom in the Greek Old Testament.[28]

Mihalios argues that Jesus announces the fulfillment of the Danielic prophecy of eschatological resurrection (Dan 12:2 // Jn 5:28-29), but with an inaugurated twist in John 5:24-25. He proposes that Jesus first declares the present reality. "Truly, truly, I say to you, whoever hears my word and believes him who sent me has eternal life. He does not come into judgment, but has passed from death to life" (Jn 5:24). The reference to eternal life tips off the reader for the next verse, in which Jesus explains the meaning. If the believer possesses eternal life now, this means that the eschatological resurrection has arrived.[29] Commentators agree broadly that the time reference ("is coming" and "now is") is significant. The voice of the Son of God in John 5:25 is distinct from the voice in John 5:28.[30] John 5:25 explains the origin of eternal life for believers, while John 5:28-29 describes the consummation

---

[26]Jesus refers to himself as "Son of Man" thirteen times in John's Gospel. The reference to Dan 7:13 is commonly acknowledged. See Stefanos Mihalios, *The Danielic Eschatological Hour in the Johannine Literature*, LNTS (London: T&T Clark, 2011), 116-17; Andreas J. Köstenberger, "John," in *CNTUOT* 442.

[27]Mihalios, *Eschatological Hour*, 31, 46. He cites the following for eschatological ὥρα in the Old Greek of Daniel: Dan 8:17, 19; 11:6, 35, 40, 45; 12:1, 13.

[28]See only 2 Macc 7:9; 4 Macc 15:3; Ps of Sol 3:12. See ibid., 109.

[29]John 5:21 shows that Jesus is speaking of resurrection with the language of "life."

[30]See references in Mihalios, *Eschatological Hour*, 113n58; C. H. Dodd, *The Interpretation of the Fourth Gospel* (Cambridge: Cambridge University Press, 1953), 364.

of the Son's judgment through a resurrection of life and a resurrection to judgment, as in Daniel 12:2. Mihalios proposes, then, that the new life in John 5:25 is the internal inauguration of the eschatological resurrection.[31] This conclusion legitimates theologizing on the raising of Lazarus. If John conceives coming to faith as participation in eschatological resurrection, then appeals to the raising of Lazarus for a theology of conversion would have support from within John's Gospel.

But our study still asks what analogy exists between spiritual and physical resurrections. According to Mihalios, "life" in John 5:24 is "a literal spiritual resurrection, which inaugurates the resurrection of 5.28-29."[32] The spiritual resurrection today participates in the general resurrection. He explains, "This interpretation is incompatible with a resurrection that is merely noetic or metaphorical, since a literal spiritual resurrection presupposes that the spiritually dead people are literally dead in their spirit, and that a spiritual resurrection literally revives their dead spirit."[33] This distinction gets to the heart of theological concepts emerging from biblical vocabulary. Mihalios seeks a clear description of the discontinuity between a spiritually dead and spiritually alive person. He rejects "noetic" or "metaphorical" as underemphasizing the radical transformation. But "literally dead in their spirit" still presupposes a fair degree of figurative language, especially what it means that a person is dead "in spirit." He proposes essentially a distinction between internal and external resurrections. Those who hear the voice of the Son of God are resurrected proleptically and partially. Christ revives "their dead spirit," presumably, so that they might fulfill the condition of belief in John 5:24 and experience eternal life.

One may object to this view based on the variety of "life" terms in John 5:24-25. Kenneth Keathley cites John 5:24 to show that possession of "eternal life" is dependent on the human response of faith. Those who hear the voice of the Son of God in John 5:25 are not the recipients of a special divine act, but those among all the hearers of the Gospel who respond in faith.[34] This

---

[31]Beale, *Biblical Theology*, 569-72, argues roughly this thesis as the central theme of New Testament theology.
[32]Mihalios, *Eschatological Hour*, 114.
[33]Ibid., 114n60.
[34]Kenneth Keathley, *Salvation and Sovereignty: A Molinist Approach* (Nashville: Broadman & Holman, 2010), 121.

view correctly notes that "eternal life" in John's Gospel refers to the experience of the benefits of the age to come. But the "voice" of the Son of God gives life both in John 5:25 and in the physical resurrection (Jn 5:28-29). The broader context (Jn 5:20-30) relates how the Son gives "life to whom he pleases" (Jn 5:21).[35] In Keathley's view, any analogy to resurrection drops out. But given John 5:28-29, "life" language in John 5:24-25 must bear some analogy to resurrection, even if this entails a greater emphasis on divine initiative.

The same double reference to resurrection now and not yet can be seen in the Lazarus story. Martha (Jn 11:23-26) understands the promise of final resurrection, but Jesus redirects her to himself as the "resurrection and the life" (Jn 11:25). This resurrection life "may take place before bodily death, and has for its result the possession of eternal life here and now."[36] Given this hint of inaugurated resurrection in John 11, it appears warranted to read Lazarus's resuscitation as a foretaste of the promised general resurrection. In addition, given the common emphasis in John 5 and John 11 on the voice of the Son of Man, it also seems appropriate to view the incomplete experience of resurrection life for Lazarus as a fulfillment of the inaugurated experience of resurrection promised in John 5:25.

Mihalios above rejects a "noetic" or "metaphorical" sense to spiritual resurrection because he wishes to highlight the eschatological time of fulfillment. A spiritual resurrection is the experience of renewed life in the age to come. But this still leaves the character of a "spiritual resurrection" underdetermined. I suggest that Mihalios's rejection of a spiritual resurrection that is "merely noetic" is a category mistake. Certainly the characters in John's Gospel experienced noetic change.[37] Jesus may describe this change as participation in the resurrection, but this does not make it any less a function of Christ's words ministered by the Spirit (Jn 6:63) convincing and transforming his hearers.[38]

---

[35]In the two previous passages Jesus gives life through his word (Jn 4:50; 5:8).
[36]Dodd, *Fourth Gospel*, 148. This is also the conclusion of Otfried Hofius, "Die Auferweckung des Lazarus: Joh 11,1-44 als Zeugnis narrativer Christologie," *ZTK* 102 (2005): 31-32.
[37]For coming to faith in the narratives of John with an emphasis on hearing, see Craig R. Koester, *The Word of Life: A Theology of John's Gospel* (Grand Rapids: Eerdmans, 2008), 164. For an emphasis on the signs and seeing, see Marianne Meye Thompson, *The God of the Gospel of John* (Grand Rapids: Eerdmans, 2001), 117-43.
[38]On Jesus as the giver of the Spirit in John, see Thompson, *God of the Gospel of John*, 173-74.

Born from above in John 3:3-5. Similar issues arise in John 3. Jesus responds to Nicodemus twice, in John 3:3 and John 3:5. Two differences stand out in his answers: the description of the "birth" and the action related to the "kingdom of God." First, one must be born "from above" (ἄνωθεν)[39] in John 3:3, and this birth is "from water and spirit" in John 3:5. In regard to the second, this birth must occur so that one is able either to "see" (Jn 3:3) or "enter" (Jn 3:5) the kingdom of God. Van Mastricht distinguishes sharply between the verbs "seeing" and "entering" in these verses. He explains the need for God's act of regeneration so that a person can perceive the kingdom.

> Here regeneration is extended to the power ("he cannot"), the reason of which is given in the following verse [Jn 3:6]: "That which is born...." For regeneration, strictly so called, finds man spiritually dead (Eph 2:2,5), into whom it infuses the first act or principle of the spiritual life, by which he has a power or ability to perform spiritual exercises.

Van Mastricht explains that this first step is expressed in John 3:3, while conversion proper is in John 3:5. "Therefore, without this [principle of spiritual life], he can neither see the kingdom of God—that is, mentally, since he is blind, and perceiveth not the things of the Spirit of God, for they are foolishness unto him... (1 Cor. 2:14)—nor, if he could see, could he enter into the kingdom of God."[40] This is, however, too fine a distinction. Many interpreters, with Calvin, assert that "seeing" and "entering are the same thing."[41] John 3:36 provides the most likely comparison, where "seeing" involves enjoying or experiencing the benefits of something. "The one who rejects the Son will not see life." There is no

---

[39] Or "born again." For an argument in favor of "born again," see Linda Belleville, "'Born of Water and Spirit': John 3:5," *TJ* 1 (1980): 138. I make no claim on the proper translation since either or both could apply.

[40] Van Mastricht, *Regeneration*, 7-8, 9, 26. Cf. John Murray, *Redemption, Accomplished and Applied* (Grand Rapids: Eerdmans, 1955), 96-97; Karl Barth, *CD* IV/4:121. New Testament scholar Ben Witherington III, *John's Wisdom: A Commentary on the Fourth Gospel* (Louisville, KY: Westminster John Knox, 1995), 95, believes "seeing" the kingdom applies to knowledge of God's dominion. Unlike the Reformed approach, for Witherington, "seeing" is a gift granted to everyone who hears and is moved by the Spirit, yet the decision to believe is not thereby determined in any sense.

[41] Calvin, *Comm. John* 3:3 (*CC* 17:108); D. A. Carson, *The Gospel According to John*, PiNTC (Grand Rapids: Eerdmans, 1991), 188; Andreas J. Köstenberger, *John*, BECNT (Grand Rapids: Baker Academic, 2004), 122n20.

distinction here between a perception of eternal or eschatological life and a participation in such life.⁴²

But once one understands both texts to refer to the same reality, there is no agreement on the proper referent.⁴³ The earliest references outside the New Testament apparently drawing on "born of water and spirit" referred this verse unequivocally to Christian baptism.⁴⁴ Much depends, however, on whether one seeks an interpretation relevant within the ministry of Jesus or if one assumes the text is crafted primarily for the context of the Christian church.⁴⁵ Protestant theologians have generally been hesitant to dismiss the sense of the text as a conversation in the ministry of Jesus. A reference to Christian baptism would be impenetrable to Nicodemus. In search of a historically plausible account, suggestion has been made that the "water" in question is that of John's baptism (see Jn 3:22-24). In this sense, entrance into the kingdom requires the baptism of John in water and baptism by the Holy Spirit, that is, joining in the ministry of Jesus.⁴⁶ The challenge for this interpretation is to relate these two actions—John's and Jesus' ministries—to the unified sense in John 3:3, where birth is singular, "from above." Better is Calvin's suggestion that water and Spirit form a hendiadys—water, that is, the Spirit.⁴⁷ Significantly, this combination of water and Spirit can be found in the eschatological promises of Ezekiel 36:25-27. Water and Spirit are linked in several Old Testament texts (e.g., Is 32:15; 44:3; cf. Jn 7:38-39), but

---

⁴²Although in many texts "seeing" refers specifically to perception (Jn 14:9; 19:35) or to a combination of perceiving and experiencing (the "kingdom of God coming in power" in Mt 16:28 // Mk 9:1 // Lk 9:27), Jn 3:36 provides the nearest reference.

⁴³Still relevant is the taxonomy by Belleville, "John 3:5," 125-34.

⁴⁴Justin, *First Apology* 61 (*ANF* 1:183; *PG* 6:420). Justin may be aware of an independent tradition, since he does not quote the Gospel of John elsewhere and because he uses ἀναγεννηθῆτε instead of γέννειν ἄνωθεν. It is sufficient that Justin applies this logion directly to Christian baptism. Irenaeus, *Fragment 34* (*ANF* 1:574), quotes Jn 3:5 as parallel to Namaan's washing in the Jordan river (2 Kings 5:14).

⁴⁵For an extreme case of the latter, see David Aune, *The Cultic Setting of Realized Eschatology in Early Christianity*, NovTSup 28 (Leiden: Brill, 1972), 8.

⁴⁶Herman N. Ridderbos, *The Gospel According to John: A Theological Commentary*, trans. John Vriend (Grand Rapids: Eerdmans, 1997), 128; G. R. Beasley-Murray, "John 3:3, 5: Baptism, Spirit and the Kingdom," *ExpTim* 97 (1986): 167-70.

⁴⁷Calvin, *Comm. John 3:5* (*CC* 17:111); Carson, *John*, 194, gives three reasons for accepting the hendiadys and seeking an OT background for the phrase: (1) the parallel with Jn 3:3 indicates one action (birth from above) rather than two types of baptism, (2) the preposition "of" governs both water and spirit, and (3) Jesus criticizes Nicodemus as "Israel's teacher" (Jn 3:10), indicating that this is something familiar to him in Jewish tradition.

the combination of the two terms as applied to God's people as an eschatological promise is particularly evident in Ezekiel 36–37.

Once the connection with Ezekiel 36 is granted, however, one needs to decide on the referent of that text, especially whether it includes personal subjective moral change. Ezekiel 36 is a promise of eschatological renewal for God's people. James Jordan (and the wider "federal vision"[48]) reads "birth from above" as an exclusively eschatological or epochal transition, rather than an existential one. For Jordan, Christian baptism introduces one into the realm or age of the Spirit. Nicodemus was not in need of internal transformation along the lines of an infusion of new qualities or the ability to "see" the kingdom. Rather, Nicodemus needed to enter into the realm of the new covenant (i.e., the realm of the Spirit) through baptism.[49]

Jordan's reading highlights the eschatological transition in these verses. He seeks to avoid a potentially "Manichean" understanding of converting change. If the distinction between flesh and Spirit in John 3:6 ("That which is born of the flesh is flesh, and that which is born of the Spirit is spirit") means that spiritual people are ontologically distinct, a charge may be made that regeneration has created a new and different species of human. This concern is legitimate, and Reformed authors (including Edwards below) attempt to avoid it by speaking of a new nature as a "moral" change.[50] Given, however, the reference to Ezekiel's prophecy that eschatological Israel will "walk in my statutes" (Ezek 36:27), it is difficult to avoid the conclusion that new birth includes personal moral change as part of the giving of the Spirit.[51]

---

[48]For the stated aim of honoring biblical language and the eschatological turn of the ages, see "A Joint Federal Vision Profession," Resources for Understanding the Federal Vision, June 2007, http://www.federal-vision.com/resources/joint_FV_Statement.pdf. For a proposed (but not undisputed) taxonomy of current conservative Reformed positions including the federal vision, see William B. Evans, "Déjà vu All Over Again? The Contemporary Reformed Soteriological Controversy in Historical Perspective," *WTJ* 72 (2010): 135-51.

[49]James B. Jordan, *Thoughts on Sovereign Grace and Regeneration: Some Tentative Explorations*, Biblical Horizons Occasional Paper 32 (Niceville, FL: Biblical Horizons, n.d.).

[50]Edwards, "Treatise on Grace," 156, 194-95. Calvin calls it a "new will" (*Institutes* 2.3.6, 297 [for full citation information for Calvin's *Institutes*, see chap. 1, n. 18]).

[51]See Craig S. Keener, *The Gospel of John: A Commentary* (Peabody, MA: Hendrickson, 2003), 1:552; Cf. Carson, *John*, 190. Jordan's wider concern is to show that the "Spiritual" person does not possess permanent and infallible characteristics, but that everyone with whom the Spirit works is in this sense "spiritual," while only some of these are given the gift of perseverance and so endure to the end in faith. "New birth" is not an infallible status given to those on whom the Spirit has come, but rather an epochal term. They are those living in the sphere of the Spirit, that is, those who have been baptized and so marked with the sign of Christ.

I proceed, therefore, concluding that birth "from above" and "of water and the Spirit" refer together to the fulfillment of promises of the new covenant in the Old Testament. The new covenant brings renewed life and salvation to God's people through their cleansing and through the presence of God's Spirit. Christ emphasizes to Nicodemus that this birth is not within natural power, but is dependent on God's saving action. The mode by which it comes about is left unstated or else shrouded in mystery.

The three main texts appropriated by Reformed theologies of salvation—John 3:3-5, John 5:25 and the raising of Lazarus—can be seen as forms of fulfillment of the eschatological new covenant promises, especially Ezekiel 36:25-27. This pushes one to read language for converting change in ways that display divine activity as primary and decisive, answering to the "passivity" criterion. This survey also makes plausible an interpretation of new-birth language throughout the New Testament as converting change. This includes instances in 1 John (1 Jn 2:29; 3:9; 4:7; 5:1, 4, 18) and references to the word as instrument in begetting believers (1 Pet 1:23; Jas 1:18). But the parallels and differences between new birth, resurrection life and physical resurrection warrant limits on the analogy between spiritual and physical resurrections. Spiritual resurrection leaves a doctrine of converting change underdetermined and requires further elaboration.

Raised with Christ: Ephesians 2 and Colossians 2

Pauline vocabulary for being made alive in Ephesians 2:5 and Colossians 2:13 brings together several questions about the application of salvation in individual lives. Central to the interpretation of each text is whether Paul is speaking about subjective converting change and whether these texts imply certain modes of causality in God's action.

Ephesians 2:1-10 serves as warrant for several doctrines related to the application of redemption. Ephesians 2:5 provides the fulcrum of interpretation since it specifies God's action as making "us" alive together with Christ. Theologians coordinate this action with the state of being "dead in trespasses" (Eph 2:5). Whatever spiritual death may mean, it is reversed when God makes one alive together with Christ. In the late sixteenth century, William Ames cited Ephesians 2:5 to warrant his claim that the *passive* receiving of Christ "is the process by which a spiritual principle of grace is generated in the will of man."⁵² John Flavel uses the same terms. To "quicken" in Ephesians 2:5 (KJV) is to "infuse the principle of the divine life into our souls."⁵³ For these Reformed orthodox theologians, "being made alive" together with Christ refers to God's action to grant a disposition toward holiness or an infused virtue.

The vocabulary of creation in Ephesians 2:10 has also drawn the attention of Reformed theologians. "Created in Christ Jesus," for Louis Berkhof, warrants a conclusion about regeneration. "The creative work of God produces a *new life*, in virtue of which man, made alive with Christ, shares the resurrection life, and can be called a new creature."⁵⁴ Within this tradition, Thomas Schreiner views God's action in Ephesians 2 as a species of his creative work. "Such a work of God is fundamentally miraculous and the product of the divine will."⁵⁵

This brief survey shows the massive theological weight built on Ephesians 2, with comparable emphasis found in treatments of the parallel text in Colossians 2:11-13.⁵⁶ For many, Ephesians 2:5 provides the best evidence for viewing God's action as a spiritual resurrection, a unique work of "infusing new life into them," which van Mastricht contrasts with the "moral" work of "teaching, offering, and persuading."⁵⁷

---

⁵²William Ames, *The Marrow of Theology*, trans. John Dykstra Eusden (Boston: Pilgrim, 1968; repr., Grand Rapids: Baker, 1997), 159.

⁵³John Flavel, *The Method of Grace in the Gospel Redemption*, in *The Works of John Flavel* (1820; repr., Carlisle, PA: Banner of Truth, 1997), 2:86. Cf. Owen, *Pneumatologia*, 285; van Mastricht, *Regeneration*, 7.

⁵⁴Louis Berkhof, *Systematic Theology* (Grand Rapids: Eerdmans, 1941), 465. Calvin interprets Eph 2:10 similarly. *Created* signifies "that all parts of good works from their first impulse belong to God" (Calvin, *Institutes* 2.3.6, 298).

⁵⁵Thomas R. Schreiner, *Paul, Apostle of God's Glory in Christ: A Pauline Theology* (Downers Grove, IL: InterVarsity Press, 2001), 247.

⁵⁶One may sidestep these metaphors by asserting that the soteriology of Ephesians is a development beyond Paul's authentic letters. It is commonplace to note that Ephesians develops a more realized eschatology than does the "authentic" Paul, perhaps focused on spatial rather than temporal categories (e.g., Udo Schnelle, *Theology of the New Testament* [Grand Rapids: Baker Academic, 2009], 571), or on the triumphal language of Christians in a "position of glory" (e.g., Ernest Best, *A Critical and Exegetical Commentary on Ephesians*, ICC [Edinburgh: T&T Clark, 1998], 220-22). But there are arguments for the authenticity of both Ephesians and Colossians on historical-critical grounds (see arguments in D. A. Carson and Douglas J. Moo, *An Introduction to the New Testament*, 2nd ed. [Grand Rapids: Zondervan, 2005], 480-86, 517-21). A Christian theologian must account for both as normative texts in Christian theology. Since they can be read in fundamental continuity with the so-called authentic Pauline letters, there is no reason to deny a unified Pauline approach.

⁵⁷Van Mastricht, *Regeneration*, 18. Ephesians 2:5 is a favorite verse for van Mastricht. In the seventy-seven pages of the English version of this treatise, he cites Eph 2:5 twenty-six times.

I maintain that Paul's language is eschatological. In converting change, believers experience the resurrection from the dead promised at the end of time in an inaugurated form. The Old Testament background is the only register in which the combination of images (spiritual circumcision, resurrection, exaltation to heaven, and baptism) can be understood. The further argument, however, that "being made alive" refers specifically to the instantaneous introduction of spiritual abilities (infusing new qualities), is tentative, especially in Colossians 2:13. As Richard Gaffin indicates, coming to life is crucially "together with Christ," that is, through a continuing union with Christ's life (death, burial, resurrection, exaltation) through faith.[58]

***Ephesians 2 and the* historia salutis.** The clearest use of resurrection language for converting change is in Ephesians 2:

> But God, being rich in mercy, because of the great love with which he loved us, even when we were dead in our trespasses, made us alive together with Christ—by grace you have been saved—and raised us up with him and seated us with him in the heavenly places in Christ Jesus. (Eph 2:4-6)

A strong argument in favor of human passivity in the first moment of God's grace is the participle phrase, "while we were dead in trespasses." Although the logical relationship of a participle phrase to a finite verb is ambiguous, the relationship here is likely temporal simultaneity. *While* we were dead, God made us alive with Christ (cf. Rom 5:8). The passage indicates that the occasion for this new life is personal conversion or coming to faith. Believers once "walked" in trespasses and sins (Eph 2:2). They were controlled by evil spiritual forces and deserved God's wrath. But God has brought about a change so that they are God's "workmanship, created in Christ Jesus for good works" (Eph 2:10). In Ephesians 2:5-6, Paul describes how God has brought about this change: believers were made alive together with Christ, raised with Christ and seated with him in the heavenly places. The addition of "with" to each verb—made alive with, raised with, seated with—indicates that the human experience parallels

---

[58]Richard Gaffin, *Resurrection and Redemption: A Study in Paul's Soteriology* (Phillipsburg, NJ: P&R, 1987; reprint from *The Centrality of the Resurrection: A Study in Paul's Soteriology* [Grand Rapids: Baker, 1978]), 127-29. For a discussion of Gaffin's approach with Reformed theological vocabulary, see Scott R. Wright, "Regeneration and Redemptive History" (PhD diss., Westminster Theological Seminary, 1999).

the experience of Christ, especially described in Ephesians 1:20-23 as his resurrection and exaltation.[59]

Reformed theologians have appropriated Ephesians 2:5 to emphasize human passivity in converting change and the instantaneous work of God to bring about this change. As seen above, they consistently call this work *regeneration*.[60] Gaffin pushes mildly against the inherited Reformed vocabulary of regeneration when he emphasizes New Testament categories and language as a sufficient description of God's action in Ephesians 2:5. Resurrection is the *"single act"* of God in the application of salvation rather than regeneration in the narrow sense.[61] All of the Christian life is "resurrection-life,"[62] understood as a participation in Christ's resurrection victory or union with Christ. For Gaffin, "the central soteriological reality is union with the exalted Christ by Spirit-created faith."[63] Christians have already participated in the resurrection with Christ in some way, and they will participate fully with him at the end of time.

Resurrection imagery plays a special role in God's revelation for Gaffin, since it literally describes converting change.

> When Paul says that believers have already been raised with Christ, we are not simply dealing with a loose, figurative adaptation of the language of resurrection, with an evocative but not strictly literal way of expressing present renewal. In terms of Paul's anthropology, the past resurrection of the inner man is to be understood as realistically and literally as future, bodily resurrection.[64]

Here is an attempt to articulate a "spiritual" resurrection with 2 Corinthians 4:16 serving as the key verse. "Though outwardly we are wasting away, yet inwardly we are being renewed day by day" (NIV). This inner renewal is just

---

[59]*Pace* Best, *Ephesians*, 215, who argues that in occurrences of the verb ζωοποιέω in the New Testament, "there is no explicit connection with resurrection." He cites 1 Cor 15:45; 2 Cor 3:6; and Jn 6:63.

[60]As with the other texts examined here, some Protestant theologians refer this raising with Christ exclusively to Christian baptism (as in Rom 6:3-4). E.g., Peter Stuhlmacher (*Biblische Theologie des Neuen Testaments* [Göttingen: Vandenhoeck & Ruprecht, 1999], 2:15-16), who cites Eph 4:5.

[61]Gaffin, *Resurrection and Redemption*, 136.

[62]Gaffin, *"By Faith,"* 68.

[63]Ibid., 43.

[64]Ibid., 67.

as real and literal as a bodily resurrection.[65] Gaffin pushes Reformed theologians to speak of salvation as a unitary event—union with Christ through faith. He acknowledges that this comes about only by the work of the Spirit, yet he challenges the exegesis of Ephesians 2:5 that identifies a distinct enlivening step prior to faith.

But even if one reads Ephesians 2:1-10 as a general description of union with Christ, one still must make sense of being "made alive."[66] The verb "made alive" stands at the head of human participation with Christ, and Paul reminds his readers that this implies "by grace you have been saved" (Eph 2:5). Divine initiative and sufficiency would seem to be in play in producing this change, hence Schreiner's conclusion that it is "fundamentally miraculous."[67] To say that believers participate in spiritual resurrection through Spirit-effected faith is still ambiguous. The experience of believers in Ephesians 2:1-10 parallels that of Christ in Ephesians 1:20-21, yet there are obvious differences between Christ's physical resurrection and converting change. A theology of converting change resists the urge to foist categories on a text without warrant (e.g., "regeneration" in the narrow sense in Eph 2:5), yet to use exclusively biblical terms may fail to discern what those terms imply. Colossians 2:11-14 further challenges a sharp delineation of the character of converting change by mixing several metaphors for the transition from death to life.

Colossians 2 and multiple metaphors. Constructing a theology of converting change based on the phrase "made alive with Christ" in Ephesians 2:5 is challenging because the only other use of the verb συζωοποιέω in the New Testament is combined with several other images.

> In him also you were circumcised with a circumcision made without hands, by putting off the body of the flesh, by the circumcision of Christ, having been buried with him in baptism, in which you were also raised with him through faith in the powerful working of God, who raised him from the dead. And

---

[65]Contrast this with N. T. Wright (*The Resurrection of the Son of God*, Christian Origins and the Question of God 3 [Minneapolis: Fortress, 2003], 239-40), for whom one's status "in the Messiah" is termed a resurrection in anticipation of the final bodily resurrection. This includes the "forgiveness of sins and a new pattern of behavior," but is not itself a resurrection.

[66]The other two verbs, "raised us up" and "seated us with him" (Eph 2:6), likely refer to the Christian's status in union with Christ and so not as clearly to subjective moral change.

[67]Schreiner, *Paul*, 247.

you, who were dead in your trespasses and the uncircumcision of your flesh, God made alive together [συνεζωοποίησεν] with him, having forgiven us all our trespasses, by canceling the record of debt that stood against us with its legal demands. This he set aside, nailing it to the cross. (Col 2:11-14)

In Colossians 2 Paul helps his readers avoid deception from "enticing arguments" (Col 2:4). Paul responds with a reminder that his readers "have been made full" (Col 2:10) in Christ. He lists the blessings believers possess in Christ including (1) a circumcision not made with hands (Col 2:11), (2) baptism as burial with Christ (Col 2:12a), (3) raising up with Christ through faith (Col 2:12b) and (4) being made alive together with Christ (Col 2:13). In addition, sin's penalty is removed through Christ's death (Col 2:13-14).

All four of the images in Colossians 2:11-13 are debatable as to their priority of importance and chronology in the life of an individual. The close association of circumcision and baptism in Colossians 2:11-12 has grounded the Reformed parallel between circumcision as the old-covenant ritual of membership and baptism within the new-covenant community.[68] But the transition from death to life could also be metaphorical for the transition from Gentile status to participation in the promises of Israel. In this case, the "circumcision of Christ" would refer to Christ's death (see Col 1:22) that renders this transition possible.[69] Alternatively, the "circumcision of Christ" could be the taking off of one's "flesh," understood as the dominant sinful inclination that characterizes humans in their fallen state.[70] This is more likely here. Although circumcision is a dominant image for Jewish status, Paul uses it as an image for spiritual renewal (Rom 2:28-29; cf. Deut 10:16; 30:6; Jer 4:4).

How one interprets circumcision in Colossians 2:11 affects how one understands Paul's analysis of the believer's former condition. In addition to

---

[68] E.g., in the Leiden Synopsis, children of covenant parents are to be baptized "from the example of circumcision, which was a seal of the same covenant and to the place of which baptism succeeded, Col 2.11" (cited in Heppe, *Dogmatics*, 621); *Heidelberg Catechism* Q. 74 cites Col 2:11 as well. See David F. Wright, *Infant Baptism in Historical Perspective: Collected Studies* (Eugene, OR: Wipf & Stock, 2007), 18-19, for an argument against the direct correspondence of baptism and circumcision.
[69] James D. G. Dunn, *The Epistles to the Colossians and to Philemon: A Commentary on the Greek Text*, NIGTC (Grand Rapids: Eerdmans, 1996), 163.
[70] Douglas J. Moo, *The Letters to the Colossians and to Philemon*, PiNTC (Grand Rapids: Eerdmans, 2008), 198-200.

"dead in trespasses," as in Ephesians 2:1, Paul also includes that they were dead in "the uncircumcision of [their] flesh" (Col 2:13a). Given the dominant use of "flesh" in Paul's letters for sinful inclination,[71] the use of "trespasses" to indicate concrete acts of sin and the position taken above regarding spiritual circumcision, it is likely that being made alive together with Christ (Col 2:13b) implies subjective moral change. This is not to deny what James D. G. Dunn affirms, that trespasses and uncircumcision are Jewish terms for outsiders and so the transition includes crossing an ethnic boundary and participating in the promises to Israel (cf. Eph 2:11-12). Indeed it appears best to affirm both. Thus being "made alive" with Christ summarizes the whole complex of metaphors for union with Christ in the previous verses. The following clauses in Colossians 2:13c-14 tell how Christ's death accomplishes objective redemption from sin's penalty. His life and ministry provide the ground for "being made alive" with him.

Because of the numerous metaphors for Christ's redemptive work in these verses, it seems unlikely that ζωοποιέω in this text should be narrowed to the definition of regeneration as an unmediated action of God to grant the ability to discern spiritual things and so respond in faith. In Colossians 2:11-14, the whole process of conversion-initiation is in view. While Colossians clearly indicates that God is the author of this move to salvation—you "were circumcised," God "made you alive"—the book itself does not clarify the mode of divine action. Paul's focus is more on the excellence of Christ's objective work. God purposed in Christ to "reconcile to himself all things" (Col 1:20), and "you" who were once strangers have been "reconciled in [Christ's] body of flesh" (Col 1:22).

Spiritual Resurrection and Its Limits

In both Johannine and Pauline texts, I have observed that converting change can be described as participation in Christ's resurrection, and so by extension as participation in the final resurrection of the body. Texts that refer to God's work of new creation give some indication of what an inaugurated experience of resurrection is like. In Galatians 6:15, Paul contrasts the "new creation" with the old situation in which circumcision carried weight in

---

[71]"Flesh" (σάρξ) in Colossians is more often the physical body, but Paul's characteristic use of "flesh" as the reign of sinful inclination within a person does appear (Col 2:18).

relation to God's promises. In two other places, he makes the same comparison but replaces new creation with "faith working through love" (Gal 5:6) and "keeping the commandments of God" (1 Cor 7:19). One may infer that the new creation, or experience of the life of the age to come, shows itself in these forms of special obedience to God's will. In Ephesians 2, God has prepared "good works" for those he has "created" in Christ Jesus (Eph 2:10). Life in the new creation, or resurrection life, includes actions in accordance with faith and love.

But what then changes in a spiritual resurrection, and when might it occur in an order of salvation? In Ephesians 2:1-10 life before God's enlivening act (Eph 2:1-3) is in bondage to sin, while life following this is freed for good works (Eph 2:4-10). Dead in trespasses and sins indicates a series of sinful acts, but also an inability to turn from these because of demonic oppression and sinful inclinations. The "passions of our flesh" and the "desires of the body and the mind" (Eph 2:3) cover the spectrum of possible faculty psychologies. The transition from "dead" to "made alive" in Christ would include, then, the cultivation of inclinations in line with Christ.

As Reformed theologians move from Ephesians 2 to a doctrine of converting change, they must ask what "made alive together" entails about the mode of God's action. One could answer that the phrase describes one's union with Christ in broad strokes, and so includes the human response of faith enacted or sealed in baptism. The redemptive-historical tradition of interpretation affirms this as an appropriate expression in the Bible's own terms—a biblical-theological conclusion.[72] One may also go further with early modern Reformed orthodox theologians and say that "being made alive" occurs invisibly by God's gift of life when the Spirit acts on a passive subject to enable faith. In other words, does our union with Christ's death and resurrection (being made alive *together*) begin by secret Spirit-wrought change, or with faith that receives Christ and his benefits? And are these terms normative entailments of Scripture's language, or may one offer other forms of causality to explain the entailments of Ephesians 2:5?

I submit that the options thus far could be enhanced. The Reformed orthodox appropriated Thomistic vocabulary to speak of "infused qualities,"

---

[72] Herman N. Ridderbos, *Paul: An Outline of His Theology*, trans. John Richard De Witt (Grand Rapids: Eerdmans, 1975), 211-14.

including an explanation of how human faculties move from potentiality to act and the necessary conditions for such to occur.[73] When these are read into texts such as John 3:5 and Ephesians 2:5, authors discover distinctions between potency and act that would likely seem foreign to Jesus, John and Paul. On the other hand, repeating only the scriptural language downplays how interpreters always construe texts and concepts in certain ways. Thus while Richard Gaffin and G. K. Beale helpfully propose the language of "spiritual resurrection" as the essence of converting change, the move to explain the features of a spiritual resurrection is somewhat lacking. We need still an ontology of converting change, that is, of spiritual resurrection and of new birth. Jonathan Edwards moves beyond the Thomistic synthesis within the Reformed orthodox tradition and yet reads the New Testament accounts with deference to biblical vocabulary. He proposes that "spiritual" refers unambiguously to the Holy Spirit. Converting change just is the presence of the Holy Spirit acting *like* a classical "habit" in the soul of the believer.

---

[73] As already noted, the Synod of Dort describes regeneration as "infusing new qualities into the soul." But the background concept is clearly that of Thomistic *habitus*. For example, see the discussion of *habitus* in the contemporary *Synopsis Purioris Theologiae*. R. T. te Velde, ed., *Synopsis Purioris Theologiae: Synopsis of a Purer Theology. Latin Text and English Translation*, Studies in Medieval and Reformation Traditions (Leiden: Brill, forthcoming), Disp. 31:§15-16.

EIGHT

Resurrection as Culmination of the Call

*We are not merely passive in it, nor yet does God do some
and we do the rest, but God does all and we do all. God produces all and
we act all. For that is what he produces, our own acts. God is the only proper
author and fountain; we only are the proper actors. We are in
different respects wholly passive and wholly active.*

JONATHAN EDWARDS

THE ABOVE QUOTATION FROM his private notebooks shows that Jonathan Edwards (d. 1758) was aware of the complex nature of divine agency and human activity in his theology of converting change.[1] Edwards wrote during a time when Enlightenment thought challenged the Reformed orthodox synthesis of the seventeenth century. He reasserted this vision with the help of John Owen, Peter van Mastricht and Francis Turretin, but also sought to communicate in language understandable to the intellectual currents of his day. Edwards reinterprets the seventeenth-century Reformed tradition on effectual calling and regeneration. He conceives God's work in regeneration as unmediated, or independent of other factors, and yet insists that it is a personal interaction. Specifically, the Spirit's personal presence is the ontological basis of converting change. The arrival of the Spirit is a spiritual

---

[1] Jonathan Edwards, "Efficacious Grace," in *Writings on the Trinity, Grace, and Faith*, ed. Sang Hyun Lee, WJE 21 (New Haven, CT: Yale University Press, 2003), 251. This passage is a bit of a wax nose in the history of interpretation. Samuel Cox, "Reply of Dr. Cox," *The Biblical Repertory and Princeton Review* 3 (1831): 494, cites it against Charles Hodge in 1831 to show that Edwards did not speak exclusively of passivity in regeneration.

resurrection.² Edwards deserves attention for formulating a doctrine of effectual calling because he views the Spirit's unconditioned or arbitrary work as particularly fitting for God's program of redemption. In addition, his understanding of the Spirit's presence moves away from the seventeenth-century acceptance of the infused habits motif in converting change.³

To see the distinctiveness of his doctrine, I first observe his fidelity to traditional interpretations of scriptural images for resurrection and new life. I then sketch his view of the new spiritual sense as the personal presence of the Spirit. This leads further into a comparison of Edwards and what I referred to in chapter two as "communicative theism."

EDWARDS AND BIBLICAL IMAGES FOR CONVERTING CHANGE

Edwards narrowed the focus of converting change into a single moment in his programmatic sermon "A Divine and Supernatural Light Immediately Imparted to the Soul," first published in 1734.⁴ He warrants this move from biblical evidence. Scripture describes this one moment with various metaphors including calling, regeneration and being born again. "By regeneration, or being begotten or born again, the same change in the state of the mind is signified, with that which the Scripture speaks of as effected in true REPENTANCE and CONVERSION."⁵ All of these portray God's action to give a person new spiritual life.⁶

---

²The same thought exists in Edwards's sources. My argument is that Edwards *emphasizes* the personal presence of the Spirit more fully by (1) using "habit" language with qualifiers and (2) by providing an argument for the fittingness of this mode. For the Spirit's presence, see Francis Turretin, *Institutes of Elenctic Theology*, ed. James T. Dennison Jr., trans. George Musgrave Giger (Phillipsburg, NJ: P&R, 1992), 15.4.39, 2:536: "Not only is [the Spirit] a certain power which exerts itself in man, but a divine person who comes into our hearts that he may dwell in them as his temples (1 Cor. 3:16; 6:19) and abide with us forever (Jn. 14:16)."
³I do not engage directly with the seminal thesis of Sang Hyun Lee, *The Philosophical Theology of Jonathan Edwards* (Princeton, NJ: Princeton University Press, 1988), who argues that Edwards holds to a "dispositional ontology" in which all entities are constituted by relational dispositions, including God. While "disposition" is clearly a fundamental term for Edwards, Lee's work stretches credibility for Edwards's time and location. See criticisms by Oliver Crisp, "Jonathan Edwards's Ontology: A Critique of Sang Hyun Lee's Dispositional Account of Edwardsian Metaphysics," *RelS* 46 (2010): 1-20, and Stephen R. Holmes, "Does Jonathan Edwards Use a Dispositional Ontology? A Response to Sang Hyun Lee," in *Jonathan Edwards: Philosophical Theologian*, ed. Paul Helm and Oliver Crisp (Aldershot: Ashgate, 2003), 99-114.
⁴Jonathan Edwards, "A Divine and Supernatural Light," in *Sermons and Discourses, 1730–1733*, ed. Mark Valeri, WJE 17 (New Haven, CT: Yale University Press, 1999), 405-26.
⁵Jonathan Edwards, *Original Sin*, ed. Clyde A. Holbrook, WJE 3 (New Haven, CT: Yale University Press, 1970), 362.
⁶Cf. Ibid., 362, 366, 369-70; Jonathan Edwards, "Treatise on Grace," in *Writings on the Trinity, Grace, and Faith*, 161, 165.

The divine and supernatural light is "immediately" imparted to the soul. This indicates both Edwards's preferred metaphor and the nature of God's action in converting change. Building on Matthew 16:16, "Flesh and blood has not revealed this to you," he interprets flesh and blood as a metonymy for all natural causes and concludes that God "imparts this knowledge immediately, not making use of any intermediate natural causes, as he does in other knowledge."[7] The final phrase indicates that Edwards is offering not a general explanation of cognitive functioning as illumination, but a unique instance of the divine light in conversion. This leads to the doctrine of the text. The divine light communicated to the soul by God is "of a different nature from any that is obtained by natural means."[8]

The light is not specific knowledge, however. In Edwards's characteristic terms, it is a new principle of action, or a new sense of the sweetness of divine things.[9] This new principle of action is the presence of God's Spirit:

> But he unites himself with the mind of a saint, takes him for his temple, actuates and influences him as a new, supernatural principle of life and action. There is this difference; that the Spirit of God in acting in the soul of a godly man, exerts and communicates himself there in his own proper nature.[10]

The Spirit communicates or shares "his own proper nature" in converting change, whereas the Spirit's operations may include a variety of influences in other circumstances. The light is neither a suggestion of new truths, nor a particular impression on one's imagination, nor an "affecting view" toward religion in general. The light is rather "a true sense of the divine excellency of the things revealed in the Word of God, and a conviction of the truth and reality of them, thence arising."[11] Here is the affective or dispositional basis of Edwards's thought on conversion. In converting change, one sees Christ as lovely. Edwards calls this knowledge a "sense of the heart," in which "the heart is sensible of pleasure and delight in the presence of the idea of it."[12]

---

[7]Edwards, "Divine and Supernatural Light," 409.
[8]Ibid., 410.
[9]Edwards, "Treatise on Grace," 174.
[10]Edwards, "Divine and Supernatural Light," 411.
[11]Ibid., 413.
[12]Ibid.

But this sense of the heart never becomes the possession of the believer. It remains dependent on the presence of God's Spirit. As noted above, regenerating grace distinguishes itself from the Spirit's common operations because the Spirit of God "communicates himself there in his own proper nature." Interpreters of Edwards have noted that he emphasizes this more than his predecessors did.[13] The Spirit's presence guarantees the life of love and faith toward God, yet the "principle of life" never becomes fully the possession of the person. The gift of grace just is the Spirit, "the very Holy Ghost dwelling in the souls acting there as a vital principle." While Edwards can say that the Sun of Righteousness makes his creatures into little suns, he grounds this continuity in God's "constitution and covenant," rather than in what might be called infused virtue, or a resident disposition.[14] In every moment one is dependent on the personal presence of the Spirit.

> All succeeding acts of grace, must be as immediately and to all intents and purposes, as much from the immediate acting of the Spirit of God on the soul as the first; and if God should take away his Spirit out of the soul, all habits and acts of grace would of themselves cease as immediately as light ceases in a room when a candle is carried out.[15]

The Spirit acts like sap for the Christian, who is like a branch. The one supplies life for the other internally. It is not as if sap were removed from the tree and put to a different purpose such as maple syrup. The Spirit rather flows like sap into branches and becomes there "a principle of life."[16] There

---

[13]Conrad Cherry, *The Theology of Jonathan Edwards: A Reappraisal* (Gloucester, MA: Peter Smith, 1974), 32; Robert W. Caldwell III, *Communion in the Spirit: The Holy Spirit as the Bond of Union in the Theology of Jonathan Edwards*, Studies in Evangelical History and Thought (Eugene, OR: Wipf & Stock, 2006), 102-20; John J. Bombaro, *Jonathan Edwards's Vision of Reality: The Relationship of God to the World, Redemption History, and the Reprobate* (Eugene, OR: Pickwick, 2012), 233-53. Caldwell and Bombaro respond to Anri Morimoto, *Jonathan Edwards and the Catholic Vision of Salvation* (University Park: Pennsylvania State University Press, 1995), who reads Edwards with concepts of uncreated and created grace. Morimoto's reading better fits the more scholastic John Owen (with the exception of Morimoto's inclusivist conclusion). See Christopher Cleveland, *Thomism in John Owen* (Farnham, UK: Ashgate, 2013), 69-89.
[14]Edwards, "Treatise on Grace," 196. "Little images of that Sun" comes from Edwards, *Religious Affections*, ed. John E. Smith, WJE 2 (New Haven, CT: Yale University Press, 1959), 201, 243.
[15]Edwards, "Treatise on Grace," 196. Cf. Morimoto, *Catholic Vision*, 30. "'Infusion' means for Edwards this self-communication and self-impartation of the nature of the Holy Spirit to humanity."
[16]Edwards, *Religious Affections*, 200-201. For the same illustration, see John Owen, ΠΝΕΥΜΑΤΟΛΟΓΙΑ [Pneumatologia], or, a Discourse Concerning the Holy Spirit, in *The Holy Spirit*, vol. 3 of *The Works of John Owen*, ed. William Goold (London: Johnstone & Hunter, 1852; repr., Carlisle, PA: Banner of

is no quantity of "Spirit" measured out and applied to a different entity. The Spirit's presence is the principle of this life, the animating force of the person just as sap is to a branch.

This sense of the heart proves legitimate by its persistence within a person. The Spirit dwells within a person and becomes an abiding principle.

> He gives his Spirit to be united to the faculties of the soul, and to dwell there after the manner of a principle of nature; so that the soul, in being indued with grace, is indued with a new nature: but nature is an abiding thing. All the exercises of grace are entirely from Christ: but those exercises are not from Christ, as something that is alive, moves and stirs something that is without life, and yet remains without life; but as having life communicated to it; so as through Christ's power, to have inherent in itself, a vital nature.[17]

Continuance is Edwards's seventh sign of truly gracious affections. A "new nature" means persistent affections or a continuous directedness of one's desires. A nature is not the set of characteristics that make a creature what kind it is. Nature is the predominant, accidental directedness of the creature.[18] To change one's nature in this sense is an ontic reality that does not alter the sense of "human nature." Edwards explains in *Religious Affections*,

> This new spiritual sense, and the new dispositions that attend it, are no new *faculties*, but are new *principles* of nature. I use the word "principles," for want of a word of a more determinate signification. By a *principle of nature* in this place, I mean that foundation which is laid in nature, either old or new, for any particular manner or kind of exercise of the faculties of the soul.[19]

Edwards affirms that the subjective change in conversion is the unmediated work of the Spirit of God acting within a person as a new principle of nature, or a new directedness for their affections. God brings this about immediately in the sense that he does not make use of "any intermediate natural causes."[20] This does not exclude natural causes entirely, but implies that God's work is neither dependent on them nor reducible to them.

Truth Trust, 1966), 475-76. Edwards cites Jn 4:14 and Jn 7:38-39 to show that the saints become a fountain of water by the power of the Spirit.

[17]Edwards, *Religious Affections*, 342.

[18]Cf. Aquinas, *ST* 3.2.12. "Nature" can be either the "essential principles of a thing" or "what he [a man] has had from his birth."

[19]Edwards, *Religious Affections*, 206.

[20]Edwards, "Divine and Supernatural Light," 409.

The Spirit's arbitrary work. In the previous chapter, I noted that Schleiermacher believed God was most honored by bringing about redemption without the use of miracle.[21] Edwards argues exactly the opposite. God reserves his greatest acts to his own unique agency apart from any secondary causes. Whereas God may choose to have various effects follow from created causes, in regeneration he chooses to act in an "arbitrary" manner.[22] Edwards links the arbitrariness of the Spirit's work to God's aim in glorifying himself. There is an ordered fittingness that the nearer one approaches God, the more one's relationship is based exclusively on the divine will. In his "rational" argument for the divine and supernatural light, Edwards concludes, "'Tis rational to suppose that God would reserve that knowledge and wisdom, that is of such a divine and excellent nature, to be bestowed immediately by himself, and that it should not be left in the power of second causes."[23] God may leave room for second causes in many effects, but it is reasonable to assume that God reserves this particular instance to his own direct activity. This is because the divine light is as close to God as one gets in the divine-human relationship. It is "a kind of emanation of God's beauty, and is related to God as the light is to the sun."[24]

Reason is engaged to recognize divine truth in this communication, but does not function as the means by which one comes to see the divine truth as attractive. The characteristic honey illustration serves as example. Reason can convince one of the beauty and good taste of honey, but reason cannot give the taste itself. So also the supernatural light communicates a taste or new sense for divine things. This occurs apart from any means precisely because this taste for the beauty of divine things is a partaking of the divine inner-trinitarian life.

---

[21] Friedrich Schleiermacher, *Christian Faith*, §§47-46. See note on citation and translation in chap. 6, n. 68.
[22] Edwards uses this term in "'Miscellanies,' no. 1263," in *The "Miscellanies" (Entry Nos. 1153-1360)*, ed. Douglas A. Sweeney, WJE 23 (New Haven, CT: Yale University Press, 2004), 201-12. Cf. Edwards, "'Miscellanies,' no. 481," in *The "Miscellanies" (Entry Nos. a-z, aa-zz, 1-500)*, ed. Thomas A. Schafer, WJE 13 (New Haven, CT: Yale University Press, 1994), 523.
[23] Edwards, "Divine and Supernatural Light," 421-22. That Edwards acknowledges secondary causes raises questions about whether he would have owned his purported occasionalism. See Edwards, "'Miscellanies,' no. 629," in *The "Miscellanies" (Entry Nos. 501-832)*, ed. Ava Chamberlain, WJE 18 (New Haven, CT: Yale University Press, 2000), 157, where he explains how means of grace operate differently than natural means.
[24] Edwards, "Divine and Supernatural Light," 422.

While earlier authors such as Owen and Turretin argue for the Spirit's unmediated work in conversion primarily by a *reductio ad absurdum* against all other explanations of the Spirit's work, Edwards argues positively that God glorifies himself through human dependence on the unmediated, unpredictable work of the Spirit in conversion.[25] Because conversion is participation in God's own happiness and blessedness, it is fitting that such come to pass through the direct operation of God. Of all his actions, "God reserved [conversion] to be bestowed by himself, according to his arbitrary will and pleasure, without any stated connection, according to fixed laws, with previous voluntary acts of men, or events in the series of natural things."[26] "Arbitrary" means that God's converting grace depends on God's sovereign will alone. But this does not mean that God's manner of working is impenetrable. God's action is still a "communication" to his creatures, particularly the communication of the Holy Spirit.

Personal communication of the Spirit. Edwards would seem to be a great friend of the "communicative" effectual call (see above, chapter two). He frequently states that God has a disposition to communicate. William Schweitzer argues that Edwards's entire theological project can be subsumed under this category. "Communicativeness is the inclination . . . to convey or transmit something of oneself."[27] Schweitzer titles his book after Edwards's comment, "God is a communicative being,"[28] that is, one who shares something about himself. What then does God share with or communicate to his human creatures? In the work of redemption, God communicates the Holy Spirit.

> True saving grace is no other than that very love of God; that is, God, in one of the persons of the Trinity, uniting himself to the soul of a creature as a vital

---

[25]One could combine Edwards's thought here with his "continuous creation" view, that God recreates the universe every moment with the appearance of change and conclude that even when God gives the appearance of natural causes, this is still an instance of his "arbitrary" action. But this is not Edwards's intent, not only in Miscellany 1263 (cited above) but also as the thesis of his *Freedom of the Will*, i.e., that all human acts of will are caused by dispositions. For occasionalism in Edwards, see Oliver Crisp, *Jonathan Edwards on God and Creation* (Oxford: Oxford University Press, 2012), 9; Crisp, "How 'Occasional' Was Edwards's Occasionalism?," in Helm and Crisp, *Jonathan Edwards: Philosophical Theologian*, 61-77.

[26]Edwards, "'Miscellanies,' no. 481," 523.

[27]William M. Schweitzer, *God Is a Communicative Being: Divine Communicativeness and Harmony in the Theology of Jonathan Edwards*, SST (Edinburgh: T&T Clark, 2012), 13.

[28]Jonathan Edwards, "'Miscellanies,' no. 332," in *"Miscellanies" (Entry Nos. a-z, aa-zz, 1-500)*, 410; Schweitzer, *Communicative Being*, 11.

principle, dwelling there and exerting himself by the faculties of the soul of man, in his own proper nature, after the manner of a principle of nature.[29]

And herein lies the mystery of the vital union that is between Christ and the soul of a believer, which orthodox divines speak so much of: Christ's love, that is, his Spirit, is actually united to the faculties of their souls. So [the Spirit] properly lives, acts and exerts its nature in the exercise of their faculties.[30]

Within the Trinity, the Spirit acts particularly as the "love" of God. When the Spirit comes to a person, this love becomes "the nature and essence of that holy principle in the hearts of the saints."[31] To have the Spirit and this love is to participate now in the eschatological promise of communion with the triune God. Indeed the entire economy of redemption focuses on this end. God communicates himself through Christ and the Spirit as knowledge, love and joy. The economy is God's *emanation* of his internal fullness to creatures that then reflect back (*remanate*) this fullness through their own experience and expression of God's knowledge, love and joy.[32]

Kyle Strobel argues that this goal of trinitarian communion shows that Edwards recognizes both God and humans as *persons* in their own ways. Regeneration renews human willing and understanding because these aspects are most appropriate to human existence as persons. The combination of knowledge, love and joy most closely approximates the divine life because this life is, in Strobel's terms, "infinite religious affection in pure act."[33] It is fitting, then, that human knowledge of God should approximate God's own knowledge of himself as Trinity, a highly "affective knowledge." This is the

---

[29]Edwards, "Treatise on Grace," 194.
[30]Ibid., 195.
[31]Ibid., 191.
[32]Edwards uses "remanation" in "Concerning the End for Which God Created the World," in *Ethical Writings*, ed. Paul Ramsey, WJE 8 (New Haven, CT: Yale University Press, 1989), 531. On sharing the inner-trinitarian life as the ultimate end of God's creation, see Walter J. Schultz, "Jonathan Edwards's *End of Creation*: An Exposition and Defense," *JETS* 49 (2006): 247-71; Schultz, "Jonathan Edwards's Concept of an Original Ultimate End," *JETS* 56 (2013): 252. "*God's glory*—taken as the ultimate end to be achieved by God's creating—is God's own intra-Trinitarian life 'dwelling within' some creatures by means of the indwelling Holy Spirit."
[33]Kyle C. Strobel, *Jonathan Edwards's Theology: A Reinterpretation*, SST 19 (London: Bloomsbury T&T Clark, 2013), 14. W. Ross Hastings, *Jonathan Edwards and the Life of God: Toward and Evangelical Theology of Participation* (Minneapolis: Fortress, 2015), 265-321, is critical of Edwards's focus on the Spirit's work to create union with God as creating an experience of the divine apart from Christ. Calling may help correct Edwards here by providing the content of the Spirit's ministry.

nature of all knowing for Edwards: "When the heart is sensible of the beauty and amiableness of a thing, it necessarily feels pleasure in the apprehension."[34] In other words, nothing could be more personal and human than leading creatures to their true human ends in union with God through participation in his knowledge, love and joy.

In his sermon "A Divine and Supernatural Light," Edwards anticipates the objection that the presence of the Spirit negates the importance of outward means and human mental capacities. The first part of the sermon demonstrates that there is a light from God qualitatively different than all other forms of knowledge. This light is not new knowledge but a new appreciation of what is in Christ. The second part of the sermon shows *how* this light comes from God. Edwards proposes that human perceptive abilities are the subject of an illumined vision rather than the cause of such a vision. "The natural faculties are the subject of this light: and they are the subject in such a manner, that they are not merely passive, but active in it."[35] By "subject" Edwards indicates that natural faculties perceive the divine light. They are not purely passive, but are enabled to see the beauty of divine things. He goes on:

> God in letting in this light into the soul, deals with man according to his nature, or as a rational creature; and makes use of his human faculties. But yet this light is not the less immediately from God for that; though the faculties are made use of, 'tis as the subject and not as the cause; and that acting of the faculties in it, is not the cause, but is either implied in the thing itself (in the light that is imparted), or is the consequence of it. As the use that we make of our eyes in beholding various objects, when the sun arises, is not the cause of the light that discovers those objects to us.[36]

The capacity for this sense is entirely dependent on the light sent from God. Yet this light produces real (in)sight on the part of the person. One's natural faculties "are not merely passive, but active in it."[37] Yet the order for Edwards is quite clear. Outward means such as the proclamation of the gospel are present, yet they do not operate by their "natural force." "The Word of

---

[34]Edwards, "Divine and Supernatural Light," 414.
[35]Ibid., 416.
[36]Ibid.
[37]Ibid.

God is only made use of to convey to the mind the subject matter of this saving instruction."[38] The light that allows a proper hearing of the gospel comes from the presence of the Spirit, who works immediately.

To express the efficacy of the Spirit's work above and beyond any means, Edwards calls this a "physical" action.[39] For Edwards, death-to-life images and the analogy with creation *ex nihilo* are appropriate for converting change because they describe an unmediated act of God in which the Spirit is sent as the principle of life to a person and awakens in that person love for God. This love imitates and ultimately participates in the love and communion among the persons of the Trinity. "Communication" in converting change, for Edwards, is the transmission of the Spirit's disposition of love toward God. The beauty and excellence of God revealed in Christ provide the occasion for the Spirit-directed response of the human creature in faith. The Spirit's presence creates this new love for divine things, a sense of Christ's excellence.

Communicative Theism and Regeneration

Communicative theism asks that theology address questions of the God-world relationship on the level of personal interaction.[40] While not excluding God's operation on the physical or atomic level (e.g., creation *ex nihilo*), communicative theism observes that Scripture registers God's interaction with the world on the level of speaking, teaching and dialogue. Can a communicative view of God's action in converting change account for the radical death-to-life imagery in Scripture?

Passivity and instantaneousness are consistent features of Reformed orthodox explanations of regeneration, primarily citing Ephesians 2:5. There is a good case for both of these in that text: a transition from death to life involves the passivity of a person while those two terms are mutually exclusive. One is not slightly alive and slightly dead at the same time and in

---

[38]Ibid. Here one would like to see some acknowledgment of the difference between human words and God's word/s.

[39]In a collection published posthumously (the original of which is lost), Edwards says that any operation of the Holy Spirit allowed to be "immediate" should also be called "physical." This sort of action is always "near akin to a miracle" ("Concerning Efficacious Grace," WJEO 37:§48). See further references in Strobel, *Edwards's Theology*, 180-81.

[40]This is the primary conclusion of Kevin J. Vanhoozer, *Remythologizing Theology: Divine Action, Passion, and Authorship*, CSCD (Cambridge: Cambridge University Press, 2010), 486-504.

the same sense. While communicative theism as articulated by Kevin Vanhoozer has resources for affirming an instantaneous transition, this view requires adjustment of the passivity criterion.

The hermeneutic gap and salvation. Edwards provides a helpful foil to the premises of communicative theism. Can Edwards agree with Vanhoozer that God's life is one of communicative action, and that the work of redemption is God's communication of himself to human creatures?[41] It appears that two senses of the term *communicative* are at work. Divine communication for Edwards happens primarily on the ontological level. The Spirit transfers his own holiness to the regenerate person. It is not an infusion of qualities *by* the Spirit, but an infusion *of* the Spirit. Communication here means union with Christ by the Spirit.

For Vanhoozer, divine communication primarily entails discourse, someone (God) saying something to someone. The Christian's union with Christ is multifaceted, but crucially includes a "dialogical" union.[42] Union results in properly ordered theodramatic participation, "a graciously enabled speaking and acting engagement in what the Father is doing in Christ through the Spirit."[43] It is to be a "willing participant in the theodrama." A dialogical union obtains when "Christ's 'voice' dominates our thinking and feeling."[44]

This sounds similar to how Edwards characterizes the Spirit's role. The Spirit's presence is like a "new principle of life" in the soul, and so Christ's voice dominates the Christian's thinking and feeling. For Edwards, a disposition to enjoy the glory of God in Christ marks true religious affection. The Spirit creates not belief *simpliciter*, but a disposition that lives in the reality of God acting in the world in Christ. A contemporary resonant voice is that of Anthony Thiselton. In his "dispositional account of belief," he includes in the concept of belief a disposition to involve oneself in showing or witnessing to its truth. When true belief occurs, it includes a "dispositional

---

[41]The comparison was first suggested by Paul Helm ("Vanhoozer IV—The Personal and the Mechanical," *Helm's Deep*, August 1, 2010, http://paulhelmsdeep.blogspot.com/2010/08/vanhoozer-iv-personal-and-mechanical.html).

[42]Vanhoozer, *Remythologizing*, 289-93. Union with Christ is eschatological (new creation), medial (neither strictly active nor passive), covenantal, dialogical, sapiential (producing wisdom) and ecclesial (communal).

[43]Ibid., 293.

[44]Ibid., 292.

reservoir," or *habit*, to respond likewise in different situations. "This dispositional reservoir becomes operative and *counts* when the believer risks *staking himself or herself on it by manifesting an appropriate stance and by performing appropriate utterances and habituated actions in the public domain*."[45] Such a description of belief would encompass both Vanhoozer's "fitting participation"[46] and Edwards's "sense of the heart."

But can Vanhoozer speak of this habit as *infused*? A Thomistic approach distinguishes between *habitus* as skill or disposition learned from practice and the infused theological virtues, which are not learned (according to Aquinas) because their end is beyond that of pure nature.[47] Within the economy of salvation, infused habits (the theological virtues) are needed because human sinful dispositions preclude their existence in a "natural" (understood as postlapsarian) human being.[48] If the gracious habit of faith is infused, then the person is passive in some sense. If it is acquired, it is based to some extent on human effort. This seems to force a decision on whether the human person is active or passive in converting change. In a nod to hermeneutics, Vanhoozer appeals to the middle voice. Drawing on Philippe Eberhard's interpretation of Hans-Georg Gadamer, Vanhoozer asserts that all forms of understanding are middle voiced. Through an active process of cognition, the "matter" (*Sache*) comes to expression as a gift or miracle. For Eberhard, faith is not something we do or receive, but something we experience or come to know from the inside.[49] In Vanhoozer's summary of Gadamer, "Understanding is a being-spoken-to, a happening that is not the result of the interpreting subject's doing, but a happening *in* language."[50] Language is the *medium* in which understanding takes place. Eberhard notes that middle-voiced verbs often express the relative location

---

[45]Anthony Thiselton, *The Hermeneutics of Doctrine* (Grand Rapids: Eerdmans, 2007), 30 (emphasis original).
[46]Kevin J. Vanhoozer, *The Drama of Doctrine: A Canonical-Linguistic Approach to Christian Theology* (Louisville, KY: Westminster John Knox, 2005), 335-44.
[47]Aquinas, *ST* 1-2.51.4.
[48]E.g., Owen, *Pneumatologia*, 218-20. A Thomistic doctrine of pure nature would assert that prelapsarian humans needed infused virtues as well.
[49]Philippe Eberhard, *The Middle Voice in Gadamer's Hermeneutics: A Basic Interpretation with Some Theological Implications*, Hermeneutische Untersuchungen zur Theologie 45 (Tübingen: Mohr Siebeck, 2004), 212.
[50]Kevin J. Vanhoozer, "Discourse on Matter: Hermeneutics and the 'Miracle' of Understanding," *IJST* 7 (2005): 28.

of the subject to the verb. "I shaved," "I got married" or "I will get baptized" show that "I" am within the action of the verb. I say, "I believe," but I can recognize that this belief is not entirely my own creation. Rather, I have participated in a process by which the true *matter*, belief, is given to me. A hermeneutic event such as belief implies both active searching and the resulting understanding as gift. "Amen" similarly expresses faith in the middle voice.[51] It is a positive affirmation, but based on the gift of recognition or understanding.

In a transposition of Gadamer, Vanhoozer proposes that all acts of understanding are dependent on the true *Sache*, Christ, giving himself to one by the Spirit. In this view one could say that all habits are infused in a rational creature, since understanding is a gift.

The hermeneutic process of coming to understanding is middle-voiced. It presupposes the effort of bringing the *Sache* to language, and yet it recognizes a distance between this reality and its expression in language. The Spirit, as presenter of Christ, leaps the gap. God brings about converting change "*precisely by bringing about understanding.*"[52] Put this way, however, it seems that a dialogical effectual call has made general hermeneutics the magisterial director of the special event of converting change, in much the same way that it has been charged that a Thomistic premotionism makes converting change the application of a general theory of action. Has Vanhoozer simply translated the Spirit's ineffable work from the register of causal language to the register of hermeneutic events?

Perhaps he has, but there may be advantages to one framework for understanding God's action over another. For him, regeneration is "medial," in the sense that "we are the subjects of our acts (i.e., believing, having faith) even as we are caught up in an encompassing action of the Spirit." Vanhoozer still affirms that the Holy Spirit is the agent giving us faith: "The Holy Spirit effects our union with Christ by giving us the faith to lay hold of him."[53] For the effectual call to count as divine discourse, he affirms that the call is more than the sum of its rhetorical parts. The Spirit ministers understanding

---

[51]Eberhard claims to go beyond Gadamer here, for whom the Christian faith presents an exception to hermeneutics in that the content of faith is "incomprehensible" (Eberhard, *Middle Voice*, 202).
[52]Vanhoozer, *Remythologizing*, 373 (emphasis original).
[53]Ibid., 290.

when and where he wills, and this leaves room, however small the space, for the language of unmediated influence of the Spirit on the soul. The Spirit fills the gap between the illocution of summoning and the perlocution of response in faith.[54] If Edwards posits that God communicates the Spirit's nature, namely, love for God, Vanhoozer posits that God communicates understanding—a persuasion or taste of God's work in Christ. But Vanhoozer wishes to add that God brings this about dialogically. "It is through Jesus' words and the Spirit's ministry of words about Jesus that God draws us into the sphere of the new covenant and hence into the fellowship of his triune life."[55] This has the advantage of locating God's action on the plane of human communication.

Nevertheless, the death-to-life images may be interpreted to mean that dialogue is impossible. When Vanhoozer speaks of prayer as a hermeneutic event in which the true matter, Christ, comes to language, he has strong ground for the middle voice.[56] The praying believer recognizes that understanding comes as a gift through participation in the event of prayer. Among the possible theological explanations for prayer's efficacy, prayer shapes believers while they pray. But converting change is not prayer. Sin intrudes, and to account for even the desire to pray requires a theological explanation. Vanhoozer provides this with a "dialogical determinism" that ensures divine efficacy. Here he lists three tenets: "(1) the dialogue between God and human creatures is real—interpersonally *genuine*; (2) the effect is *communicative*; (3) the outcome is divinely *determined*."[57] Again it may be asked if such a communicative register is sufficient to overcome sin. If God's action is dialogical, it seems to assume that what is true, good and beautiful will turn stony hearts into fleshly ones. "Communicative action brings about its effects irresistibly yet non-coercively, through reasoned discourse that, because it is true, good, and beautiful, resonates with human minds and hearts (i.e., is internally persuasive)."[58] But does not total depravity eliminate this very possibility? Yes, but this is the location of the miracle. Edwards can say

---

[54]Ibid., 374. See the appropriation of these terms in Michael S. Horton, *The Christian Faith: A Systematic Theology for Pilgrims on the Way* (Grand Rapids: Zondervan, 2011), 614.
[55]Vanhoozer, *Remythologizing*, 292.
[56]Ibid., 382-83.
[57]Ibid., 384.
[58]Ibid., 383-84.

that "one sight" (in its full affective sense) of the beauty of Christ sets a trajectory for a person that results in union with Christ and ultimate glorification.[59] The Spirit makes such a vision possible by sharing a taste of his own love for God.

Vanhoozer's communicative theism emphasizes that this work takes place within God's communicative action. Without diminishing the divine decree as governing the outcome of events, a dialogical effectual call locates the Spirit's unmediated work within the process of understanding. The Spirit crowns the word spoken in the gospel with its proper effect—affectional understanding. As Calvin stated against Albert Pighius, "God by his Spirit engraves on human hearts what he speaks through his mouth to their ears, not before or after but at the same time."[60] The "dead" in John 5:25 medially hear a voice and live.

The middle voice may present a way forward, but the Reformed tradition has insisted that a person is *passive* in the first moment. The creation of the world, the begetting of a child, the incarnation, Christ's resurrection and the raising of Lazarus all presuppose a passive object. This passivity may be only for a moment, but such may be the line separating Reformed orthodoxy from synergistic alternatives.[61] Passivity reflects an additional premise. The classical Arminian might agree that there is "passivity" in human response, since God is always the initiator in the process of salvation. God calls to sinners and provides prevenient grace before or with the call in order to restore libertarian freedom. Roger Olson compares this to a person trapped in the bottom of a pit ("dead" in sin). God floods the pit and those who let themselves float find that they have risen to the top. "It takes a decision, but not an effort."[62] Is this the "middle-voiced" mode of communicative theism?

---

[59]Edwards, "Divine and Supernatural Light," 420. "If the difference [of divine things] were but seen, it would have a convincing, satisfying influence upon anyone, that they are what they are, viz. divine."

[60]John Calvin, *The Bondage and Liberation of the Will: A Defense of the Orthodox Doctrine of Human Choice Against Pighius*, ed. A. N. S. Lane, trans. G. I. Davies, TSRPrT 2 (Grand Rapids: Baker, 1996), 164-65.

[61]Among alternatives, Kathryn Tanner (*Christ the Key*, Current Issues in Theology [Cambridge: Cambridge University Press, 2010], 4) suggests that "a simple contrast between activity and passivity will not do for creatures' relations with God because no matter how active one is as a creature, one is never anything other than the recipient of God's active grace—God remains active over all."

[62]Roger Olson, *Against Calvinism* (Grand Rapids: Zondervan, 2011), 172.

Reformed theology means by passivity that humans are radically dependent for the first and decisive act of God, yet has sought to leave room for the continued use of human reason and consciousness. Spiritually dead does not mean the same thing as Lazarus's deadness. A communicative approach to the effectual call agrees that there is dependence on God for the first moment of new spiritual life (and every subsequent moment), but this must be understood to mean that no living person is passive in every sense. God the Spirit takes up a person's activity and channels or directs it to appropriate ends by means of a convincing and transforming encounter with the divine word of witness. The Spirit bridges the hermeneutic gap in converting change. This is unmediated in the sense that no independent entity stands in between, but it takes place within the medium of speaking, hearing and coming to understand.

Two communications: Edwards and regeneration after the hermeneutic turn. Communicative theism posits that God authors the world in several ways: in creation from "outside" (*ex nihilo*), from within history by speaking and acting, and in the production of Scripture through human authors.[63] The crux of the matter in discussion with Edwards is whether God's authoring of redemption falls in the first or second category. As Edwards asks, for the person who believes in creation *ex nihilo*, why would it be difficult to affirm supernatural, unmediated, "arbitrary" agency in the work of redemption?[64]

At the same time, Reformed accounts have sought to emphasize the unity and indispensability of both Word and Spirit in converting change. Edwards in particular emphasizes that the Spirit's personal presence brings about converting change. The Spirit takes what is in Christ, namely, God's glory and excellence displayed, and applies this to the sinful human heart. The relationship is "immediate" and "physical," in the sense that the Spirit's work is not dependent on natural causes and that it works effectively to accomplish God's plan. The difficulty is to explain the place of the word, understood both as the semantic content of the gospel and as God's address.

Communicative theism makes explicit that God's personal address is decisive. If for Edwards the "Word," understood as the gospel, provides the

---

[63]Vanhoozer, *Remythologizing*, 349. He adds God's causing of physical events as a fourth category (ibid., 349n29). I am grouping this with the first category of creation above.
[64]Edwards, "Treatise on Grace," 177.

occasion for the Spirit's work, communicative theism argues that the divine word, divine speaking, is the proper and fitting mode for the Spirit's work.

The emphasis on dialogue introduces a category left unstated in many Reformed accounts—that the Spirit's work in effectual calling is tailored to the individual person. The Puritan tradition of "preparationism" in its best sense sought to leave room for just this.[65] The hermeneutic turn of the twentieth century to a large extent simply makes this plain. Humans are formed and develop through dialogue. We require the view of those outside us in order to understand ourselves. As Mikhail Bakhtin notes, "In dialogue a person not only shows himself outwardly, but he becomes for the first time that which he is."[66] God's *call* is the means by which he brings about understanding and faith in a way that is personal, individual and communicative.

CALLING AND REGENERATION

As throughout this book, I have tried to bring together two registers of discourse (biblical theology and systematic theology) in order to offer an account of the call to salvation, particularly in evaluating a communicative or dialogical effectual call.

Death-to-life and new-birth imagery for salvation in the New Testament presents a variety of options for theological interpreters. I have argued for the broad utility of inaugurated eschatology to make sense of these images on their own terms. A doctrine of converting change ought then to include a statement about participation in the new creation, understood as the inbreaking of the eschatological age into today in the lives of those whom God calls. The quintessential blessing of the age to come, resurrection, takes place now in inaugurated form as Christians are united to Christ and experience the Spirit. But for specifics on what this participation in a spiritual resurrection entails, I turned to Jonathan Edwards.

---

[65]Owen, *Pneumatologia*, 213-14. "Great variety there is in the application of the outward means which the Holy Spirit is pleased to use and make effectual towards the accomplishment of this great work." The English delegation at the Synod of Dort warranted God's preparatory work on the ground that God uses humans as his instruments (George Carleton et al., "The Collegiate Suffrage of the British Divines," in *The British Delegation and the Synod of Dort (1618–1619)*, ed. Anthony Milton, Church of England Record Society 13 [Woodbridge: Boydell, 2005], 253).

[66]M. M. Bakhtin, *Problems of Dostoevsky's Poetics*, trans. Caryl Emerson (Minneapolis: University of Minnesota Press, 1984), 252.

In Edwards, the Spirit is a principle of life and acts like a habit of nature in a converted person. The Spirit's presence reorders human affections and introduces a new sense or taste for divine things. Edwards emphasizes human dependence on God and so defends the "arbitrary" or unconditioned work of the Spirit. God chooses to work in regeneration apart from any created means in order to display this relationship as the closest analogue to divine life. The Spirit testifies to Christ, but the decisive work of the Spirit occurs on the level of disposition. Regeneration is a "communication" of the Spirit's holiness or a participation in the Spirit's nature. The primary focus for Edwards is to say that the Spirit does not stand to the side in converting change. The Spirit does not set off a chain reaction that leads to gracious affections. Rather, when the Spirit is present, gracious affections result. The Spirit's activity in converting change just is his presence. Because the Spirit communicates his own love and joy by being present, Edwards counts this as a "personal" action—the Spirit leads us to the ultimate human and personal goal. Thus, when interpreting biblical texts on the giving of life, Edwards speaks of regenerate people as "new creatures" and means that the presence of the Spirit acts as a ruling principle for their affections that is opposite to their state while dead in trespasses and sins.[67]

The dialogical effectual call affirms Edwards's definition of spiritual life as the Spirit's presence producing a disposition of love to God in Christ. The burden of a communicative effectual call is to assert that this comes about through the display and announcement of the crucified and risen Lord Jesus Christ. The Spirit gives new life by an overwhelming impression of the truth, goodness and beauty of God's action in Christ. In the divine economy of salvation, the Spirit restores our created capacities to right functioning through the creative voice of God. The Spirit's action is within the event of understanding, and so "we are in different respects wholly passive and wholly active."[68]

Having relocated the Spirit's "unmediated" work to the event of understanding, it is now possible to locate the dogmatic term *regeneration* in relation

---

[67]Cf. Calvin, *Institutes* 2.5.14, 334. "Hence it appears that God's grace, as this word is understood in discussing regeneration, is the rule of the Spirit to direct and regulate man's will." (For full citation information for Calvin's *Institutes*, see chap. 1, n. 18.)
[68]Edwards, "Efficacious Grace," 251.

to the effectual call. Edwards views these two as a single event. Whether it is referred to as calling, new birth, new creation, regeneration or even conversion, there is one indistinguishable reality—the presence of the Spirit imparting life and light immediately to the human soul. For Richard Gaffin and the redemptive-historical tradition, the "regeneration" is the new world of resurrection. Thus new birth (Jn 3:3-5), new creation (2 Cor 5:17) and regeneration (Tit 3:5) all refer to participation in the resurrection as the beginning of salvific life. I affirm that a doctrine of converting change needs to include (to the extent it attempts to follow the biblical story line) a statement of the eschatological transition that takes place in Jesus Christ. Jesus explains to Nicodemus that the time of fulfillment of the Ezekiel promises has arrived. In Ephesians 2 and Colossians 2, Paul shows that the believer's experience of spiritual life is a participation in resurrection life through union with Christ. Thus it would seem too narrow to define *regeneration* exclusively as "the subjective change wrought in the soul by the grace of God."[69] Yet even the most strident biblical theologians affirm that there is a subjective change made in the soul by the grace of God to which John's Jesus, Paul, Peter and James all make reference with terms for new life, resurrection and new birth. An account of regeneration, then, will include both the eschatological transition in play and the reality of subjective change.[70]

A communicative or dialogical approach to the effectual call builds on the insight that God's action as portrayed in Scripture to win the hearts of human beings comes about as God speaks with his creatures, either directly or through authorized witnesses. When and where God wills, he chooses to speak authoritatively and delightfully through human characters with irresistible persuasiveness tailored for the individual whom he calls. The result of divine speaking is a sharing or participation in the Spirit of Christ, who communicates God's love. The result of God's call is participation in "the regeneration," and because it reorients one's affections it may be referred to as new birth, resurrection or, as in 2 Corinthians 5:17, the "new creation."

This conception of effectual calling locates the power or efficacy that produces regeneration in God's effective voice—crucially, not simply the

---

[69]Charles Hodge, *Systematic Theology* (New York: Scribner, 1871; repr., Grand Rapids: Eerdmans, 1940), 3:3.
[70]I treat the order of salvation (*ordo salutis*) in chap. 10.

semantic content, but in the whole range of factors orchestrated by the divine Author. There is still ineffability here and even immediacy. But the dialogical effectual call specifies the immediacy as a personal interaction, in which the Spirit effectively persuades human creatures of the glory of Christ.

The relocation of divine efficacy in converting change to communicative categories is nearly complete. In chapter four I argued that the effectual call has semantic content both in its concrete expression and in its theoretical construal. The whole Trinity participates in announcing, "Jesus is your saving Lord," through which God summons hearers to respond in repentance and faith. In chapter six I noted that light and illumination convey the authority of the effectual call. As an analogue to the testimony of the Holy Spirit in a doctrine of Scripture, soteriological illumination is the Spirit's work to appropriate human witnesses who bear Christ's attunement in order to display a picture or image (interpreted no doubt, and still "through a glass dimly") of the exalted Christ Jesus as authority and Lord of the in-breaking eschatological kingdom. The previous chapter canvassed death-to-life and new-birth images in order to explain the change that occurs in calling. Reformed theologians have called this change regeneration or spiritual resurrection. With the help of Jonathan Edwards, I point to the presence of the Spirit providing understanding as the crucial change made in the effectual call. This renewed understanding, in its full affective self-involved sense, is the experience of spiritual resurrection. This is so precisely because God is "infinite religious affection in pure act."[71] Humans join in sharing God's knowledge, love and joy as God has revealed himself in the economy of salvation.

---

[71]Strobel, *Edwards's Theology*, 14.

Triune Rhetoric and Converting Change

IN THE PREVIOUS CHAPTER I argued that a communicative effectual call stands in continuity with the Reformed orthodox confessional statements and yet has the advantage of locating the Spirit's decisive operative grace within the process of understanding rather than as separate from that process. This chapter presents an analogy to explain how the effectual call entails that God has a speaking part in the drama of converting change. I propose that the effectual call may be described as an instance of *triune rhetoric*, a unique work of divine speech to bring about the disposition of faith that unites a person to Christ. Conceived thus, to have faith is to be persuaded. It is to possess a high degree of committed disposition toward God's work in Christ.[1] Such a definition of faith can account both for the predominantly religious orientation of "trust" often present in New Testament texts that use πίστις (drawn from the LXX) and the rhetorical background of the term for persuasive proof.[2]

---

[1] Following Anthony Thiselton's "dispositional account of belief" (*The Hermeneutics of Doctrine* [Grand Rapids: Eerdmans, 2007], 21-34).

[2] Πίστις referred to "proof" in Aristotle and the rhetorical tradition. But James L. Kinneavy, *Greek Rhetorical Origins of Christian Faith: An Inquiry* (New York: Oxford University Press, 1987), overstates the rhetorical background in the New Testament. George A. Kennedy, *Classical Rhetoric and Its Christian and Secular Tradition from Ancient to Modern Times*, 2nd ed. (Chapel Hill: University of North Carolina Press, 1999), 146, is more modest to conclude that πίστις "implied at the very least that faith came from hearing speech." For the LXX background of πίστις, see David M. Hay, "Paul's Understanding of Faith as Participation," in *Paul and His Theology*, ed. Stanley Porter, Pauline Studies 3 (Leiden: Brill, 2006), 45-76.

To propose rhetoric as an analogy is risky because rhetoric is typically the *human* art of persuasion. In what follows, however, I propose that the effectual call is a revealed instance of divine rhetoric in relation to which human rhetoric is a limited analogue. God does not copy human rhetoric. Rather, what we call human rhetoric is a limited participation in the effectiveness of God's speech—especially God's speech in the economy of redemption. After warranting such an approach by answering objections, noting speech-act theory as an alternative, and displaying hints of such a move in Reformed sources, I appropriate the classical division of the means of persuasion (*logos*, *ethos* and *pathos*) as an ad hoc analogy for the trinitarian appropriations in the effectual call.

Rhetoric in Contemporary Theology

Let rhetoric be [defined as] an ability, in each [particular] case, to see the available means of persuasion. (Aristotle, *Rhetoric* 1.2.1)[3]

Rhetoric may be understood broadly as the art of persuading through words.[4] In Christian theology there is contemporary discussion of rhetoric in primarily two fields: the rhetoric of New Testament authors and rhetoric as a mode of theological discourse. The first confirms the observation that the New Testament writers participate in reasoned discourse and persuasion. The second represents a response to late- or postmodern suspicion of overconfident modes of discourse. Both streams raise questions about the applicability of a rhetorical analogy for God's action.

New Testament rhetoric. Rhetorical criticism attempts to identify the rhetorical strategies of New Testament writers using the vocabulary of formal rhetoric common in New Testament times.[5] This stream of research

---

[3] Aristotle, *On Rhetoric: A Theory of Civic Discourse*, trans. George A. Kennedy (New York: Oxford University Press, 1991), 36.
[4] Among histories of rhetoric, I note George A. Kennedy, *A New History of Classical Rhetoric* (Princeton, NJ: Princeton University Press, 1994); Kennedy, *Classical Rhetoric*; Craig R. Smith, *Rhetoric and Human Consciousness*, 4th ed. (Long Grove, IL: Waveland, 2013); Jeffrey Walker, *Rhetoric and Poetics in Antiquity* (Oxford: Oxford University Press, 2000).
[5] I primarily assess the projects of George A. Kennedy, *New Testament Interpretation Through Rhetorical Criticism* (Chapel Hill: University of North Carolina Press, 1984), and Ben Witherington III, *New Testament Rhetoric: An Introductory Guide to the Art of Persuasion in and of the New Testament* (Eugene, OR: Cascade, 2009). The related "sociorhetorical" criticism of Vernon Robbins "focuses on values, convictions, and beliefs both in the texts we read and in the world in

is helpful for the fairly commonplace conclusion that the apostles viewed the proclamation of the gospel as a form of persuasion. Although the discipline continues to discuss whether the New Testament writings are organized according to rhetorical conventions on the level of whole books ("macro-rhetoric"), there is broad agreement both that the New Testament writers use a style intended to persuade and that they use tropes often associated with the classical discipline of rhetoric ("micro-rhetoric"). Augustine can identify New Testament texts that correspond roughly to Cicero's three styles, all intended to teach, delight and sway their audiences.[6]

In Acts, Paul intends to "persuade" the Jews in the synagogue (Acts 18:4; 19:8; 28:23). Both Jews and Gentiles "were persuaded" (Acts 17:4) and joined the apostolic missionary band. In 2 Corinthians 5:11, Paul views his task as persuading people through bold and open proclamation (see 2 Cor 4:2).[7] Although Paul speaks against certain forms of argument that seek only the approval of the audience (Gal 1:10; 1 Cor 1:17), he conceives his missionary task under the general category of persuasion through witness.

While New Testament writers clearly seek to persuade, it is plain that both the Old and New Testaments employ modes of persuasion that differ from those common in the Greco-Roman rhetorical tradition. Classicist George Kennedy analyzes rhetoric in the Bible and reformulates Aristotle's modes of persuasion (*logos*, *ethos* and *pathos*) as *logos*, *authority* and *grace*. The Old Testament prophets are paradigmatic in that they base their appeal primarily on their authority as God's messengers. The apostolic witness continues this practice. "Christian preaching . . . is thus not persuasion but proclamation, and is based on authority and grace, not on proof."[8] Kennedy

---

which we live" (*Exploring the Texture of Texts: A Guide to Socio-rhetorical Interpretation* [Valley Forge, PA: Trinity Press International, 1996], 1). This latter is marked by greater appropriation of contemporary social-scientific disciplines. Within theology, this focus on social status may be seen in Don H. Compier, *What Is Rhetorical Theology? Textual Practice and Public Discourse* (Harrisburg, PA: Trinity Press International, 1999).

[6]The triad is from Marcus Tullius Cicero, *Orator*, trans. H. M. Hubbell, LCL 342 (Cambridge, MA: Harvard University Press, 2001), 21.69, 357. Cf. Augustine, *Teaching Christianity: De Doctrina Christiana*, trans. Edmund Hill, WSA I/11 (Hyde Park, NY: New City, 1996), 4.12.27, 215 (hereafter *Doctr. chr.*).

[7]This is likely through evangelistic preaching. See Paul Barnett, *The Second Epistle to the Corinthians*, NICNT (Grand Rapids: Eerdmans, 1997), 279-81. Pace Murray J. Harris, *The Second Epistle to the Corinthians: A Commentary on the Greek Text*, NIGTC (Grand Rapids: Eerdmans, 2005), 413.

[8]Kennedy, *Classical Rhetoric*, 146.

cites 1 Corinthians 1:22-31—an important text for the effectual call—as an example of minimizing persuasive argument. "The message is proclaimed, not proved; it is persuasive to those who are called or chosen by God."[9] Kennedy calls this form of discourse "radical Christian rhetoric."[10] He is certainly correct that early Christians developed their own rhetoric, but this does not mean that the apostles and prophets never used arguments in their proclamation. As observed throughout this study, an acknowledgment of dependence on the Spirit's work did not forestall human proclamation and discussion (e.g., 2 Tim 2:24-26). In addition, both the Old Testament prophets generally and the apostles in their preaching to Jews could assume certain premises within the covenantal context of the Old Testament. While rhetoric in the Bible is distinct from Cicero's legal context, for example, it still participates in the human task of persuasion.

For the purposes of this chapter, rhetorical criticism of the New Testament establishes the human side of gospel proclamation as a species of persuasion. From the New Testament witness I conclude that God authorizes persuasion as the mode in which gospel proclamation takes place. It will require a further step to propose that God participates with a form of persuasion or rhetoric.

Rhetoric in theology: Limits of human discourse. Several theologians criticize the argumentative language of modernity as unduly confident that it can attain absolute knowledge. David Cunningham, Theo Hobson and Stephen Webb each argue that Christian theology ought to be conceived as a form of rhetoric rather than as a deductive science.[11] Rhetoric is attractive because the classical tradition applies rhetoric to situations in which a question is in doubt and the answer is not self-evident. The three situations of classical rhetoric—epideictic, forensic and deliberative—all use as their paradigm cases questions in which there may be disagreement: the funeral

---

[9]Ibid., 150.
[10]Ibid., 147. The Gospel of Mark serves as his primary example. See also Kennedy, *Rhetorical Criticism*, 7; Kennedy, *A New History of Classical Rhetoric*, 258.
[11]David S. Cunningham, *Faithful Persuasion: In Aid of a Rhetoric of Christian Theology* (Notre Dame, IN: University of Notre Dame Press, 1991); Theo Hobson, *The Rhetorical Word: Protestant Theology and the Rhetoric of Authority* (Aldershot: Ashgate, 2002); Stephen Webb, *The Divine Voice: Christian Proclamation and the Theology of Sound* (Grand Rapids: Brazos, 2004). Cf. Peter M. Candler Jr., *Theology, Rhetoric, Manuduction, or Reading Scripture Together on the Path to God*, Radical Traditions (Grand Rapids: Eerdmans, 2006).

oration assigning praise and blame, the speech at a legal trial and the speech before a legislature.

Rhetoric as a stance of epistemic humility responds to a postmodern criticism that all rhetoric is a form of power play. David Jasper, for instance, challenges the rhetoric of the apostle Paul with a hermeneutic of suspicion. "In his letters . . . St. Paul opens with words that soothe and flatter: some might call it buttering your audience up." Although human orators maintain that their goal is persuasion, they "quietly accede to the end justifying the means."[12] According to Jasper, significant power plays are at work in the early Pauline letters that compromise a straightforward reading of Paul's arguments. Authority is a concept too dangerous to allow as a means of persuasion, yet this is the dominant form of argument in the New Testament.[13] He proposes that a self-effacing irony should dominate Christian theological discourse and that Paul discovered this for himself in his epistle to the Romans.[14] The historical argument is only secondary, however, to his point that authoritative rhetoric is susceptible to deconstruction.

Hobson attempts to rebuild after such a demolition. He acknowledges that Christian discourse comes as "authoritative" rhetoric. It speaks confidently and demands response in action. But he believes that Christian theology has the resources for an authoritative rhetoric that subverts itself, or contains within itself its own limitations. Though it may be misunderstood as overconfident, Christian rhetoric recognizes that human speakers use merely human words. For Hobson, "dialogism" describes a self-criticism in which one invites opposing voices to respond and temper one's claims.[15] Theology is "a form of *rhetorical* performance" and "is simply the discourse of faith at its most reflective and intellectually open."[16] He thus calls for a self-involving theology that maintains the boldness of *credo*. Theological discourse must be spoken in a certain mood in order to preserve the Christian faith.

---

[12]David Jasper, *Rhetoric, Power and Community: An Exercise in Reserve*, Studies in Literature and Religion (London: Macmillan, 1993), 124-25.
[13]Ibid., 39-40.
[14]Ibid., 47-48. He posits unconvincingly that "Owe no one anything, except to love one another" (Rom 13:8) undercuts Paul's previous plays on authority.
[15]Hobson, *Rhetorical Word*, 199.
[16]Ibid., 200.

That mood is one of dialogue, or even a polyphony of seemingly contradictory viewpoints. "Divine authority [in Scripture] is communicated by various rhetorical strategies, and often through the dramatisation of conflicting voices. It is communicated *through* dialogue, not at the expense of it."[17] Problems arise when human voices presume to communicate the authority of God with certainty. Because of God's freedom, Christians cannot assume that their words carry God's authority. Yet they are called to testify to Christ. Hence, Christian discourse "sounds hopelessly self-defeating." This is, for Hobson, the primary point. To the extent that Christian proclamation recognizes its own inability to properly portray the authority of God, it succeeds. In other words, "it relies upon the constant miracle of God."[18] Rhetoric serves as a humbled stance for the Christian theologian. Similarly for Cunningham, Christian theology "claims to speak about a truth to which, by its own admission, it has no definitive access."[19] Because of this tentativeness, the genre of Christian theology ought to be persuasive rhetoric.

I agree that Christians acknowledge their limited perspective and even uncertainty. The rhetoric of the martyr remains that of testimony. Polycarp confesses, "For eighty-six years I have been his servant, and he has done me no wrong. How can I blaspheme my King who saved me?"[20] If Cunningham's term "faithful persuasion" means that theologians always recognize that they are speaking from their own point of view, all is well and good. Yet Cunningham goes further. Christian theology is individualized to the theologian. There does not seem to be a stable core to the content of theology since a theologian does not bow to rules of logic and deduction. Rather, "a doctrine describes how a speaker (often a doctrinal authority of some sort) attempts to persuade an audience (the faithful) of a particular way of understanding the faith."[21] While this is certainly one of several goals in most genres of theological writing, John Thiel asks in a review what "faithful persuasion" is faithful to?[22]

---

[17]Ibid., 20.
[18]Ibid., 21. He appeals to Karl Barth's doctrine of the Word of God. "Barth shows that theology can reaffirm its authoritative rhetorical basis and be fully self-critical about the potential dangers of religious rhetoric" (ibid., 137). Cf. Webb, *Divine Voice*, 165-97.
[19]Cunningham, *Faithful Persuasion*, 4.
[20]*Martyrdom of Polycarp* 9.3; Michael W. Holmes, ed., *The Apostolic Fathers: Greek Texts and English Translations*, trans. J. B. Lightfoot, 2nd rev. ed. (Grand Rapids: Baker, 1999), 235.
[21]Cunningham, *Faithful Persuasion*, 212.
[22]John Thiel, review of *Faithful Persuasion*, by David Cunningham, *TS* 54 (1993): 368.

There are both strong and weak applications of rhetoric to Christian theology; that is, rhetoric may function in either a ministerial or magisterial role. The strong or magisterial approach views rhetoric as the only context for human discourse. Since rhetoric is enmeshed within imperfect language use, truth claims fail to reach beyond the belief state of the speaker. A more restrained use of rhetoric as the genre for Christian theology and proclamation contrasts itself with a positivist, or modern scientific approach. Rhetoric in a ministerial role acknowledges that human decision-making involves whole persons, not just discursive reason. It also recognizes that the primary topics of Christian theology are not susceptible to irrefutable proof and so lie in the realm of persuasion and rhetoric. I accept the reminder that theology is a form of rhetoric from Cunningham, but believe one may ask further how human rhetoric takes part in the divine plan, and how it may be related to God's own mode of persuasion.

Both strands of rhetorical research, whether applying classical rhetoric to early Christian texts or appropriating classical rhetoric as a genre for theological discourse, argue that persuasive rhetoric is the natural genre for Christian proclamation. Given this Christian rhetoric of witness, one may ask whether such can be applied to God as he has revealed himself in the economy of salvation.

Divine Rhetoric: Persuasion and Accommodation

Since rhetoric is typically a study of human discourse, one must be careful not to project a picture of an exalted human orator in place of God. Francis Turretin was attuned to this danger in response to the theology of Claude Pajon.

> If the entire action of the Spirit is dispensed by the word with certain circumstances, in no other way would Christians be brought into the church than philosophers into their schools; nor will the action of God, converting sinners, differ from the action of the orator drawing men by his eloquence to assent, or of a master teaching his disciple.[23]

It will not do, for Turretin, to conceive of God as the greatest orator, philosopher or teacher.[24] If God's grace consists in the arranging of circumstances

---

[23] Francis Turretin, *Institutes of Elenctic Theology*, ed. James T. Dennison Jr., trans. George Musgrave Giger (Phillipsburg, NJ: P&R, 1992), 15.4.44, 2:538. For Claude Pajon, see chap. 6 above.

[24] It is interesting that Turretin still affirms Augustine's description that God "teaches" his elect (*Institutes* 15.6.13, 2:550).

and words, nothing separates the effectiveness of God's speaking from that of human speakers. Orators use circumstances outside their control in order to persuade: the predispositions of the audience, their beliefs and the history of events relevant to them. Orators operate with what they are given, since they achieve their goal only if people respond. They never have absolute certainty that their words will persuade. Such would be an improper picture of God. In the background of Turretin's argument is the theology of Robert Bellarmine and other Molinists who proposed that God experiences free human decisions in much the same way as humans do, although with perfect foreknowledge of all possible outcomes. God's creatures, like the jury in a courtroom, have dispositions and beliefs that exist independent of the lawyer. The Molinist states that in God's case, however, he knows all these dispositions perfectly and how each member of the jury would respond in any possible situation. Turretin asks, "Now who would say that the invincible grace of God does not differ in any way from the ordinary mode of acting of weak men?"[25] God's speech must be distinct from human speech.

Turretin registers a strong claim that any talk of God persuading or convincing must deal on the level of loose analogy. Yet one could bring forward examples in Scripture in which God interacts with human characters and uses his speech and actions to form appropriate responses from them.[26] Such an inductive account would show that in significant moments in the economy of redemption God works by speaking. This warrants an analogy between original divine speech and human speech. If God chooses to record his interaction with humanity as a form of speaking, it follows that in some way God's speaking is analogous to human speaking. To provide categories for relating divine and human speech, I turn first to Augustine for the stance of the Christian preacher toward divine assistance and then to John Calvin to warrant the claim that God enters into human discourse. Augustine provides a theological rationale for why one may attribute to God's action any teaching or learning that comes about through human witnesses to Christ. Calvin's use of "accommodation" language shows that God considers the situation or capacity of his human

---

[25]Turretin, *Institutes* 15.4.44, 2:539.
[26]Kevin J. Vanhoozer, *Remythologizing Theology: Divine Action, Passion, and Authorship*, CSCD (Cambridge: Cambridge University Press, 2010), 36-57, provides such an index.

creatures when choosing how to speak with them. Both of these elements—learning through mediated human witness and taking account of creaturely capacities—give evidence that God speaks in ways that move his creatures toward his ends.[27] Hence *rhetoric* is a possible description for God's action in the economy of redemption.

Human rhetoric and divine aid: Augustine and On Christian Teaching. In *De doctrina christiana* (*On Christian Teaching*), his treatise on Christian hermeneutics and rhetoric, Augustine blends his earlier rhetorical training with a Christian focus on submission to Scripture.[28] While the first three books outline how one ought to read Scripture, book four teaches how one should declare what one has discovered for the benefit of the church. Appropriating Cicero's goals in rhetoric, Augustine advises Christian preachers how to teach, delight and move their audience, namely, the church.[29]

It is particularly relevant to consider whether a rhetorical analogy may be applicable to God's action in converting change. Several studies have suggested this as an interpretation of *De doctrina*.[30] John Cavadini calls book four "less a theory of rhetoric *per se* than a theory of conversion." Augustine recognizes that Christian preachers will be successful only when they speak sweetly and persuasively.[31] Cavadini assumes the same is true for

---

[27]I make no claim about dependence of Calvin on Augustine here. David F. Wright, "Was John Calvin a 'Rhetorical Theologian'?," in *Calvin Studies IX: Papers Presented at the Ninth Colloquium on Calvin Studies*, ed. John H. Leith and Robert A. Johnson (Davidson, NC: Davidson College, 1998), 55-56, notes that others have made this connection, but he doubts its historical grounding.

[28]For Augustine and classical rhetoric, see Richard Leo Enos et al., eds., *The Rhetoric of Saint Augustine of Hippo*: De Doctrina Christiana *and the Search for a Distinctly Christian Rhetoric*, Studies in Rhetoric and Religion 7 (Waco, TX: Baylor University Press, 2008); Duane W. H. Arnold and Pamela Bright, eds., De Doctrina Christiana: *A Classic of Western Culture*, ChJA 9 (Notre Dame, IN: University of Notre Dame Press, 1995).

[29]Augustine, *Doctr. chr.* 4.1.1, 2.37.55. For the ecclesial setting, see James A. Andrews, *Hermeneutics and the Church: In Dialogue with Augustine*, Reading the Scriptures (Notre Dame, IN: University of Notre Dame Press, 2012).

[30]Mark F. M. Clavier, "Eloquent Wisdom: The Role of Rhetoric and Delight in the Theology of Saint Augustine of Hippo" (PhD diss., Durham University, 2010); John C. Cavadini, "The Sweetness of the Word: Salvation and Rhetoric in Augustine's *De Doctrina Christiana*," in Arnold and Bright, De Doctrina Christiana, 164-81; J. Patout Burns, "Delighting the Spirit: Augustine's Practice of Figurative Interpretation," in Arnold and Bright, De Doctrina Christiana, 182-94; Robert W. Bernard, "The Rhetoric of God in the Figurative Exegesis of Augustine," in *Biblical Hermeneutics in Historical Perspective: Studies in Honor of Karlfried Froehlich on His Sixtieth Birthday*, ed. Mark S. Burrows and Paul Rorem (Grand Rapids: Eerdmans, 1991), 88-99. *Pace* Kennedy, *Classical Rhetoric*, 180, who reminds us that the audience is Christian preachers in established churches, rather than in a missionary context.

[31]Augustine, *Doctr. chr.* 4.14.30; Cavadini, "Sweetness of the Word," 164-65.

God. He points to Christ's death as the apex of God's rhetoric.[32] This goes beyond Augustine's focus on human rhetoric in book four. Yet it is not unfounded since Augustine, in the final pages of the book, discusses how human rhetoric depends on divine agency.

After his discussion of the styles of rhetoric, their uses, and examples from Scripture and earlier bishops, Augustine reminds his readers to be aware of divine agency. One should prepare diligently, but "at the actual moment he is due to speak" the Christian preacher should remember Christ's words that "it will be given to you in that hour what you are to speak" (Mt 10:19-20). "If the Holy Spirit is speaking in those who are handed over [*traduntur*] to the persecutors on Christ's account, why not also in those who are handing [*tradunt*] Christ over to the learners?"[33] Augustine counsels the Christian *orator* to be one consumed with *oratio*, prayer.[34] This is needed because regardless of the speaker's finesse, the outcome remains under God's control just as a doctor's use of medicine assumes that God will grant the medicine to work in this case. "The assistance of sound doctrine provided by a human teacher is only then any good to the soul when God is at work to make it any good, seeing that he was able to give the gospel to man, even without its coming from men or through man."[35]

But may one conclude that God also speaks in this way? God does not speak directly in book four. Rather, Christian preachers hope, expect and pray that God would speak through their words. In the prologue to the entire work, Augustine addresses those who might find his treatise useless because they believe the Spirit's gift of understanding bypasses the study of rules and method.[36] Augustine responds that the Spirit chooses to speak through human witnesses and through the process of learning. He points to the processes of learning to speak, read and write. Cornelius (Acts 10) and the Ethiopian eunuch (Acts 8:26-40) show that God uses human messengers even when supernatural agency is also involved.[37] "And it could all, of

---

[32]Cavadini, "Sweetness of the Word," 171.
[33]Augustine, *Doctr. chr.* 4.15.32 (WSA 11:219), in *Opera omnia*, ed. J.-P. Migne, PL 34 (Paris: Migne, 1887), 103.
[34]Augustine, *Doctr. chr.* 4.30.63; Clavier, "Eloquent Wisdom," 115.
[35]Augustine, *Doctr. chr.* 4.16.33 (WSA 11:220).
[36]Augustine, *Doctr. chr.* prologue 2 (WSA 11:101).
[37]Augustine, *Doctr. chr.* prologue 5-7.

course, have been done by the angel [in the case of Cornelius]; but then no respect would have been shown to our human status, if God appeared to be unwilling to have his word administered to us by other human beings."[38] God chooses to use human witnesses in part because this affirms something about humans as the particular creatures they are created to be.

Augustine further notes that dependence on one another for teaching and growing helps draw people together in love. "Charity itself, which binds people together with the knot of unity, would have no scope for pouring minds and hearts in together, as it were, and blending them with one another, if human beings were never to learn anything from each other."[39] God speaks to his people through other people preeminently in the church. Yet this is not new or original speech from God. Rather, as is evident throughout *De doctrina*, Christian preachers speak only after discovering the matter in Scripture. God reveals his will in Scripture, but this requires preaching in order to move the congregation to respond appropriately.[40]

Augustine envisions a divine economy of communication in which Christian preachers utilize the best available training in how to teach, delight and move their audiences toward action in line with Christian doctrine.[41] In the midst of this process, they recognize that God must choose to speak through them in order for their words to have effect. Ultimately, God is accomplishing his will through them while achieving additional ends such as respecting humans as communicative creatures and binding them together in love through mutual dependence. While Augustine nowhere calls God the "ideal orator,"[42] he views Scripture and its proclamation as parts of God's plan to bring about his purposes. In addition, God chooses to work in his people through human proclamation and so may be said to take part in human discourse.

Calvin and accommodation. Augustine shows that part of God's action in the economy of redemption is his empowerment of human witnesses to transform other people through rhetorical means. To see further how God

---

[38] Augustine, *Doctr. chr.* prologue 6 (WSA 11:103).
[39] Augustine, *Doctr. chr.* prologue 6 (WSA 11:103).
[40] Andrews, *Hermeneutics and the Church*, 150, 230.
[41] Augustine, *Doctr. chr.* 4.13.29 (WSA 11:217).
[42] Clavier, "Eloquent Wisdom," 116, overstates this as an interpretation of Augustine. As a constructive proposal, however, it is entirely defensible.

participates in human discourse, I note with Calvin that God "accommodates" his speech to accord with human capacity.[43] Calvin recognizes that in Scripture God meets people where they are and works from that point. Because God matches his accommodated speech to human capacities, I maintain that one may speak of a divine eloquence or rhetoric.[44]

When introducing the doctrine of the Trinity, Calvin takes anthropomorphic language for God as evidence that "God is wont in a measure to 'lisp' in speaking to us," just as a nurse speaks with an infant. Such descriptions "accommodate the knowledge of him to our slight capacity."[45] The level of accommodation God employs reflects both human capacity and God's communicative goals. Calvin notes the plain style of God's discourse in Scripture as a form of accommodation. Commenting on 1 Corinthians 1:17, in which Paul disparages "words of wisdom," Calvin affirms that "the Spirit of God, also, has an eloquence of his own, but of such a nature as to shine forth with a native luster peculiar to itself, or rather (as they say) intrinsic, more than with any adventitious ornaments."[46] This applies especially to the eloquence of the Spirit through the writers of Scripture. Both anthropomorphic language for God and the plain style of Paul's letters indicate to Calvin that God tailors his communication to his creatures. The sheer fact that the Spirit accommodates his eloquence for the sake of certain

---

[43]The standard account of Calvin on accommodation is Ford Lewis Battles, "God Was Accommodating Himself to Human Capacity," *Int* 31 (1977): 19-38. More recent discussion that criticizes Battles for speculation about Calvin's appropriation of the rhetorical tradition includes Arnold Huijgen, *Divine Accommodation in John Calvin's Theology: Analysis and Assessment*, Reformed Historical Theology 16 (Göttingen: Vandenhoeck & Ruprecht, 2011); Jon Balserak, *Divinity Compromised: A Study of Divine Accommodation in the Thought of John Calvin*, Studies in Early Modern Religious Reforms 5 (Dordrecht: Springer, 2006); David F. Wright, "Calvin's Accommodating God," in *Calvinus Sincerioris Religionis Vindex: Calvin as Protector of the Purer Religion*, ed. Wilhelm H. Neuser and Brian G. Armstrong, Sixteenth Century Essays and Studies 36 (Kirksville, MO: Sixteenth Century Journal, 1997), 3-19.

[44]Wright, "Rhetorical Theologian," 59-63, is correct to criticize the use of "rhetorical" in theology as a way to minimize truth claims. In relation to Calvin, this can be seen in Serene Jones, *Calvin and the Rhetoric of Piety*, CSRT (Louisville, KY: Westminster John Knox Press, 1995), 28, and E. David Willis, "Rhetoric and Responsibility in Calvin's Theology," in *The Context of Contemporary Theology: Essays in Honor of Paul Lehmann*, ed. Alexander J. McKelway and E. David Willis (Atlanta: John Knox, 1974), 53. I am in fundamental agreement that Calvin's God accommodates himself for pedagogical goals (Huijgen, *Divine Accommodation*, 112). I call this "rhetorical" because it takes part in human discourse.

[45]Calvin, *Institutes* 1.13.1, 121 (for full citation information for Calvin's *Institutes*, see chap. 1, n. 18).

[46]Calvin, *Comm. 1 Cor. 1:17* (CC 20:77-78).

ends implies, I submit, that God enters into the realm of human discourse when he reveals himself by speech.

But one must also respect the variety of ways that Calvin uses accommodation language. God may make it easier for his people to believe him or he may make life more difficult so that they rely on him more fully. When God hides himself so that his people do not fall asleep in comfort, God's "purposes in accommodation actually run counter (at times) to any revelatory objective."[47] Accommodation for Calvin is not simply God's condescension to humanity in revelation. Rather, accommodation is a characteristic of God's action in the whole economy of salvation.

David Wright concludes that Calvin wishes to show God's "kindly considerateness" in coming to us in ways that we may understand. He cites Calvin's commentary on Jesus' pleading lament, "How often would I have gathered your children together, like a hen gathering her chicks" (Mt 23:27):

> It is a wonderful and incomparable proof of his love that God did not mind condescending to endearments to win rebels to his service. . . . Whenever the Word of God is set before us, he bares his breast to us with motherly kindness, and not content with that, condescends to the humble affection of a hen fostering her chicks. . . . When he assumes a mother's role, he comes a great way down from his glory; how much further when he takes the guise of a hen, and deigns to treat us as his chicks![48]

God's condescension and accommodation are aspects of his love for his creatures. Such is the case especially in regard to the means by which God works out salvation. The law, angels, providential care and even baptism are accommodated aids to bring humans to salvation. "Calvin explains that when God was ordaining them, he chose to accommodate them to human *captus* [capacity]—thus, God's stooping to human capacity is exhibited in his establishing of the order of salvation."[49] While accommodation may have implications for questions about God's revelation in general,[50] at the

---

[47]Jon Balserak, "'The Accommodating Act Par Excellence?': An Inquiry into the Incarnation and Calvin's Understanding of Accommodation," *SJT* 55 (2002): 415.
[48]Calvin, *Comm. Matt. 23:27* (translation from Wright, "Calvin's Accommodating God," 14).
[49]Balserak, *Divinity Compromised*, 155.
[50]Edward A. Dowey Jr., *The Knowledge of God in Calvin's Theology*, exp. ed. (Grand Rapids: Eerdmans, 1994), 17, calls accommodation the "horizon of Calvin's theology." J. Todd Billings, *Union*

least it is evident that God's use of means in the economy of salvation shows that he fashions his ways in order to work in and with his creatures.

If God accommodates his speaking to human capacity, may one conclude that God participates in human communication involving rhetoric? From the records of divine speech in Scripture, I maintain that because God chooses to communicate in ways that can be observed and understood, these are accommodations to human finitude and sinfulness. God engages his creatures in ways appropriate to them, including how he speaks with them. I contend God's decision to work patiently with his creatures according to their capacities means that God's speech is effective in different ways.[51] Not all of God's speech includes the creative force of "Let there be light!" Scripture portrays an array of approaches God chooses to take in order to guide his people and effect his salvation and judgment. Calvin recognizes from the biblical record that God's interaction with the world takes various forms, especially including his decision to speak with his creatures in ways they can be made to understand. In other words, accommodation shows that God participates in communication. He is Lord of the communicative word, but in his grace this word often takes the form of a servant.

Speech acts and rhetorical acts. Augustine and Calvin agree that God speaks to his creatures in ways appropriate to them. God's speech displays his loving intent to accommodate himself to human finitude and sinfulness. The expectation that God speaks through human words locates much of God's redemptive action within the realm of speech. I next move to evaluate the contemporary use of speech-act theory for God's speaking, particularly in regard to the effectual call.

Speech-act theory has provided an interpretive grid for theologians asking what it means that God speaks. The identification of the illocutionary act as the locus of sentence meaning has helped biblical interpreters recognize that human discourse cannot be explained apart from the human action in which it participates—that is, propositions cannot be abstracted from their speakers and contexts. The same may be true for God. Scripture records that God performs characteristic speech acts such as promising,

---

with Christ: Reframing Theology and Ministry for the Church (Grand Rapids: Baker Academic, 2011), 80-84, challenges this by showing that Calvin hints at an unaccommodated beatific vision.
[51]For this variety in Calvin, see Balserak, *Divinity Compromised*, 60-64.

commanding and asserting. Kevin Vanhoozer takes a further step and applies the elements of a speech act—locution, illocution and perlocution—as an analogy for the specific actions of the Trinity. The Father speaks, the Son is spoken and the Spirit brings about the results (perlocutionary effects) of this speech.

> As Voice, the Father is the speaking subject who initiates the process of communication. As Word, the Son is what the Father speaks, the content of the communicative act. As the Breath that accompanies and conveys the Father's Word, the Spirit is the channel or medium of the communicative act as well as its efficacy.[52]

This is the case in relation to Scripture first of all. "The Spirit speaks in and through Scripture precisely by rendering its illocutions at the sentential, generic and canonic levels perlocutionarily efficacious."[53] The division between illocution and perlocution allows Vanhoozer to affirm Scripture as God's Word and as God's speech apart from the event in which it is received as such by a person. The illocution may exist without the appropriate response and results.[54]

But how might the speech-act taxonomy apply to the effectual call? As I will argue, speech-act theory accounts well for sentence meaning in the context of human action, but it struggles to account for the phenomenon of conversation. The theory on its own does not account for the various possible links between an illocutionary act and its perlocutionary effects. An analysis of how God brings about the effectual call requires a further layer of description to account for the results of the call.

Perlocutionary acts and effects. Speech-act theory gained a hearing by isolating the *illocutionary act*, what someone does *in* saying something. But there remains the question of *perlocutionary effects*, what one does *by* saying something. The relationship between these two is a potential problem for speech-act theory. Certainly both presuppose a *locution*, the spoken medium in which something is said. And one can accomplish either the illocution or

---

[52]Vanhoozer, *Remythologizing*, 261, 374.
[53]Kevin J. Vanhoozer, "From Speech Acts to Scripture Acts: The Covenant of Discourse and the Discourse of the Covenant," in *First Theology: God, Scripture and Hermeneutics* (Downers Grove, IL: InterVarsity Press, 2002), 200.
[54]Vanhoozer, *Drama of Doctrine*, 66.

the perlocution by means other than a locution. But there is also a natural fit for the hierarchy, according to William Alston, since one can bring about a result by performing a corresponding illocutionary act.[55] There is no natural fit when someone yells, "Don't wake up!" to a sleeping person. But when there is a proper and conventional fit, J. L. Austin spoke of a perlocutionary "object" as the natural result of an illocutionary act. When the perlocutionary object obtains, a person performs a "perlocutionary act."[56] Some theorists, however, have challenged the notion of a perlocutionary act because it is impossible to know the results of a speech act before it is enacted.[57] Yueguo Gu argues that it is improper to assign perlocutionary causality to a speaker, since the speaker's language can only function as a trigger for certain responses from the hearer. Since there is a finite yet large number of possible effects that may result from performing any illocutionary act, for which of these is a speaker accountable? Or more pointedly, may one say that the speaker caused these effects at all?

In the specific case of persuasion, Elise Springer answers in the negative. "If a robustly dialogical encounter persuades someone of something, this resolution has emerged in the process of conversation; there is no distinct speech-cause to which it corresponds as perlocutionary effect."[58] Springer views speech-act theory as a "ballistic" metaphor for persuasion, as if one could measure the effects of an utterance like one measures the trajectory of a canon ball.[59] In Austin's classic ballistic example, one person persuades another to fire a gun by saying, "Shoot her."[60] The illocutionary act consists in one person urging or ordering another to shoot her. The perlocution is the result; he persuades or forces the other person to fire the gun. Springer objects that one cannot move from a discrete act to its result of persuasion so easily. "How things go with a hearer are never simply *effects* of a speaker's

---

[55] William Alston, *Illocutionary Acts and Sentence Meaning* (Ithaca, NY: Cornell University Press, 2000), 31.
[56] J. L. Austin, *How to Do Things with Words*, 2nd ed. (Cambridge, MA: Harvard University Press, 1975), 109.
[57] Daniel Marcu, "Perlocutions: The Achilles' Heel of Speech Act Theory," *JP* 32 (2000): 1719-41; Yueguo Gu, "The Impasse of Perlocution," *JP* 20 (1993): 405-32; Dennis Kurzon, "The Speech Act Status of Incitement: Perlocutionary Acts Revisited," *JP* 29 (1998): 571-96.
[58] Elise Springer, *Communicating Moral Concern: An Ethics of Critical Responsiveness* (Cambridge, MA: MIT Press, 2013), 105.
[59] Ibid., 101.
[60] Austin, *How to Do Things with Words*, 100-103.

utterance; they are responses that emerge in overlapping tandem with a speaker's words."[61] The Socratic dialogues serve as an example. Socrates's interlocutors do not know when they have moved over to his side.

A danger may exist in isolating discrete speech acts without consideration of an interlocutor's response. With the exception of strong performatives such as, "I now pronounce you husband and wife," the analysis may ignore the diachronic and dialogical nature of human interaction. But speech-act theory could still use the vocabulary of perlocutions for the effects of an illocutionary act while acknowledging that understanding, persuasion and other effects come about in processes or through extended activities. One could conceive of the locution-illocution-perlocution structure as an observation of speech acts and their effects, rather than as a mechanics explaining how they work. People do, or attempt to do, things with words. We attribute agency to those who persuade us of a viewpoint, and so it is natural to attribute perlocutionary effects to that person. But no human speech act on its own counts as the perlocutionary act of persuasion apart from the response of the other person. If, as I have maintained, the effectual call is a summons rather than a pure declarative, analyzing its effects requires a special category of divine speech that goes beyond what speech-act theory on its own can explain.

Moving beyond speech-act theory. A need to move beyond speech-act theory arises from two primary arguments seen above: the difficulty of defining a perlocutionary act, and a "ballistic" view of speech acts that ignores diachronic persuasion. On the first, the theory reaches its limit if it postulates the mechanism by which illocutionary acts produce perlocutionary effects. Speech-act theory on its own does not tell us why certain illocutions produce certain perlocutions. To account for the efficacy of persuasion it is necessary to add an additional factor such as the Spirit's gift of understanding. For the second, speech-act theory on its own presses one toward a *fiat lux* conception of the effectual call, as if God interacts with humans in the same way that he first spoke to the unformed world. While the Reformed

---

[61]Springer, *Moral Concern*, 103-4. Gu, "Impasse of Perlocution," 420-22, criticizes speech-act theory on this point for eliminating the agency of the person who hears a persuasive speech act. Vincent Brümmer, *Speaking of a Personal God: An Essay in Philosophical Theology* (Cambridge: Cambridge University Press, 1992), 68-89, makes this same argument against the conclusions of the Synod of Dort.

tradition affirms that converting change can be focused in one event and even one moment, I have offered here a theological statement of God's purposes in the processes that lead up to and effect converting change. Thus I choose to leave behind speech-act vocabulary for a discussion of persuasion or transformation in a dialogical encounter.

Before introducing rhetoric as a framework for the effectual call as trinitarian discourse, it is helpful to note that some early modern Reformed orthodox theologians included persuasion as an analogical description of God's action in converting change.

The tender necessity of persuasion. The Synod of Dort denies that regeneration comes about "by moral suasion" (*morale suasionem*), which it defines as a mode of operating that, "after God has done his work, it remains in man's power whether or not to be reborn or converted."[62] The focus throughout is on the certain success of God's work in regeneration. John Cameron, who subscribed to Dort but was widely suspect among the Reformed for his intellectualist view of converting change, appealed to "persuasion" as the distinctive attribute of faith.[63] Cameron found sympathetic ears in surprising places—notably in two stalwarts of Reformed orthodoxy toward the end of the seventeenth century: Francis Turretin and Herman Witsius (d. 1708).[64]

---

[62] *The Canons of the Synod of Dort* 3/4.12, in Philip Schaff, ed., *The Creeds of Christendom: With a History and Critical Notes*, 6th ed. (Harper & Row, 1931; repr., Grand Rapids: Baker, 1983), 3:567. The Jaroslav Pelikan and Valerie Hotchkiss translation (*Creeds and Confessions of Faith in the Christian Tradition* [New Haven, CT: Yale University Press, 2003], 2:586) says "moral persuasion," which will be significant immediately below. "Persuade" also appears in the document (*Dort*, concl.; Pelikan and Hotchkiss, *Creeds*, 2:598) with the sense of successful persuasion.

[63] Brian Armstrong, *Calvinism and the Amyraut Heresy: Protestant Scholasticism and Humanism in Seventeenth-Century France* (Madison: University of Wisconsin Press, 1969), 66-69. In Cameron's inaugural lecture on Phil 2:12-13, he attributes "willing" and "doing" to the results of "persuasion." As noted in chap. 6, Erasmus distinguished *persuasion* from *suasion* by its efficacy.

[64] For various treatments of *suasion* and *persuasion* among the Reformed orthodox, see George Carleton et al., "The Collegiate Suffrage of the British Divines," in *The British Delegation and the Synod of Dort (1618–1619)*, ed. Anthony Milton, Church of England Record Society 13 (Woodbridge: Boydell, 2005), 262-63; Heinrich Heppe, *Reformed Dogmatics*, ed. Ernst Bizer, trans. G. Thomson (Grand Rapids: Baker, 1978), 522. John Owen, ΠΝΕΥΜΑΤΟΛΟΓΙΑ *[Pneumatologia], or, a Discourse Concerning the Holy Spirit*, in *The Holy Spirit*, vol. 3 of *The Works of John Owen*, ed. William Goold (London: Johnstone & Hunter, 1852; repr., Carlisle, PA: Banner of Truth Trust, 1966), 3:309, considers, but ultimately rejects, "persuasion." In the nineteenth century, Charles Hodge defines "moral suasion" as "the influence exerted by one mind over the acts and states of another mind, by the presentation of truth and motives, by expostulations, entreaty, appeals, etc." (Charles Hodge, *Systematic Theology* [New York: Scribner, 1871; repr., Grand Rapids: Eerdmans, 1940], 2:684).

Turretin wishes to balance God's effectual call with the voluntary assent of human creatures. "Our calling is a work of divine omnipotence, that no one may make it resistible; and it claims us for itself by a loving and most tender necessity of persuasion [*suavissima persuasionis necessitate*], that no one may imagine it to be forced or involuntary."[65] Turretin cites the difference between *suasion* and *persuasion* when discussing John 6:44, "No one can come to me unless the Father who sent me draws him." He focuses on God the Father's action to draw or attract.[66]

> The institution of men differs from that of God. Men do not draw by teaching since they can exercise suasion but not persuasion [*suadere quippe possunt, sed non persuadere*]; while they who are taught of God are drawn (i.e., they necessarily follow and obey because they are taught not only mediately by the word, but immediately and internally by the Spirit [1 Jn 2:20] and by being taught they are drawn).[67]

Only God persuades, but he does so through discourse. While I have sought to restate Turretin's insistence on an "immediate" work of the Spirit in terms of dialogue and the process of understanding, his use of "persuasion" shows that he believes God's mode of acting respects the particular capacities God has created in humans.

Writing two years before Turretin, Witsius portrays effectual calling as an instance of persuasion: "It is a violence, indeed, but that of heavenly love, the greater the sweeter."[68] In calling, God makes his people willing, "bringing his truths so clearly to their understanding that they cannot but assent, so effectually gaining upon their will by the charms of his goodness, that they are not able to reject them; but yield themselves conquered, and that with

---

[65]Turretin, *Institutes* 15.4.21, 2:526 (*Institutio theologiae elencticae, in qua status controversiae perspicuè exponitur, praecipua orthodoxorum argumenta proponuntur & vindicantur, & fontes solutionum aperiuntur* [Geneva: Apud Samuelem De Tournes, 1688], 2:573) (critical text is hereafter cited as *Institutio* following the translation citation).

[66]A challenge for this interpretation is that ἕλκω (to attract, drag) appears without a connotation of efficiency in Jn 12:32, where Christ's "lifting up" will "draw [ἑλκύσω] all people" to himself. For this argument, see Roger Olson, *Against Calvinism* (Grand Rapids: Zondervan, 2011), 163-64. But the verse concludes with a promise, "and I will raise him in the last day" (Jn 6:44), likely referring to all those who are "drawn" by the Father.

[67]Turretin, *Institutes* 15.6.13, 2:550 (*Institutio*, 2:600).

[68]Herman Witsius, *The Economy of the Covenants Between God and Man: Comprehending a Complete Body of Divinity*, trans. William Crookshank (1693; Edinburgh: Thomas Turnbull, 1803), 1:358.

the highest complacency."⁶⁹ Witsius calls this action "πειθανάγκη, the contracting persuasion of God, who calls."⁷⁰ The Greek term, with its etymology of "persuade" (πείθω) and "necessity" (ἀνάγκη), may not be the best analogy of God's call. According to the LSJ citations, it functions more, as we say, as "an offer you cannot refuse." Cicero fears the πειθανάγκη of Pompey because "the requests of despots have an element of compulsion."⁷¹ Is the effectual call an instance of πειθανάγκη, a request or summons functioning as a veiled threat?

In one sense it is. What David Jasper and other postmoderns lament as the subversive power of authoritative speech is for the Christian a reality when God speaks. And yet consequences are a regular part of education and moral discernment. What makes the threat illegitimate or evil is the right of the speaker to ask for such a response. The examples of πειθανάγκη, however, involve the coercive power of a political leader demanding personal sacrifice on the part of a subordinate based on this power alone. The persuasive rhetoric comes with tongue in cheek, since the real power to persuade comes from the compulsion of threats to life or property. When Witsius and Turretin appeal to πειθανάγκη, they have a different sense in mind. Turretin's nineteenth-century translator glosses it as "forcible conviction," completing Turretin's thought that "by influencing" us, the gospel "persuades and turns to obedience."⁷²

So despite the coercive connotations of πειθανάγκη, Turretin does not conclude that the primary means of persuasion in calling is the threat of retaliation. Rather, he appeals to God as teacher: "When God teaches, he demonstrates (i.e., not only exhorts and moves, but persuades and carries through); when man learns from God, he is not indeed drawn with twisted neck, but is conquered by the truth and vanquished by a triumphant delight, than which nothing is sweeter, nothing more efficacious."⁷³

---

⁶⁹Ibid., 1:358-59.
⁷⁰Ibid., 1:359. Witsius and Turretin (*Institutes* 15.6.13, 2:550) are drawing on an unidentified source, since the term does not appear in the standard ancient authors on rhetoric (Aristotle, Cicero [with the exception below in a letter], Isocrates, Quintilian). The Digital Library of Classic Protestant Texts gives only one reference earlier than Turretin among Protestant sources, in which it is viewed negatively.
⁷¹Marcus Tullius Cicero, *Letters to Atticus* 180.4, in *Letters to Atticus, Volume III*, trans. D. R. Shackleton Bailey, LCL 97 (Cambridge, MA: Harvard University Press, 1999), 76-77. Cicero uses the Greek term (LSJ 1353).
⁷²Turretin, *Institutes* 15.6.13, 2:550.
⁷³Turretin, *Institutes* 15.6.13, 2:550.

This appeal to a "triumphant delight" establishes the possibility in Turretin and Witsius that God's work in calling may be characterized as "persuading" his elect, understood as efficaciously bringing someone to a conviction about something.

TRIUNE RHETORIC: TRINITARIAN THEOLOGY AND RHETORIC

> 'Tis rational to suppose, that when God speaks to the world, there should be something in his word or speech vastly different from men's word.[74]

To present God's actions in the economy of salvation as a trinitarian word or communication is not unusual. Martin Luther does something similar in his table talk:

> The Father is in divine things and matters the grammar, because he gives the words and is the source from which flow good, fine and pure words which one should use in talking. The Son is the dialectics, because he provides the disposition how one should put matters in an orderly fashion one after the other, so that it concludes and follows with certainty. The Holy Spirit, however, is the rhetoric, the orator, who performs it well, breathes and drives it, enlivens and strengthens it so that it impresses and captures the hearts.[75]

Luther compares the work of the Trinity to the *trivium* with emphasis on how all three elements combine to capture the hearts of God's people. This is a trinitarian order of redemptive action conceived as God's speech. As I mentioned above in this chapter, George Kennedy proposes that early Christians modified the three Aristotelian modes of persuasion in their rhetoric. Christian rhetoric maintains the importance of *logos*, but replaces the *ethos* of the speaker with the authority of God and appeals not to an emotion in the hearer (*pathos*), but to God's grace that transforms the hearer. Kennedy's "radical Christian rhetoric" helps explain the three main loci of speech, author and hearer in rhetorical terms.

I propose a trinitarian taxonomy of *logos*, *ethos* and *pathos* as a way to organize the triad of what is spoken, the speaker and the audience. I am not

---

[74]Jonathan Edwards, "A Divine and Supernatural Light," in *Sermons and Discourses, 1730–1733*, ed. Mark Valeri, WJE 17 (New Haven, CT: Yale University Press, 1999), 420.
[75]Martin Luther, WA *Tischreden* 1:564. Translation from Christoph Schwöbel, "God as Conversation: Reflections on a Theological Ontology of Communicative Relations," in *Theology and Conversation: Towards a Relational Theology*, ed. Jacques Haers (Leuven: Peeters, 2003), 62-63.

conceiving the triune God as any particular rhetorician in the tradition of classical rhetoric. Experts in human rhetoric such as Cicero or Augustine only dimly reflect effective divine speech. Rhetoric simply recognizes that God appropriates fitting means to persuade and transform his audience through his speaking.

Rhetoric as an analogy for the effectual call offers several advantages. First, it recognizes God as a speech agent. This respects the biblical evidence that God enacts his will in history through his own speech and through the appropriated speech of his witnesses. Second, the rhetorical tradition allows God's action with words to encompass what Friedrich Schleiermacher calls the word "in the widest sense."[76] This allows one to respect the New Testament witness that, for instance, Paul's person and deeds (*ethos*) participated in God's persuasive and transforming work (e.g., Rom 15:18-19; 1 Thess 2:1-10). Third, rhetoric allows one to give respect to the gospel as a personal announcement. The content (*logos*) of the gospel ought to be persuasive on its own, but rhetoric allows one to acknowledge that belief emerges from a combination of factors including a changed perspective in those who hear the message. This locates the authority and power of gospel proclamation in the divine speaker, rather than exclusively in the content of the message.

The Father as source of authority. God the Father represents the *ethos* of the effectual call, its efficacy based on the character of the speaker.[77] For Aristotle, hearers come to trust a speaker when the speaker shows practical wisdom, virtue and goodwill.[78] Augustine likewise emphasizes the preacher's quality of life above other factors. "But for us to be listened to with obedient compliance, whatever the grandeur of the speaker's utterances, his manner of life carries more weight."[79] In calling, God the Father moves his people through a display or sense of his character both as Creator and as

---

[76]Schleiermacher, *Christian Faith*, §108.5 (*CF* 491). See note on citation and translation in chap. 6, n. 68.
[77]Aristotle, *Rhetoric* 1.2.4, 1.9.1, 2.1.5-7. See James S. Baumlin, "Ethos," in *Encyclopedia of Rhetoric*, ed. Thomas O. Sloane (Oxford: Oxford University Press, 2001), 263-77. Jakob Wisse, *Ethos and Pathos: From Aristotle to Cicero* (Amsterdam: Adolf M. Hakkert, 1989), 240-49, argues that for Aristotle, ethos centers on the speaker's *trustworthiness*, while for Cicero emphasis is on the speaker's *sympathy*. I present the divine analogy more in line with Aristotle since sympathy toward God is not the goal of the effectual call.
[78]Aristotle, *Rhetoric* 2.1.5 (Kennedy, 121).
[79]Augustine, *Doctr. chr.* 4.27.59 (WSA 11:237).

faithful covenant keeper. Illumination in John Owen, for instance, produces the conviction that God is speaking in Scripture. Because the quality of the speaker determines the trustworthiness of the Word, one is convinced of Scripture's truthfulness when one recognizes that the true God is speaking in Scripture.

But how may one speak of God's use of *ethos* in the effectual call? Aristotle suggests that orators construct their *ethos* through their speech. Cunningham relativizes this for the Christian theologian: "The character of the speaker is a constructed reality. It is not an essence, waiting to be truthfully revealed; rather, it is actively constructed by a particular audience in a specific rhetorical context."[80] If one transposes this to God without caveat, one might suppose that God's character exists only in its construction by an audience. Cunningham's comment is nevertheless helpful for pointing out that an audience knows the speaker's character only through what the speaker says and does. Scripture presents an analogy for this in that God constructs his character through the *economy*, that is, through his covenant faithfulness most clearly displayed in Jesus Christ. As Creator, God possesses an unrivaled authority. Yet he chooses also to establish his authority as redeemer through the history of Israel and in the ministry of Jesus. Because "the character of the speaker is grafted onto the argument and becomes a part of its persuasive force,"[81] *ethos* in this trinitarian exposition is properly ascribed to God the Father. In the effectual call, God the Father brings the presentation of his character as the one who possesses trustworthy authority to a climax in a summons to Christ and the gospel. Attributing *ethos* to God the Father respects him as source and goal of the effectual call. The call comes from the one who summons his people to himself.

Divine speaking in the effectual call involves the entire Trinity in unified action. Yet one may attribute the actual speaking to God the Father as the origin or source of all God's actions. Two reasons allow for this: first, God the Father is most often the referent of "God" *simpliciter* as agent in Scripture, and second, because Christian theology has affirmed the Father as the source of divine actions on the basis of the relationship between the Father and the Son revealed in the economy. The summary of Dutch Reformed

---

[80]Cunningham, *Faithful Persuasion*, 146.
[81]Ibid., 125.

theology, the *Synopsis Purioris Theologiae*, divides the effectual call thus: "The primary efficient cause of the Gospel-call is God the Father, in the Son and through the Holy Spirit."[82] The *Synopsis* cites Ephesians 1:17-18, in which the "Father of glory" is the "God of our Lord Jesus Christ." In addition, the Father is here the source of the "Spirit of wisdom and revelation," as well as the gift of illumination.[83]

I thus take exception with Karl Barth's exposition of the call.[84] He argues that Jesus Christ is the one who calls.

> The vocation [*Berufung*] of man consists decisively in the fact that the living Jesus Christ encounters definite men at definite times in their lives as their Contemporary, makes Himself known to them as the One He is, i.e., as the One He is for the world, for all men, and therefore for them too, and addresses and claims them as partners in His covenant and sinners justified and sanctified in Him. He does this in the witness of the prophets and apostles. But in this witness it is He, Jesus Christ, who does it.[85]

Barth recognizes that many texts refer to God *simpliciter* as the one who calls, and that no texts expressly refer thus to Jesus Christ.[86] Nevertheless, he notes that in the Gospels the call of each disciple is recounted as a conversation with Jesus Christ. He then describes the concrete form of God's call. "It is Jesus who does it in all the concreteness of His humanity. And to

---

[82] R. T. te Velde, ed., *Synopsis Purioris Theologiae: Synopsis of a Purer Theology. Latin Text and English Translation*, Studies in Medieval and Reformation Traditions (Leiden: Brill, forthcoming), Disp. 30:§10. The clearest texts for God the Father as the one who calls are Rom 8:29-30; 1 Cor 1:9; and 2 Tim 1:8-9.

[83] Although the choice between the divine Spirit and the human spirit is often ambiguous, the close parallel with Is 11:2 LXX strongly favors the divine Spirit in Eph 1:17.

[84] Barth examines *vocatio* as Christian conversion in *CD* IV/3.2:481-554, "§71 The Vocation of Man [*Des Menschen Berufung*]," and *vocatio* as one's response to the command of God in *CD* III/3:595-647, "§56.2 Vocation [*Der Beruf*]." See Rhys Kuzmič, "*Beruf* and *Berufung* in Karl Barth's *Church Dogmatics*: Toward a Subversive Klesiology," *IJST* 7 (2005): 262-78.

[85] Barth, *CD* IV/3.2:502.

[86] Barth, *CD* IV/3.2:503. He cites Rom 1:6 and 1 Cor 7:17 as possible exceptions. In Rom 1:6, the κλητοὶ Ἰησοῦ Χριστοῦ could be either those called *by* Jesus Christ, in the same way that Paul received his apostleship from him (Rom 1:5), or those called *to belong to* Jesus Christ (Moo, *Romans*, 54). First Corinthians 7:17 is less likely to indicate Christ as the one who calls: "Only let each person lead the life that the Lord has assigned to him, and to which God has called him." Barth might have added Acts 16:14, where the "Lord" opens Lydia's heart. Given that she explains her belief "in the Lord" in the next verse (Acts 16:15), it is likely referring to the Lord Jesus. In the book of Acts, κύριος is characteristic of Christ (Acts 2:36), but can refer simply to God when an Old Testament context is in view (Acts 2:39; cf. Joel 3:5 LXX [Joel 2:32 ET]).

the question how He does it, the only answer is obviously that in what this man does God is at work in His eternal mercy and omnipotence."[87] Barth affirms that in the words and actions of Jesus Christ, God is active in all three persons of the Trinity, just as Scripture ascribes the resurrection of Christ to the Father, to Christ himself and possibly to the Holy Spirit (Barth cites Rom 1:4). Yet Barth insists that specifically Christ calls.

Barth offers Christ as the one who calls in order to avoid any abstraction in the agent of the call. "Is there not needed a good deal of mythology, and much naivety, to understand and take seriously the vocation of man without the concrete person of Jesus Christ who as the Son of God calls him by the Holy Spirit?"[88] Barth wishes to maintain the contemporaneity of the call for an individual while ensuring that particular cultural assumptions about "God" do not cloud the uniqueness of Christ's call. This is an acceptable goal, and Barth is correct to note Christ as the instrument through which God calls during his ministry. But even here one must take account of Christ as one sent and acting on behalf of the Father, the God of Israel. We may speak then of Christ as coauthor of the call, but I submit that the *ethos* of God's call takes up his covenantal history not only in Jesus Christ but also in his promises to Israel.

In Paul's Damascus road experience, for example, he hears Christ. Yet Christ comes to him with an authority Paul has already met in the God of Israel.[89] When Luke records Paul's further reflection on his call, Paul defends his conclusion that the God of Israel is working salvation for his people and for the world (e.g., Acts 22:14-15; 26:6-7, 22-23). Acknowledging God the Father as the one who calls answers Barth's criterion of specificity. The Creator God who covenanted with Israel and has now broadcast his steadfast love to the world in a new way through Jesus Christ calls as one who is faithful and who possesses authority. He calls individuals through contemporary human witnesses—including the incarnate Son of God. Ultimately, as Barth acknowledges, "where the New Testament speaks generally of κλῆσις as the historical beginning of the Christian state, in obvious

---

[87]Barth, *CD* IV/3.2:503.
[88]Barth, *CD* IV/3.2:504.
[89]Acts 9:20 describes Paul's immediate ministry as proclaiming Jesus "Son of God" in the synagogue, pointing to a fulfillment of messianic expectations.

agreement with the Old it calls God Himself the great καλῶν."[90] My presentation parallels Barth's in that he also affirms that God's call happens "in the witness of the prophets and apostles."[91] Yet identifying God the Father as the one who calls best accords with New Testament testimony and brings in the ethos of the covenant-keeping God of Israel as part of God's means of transforming and persuading his people toward faith.[92]

To speak of God the Father as providing the *ethos* of the effectual call means that when God calls, he invests the words of the gospel with his own authority. This authority is not separate from a personal relationship since it invites the hearer to respond to God's trustworthiness in Christ. The effectual call communicates the *ethos* of God as Creator, but also as trustworthy covenant-keeper both to Israel and to all humanity in Jesus Christ.

The Son as the argument.

In these last days he has spoken to us by his Son. (Heb 1:2)

The effectual call is an instance of divine address in which God speaks a particular word, "Jesus Christ is your saving Lord." The rhetorical category of *logos*, the argument, adds that this distilled statement includes history and context that give it meaning. One may isolate the effectual call from a broader argument, but the call does not exist without the argument.

Although the Gospel of John likely does not have rhetorical vocabulary in view with λόγος in John 1:1, the New Testament makes clear that the incarnate Jesus Christ is the content of God's argument. The apostle preaches "Christ crucified," and Christ is the "power and wisdom of God" (1 Cor 1:23-24). Jesus identifies himself as the serpent lifted up in the wilderness so that he may be seen (Jn 3:14-16) and as one who will be lifted up in order to draw all people to himself (Jn 12:32). Ignatius of Antioch, the early bishop and martyr, calls Christ the "unerring mouth by whom the Father has spoken truly."[93] Jesus Christ may be identified so strongly with God's argument that, as Stephen Webb and others have noted, Erasmus of Rotterdam translated John 1:1 with *sermo* (speech) instead of *verbum*. Erasmus's

---

[90]Barth, *CD* IV/3.2:503.
[91]Barth, *CD* IV/3.2:502.
[92]It may be significant that Barth does not reference Jn 6:44-45 in his discussion of calling, since here the "Father" draws people to Christ.
[93]Ignatius, *To the Romans* 8.2; Holmes, *Apostolic Fathers*, 175.

interpretation recognizes Christ as the means by which God communicates as a speaker.[94]

Christ's person and work are the argument of triune rhetoric in the effectual call. If the Father functions as the *ethos* of the call by grounding its authority and trustworthiness, Christ's person and work are the argument itself, the point on which God focuses human attention. As with *ethos*, the argument in effectual calling also extends to the messengers empowered by God's Spirit for the task of proclamation. "Divine self-communication comes through Jesus' manner of living and speaking as well as what he says [and does!] through others appointed to serve the economy of divine self-communication."[95]

To be sure, identifying Christ with *logos* as a mode of persuasion by no means diminishes his status as the *Logos*, second person of the Trinity. This proposal affirms the essential incarnational shape of the Son's mission. The rhetorical analogy highlights, however, that in the particular mode of the Son's mission in redemption and reconciliation, the *Logos* functions as a form of *logos*. Oscar Cullmann reflects on how the Word's "words" participate in his identity as the one sent from the Father.

> Jesus not only *brings* revelation, but in his person *is* revelation. He brings light and at the same time he is Light; he bestows life, and he is Life; he proclaims truth, and he is Truth. More properly expressed, he brings light, life and truth just because he himself is Light, Life, and Truth. So it is also with the Logos: he brings the word, because he is the Word.[96]

Christ does not stand mute in the effectual call. I have argued that God the Father should be identified as the one who calls, but this is primarily to highlight his authority as Creator and covenanter. The call may come about through a myriad of witnesses including Christ. This does not limit Christ's role as divine *Logos* to a witness, since Christ's works include other actions such as creation, atonement and intercession. But it represents a fully trinitarian economy of salvation that originates with the Father, is enacted by the Son and is made perfect by the Spirit.

---

[94]Webb, *Divine Voice*, 131. Cf. Marjorie O'Rourke Boyle, "Religion," in Sloane, *Encyclopedia of Rhetoric*, 667.
[95]Vanhoozer, *Remythologizing*, 197.
[96]Oscar Cullmann, *The Christology of the New Testament*, trans. Shirley C. Guthrie and Charles A. M. Hall (Philadelphia: Fortress, 1959), 259.

To organize what might be said about the *logos* of the call, I note Aristotle's two modes of argumentation in rhetoric: the enthymeme and the paradigm.[97] An enthymeme is any logical argument in which not every premise is specified. Orators assume premises with which their audience can agree in order to speak more poignantly. A *paradigm*, in this technical sense, is an example used to prove a point. One may examine how Christ serves as the argument of the effectual call both as enthymeme and as paradigm.

Christ the enthymeme of the Father. Apostolic preaching is full of enthymemes, that is, short arguments with assumed premises or implied conclusions. Witherington cites 1 Timothy 5:17-18, in which the conclusion that church teachers should be paid presumes that the audience can see the connection between an ox threshing grain and elders teaching.[98] How might Christ serve as the enthymeme of the effectual call? The sending of the Son for humanity supplies both the premises and the conclusion of an argument. Christ's witness to humanity's plight and his mission of redemption serve as the premises. These lead to the conclusion that Jesus is the saving Lord.

Because Aristotle's orator searches for any argument that an audience would deem valuable, enthymemes display great variety. Divine rhetoric is distinct. Among many hearers, the gospel of a crucified Messiah looked either foolish or shameful (1 Cor 1:22-23). Apostolic rhetoric is not directly tailored to persuade people of what they already believe and know. Yet Luke records that Paul proclaimed Christ to Jews with appeals to their own Scriptures (Acts 13:14-43) and to Gentiles on the basis of their recognition of divine factors operative in the world (Acts 17:15-34). Therefore to speak of divine rhetoric is to acknowledge that God opens up the drama of redemption for observation. In this regard the mission of the Son is a public event. Paul displayed Christ crucified "publicly" in his preaching before their "eyes" (Gal 3:1).[99] Jesus answers objections to his claim to be the fulfillment of Israel's history, and the early Christians offered arguments for associating him with the God of Israel. A dogmatic account of the effectual call confesses that God works in the covenantal

---

[97] Aristotle, *Rhetoric* 1.2.8 (Kennedy, 40).
[98] Witherington, *New Testament Rhetoric*, 224.
[99] Paul could indicate his own suffering here, which would prove my point. Although I agree that the ministry of Christ's servants is part of the rhetorical *logos*, Paul likely has in mind proclamation about Christ's sufferings in this text.

history, in the ministry of Jesus Christ and in the witness of the church in syllogistic-like ways.

Christ as enthymeme or argument implies that the effectual call gives reasons for accepting Christ as saving Lord. In particular, apostolic preaching displays Christ and so is the instrumental means of the effectual call. The Westminster Shorter Catechism assigns the power of the call to God's Spirit, but the Spirit "persuades and enables us to embrace Jesus Christ, freely offered to us in the gospel."[100] That God commissioned the apostles with a gospel to proclaim warrants the affirmation that the effectual call has an argument associated with it. If the effectual call includes a form of argument, and if this is expressible from one human to another, then human proclamation has been taken up into divine rhetoric. "Preaching is commissioned human speech in which God makes his appeal."[101] Christ's words, Scripture's words and contemporary preaching all participate in the enthymemes of divine rhetoric in effectual calling. As in rhetoric, the form of the enthymemes varies, but the content remains Christ freely offered in the gospel.

Christ as paradigm. For Aristotle, a paradigm gives evidence for a conclusion by use of examples. These examples serve as collaborating witnesses to one's previous arguments. He concludes, "A witness is everywhere persuasive."[102] Christ acts as paradigm or example in divine rhetoric as the goal of God's creation. He not only witnesses to the coming kingdom but also enacts the kingdom in himself as the firstfruits of the new creation. If Christ as the enthymeme of the effectual call announces how he enacts the divine will in redemption, Christ as paradigm enacts the human response to God's kingdom. Christoph Schwöbel explains,

> The incarnation of the word of God is the way in which the divine word takes the form of embodied human discourse so that God's word becomes audible in a human voice. God's word incarnate is at the same time the perfect human response to God's word, the carnal being of humanity turned into the voice answering to God's address.[103]

---

[100] *WSC* Q. 31.
[101] John Webster, *The Domain of the Word: Scripture and Theological Reasoning* (London: T&T Clark, 2012), 26. Cf. Schwöbel, "God as Conversation," 49.
[102] Aristotle, *Rhetoric* 2.1.9 (Kennedy, 181).
[103] Schwöbel, "God as Conversation," 57.

Christ serves not as a model for imitation in this sense, but as the one who goes before the rest of humanity as champion and guide. The rhetoric of the effectual call says that because this one has been exalted as Lord and Christ, there is hope for all who are joined to him by faith.

Jonathan Edwards pictures Christ as the object of sight in conversion through a reading of 2 Corinthians 4:4-6. He speaks of Christ's beauty.

> He that has his eyes opened to behold the divine superlative beauty and loveliness of Jesus Christ, is convinced of his sufficiency, to stand as mediator between him, a guilty hell-deserving wretch, and an infinitely holy God, in an exceeding different manner than ever he can be convinced by all the arguments that are made use of, by the most excellent authors or preachers. When he once comes to see Christ's divine loveliness, he wonders no more that he is thought worthy by God the Father, to be accepted for the vilest sinner.[104]

Edwards here disparages "arguments" as insufficient for converting change. My account of the effectual call agrees with this when arguments are conceived narrowly along the lines of enthymemes or logical syllogisms. Indeed, divine rhetoric moves beyond human rhetoric. But it seems appropriate to call the sight of Christ as crucified and exalted Lord a strong *argument* for the response of repentance and faith.

To refer to Christ as the paradigm of divine rhetoric in the effectual call stretches Aristotle's categories. Yet Aristotle acknowledges that a trustworthy witness proves persuasive to all sorts of people. I take up Christ here as human witness to and participant in the enactment of God's saving economy through his passion, resurrection and ascension. But this christological sketch returns us to the question asked above about whether Christ has a speaking part in the effectual call.

"Jesus is your saving Lord" and rhetoric. In chapter four I argued that the effectual call has as its content the summons, "Jesus is your saving Lord!" This statement coordinates closely with a rhetorical emphasis since it is a form of enthymeme grounded on the covenant faithfulness of the God of Israel and his determination to save people from their sins. "Saving Lord" can also imply that Christ is the goal of creation. He is both a witness to God's saving

---

[104]Jonathan Edwards, "True Grace, Distinguished from That of Devils," in *Sermons and Discourses, 1743–1758*, ed. Wilson H. Kimnach, WJE 25 (New Haven, CT: Yale University Press, 2006), 635.

work and the one who brings it about. But does this account of the effectual call give opportunity for the *Logos*, eternal Son of the Father, to act? In other words, if Christ is primarily the content of the effectual call, has this proposal denied that one's relationship with Christ is a personal relationship?

Modern theology after Barth has brought this question into sharper relief through a doctrine of the Word of God. In a broad sense, if the church is the sphere in which Christ reigns as Lord, then we expect him to speak. John Webster explains, "Jesus Christ is present to the church as the Word of God. As the eternal divine Word he is in himself eloquent, and he now addresses himself to the church, setting himself in the midst of the fellowship of the saints clothed with his gospel."[105] Christ speaks through Scripture and the visible words of the sacraments. But even in the beginning stages of the application of redemption, Christ himself comes near. "His reconciling presence sets aside the estrangement and hostility of mind of corrupt creatures, and brings into existence a place in which he makes himself known."[106] In this view, the effectual call is Christ's saying to us, "I am your saving Lord." The act of revelation, as with Barth, creates reconciliation.

Similarly, we have observed this emphasis in Schleiermacher, but for nearly opposite reasons. The moment of converting change is a direct encounter with Jesus Christ in the form of the attunement or feeling of Christ's witnesses. This form of Christ's presence ensures an organic continuity between Christ's God-consciousness and the experience of Christians today. Schleiermacher aims to show that "everything that in any way contributes to conversion, from the first impression made on the soul to its final establishment in faith, is the work of Christ."[107] For Barth, it is entirely miracle; for Schleiermacher, it is entirely natural. Both streams here press an effectual call to account for the part played by human instruments today as extensions of God in Christ.

Scripture demands that Christ has a speaking part in redemption, particularly in the effectual call. After all, the dead will hear the voice of the "Son of God" (Jn 5:25). So when Barth argues that Christ calls, he is correct

---

[105] John Webster, "Prolegomena to Christology: Four Theses," in *Confessing God: Essays in Christian Dogmatics II* (London: T&T Clark, 2005), 146.
[106] Ibid., 138.
[107] Schleiermacher, *Christian Faith*, §108.5 (*CF* 492).

to a significant degree. God calls through Christ by the power of the Spirit. But we may also say that God calls through other human witnesses empowered and directed by the Spirit who shows them Christ.[108]

The content or argument of the call is Christ's particular office in his exalted state. The divine light, as observed in chapter five, shows the glory of God "in the face of Christ" (2 Cor 4:6). Yet the origin and authority of the call belong to the Father. Christ's authority is delegated from the Father (Mt 28:18). In his final commission, Christ gives his disciples confidence that their proclamation will be invested with his delegated authority. The apostolic missionary groups summoned people as official representatives of Christ and as an enactment of God's appeal, "Be reconciled to God" (2 Cor 5:20). Christian witnesses thus go out with the authority of God on behalf of Christ.[109]

A further concern is to show that the effectual call is a personal interaction. When Edwards presents the "sight of Christ" as the power of converting change, does one encounter Christ personally in the call? The call issued by the Father is a word about Christ and is communicated through the medium of his witnesses who display his way of being in the world by the power of his Spirit. The Gospels record Christ summoning, "Come to me, all who are weary" (Mt 11:28). In this he participates as the human medium of God's address. Yet an account of the effectual call concludes that in gospel proclamation ministered by the Spirit, God the Father speaks the word about Christ. He shows Christ in his glory to particular persons. Schleiermacher and Barth are at least correct that in the effectual call one sees and hears the invitation of Christ through his witnesses. Yet a dogmatic account concludes that Christ and his witnesses act as agents for the purpose of God the Father, who calls his people into fellowship with his Son by the power of the Spirit. To say that the effectual call is personal affirms that the call comes from a personal source, namely, God, and that it introduces one to a person, namely, Christ. Further participation (i.e., communion) with

---

[108] I resist here Schleiermacher's reduction of the Spirit to exclusively the "Spirit of Christ" (Rom 8:9; Phil 1:19) and hence the continuing presence of Christ's way of being in the world (attunement).

[109] Harris, *2 Corinthians*, 446-47, concludes that "on behalf of Christ" (ὑπὲρ Χριστοῦ), when linked with the image of an official representative, suggests "in the place of" as well. Cf. Barth, *CD* IV/2:209, 601. But the passage distinguishes "God" from "Christ" throughout. God calls through the apostolic witness to Christ.

Christ takes on other dimensions as in the Lord's Supper or in prayer, but the effectual call itself is one's introduction by the Father to the Son.

As Edwards makes clear above, the persuasive change in the effectual call must involve a new delight or love for God in Christ. To the extent that sin hinders this possibility in fallen humans, one must speak of the work of the Spirit to bring God's rhetoric to fruition.

The Spirit creates an audience by grace. To the Spirit is assigned the operation of effectively bringing about what comes from the Father and is enacted through the Son. The Holy Spirit provides the principle of particularity in his mission to the world.[110] In the economy of salvation, "the Spirit empowers and makes effective the speech of God."[111] Since *pathos* relates primarily to shaping the perception of an audience, in divine rhetoric this task may be assigned to the Spirit.

An argument from *pathos* traditionally evokes a certain perception from an audience, especially their more violent emotions. Whereas Cicero and his heirs viewed *pathos* as strong emotion and *ethos* as relating to weaker emotions,[112] Aristotle gives a much wider realm to *pathos*. He defines persuasion by *pathos* as "disposing the listener in some way," or by leading the listener "to feel emotion [*pathos*] by the speech."[113] In what follows, I take this wider sense of *pathos*. Implicit here is the conclusion that all persuasive arguments appeal to *pathos* or emotions in order to create a sympathetic hearing.[114] Augustine recognizes this when he advises Christian orators to move their audience toward proper action by a love of good things.[115] If human rhetoric seeks to create the audience the speaker wishes, divine rhetoric more radically creates the audience God

---

[110] Colin Gunton, *The One, the Three, and the Many: God, Creation, and the Culture of Modernity* (Cambridge: Cambridge University Press, 1993), 189.

[111] Vern S. Poythress, "Reforming Ontology and Logic in the Light of the Trinity: An Application of Van Til's Idea of Analogy," *WTJ* 57 (1995): 201.

[112] See discussion in Lawrence D. Greene, "Pathos," in Sloane, *Encyclopedia of Rhetoric*, 560-61; Emanuele Narducci, "*Orator* and the Definition of the Ideal Orator," in *Brill's Companion to Cicero: Oratory and Rhetoric*, ed. and trans. James M. May (Leiden: Brill, 2002), 434; Wisse, *Ethos and Pathos*, 242.

[113] Aristotle, *Rhetoric* 1.2.2-4 (Kennedy, 37-38).

[114] Jeffrey Walker, "*Pathos* and *Katharsis* in 'Aristotelian' Rhetoric: Some Implications," in *Rereading Aristotle's* Rhetoric, ed. Alan G. Gross and Arthur E. Walzer (Carbondale, IL: Southern Illinois University Press, 2000), 74-92, argues that even if Aristotle would not say as much, his *Rhetoric* entails this conclusion.

[115] Augustine, *Doctr. chr.* 4.13.29 (WSA 11:217).

wishes through the work of the Spirit, which I associate most closely with the miracle of understanding.

Human orators dimly reflect divine rhetoric when they form their audience through the use of images that the audience identifies with certain emotions, through evocative words and phrases, and through tones and body movements that communicate the needed feelings. These are so liable to be deceptive and manipulative that a *pathetic* appeal is often denigrated in comparison with a logical appeal. Yet in its ideal form, an argument from *pathos* leads an audience to feel what is appropriate for a given situation and so be moved to respond in appropriate ways.

In the effectual call the Spirit forms the audience through encounter with God's speech mediated through human witnesses including the incarnate Christ, the apostolic witnesses and contemporary human preachers. The Spirit's ministry here is to impress the proper loves or delights that correspond to the excellence of Christ in the gospel. The visible and auditory proclamation of human witnesses and the invisible and accompanying work of the Spirit combine to establish both human responsibility and dependence.

For Webb, "it is the Spirit who makes the Bible sound like God."[116] A doctrine of calling recognizes that in and through hearing Scripture and gospel proclamation, the Spirit gives people understanding and love of divine things. Such a position highlights that converting change takes place within the human processes of discernment and reasoning.[117]

How then does the Spirit shape the audience, especially recognizing the reality of total depravity? A seventeenth-century Dutch disputation postulated that "the efficacious call is the gracious act of God in which he raises those who are dead in sin to spiritual life."[118] I have sought to affirm such definitions while recognizing that the death-to-life metaphor presupposes

---

[116]Webb, *Divine Voice*, 174.

[117]This also entails that the Spirit's *pathos* work occurs within the context of gospel proclamation. Such an approach affirms the *filioque*. Because Son and Spirit work together on their missions according to their order in the immanent Trinity, the effectual call does not expect a work of the Spirit apart from the proclaimed gospel of Christ. This claim is central for John Owen (*Pneumatologia*, 60-61). See Carl Trueman, *The Claims of Truth: John Owen's Trinitarian Theology* (Carlisle, UK: Paternoster, 1998), 145-48. For criticism of the *filioque* on this point, see Jürgen Moltmann, *The Spirit of Life: A Universal Affirmation* (Minneapolis: Fortress, 1992), 7-8.

[118]Cited in Henk van den Belt, "The *Vocatio* in the Leiden Disputations (1597–1631): The Influence of the Arminian Controversy on the Concept of the Divine Call to Salvation," *CHRC* 92 (2012): 550.

an active and living human subject. Augustine in particular suggests that the Spirit's work is to give a delight in spiritual things that overcomes the desire for lesser things. Thus the Spirit's persuasion through *pathos* is to reorient human loves through this gift of delight in Christ.

Delectatio victrix. Augustine referred to a "delight in righteousness" that, by God's grace, conquers the love of earthly things.

> For the good begins to be desired when it begins to become sweet.... And so, the blessing of sweetness is the grace of God by which he brings it about in us that we find delight in and we desire, that is, that we love, what he commands us. If God does not go before us with this grace, we not only do not complete, but we do not even begin to do what he commands.[119]

Augustine's focus on changed loves in conversion allows that God conquers human hearts by exciting a love of righteousness.[120] God's grace makes righteousness appear sweet. Catholic Augustinian Cornelius Jansen (d. 1638) appropriated this vocabulary as a description of God's manner of bringing about saving faith. Victorious delight, in Jansen's moral psychology, determines the will and leads to saving faith.[121] Some Protestant theologians

---

[119] Augustine, *Against Two Epistles of the Pelagians* 2.21, trans. Roland J. Teske, in *Answer to the Pelagians, II*, ed. John E. Rotelle, WSA I/24 (Hyde Park, NY: New City, 1998), 157. For other citations and the connection in Augustine with Rom 5:5, see J. Patout Burns, *The Development of Augustine's Doctrine of Operative Grace* (Paris: Études Augustiniennes, 1980), 41-43.

[120] Augustine uses the exact phrase "victorious delight" (*victrix delectatio*) in just one passage, and not about operative grace in converting change. Augustine, *On the Forgiveness of Sins* 2.19.32 (*NPNF¹* 5:57). On *delectatio victrix* in Augustine, see Carol Harrison, "Delectatio Victrix: Grace and Freedom in Saint Augustine," *SP* 28 (1993): 298-302; Cornelius P. Mayer, "Delectatio (Delectare)," in *Augustinus-Lexikon*, ed. Cornelius P. Mayer (Basel: Schwabe, 1986), 2:280-81; Robert J. O'Connell, *Images of Conversion in St. Augustine's Confessions* (New York: Fordham University Press, 1996), 183, 239-43; Eugene TeSelle, "Exploring the Inner Conflict: Augustine's Sermons on Romans 7 and 8," in *Augustine: Biblical Exegete*, ed. Frederick Van Fleteren and Joseph C. Schnaubelt, Augustinian Historical Institute (New York: Peter Lang, 2004), 313-45.

[121] Jansen's magnum opus, a commentary on Augustine, was published in 1640 just after his death. "Jansenism" took on several streams during the next 150 years. My interest is only in his doctrine of grace, which is recognized as consistent with the Dutch Calvinism of the Synod of Dort. See Brian E. Strayer, *Suffering Saints: Jansenists and Convulsionnaires in France, 1640-1799* (Brighton: Sussex Academic Press, 2008), 22-26, 47-74; William Doyle, *Jansenism: Catholic Resistance to Authority from the Reformation to the French Revolution*, Studies in European History (London: Macmillan, 2000); Diana Stanciu, "The Feelings of the Master as Articles of Faith or Medicine Against Heresy? Jansenius' Polemics against the 'New Pelagians,'" *Ephemerides Theologicae Lovanienses* 87 (2011): 393-418. For representative Catholic polemic against him, see Henri de Lubac, *Augustinianism and Modern Theology*, trans. Lancelot Sheppard (New York: Herder and Herder, 1969), 36-58. For Protestant appropriation, see Herman Bavinck, *Reformed Dogmatics*, ed. John Bolt, trans. John Vriend (Grand Rapids: Baker Academic, 2003), 3:514.

appropriated this vocabulary for God's grace in conversion. John Flavel understands it to mean that God works by "a most efficacious sweetness."[122] Alongside his close argument for the Spirit's work as "immediate," Turretin appeals to the same concept.

> That immediate operation has in view nothing else than to impress the proposed word upon the heart, captivating the blind reason into the obedience of Christ and so changing by victorious delight [*victrice delectatione*] the strength or propensity of the will to evil; that what was before followed with hatred and contempt as the highest evil is now pursued with the most ardent love as the highest good.[123]

Turretin makes clear that the Spirit ministers the gospel to a person's heart. In this action, the Spirit fills the person with delight to follow the divine will. He returns to the same idea under the metaphor of teaching, as noted above. "When man learns from God, he is not indeed drawn with twisted neck, but is conquered by the truth and vanquished by a triumphant delight [*victrice delectatione*], than which nothing is sweeter, nothing more efficacious."[124] Turretin goes beyond what Augustine says explicitly to describe the manner in which this delight conquers. God speaks, demonstrates and persuades by showing a person the sweetness of Christ.

This delight in righteousness, or a realization of the sweetness of Christ, can be described as part of human emotion or affection. Faith is here an emotional transformation. One now loves God revealed in Christ. According to Matthew Elliott's construction of emotions as "concern-based construals," emotions enact cognitive perceptions of the world.[125] For God to grant that spiritual things now appear lovely and desirable is a function of *pathos*, a rhetorical construction of the audience by eliciting various emotions. The Spirit's persuasion through *pathos*, then, is the giving delight in Christ to a person as Christ is revealed in Scripture and testified to through the church's witness.

The Reformed objection to persuasion. The discussion of *pathos* brings up the most significant objection to an analysis of divine rhetoric in the economy

---

[122] John Flavel, *The Method of Grace in the Gospel Redemption*, in *The Works of John Flavel* (1820; repr., Carlisle, PA: Banner of Truth, 1997), 2:70.
[123] Turretin, *Institutes* 15.4.50, 2:540 (*Institutio*, 2:589).
[124] Turretin, *Institutes* 15.6.13, 2:550 (*Institutio*, 2:600).
[125] Matthew Elliott, *Faithful Feelings: Emotion in the New Testament* (Leicester, UK: Inter-Varsity Press, 2005).

of salvation. Does not rhetoric presuppose a certain disposition in the audience that the speaker activates? In Aristotle's treatment of *pathos*, he uses the audience's susceptibility to emotions such as pride, hate and ambition in order to sway them. *Pathos* as a mode of persuasion is not instruction about something new. Rather, a persuasive speech seeks to tailor words to sync with the ambitions or dispositions of the audience. Orators modify themselves to the place of the audience, rather than vice versa. "Speech is 'like a feast, at which the dishes are made to please the guests, and not the cooks.'"[126]

At this point a Reformed account of the effectual call must distinguish between divine and human speech.[127] As with all teaching, the Spirit shapes and brings about this moment of understanding. The effectual call highlights that God provides appropriate means and reasons for a given person to be shaped and transformed by irresistible divine grace, but God's speech still determinatively shapes human hearts. The *pathos* of the Spirit creates the audience by grace. So although it is theologically significant that the process of coming to faith can be named as "persuasion," the final outcome must be left to the Spirit's gift.

Lydia and Divine Rhetoric

A final example may be found in the brief account of Lydia's conversion during Paul's preaching in Philippi.[128]

> And on the Sabbath day we went outside the gate [of Philippi] to the riverside, where we supposed there was a place of prayer, and we sat down and spoke

---

[126]Chaim Perelman and Lucie Olbrechts-Tyteca, *The New Rhetoric: A Treatise on Argumentation*, trans. John Wilkinson and Purcell Weaver (Notre Dame, IN: University of Notre Dame Press, 1969), 24. Quoting seventeenth-century Jesuit Baltasar Gracián.

[127]Given Jn 3:8, there is an appeal to mystery in every doctrine of grace. "Therefore they are disappointed who would wish the mode of its [the Spirit's] operation to be accurately described to them and what its secret movements are, what and how great that heart-turning power of the Spirit acting in the hearts of the elect, and in what degrees and moments he carries forward his work" (Turretin, *Institutes* 15.4.11, 2:521).

[128]Lydia is a consistent example of the effectual call: Calvin, *Institutes* 3.24.13, 980; Turretin, *Institutes* 15.4.35, 2:533; Herman Bavinck, *Saved by Grace: The Holy Spirit's Work in Calling and Regeneration*, ed. J. Mark Beach, trans. Nelson D. Kloosterman (Grand Rapids: Reformation Heritage, 2008), 61. For the use of Lydia in theology, see Charles Cohen, "Two Biblical Models of Conversion: An Example of Puritan Hermeneutics," *CH* 58 (1989): 182-96. For historical-critical work, see Richard Ascough, *Lydia: Paul's Cosmopolitan Hostess* (Collegeville, MN: Liturgical, 2009); David Matson, *Household Conversion Narratives in Acts: Pattern and Interpretation* (Sheffield: Sheffield Academic Press, 1996), 149.

to the women who had come together. One who heard us was a woman named Lydia, from the city of Thyatira, a seller of purple goods, who was a worshiper of God. The Lord opened her heart to pay attention to what was said by Paul. And after she was baptized, and her household as well, she urged us, saying, "If you have judged me to be faithful to the Lord, come to my house and stay." And she prevailed upon us. (Acts 16:13-15)

How is Lydia's conversion an instance of divine rhetoric? Or is it a conversion at all? Lydia "feared God," a common term in Acts for Gentiles who associated with Jewish worship of the God of Israel (Acts 13:26, 50; 17:4).[129] Although Luke does not use characteristic terms such as "repent" or "turn to God," however, the results of Lydia's experience parallel other conversion accounts in Acts.[130] Similarly, although she was already a Godfearer, Luke considers this to be only preparatory for gospel conversion.[131] Her encounter with Paul's preaching is the determinative moment and produces a change in her allegiances—a conversion. Luke presents her as a paradigmatic new member of the Christian community who receives Paul's message about Jesus Christ and demonstrates her allegiance through the act of hospitality. What part, then, did God play in this conversion?

One could read the passage with an assumption that her autonomous decision was foremost, and that after the Lord opened her heart she had no determining inclination either to reject or accept Paul's message. In an Arminian interpretation, the opening of her heart was prevenient grace. Objections to this would include that it presupposes a libertarian freedom that is susceptible to the "grounding objection." If prevenient grace placed Lydia at a point of absolute neutrality with regard to listening or not listening to Paul, then she would have no sufficient reason to choose either way. Confessional Lutherans, on the other hand, would explain her acceptance as the result of her nonresistance to the grace given through the preaching of the word. When asked what explains Lydia's nonresistance in contrast to the other

---

[129]Dietrich-Alex Koch, "The God-Fearers Between Facts and Fiction," *Studia Theologica* 60 (2006): 62-90.
[130]Acts highlights the conversion of prominent Gentile women (Acts 17:4, 12), believing and "turning" to the Lord (Acts 11:21; 14:15; 15:3, 19), and showing hospitality to the gospel messengers (Acts 10:48; cf. Lk 10:7-8).
[131]Christoph Stenschke, *Luke's Portrait of the Gentiles Prior to Their Coming to Faith* (Tübingen: Mohr Siebeck, 1999), 386-87, notes that not all Godfearers believed (e.g., Acts 13:50).

women present (presumably not all believed that day), Lutheran Francis Pieper might respond that this is the limit of mystery.[132]

I contend, however, that when one considers how Luke uses the term "opening" in Luke 24:31-32 for the giving of hermeneutic understanding of Jesus' identity in the Old Testament, the divine action to "open" Lydia's heart in Acts 16:14 can be understood as both necessary and sufficient.[133] The opening of her heart resulted inevitably in her paying attention to Paul's message. Like the disciples on the road to Emmaus and the Twelve later that evening, the Lord "opened" Lydia's heart within the process of discernment and understanding.[134] The main verb in Acts 16:14 is ἤκουεν, which is ambiguous as to whether she actively "listened" (cf. Acts 15:12; 22:22) or passively "heard" (cf. Acts 2:6; 10:46). The ambiguity of "to hear" challenges a clear subject-object dichotomy. No doubt she had an interest in the God of Israel so much so that she joined the other women for prayer. Yet to hear Paul's words is a middle-voiced action—they come to her unbidden and yet require her attention for understanding. The verse records that the Lord provided the necessary attention[135] to the words that Paul spoke by opening her heart.

The text itself does not ascribe actions to members of the Trinity apart from the "Lord" as the agent opening her heart. The proposal above assigns elements of rhetoric to the divine persons according to the missions of the Son and Spirit. In Lydia's case even the brief encounter can be understood as an instance of divine rhetoric. First, Lydia's response is a form of persuasion in that she decides to accept baptism from the apostolic band (Acts

---

[132] Pieper does not cite Acts 16:14 or refer to Lydia in his treatment of conversion (Franz Pieper, *Christian Dogmatics*, trans. Theodore Engelder [St. Louis: Concordia, 1950], 2:454-95). *Solid Declaration of the Formula of Concord* 2.26; Robert Kolb and Timothy J. Wengert, eds., *The Book of Concord: The Confessions of the Evangelical Lutheran Church* (Minneapolis: Fortress, 2000), 549, cites Acts 16:14 to show the necessity of divine action in converting change.

[133] The only other instance of "open the heart" is 2 Macc 1:3-4, where it means to order the inclination or affections, "May [God] give you all a *heart* to worship him and to do his will with a strong *heart* and a willing spirit. May he *open your heart* to his law and his ordinances, and may he bring peace" (NETS).

[134] The Lord opens the disciples' *eyes* on the road to Emmaus and the *minds* of the Twelve. This may allow for some distinction, although the terms are fluid. Jesus criticizes the disciples on the road for being slow of "heart" (Lk 24:25), and they acknowledge that their "hearts" were burning while he was speaking (Lk 24:32). I note only that the gracious "opening" takes place for each group in the midst of attempting to understand Christ.

[135] See Acts 8:6 for προσέχειν as "pay attention."

16:15). Second, Paul's proclamation, if it is consistent with the missionary preaching recorded throughout Acts, would appeal to the Scriptures of Israel and to their interpretation through the events of Christ's death and resurrection. This accounts for both the authority of God as authorizing the call (*ethos*) and for Christ as the content toward which Paul points (*logos*). *Pathos* is the shaping of an audience. While Paul's own rhetoric sought to do this, Luke records that divine action to "open the heart" was a necessary component to complete the efficacy of the preached message. Given a doctrine of providence in which God ordains that circumstances fit with a plan to bring about the salvation of God's people, one may conclude that the Lydia episode illustrates the unique, yet analogous, form of divine rhetoric. The communicative effectual call thus works "not on or against but in and through Lydia's nature and personhood" to bring about understanding, persuasion and therefore faith.[136]

This approach maintains the uniqueness of divine rhetoric since only God's speech opens hearts, or better, God's use of Paul's speech opens hearts. We are now in a position to answer Turretin's objection against Claude Pajon about God's providence. He asks, "Now if the providence of God (which is concerned about evil by the arrangement of objects and circumstances) did not make him the author of sin, why should the arranging of objects and circumstances which draw us to Christ make him the author of our conversion?"[137] This confronts all theologians who wish to maintain that God authors salvation in ways that are distinct from how he ordains or permits evil.

A dialogical conception of the effectual call affirms that God arranges "objects and circumstances" and that these act as means to bring about saving faith. But it preserves the distinctiveness of divine speech. The divine interjection is not the same as an "object and circumstance," even if humans encounter it through the witness of other humans. That Philip would encounter the Ethiopian on the road to Gaza or that Paul would be the first Christian to preach to the Thessalonians is certainly a result of divine ordering of circumstances. Yet in each instance God chooses to speak through his human messengers and by grace the Spirit introduces these people to the exalted and saving Christ.

---

[136]Vanhoozer, *Remythologizing*, 372.
[137]Turretin, *Institutes* 15.4.45, 2:539.

Flavel points to the Spirit's crucial agency in all that goes into a saving hearing of the gospel: "It is the Spirit that gives the word all that virtue it hath, he is the Lord of all saving influences: he hath dominion over the *word*, over our *souls*, over the *times* and *seasons* of conversion."[138] Flavel does not shy away from the conclusion that if someone hears the gospel and yet rejects it, Christians may conclude that Christ was not present in his Spirit—like Christ's healing presence would have prevented Lazarus's death. Yet because a communicative conception of the effectual call locates the Spirit's work of *pathos*-persuasion within the process of communication and understanding, it includes circumstances and speech among God's means to bring about faith.

DIVINE RHETORIC AND EFFECTUAL CALLING

Human rhetoric is the practice of knowing the means of persuasion in any case. In the hands (or on the lips) of sinful humans such a tool is liable to damage and destroy. Yet a theological account of rhetoric recognizes that language is created and appropriated by God for his good ends. Christian theologians expect that God speaks both through Scripture and through gospel witness. This gives hope to the partial success of communication even in a postlapsarian world. In the face of postmodern suspicion of power plays disguised as preaching, Christians testify to Christ in the mode of praise and prayer, always refining yet never attaining a complete grasp of God and his ways.[139]

A divine rhetoric in the economy of redemption should be understood as the archetype of human rhetoric. If God reveals himself as one who enters into the process of discourse, and if the specific work of applying Christ's benefits to men and women through converting change evidences itself as a work of speech and understanding, Christians have warrant to draw analogies between God's speech and their own.

Positioning the effectual call under the banner of rhetoric means that the call is a type of persuasion. Better, the closest human analogue for what God is doing in calling his elect is a unique form of persuasion. Here persuasion

---

[138]Flavel, *Method of Grace*, 2:58-59.
[139]James K. A. Smith, "Between Predication and Silence: Augustine on How (Not) to Speak of God," *HeyJ* 41 (2000): 66-86.

is understood as in Turretin, as a change in affections or dispositions that correspond with particular beliefs about God in Christ. Persuasion is the creation of a dispositional form of love for God in Christ through the presence of the Spirit ministering an effective witness to Christ.

God's rhetoric is a work of the entire Trinity. God the Father issues the summons. The Son is the content of the call, but also the form it takes historically in the incarnation. The Spirit is the energy of the effectual call. I proposed further that rhetorical terms help show more clearly in what ways God's summons is effective.

Appropriating *logos, ethos* and *pathos* as means of persuasion in rhetoric, the effectual call is God's overwhelming use of these paths in sovereign and effective ways that are tailored to the individual and come through human witnesses.[140] Although the biblical vocabulary does not allow insistence on trinitarian appropriations, I suggest the following based on the trinitarian order *from* the Father, *through* the Son, *by* the Holy Spirit. *Logos*, the argument, is the role of the Son. We may say that the effectual call utilizes *enthymemes* deducing the necessity of faith from God's covenant history with Israel and from general premises. Jesus Christ also functions as a *paradigm*, example or as the goal of the divine economy—hence his title in the call as the "saving Lord." The Father persuades by means of *ethos*. The creator of the world and covenant God of Israel speaks with authority. Yet while the Father is ascribed the leading and originating authority, he shares this authority with the Son. Paul's vision of the exalted Jesus Christ receives its authority from Christ's enactment of God the Father's plan. *Pathos* is the means of shaping an audience emotionally. In the trinitarian economy, the Spirit forms the audience to be those who can respond to the gospel by granting them understanding. Viewing the Spirit's work in terms of providing understanding allows the effectual call to place the Spirit's work within the process of human activity. The Spirit's work both presupposes universal human capacities and restores these according to the Spirit's will.

Rhetoric provides an analogical framework for the effectual call. It acknowledges (1) that God is a speech agent in the economy of redemption, (2) that converting change, while it may be marked as instantaneous, takes

---

[140]One cannot exclude direct revelation, but the New Testament gives no expectation of such.

place within the process of coming to understanding, and (3) that this work involves the whole Trinity while acknowledging scriptural distinctions in the roles of the persons. Although *persuasion* is not the primary term used by Reformed sources for the effectual call, Reformed orthodox sources appropriate it as a way to emphasize the efficacy of God's call in contrast to human *suasion*. The dialogical effectual call presented here is thus an example of the "tender necessity of persuasion."

TEN

God's Call and the Church

Several scriptural metaphors for converting change inform the effectual call. This study has presented a dogmatic account of the effectual call that probes the scriptural warrant for the doctrine and then asks why it is significant that God's action is revealed in the New Testament as a call. The goal has not been to defend the Reformed doctrines of operative grace in conversion against all objections. Rather, this project has analyzed and in some cases modified classic Reformed expressions toward the goal of articulating the effectual call freshly.

In addition to the specific focus on the effectual call, the conclusions offered here about God's use of means in salvation resonate with a broadly evangelical focus on the necessity of conversion. The effectual call entails affective change in an individual. God's call is not merely a declaration of what is already the case, but a convincing announcement about Christ who also draws near to us by the Holy Spirit. The Spirit's work is precisely in this convincing, persuading motion. After summarizing the contribution of this study, I examine two broader issues in soteriology for which the effectual call may be significant.

A primary contribution of this study is a definition of the effectual call:

> The *effectual call* is an act of triune rhetoric in which God the Father appropriates human witness to Christ the Son in order to convince and transform a particular person by ministering, through the presence of God the Spirit, understanding and love of Christ.

This definition emphasizes that calling is a literal description of God's action, although God's speech differs from human speech. The disjunction with human speech is most clear in that God's speech always accomplishes its goal. But "calling" in the New Testament is not metaphorical; that is, the term is not a cipher for the positional change God accomplishes in conversion. The Reformed tradition has distinguished between an external and internal call, God's work through public proclamation and his work through internal influence. While my definition maintains such a distinction by including the "presence of God the Spirit," it notes that the external/internal dynamic exists within one unified call of God. The general call becomes a special or internal call because of God's use of it in the economy of salvation.

I have proposed three questions for a dogmatic account of the effectual call that get at the nature of the calling metaphor. First, who calls? I have maintained that God the Father is best assigned the agency of the call. As in all triune acts, God calls through the Son and by the Spirit. The effectual call comes about primarily through God's providential use of human speech to summon individuals.[1] To say that God uses human speech means both that God enables proclamation and that the Holy Spirit ministers these words in order to create faith.

Second, what is the semantic content of the call? The effectual call is individualized in each case, since God's use of words not only fits languages and cultures but also utilizes social and personal factors. Nevertheless, the New Testament generalizes about God's action in converting change and about the results that emerge. Peter can speak of God's work to call his readers "out of darkness into his marvelous light" (1 Pet 2:9). In this case, God directs everyone whom he calls toward an identical goal—experiencing the light. This warrants generalizing about the content of the effectual call. I concluded in chapter four that such content must be expressible orally, have cognitive content, come in the form of a summons, elicit human response and lead to belief or faith. "Jesus is your saving Lord" serves as an attractive distillation of what God is saying (the semantic content) in the effectual call.

One may also ask if God says the same thing to both elect and nonelect individuals. In other words, does God whisper special semantic content to the elect? Bavinck answers, "The Word that God causes to be proclaimed by the external call is the same Word that He causes, in the internal call by the

---

[1]This is seen specifically in 2 Thess 2:14.

Holy Spirit, to be inscribed on the heart."[2] Bavinck thus affirms that the semantic content is identical. This is essential if one wishes to maintain a belief in the "well-meant offer," that God's announcement of the gospel is genuine and sincere. But there is also a sense in which the content of the call is personalized. "Jesus is your saving Lord" is not the uniform locution of the call. God summons his people in various forms. Because I have maintained that the call is expressed orally, I reject Karl Barth's conclusion that a dead dog or Russian Communism might be the form that God's call takes.[3] Yet the human messengers God uses will be imperfect, may be improperly motivated (Phil 1:12-19) and may not be conscious of their use in God's program—as is the case when God's call evokes memory of a word heard earlier. In the way I have construed the effectual call as coming through human witnesses, I maintain that the general call has the same content as the effectual call, yet the effectual call adds an element of divine persuasion or rhetoric. A Christian witness may say, "Jesus is your saving Lord" provisionally, as reflecting the well-meant offer. But the effectual call is triune discourse that announces and summons one into this reality definitively through effective and transformative persuasion.

A third question was, what changes in the effectual call? Subjectively considered, a person expresses faith in Christ. Objectively, this means that they are united to Christ by faith. The Westminster Shorter Catechism reflects this conclusion when it names effectual calling as the means by which one is united to Christ.[4] New Testament texts also identify this change as an eschatological or epochal transition. New birth and the coming of the Spirit both represent participation in the eschatological blessings of the new age. It is appropriate to call the result a "spiritual resurrection,"[5] but this does not answer several further questions about how God works in converting change. As Reformed theologians have noted with the distinction between act and ability, an act of faith is a flower that grows from roots deeper within the individual. Jonathan Edwards helpfully focuses attention on the presence

---

[2] Herman Bavinck, *Saved by Grace: The Holy Spirit's Work in Calling and Regeneration*, ed. J. Mark Beach, trans. Nelson D. Kloosterman (Grand Rapids: Reformation Heritage, 2008), 149.
[3] Karl Barth, *CD* I/1:55.
[4] *WSC* Q. 30-31. Cf. 1 Cor 1:9.
[5] E.g., Richard Gaffin, *"By Faith, Not by Sight": Paul and the Order of Salvation* (Waynesboro, GA: Paternoster, 2006), 64, who points primarily to 2 Cor 4:16.

of the Spirit superintending over human affections in order to give his people a sense of the divine beauty of God revealed in Christ. This locates converting change primarily on the level of one's disposition, affections, attunement or, more simply, in the "heart." How then does this analysis of subjective change relate to the concept of spiritual resurrection? Renewed affections that are disposed toward God are the mark of the age to come because this disposition participates in God's own affective, delightful communion within the Trinity.

In order to preserve the effectual call as a communicative act, I appealed to rhetoric as an analogical framework. Rhetoric specifies that the effectual call is argumentative and persuasive rather than physical or "creative." Rhetoric also helps clarify that God presents definite content (*logos*) in Jesus Christ. God the Father speaks the word "Jesus is your saving Lord" through his appointed witnesses including the incarnate Christ and his commissioned disciples. The Spirit makes use of various arguments including the history of redemption and the reflection of Christ in his disciples to bring about understanding and ultimately persuasive delight. The Spirit appropriates all manner of circumstances to this end and impresses Christ's excellence on the human heart so that one sees Christ and delights in him. This rhetorical account of the effectual call offers a means for exploring the trinitarian implications of a dialogical call. I emphasize God the Father as the originator and *ethos* of the call in contrast to Barth and Schleiermacher, who see Jesus Christ as the one who calls. Nevertheless, the rhetorical analogy finds surprising connections with these theologians by viewing God's work in converting change as empowered by divine personal presence. Barth's doctrine of the Word of God emphasizes the need for God's act in each moment of contemporary revelation. The effectual call is such a moment, but a trinitarian account that includes God the Father as *ethos* of the call helps locate God's work within the covenantal economy of salvation.

THE EFFECTUAL CALL IN PRACTICE

Because the effectual call is "the first act of election shown and exercised in man himself,"[6] it serves as a flashpoint for a range of doctrinal questions. I

---

[6]William Ames, *The Marrow of Theology*, trans. John Dykstra Eusden (Boston: Pilgrim, 1968; repr., Grand Rapids: Baker, 1997), 157. Cf. *WCF* 10.1.

here mention two questions in which the effectual call implies further conclusions about soteriology. First, the doctrine of salvation has historically addressed the question of children who die in infancy.[7] My account of the dialogical effectual call urges that the case of infants not be made into the standard for a doctrine of converting change. Second, because the effectual call is cited consistently within an order of salvation (*ordo salutis*), it is important to explain and defend the construction of such an order. A dogmatic account must also answer how the effectual call relates to the related term *regeneration* in an order of salvation.

Infant salvation and regeneration. A challenge to a dialogical effectual call emerges from what is acknowledged by all Protestants as an exception—the salvation of infants who die within a short time of being born. Christians have attempted to affirm God's grace to at least some of those who die in infancy, either from a theology of baptismal regeneration (Augustine), from an argument for the promise of God to covenant children (Reformed), from the work of the gospel on unresisting infants in baptism (Lutheran), from a doctrine of prevenient grace not yet consciously transgressed (the so-called age of accountability) or from a claim to a special dispensation of God's grace impenetrable to us but witnessed in biblical texts.[8] The challenge for a doctrine of effectual calling as presented here is that any view of infant salvation appears to bypass conscious faith in Christ and cognitive understanding of the gospel. I do not intend to present a theology of infant salvation, but I note that a doctrine of effectual calling implies that the situation of infant mortality and salvation serves as an exception rather than as the rule.

Both the Synod of Dort and the Westminster Confession of Faith assure Christian parents that some children who die in infancy are saved in an extraordinary way. Significantly, the Westminster statement on infant

---

[7]For contemporary views, see Myk Habets, "'Suffer the Little Children to Come to Me, for Theirs Is the Kingdom of Heaven': Infant Salvation and the Destiny of the Severely Mentally Disabled," in *Evangelical Calvinism: Essays Resourcing the Continuing Reformation of the Church*, ed. Myk Habets and Bobby Grow (Eugene, OR: Wipf & Stock, 2012), 287-328. Despite insightful analysis throughout, his appeal to the "vicarious humanity" of Christ in conclusion appears to prove too much. If Christ's vicarious humanity is good enough for infants, why not for everyone?

[8]Scripture testimonies are indirect, but one may argue that children belong especially to God or to the kingdom (Ezek 16:21; Mt 2:18; 19:14; Mk 10:13-16), that their postmortem state is viewed positively (2 Sam 12:23; 2 Kings 4:26), that they may be set apart and made holy while still in the womb (Jer 1:5; Lk 1:44), or that God's justice limits the transfer of guilt (Deut 1:39; such an appeal requires a reworking of original sin to exclude original *guilt*). For these texts, see ibid., 290-91.

salvation occurs in the article on effectual calling.[9] These confessional documents ask implicitly how the salvation of infants who have died is similar to the effectual call. Westminster and Dort primarily respond to different questions. Dort sought to counter a Remonstrant argument that unconditional election implies that God arbitrarily chooses which infants would be given eternal life.[10] The theologians at Dort responded that because the children of Christian parents are holy (1 Cor 7:14), "godly parents ought not to doubt the election and salvation of their children whom God calls out of this life in infancy."[11] This has stimulated questions, however, about whether such children are regenerate. As observed in chapter two, Abraham Kuyper and some earlier Reformed representatives (e.g., Gisbertus Voetius) argued that the church baptizes the infant children of Christian parents because within the covenant of grace these children already possess a seed of regeneration and so are regenerate.[12] Kuyper builds his doctrine of regeneration from the presumed regeneration of infants. God gives a seed of regeneration or a faith faculty apart from external means, and this faculty may lie dormant for much of one's life. As I argued in chapter two, the effectual call challenges this view because it bypasses God's ordinary means of working through understanding. The statement of Dort, however, argues from the generational implications of the covenant of grace. Thereby it avoids drawing a conclusion about the status of the children of Christian parents in regard to regeneration. The hope of Christian parents is ultimately set on truths about God and his promises, rather than on an understanding of the mechanics of God's ways.

---

[9] *WCF* 10.3; *The Canons of the Synod of Dort* 1.17. See Cornelis P. Venema, "The Election and Salvation of the Children of Believers Who Die in Infancy: A Study of Article I/17 of the Canons of Dort," *MJT* 17 (2006): 57-100.

[10] Venema, "Election and Salvation," 60-64. See *Dort, Rejection of False Accusations*; Jaroslav Pelikan and Valerie Hotchkiss translation (*Creeds and Confessions of Faith in the Christian Tradition* (New Haven, CT: Yale University Press, 2003), 2:598.

[11] *Dort* 1.17; Pelikan and Hotchkiss, *Creeds*, 2:575. "Since we must make judgments about God's will from his word, which testifies that the children of believers are holy, not by nature but by virtue of the gracious covenant in which they together with their parents are included, godly parents ought not to doubt the election and salvation of their children whom God calls out of this life in infancy." Benjamin B. Warfield, "The Development of the Doctrine of Infant Salvation," in *Two Studies in the History of Doctrine* (New York: Christian Literature Crusade, 1897; repr., Eugene, OR: Wipf & Stock, 2001), 214, notes that the synod chose not to make a statement regarding the salvation of all children who die in infancy.

[12] See discussion in Bavinck, *Saved by Grace*, 63-68.

The Westminster Confession is more modest when it declares that "elect infants, dying in infancy, are regenerated, and saved by Christ, through the Spirit, who works when, and where, and how He pleases: so also are all other elect persons who are incapable of being outwardly called by the ministry of the Word."[13] This position acknowledges that God's salvation of infants who have died is an exception, standing outside the ordinary mode of hearing the gospel proclaimed. It primarily protects God's freedom to elect and save in the manner he pleases. Yet the confession seeks to find continuity between the grace of regeneration in adults and in those who die in infancy by including the term *regeneration*.

I submit that the discussion of infant salvation ought to be kept separate from a doctrine of effectual calling because of the limited biblical evidence. That said, at least one text hints that God may direct his saving work to people of all ages. Luke records that John the Baptist was filled with the Holy Spirit from his mother's womb (Lk 1:15). One could argue that "filled with the Holy Spirit" indicates God's intention to include John in a crucial redemptive-historical role, just as Paul was "set apart" from birth (Gal 1:15).[14] Nevertheless, this one example of the Holy Spirit's indwelling presence apart from cognitive awareness calls into question a wholesale rejection of "immediate" or unmediated grace.[15] It appears that God may work his grace when, where and how he wishes.[16] Yet there is a temptation to make the exceptional experience of John into the norm for a definition of converting change.

An insistence that operative grace is identical in all the elect could lead to the following argument: The working of God's grace in regeneration is identical in different groups of people and in different times. John the Baptist was regenerated apart from external means. Therefore God's grace of regeneration comes to us apart from any external means. A similar argument

---

[13] *WCF* 10.3.
[14] John the Baptist's birth clearly evokes Old Testament calls to prophet-like service. E.g., Judg 13:5, 7; Is 49:1; Jer 1:5. "Filled" with the Spirit indicates empowerment for proclamation in Lk 1:41-45, 67-79. See James Hamilton, *God's Indwelling Presence: The Holy Spirit in the Old and New Testaments*, NAC Studies in Bible and Theology (Nashville: Broadman & Holman, 2006), 200.
[15] Bavinck, *Saved by Grace*, 106.
[16] English Puritan Thomas Goodwin (d. 1680) concludes, "Therefore an infant is as capable of all the essentials of regeneration as a man grown up; and therefore of baptism" (*The Work of the Holy Ghost in Our Salvation*, vol. 6 of *The Works of Thomas Goodwin* [Edinburgh: J. Nichol, 1863], 412).

would constrain the effectual call based on the salvation of infants who die young: God regenerates infants who die young.[17] Since infants who die young do not have mature cognitive functioning in any way that we can compare to adults, this regeneration takes place apart from a conscious hearing and acceptance of the gospel. Regeneration in infants is significantly similar to regeneration in adults. Therefore converting change in adults also occurs apart from conscious hearing and acceptance of the gospel.[18]

In the above hypothetical arguments, the exceptional case of infants becomes the norm for marking converting change. But this use of the exception goes against the tenor of the biblical material. Bavinck cautions,

> Scripture is of course appointed for the instruction of those who have come to years of discretion, but it treats the state of children hardly at all, nor was it given us for the purpose that we might discover answers to all sorts of questions arising from our curiosity. Therefore the route that God in His sovereignty travels with children cannot without any further qualification be fixed as the example and rule for the way God deals with adults.[19]

If a doctrine of effectual calling insists that converting change occurs within the process of human understanding, one ought to acknowledge ignorance of the mode of infant salvation. Scripture testifies to God's sanctifying work even in the womb in the case of John the Baptist, yet this isolated case does not give one warrant to draw conclusions about God's work in converting change in general.

When appropriately separated from the exception of children who die in infancy, affirmation of the effectual call entails that God brings one

---

[17] Either (1) infant children of believing parents because of the covenant of grace (Dort), (2) some infants based on sovereign election (Westminster) or (3) all infants who die young because of texts that say children belong to God or because of arguments from the justice of God. A classic Reformed account that affirms universal infant salvation for those who die is Warfield, "Doctrine of Infant Salvation." For a challenge against Warfield, see David K. Clark, "Warfield, Infant Salvation, and the Logic of Calvinism," *JETS* 27 (1984): 459-64.

[18] Francis Turretin, *Institutes of Elenctic Theology*, ed. James T. Dennison Jr., trans. George Musgrave Giger (Phillipsburg, NJ: P&R, 1992), 15.4.32, 2:532, makes this argument and concludes about adult conversion, "Nothing stands in the way of the Spirit operating in them distinctly from the word." John Gill offers the same argument on behalf of eternal justification. In his view, faith is only the "sense, perception, and evidence of our justification" (John Gill, "The Doctrine of Justification," cited in Jonathan Anthony White, "A Theological and Historical Examination of John Gill's Soteriology in Relation to Eighteenth-Century Hyper-Calvinism" [PhD diss., Southern Baptist Theological Seminary, 2010], 97).

[19] Bavinck, *Saved by Grace*, 109.

to saving faith in the process of understanding. This results in new dispositions in the heart of a person who now loves God in Christ and places faith in Christ's provision for sin and salvation. Although such a conversion theology sets up the potential for uncertainty and consequently speculation about God's work in the salvation of infants who die young as well as among the severely mentally disabled, a doctrine of effectual calling based on the missionary preaching of the New Testament implies that these cases are exceptions to the general pattern of conscious, adult conversion.

The order of salvation. The validity of an order of salvation (*ordo salutis*) is hotly debated in Reformed theology.[20] As Richard Muller notes, the term *ordo salutis* emerged in Lutheran discussions in the early eighteenth century.[21] But earlier Reformed theologians and exegetes appropriated Romans 8:28-30 to explain the logical structure of Christ's benefits in the covenant of grace or redemptive history.[22] Known as the "golden chain" or "golden bracelet," these verses provided an outline of God's work in applying redemption to individuals. The effectual call played a major role in Reformed expositions of this order. A. T. B. McGowan notes, "Rather than predestination, the key to the *ordo salutis* in early Reformed theology was effectual calling."[23] Yet this focus on God's call of individuals has raised the most significant objection to the concept of an order.

Individualistic focus of the order. Karl Barth criticized the order of salvation because of its individualistic focus. As Markus Matthias notes, the German Pietist tradition developed an *ordo salutis* with specific focus on

---

[20]The best recent defense of the concept is Richard A. Muller, *Calvin and the Reformed Tradition: On the Work of Christ and the Order of Salvation* (Grand Rapids: Baker Academic, 2012), 160-201. See also A. T. B. McGowan, "Justification and the *Ordo Salutis*," in *Justification in Perspective: Historical Developments and Contemporary Challenges*, ed. Bruce L. McCormack (Grand Rapids: Baker Academic, 2006), 147-63; John V. Fesko, *Beyond Calvin: Union with Christ and Justification in Early Modern Reformed Theology (1517–1700)*, Reformed Historical Theology 20 (Göttingen: Vandenhoeck & Ruprecht, 2012); John V. Fesko, "Romans 8.29-30 and the Question of the *Ordo Salutis*," *JRT* 8 (2014): 35-60. For the Lutheran history, see Markus Matthias, "Ordo Salutis—Zur Geschichte eines dogmatischen Begriffs," *ZKG* 115 (2004): 318-46. For recent criticism, see William B. Evans, *Imputation and Impartation: Union with Christ in American Reformed Theology*, Studies in Christian History and Thought (Colorado Springs, CO: Paternoster, 2008), 52-57.
[21]Muller, *Reformed Tradition*, 163.
[22]Ibid., 166.
[23]McGowan, "Ordo Salutis," 151.

personal development.²⁴ Barth viewed this tendency as a precursor to Enlightenment theology and its characteristic temptation to make anthropology the true object of theology.²⁵ The *ordo*, especially as seen in the Lutheran David Hollatz (d. 1713),²⁶ is a "psychological and biographical description of the evolution of the Christian."²⁷

G. C. Berkouwer similarly criticizes the concept of an *ordo salutis*. For him, it is dangerous to make the "subjective life of faith" into an "independent area of study."²⁸ An order of salvation must not turn into an occasion for self-analysis. For example, if faith is allowed to stand as a point in a sequence, it loses its place as the dominant life characteristic of a believer. Berkouwer prefers the term *way* of salvation because this stresses the continuity of God's action in conversion. This way of salvation "is only meant to illuminate *sola fide* and *sola gratia*. For only thus can it be confessed that *Christ is the way*."²⁹ Berkouwer and Barth criticize the order of salvation because it becomes an end in itself rather than pointing to a larger reality— God's redemptive work to bring about the believer's union with Christ.³⁰

Endurance of an order. The above criticisms warn against dangers present in any effort to systematize. But given texts such as Romans 8:28-30, it is difficult to avoid asking how calling, justification and glorification relate to one another in God's design. The order of salvation, I maintain, is a way of speaking about the Christian's union with Christ in order to clarify the relationships among various doctrines.³¹ "Every element in the classical *ordo salutis* is thus a further perspective on the one reality of the believer's union

---

²⁴Matthias, "*Ordo Salutis*," 333, shows that the transition to an anthropological view took place at the end of the seventeenth century. He discovered, however, that the term *ordo salutis* occurs in several texts from the seventh to twelfth centuries (ibid., 322).
²⁵Barth, *CD* IV/2:502.
²⁶As noted in chap. 5, Hollatz claimed to find all nine stages of his order of salvation in Acts 26:17-18. Cited in Barth, *CD* IV/3.2:505.
²⁷Barth, *CD* IV/3.2:506.
²⁸G. C. Berkouwer, *Faith and Justification*, Studies in Dogmatics (Grand Rapids: Eerdmans, 1954), 26.
²⁹Ibid., 33.
³⁰This finds resonance in conservative Reformed theologians as well. E.g., Sinclair B. Ferguson, *The Holy Spirit*, Contours of Christian Theology (Downers Grove, IL: InterVarsity Press, 1996), 99; John Frame, *Systematic Theology: An Introduction to Christian Belief* (Phillipsburg, NJ: P&R, 2013), 936-37.
³¹McGowan, "*Ordo Salutis*," 163. This is Muller's explanation for the use of the *ordo* in early Reformed sources (*Reformed Tradition*, 199-201). Romans 8:28-30 receives particular attention over other texts (1 Cor 1:30; 6:11) because it relates the terms logically to one another by referring to the previous term.

with Christ."³² Paul explicitly attributes our "fellowship" or partaking in Jesus Christ to God's call (1 Cor 1:9), and so calling provides a crucial link within the order.

If one understands the order of salvation as explaining how God brings one into fellowship with Christ, it is not then a handbook for moving through stages of enlightenment, or a "way of salvation" as in the Wesleyan tradition,³³ or even as a checklist for God's work within a person toward regeneration. The goal of an order of salvation is to organize the relationships between the various terms for God's action in salvation. This theocentric focus accepts Barth's advice that an order must not be approached "from below."³⁴ This can be seen most clearly by the fact that the order of salvation is arranged not *temporally*, but logically. As mentioned at the beginning of this work, soteriology seeks to trace God's action to its root in the divine decision and forward through the history of God's dealings with humanity in Christ. Thus understood, a dogmatic account of effectual calling cannot avoid an order of relationships among God's actions and their results.

Statement of the ordo salutis. If one accepts my thesis of a dialogical effectual call ministered through human witness as a species of triune rhetoric, certain implications follow for the order of salvation. To the extent that the call is effective, it gains this effectiveness from the purpose of God in election. Its efficacy is shown in both a change of status before God and a change of disposition subjectively in the person. Because the effectual call is God's action and because it includes gospel proclamation in time, the call logically precedes the human response of faith. With the Augustinian and Reformed tradition I also affirm that for the call to be effectual it must elicit or create a disposition leading to faith. If faith is an affective disposition, and if this disposition is morally impossible for fallen humans because of slavery to sin, then a form of dispositional change must occur in order to bring about the response of faith. Thus the effectual call precedes and empowers the human response of faith.

---

³²Ferguson, *Holy Spirit*, 106.
³³Wesley objected to the "order of salvation" because it did not allow room for synergism at the various stages. But he affirmed an "order" of changes that occur within a person (Kenneth J. Collins, *The Scripture Way of Salvation: The Heart of John Wesley's Theology* [Nashville: Abingdon, 1997], 186-87).
³⁴Barth, *CD* IV/3.2:508.

Within Reformed theology, a discussion continues about the relationship between effectual calling and regeneration.[35] In chapter two I outlined several possibilities for this relationship. Regeneration could logically precede the effectual call.[36] Although a person may hear and understand the gospel proclaimed earlier, and so have heard the general call, this call cannot become *effectual* until God grants new spiritual life or regeneration. Such an approach denies that the effectual call functions in any way to bring about converting change. Rather, the call gives occasion for regeneration to display its results. A second option is that they occur simultaneously in time, but have no logical relationship. God chooses sovereignly to perform his regenerating act during certain events of proclamation, but the proclamation and the change of regeneration are not essentially linked. A third option, which represents a wide swath of Reformed thinkers, posits that effectual calling and regeneration are functionally identical. "Regeneration in the active sense, the regenerative activity of God, is only another name for the call: the efficacious call of God."[37] To say that God calls is to say that God regenerates or gives new life. The benefit of such a position is that it places God's gift of new life within the framework of God's speaking through calling. In such an approach, one may even explain the difference in vocabulary between "new birth" and "calling" as reflecting Johannine and Pauline preferences. While my proposal for the effectual call is consistent with this last view, I believe it is significant that New Testament writers chose a term involving speech as a primary metaphor for converting change.

Two texts directly name God's word as the instrumental cause of new birth, either the "living and enduring word of God" (1 Pet 1:23) or the "word of truth" (Jas 1:18). To show this instrumental relationship of God's word, effectual calling should be placed logically prior to regeneration in an order of salvation. This clarifies that the call regenerates, in other words, that

---

[35]There is no biblical text that explicitly links calling with new birth or regeneration. When the New Testament combines the vocabulary of "calling" with that of "life," it speaks of the not-yet eschatological reality. Calling is nowhere linked with a *present* experience of resurrection life, thus leaving the relationship open to interpretation. God "called" Christians to eternal life (1 Tim 6:12) or into eternal glory (1 Pet 5:10), and he calls Christians to inherit a blessing (1 Pet 3:9).
[36]Bavinck, *Saved by Grace*, 54-65, shows that this was a minority opinion among the Reformed.
[37]Herman Bavinck, *Reformed Dogmatics*, ed. John Bolt, trans. John Vriend (Grand Rapids: Baker Academic, 2003), 4:77.

divine speaking brings about new life. Triune rhetoric ushers in new understanding by the presence of the Holy Spirit. The new age is inaugurated in and through God's speaking in the effectual call. This new life consists in changed dispositions that now love or delight in God as revealed in Christ for our sins. Placing regeneration after calling in an order of salvation solidifies the insight of this project that God's gift of new spiritual life occurs within active human life and thought.

A primary contribution of this study is to note that the effectual call cannot be reduced to the semantic content of the gospel. I have argued that the effectual call is effective not because of the specific words used, but because of who speaks these words—namely, the triune God. Here I lean on the redemptive-historical trajectory of contemporary Reformed thought. Regeneration indicates the new creation. To be regenerated is to participate now in an inaugurated fashion in the world to come. Such life in fellowship with God and ultimately vindicated through the redemption of one's body is the goal of God's salvific work. The indwelling Holy Spirit serves as the guarantee of that full possession and as the present experience of one's union with Christ. The coming of the Spirit to a person is regeneration, an experience of "the regeneration" or "new creation." Proponents of this redemptive-historical view stop, however, with the biblical vocabulary of new creation. I have asked how God brings about this experience of the new age. The effectual call provides an answer: God calls or summons people into his kingdom. God opens hearts to see the glory of Christ and respond in faith. God regenerates *by* calling. In other words, God grants participation in the age to come by summoning one into union with Christ by faith. This faith comes about through God's sovereign use of human witnesses that testify to God's glory in Christ. God's human creatures receive this testimony because in and through it the Spirit grants one insight or understanding of God's greatness in Christ.

Effectual Calling and the Church

Theology is the church's joyful and reasoned reflection on what God is doing to reconcile the world to himself. It also seeks to speak well of God and his ways in a given context. This means that theology seeks to foster "fitting participation" in the drama of redemption. How might a doctrine of the dialogical effectual call contribute to this participation?

First, the effectual call helps the church confess the nature of God's works in the application of redemption. God chooses to reveal converting change through various metaphors in Scripture. I have examined hearing, seeing and coming to life. Calling, I maintain, provides additional insights that illumination and spiritual resurrection on their own would not. If Christians confess that God has called them, this implies that God's saving work encounters them on the level of cognitive and personal interaction. Proclamation and hearing are the medium or context in which God effectually calls.

Second, the effectual call provides an example for the church's reflection on moving from biblical concepts to contemporary theological expression. I conclude that the three primary terms for converting change—*calling, illumination* and *regeneration*—refer to different aspects of the same phenomenon. Calling primarily stresses instrumental divine action. Regeneration primarily stresses the results of divine action. Illumination speaks more generally to the process. All three speak about converting change as the coming of the eschatological kingdom of God. This encourages the church to recognize that the metaphors are themselves constitutive of the doctrine and so cannot be separated from it. At the same time, it also calls the church to confess God's action in converting change with more than mere repetition of the biblical metaphors.

Finally, despite a tendency to use physical or mechanical language, the Protestant tradition uses communicative categories for the effectual call. Historic Reformed authors and confessions of faith recognize the instrumental necessity of personal proclamation and dispositional change within the process of understanding. This implies the usefulness of persuasive speech and reasoning in evangelism. It also militates against the danger of hyper-Calvinism or a denial of the well-meant offer. Norman Shepherd describes a form of "evangelism for regeneration": "The climax of the gospel appeal is reached when the hearer is urged to ask God for a new heart with which to lay hold of the grace of Christ."[38] There may be practical cases in which persons are uncertain and can recognize conflicted affections within themselves. In such a case, any form of prayer that seeks God's grace in

---

[38]Norman Shepherd, *The Call of Grace: How the Covenant Illuminates Salvation and Evangelism* (Phillipsburg, NJ: P&R, 2000), 97.

changing or affirming one's conviction cannot be denied. "I believe; help my unbelief" would give biblical warrant (Mk 9:24). But the practice Shepherd cites places such a prayer as the primary goal of evangelism. Despair becomes the ideal outcome of gospel proclamation. A doctrine of effectual calling argues differently. Human transformation occurs within the process of coming to understand. Hence Christian evangelists may assume (in hope) that their words will serve as the instrument by which the Spirit brings about faith. Their own declaration, "Jesus is your saving Lord," may in this case also carry the Spirit's presence and awaken faith.

Bibliography

Abasciano, Brian J. *Paul's Use of the Old Testament in Romans 9.1-9*. LNTS 301. London: T&T Clark, 2005.

———. *Paul's Use of the Old Testament in Romans 9.10-18: An Intertextual and Theological Exegesis*. LNTS 317. London: T&T Clark, 2011.

Achtemeier, Paul J. *1 Peter*. Hermeneia. Minneapolis: Fortress, 1996.

Allen, R. Michael. *The Christ's Faith: A Dogmatic Account*. SST. London: T&T Clark, 2009.

Allen, R. Michael, and Scott R. Swain. "In Defense of Proof-Texting." *JETS* 54 (2011): 589-606.

Alston, William. *Illocutionary Acts and Sentence Meaning*. Ithaca, NY: Cornell University Press, 2000.

Ames, William. *The Marrow of Theology*. Translated by John Dykstra Eusden. 1968. Reprint, Grand Rapids: Baker, 1997.

Andrews, James A. *Hermeneutics and the Church: In Dialogue with Augustine*. Reading the Scriptures. Notre Dame, IN: University of Notre Dame Press, 2012.

Aquinas, Thomas. *Summa Theologiae*. 61 vols. New York: McGraw-Hill, 1964–1981.

Aristotle. *On Rhetoric: A Theory of Civic Discourse*. Translated by George A. Kennedy. New York: Oxford University Press, 1991.

Armstrong, Brian. *Calvinism and the Amyraut Heresy: Protestant Scholasticism and Humanism in Seventeenth-Century France*. Madison: University of Wisconsin Press, 1969.

Arnold, Duane W. H., and Pamela Bright, eds. *De doctrina christiana: A Classic of Western Culture*. ChJA 9. Notre Dame, IN: University of Notre Dame Press, 1995.

Ascough, Richard. *Lydia: Paul's Cosmopolitan Hostess*. Collegeville, MN: Liturgical, 2009.

Asselt, W. J. van, J. Martin Bac and Roelf T. te Velde, eds. *Reformed Thought on Freedom: The Concept of Free Choice in Early Modern Reformed Theology*. TSRPrT. Grand Rapids: Baker Academic, 2010.

Augustine. *Against Two Epistles of the Pelagians*. In *Answer to the Pelagians, II*. Edited by John E. Rotelle. Translated by Roland J. Teske. WSA I/24. Hyde Park, NY: New City, 1998.

———. *The Confessions*. Translated by Maria Boulding. WSA I/1. Hyde Park, NY: New City, 1997.

———. *Miscellany of Questions in Response to Simplician*. In *Responses to Miscellaneous Questions*, edited by Raymond Canning, translated by Boniface Ramsey, 174-231. WSA I/12. Hyde Park, NY: New City, 2008.

———. *Opera omnia*. Edited by J.-P. Migne. PL 34. Paris: Migne, 1887.

———. *Teaching Christianity*. Translated by Edmund Hill. WSA I/11. Hyde Park, NY: New City, 1996.

Aune, David. *The Cultic Setting of Realized Eschatology in Early Christianity*. NovTSup 28. Leiden: Brill, 1972.

Austin, J. L. *How to Do Things with Words*. 2nd ed. Cambridge, MA: Harvard University Press, 1975.

Bakhtin, M. M. *Problems of Dostoevsky's Poetics*. Translated by Caryl Emerson. Minneapolis: University of Minnesota Press, 1984.

Balla, Peter. "2 Corinthians." In *CNTUOT* 753-83.

Balserak, Jon. "'The Accommodating Act Par Excellence?' An Inquiry into the Incarnation and Calvin's Understanding of Accommodation." *SJT* 55 (2002): 408-23.

———. *Divinity Compromised: A Study of Divine Accommodation in the Thought of John Calvin*. Studies in Early Modern Religious Reforms 5. Dordrecht: Springer, 2006.

Barclay, John M. G. "Why the Roman Empire Was Insignificant to Paul." In *Pauline Churches and Diaspora Jews*, 363-87. WUNT 275. Tübingen: Mohr Siebeck, 2011.

Barnett, Paul. *The Second Epistle to the Corinthians*. NICNT. Grand Rapids: Eerdmans, 1997.

Barrett, C. K. *A Critical and Exegetical Commentary on the Acts of the Apostles*. 2 vols. ICC. Edinburgh: T&T Clark, 1998.

Barrett, Matthew. *Salvation by Grace: The Case for Effectual Calling and Regeneration*. Phillipsburg, NJ: P&R, 2013.

Barth, Karl. *Church Dogmatics*. Edited by Geoffrey W. Bromiley and Thomas F. Torrance. 4 vols. in 14 parts. Edinburgh: T&T Clark, 1956–1975.

Barth, Markus. *Ephesians*. 2 vols. AB 34. Garden City, NY: Doubleday, 1974.

Battles, Ford Lewis. "God Was Accommodating Himself to Human Capacity." *Int* 31 (1977): 19-38.

Baumlin, James S. "Ethos." In *Encyclopedia of Rhetoric*, edited by Thomas O. Sloane, 263-77. Oxford: Oxford University Press, 2001.

Bavinck, Herman. *Reformed Dogmatics*. Edited by John Bolt. Translated by John Vriend. 4 vols. Grand Rapids: Baker Academic, 2003.

———. *Roeping en Wedergeboorte*. Kampen: Zalsman, 1903.

———. *Saved by Grace: The Holy Spirit's Work in Calling and Regeneration*. Edited by J. Mark Beach. Translated by Nelson D. Kloosterman. Grand Rapids: Reformation Heritage, 2008.

Bayer, Oswald. *Living by Faith: Justification and Sanctification*. Grand Rapids: Eerdmans, 2003.

———. *Martin Luther's Theology: A Contemporary Interpretation*. Translated by Thomas H. Trapp. Grand Rapids: Eerdmans, 2008.

———. *Promissio: Geschichte der reformatorischen Wende in Luthers Theologie*. Göttingen: Vandenhoeck & Ruprecht, 1971.

———. *Theology the Lutheran Way*. Translated by Jeffrey Silcock and Mark Mattes. Grand Rapids: Eerdmans, 2007.

Beale, G. K. *1-2 Thessalonians*. IVPNTC. Downers Grove, IL: InterVarsity Press, 2003.

———. *A New Testament Biblical Theology: The Unfolding of the Old Testament in the New*. Grand Rapids: Baker Academic, 2011.

Beasley-Murray, G. R. "John 3:3, 5: Baptism, Spirit and the Kingdom." *ExpTim* 97 (1986): 167-70.

Beeke, Joel R., and Mark Jones. *A Puritan Theology: Doctrine for Life*. Grand Rapids: Reformation Heritage, 2012.

Belleville, Linda. "'Born of Water and Spirit': John 3:5." *TJ* 1 (1980): 125-41.

Belt, Henk van den. "Herman Bavinck and His Reformed Sources on the Call to Grace: A Shift in Emphasis Towards the Internal Work of the Spirit." *SBET* 29 (2011): 41-59.

———. "The *Vocatio* in the Leiden Disputations (1597–1631): The Influence of the Arminian Controversy on the Concept of the Divine Call to Salvation." *CHRC* 92 (2012): 539-59.

Berkhof, Louis. *Systematic Theology*. Grand Rapids: Eerdmans, 1941.

Berkouwer, G. C. *Faith and Justification*. Studies in Dogmatics. Grand Rapids: Eerdmans, 1954.

———. *Faith and Sanctification*. Studies in Dogmatics. Grand Rapids: Eerdmans, 1952.

Bernard, Robert W. "The Rhetoric of God in the Figurative Exegesis of Augustine." In *Biblical Hermeneutics in Historical Perspective: Studies in Honor of Karlfried Froehlich on His Sixtieth Birthday*, edited by Mark S. Burrows and Paul Rorem, 88-99. Grand Rapids: Eerdmans, 1991.

Best, Ernest. *A Critical and Exegetical Commentary on Ephesians*. ICC. Edinburgh: T&T Clark, 1998.

Bieder, Werner. *Die Berufung im Neuen Testament*. Zürich: Zwingli, 1961.

Billings, J. Todd. *Union with Christ: Reframing Theology and Ministry for the Church*. Grand Rapids: Baker Academic, 2011.

Blumenberg, H. "Light as a Metaphor of Truth." In *Modernity and the Hegemony of Vision*, edited by David Kleinberg-Levin, 30-62. Translated by Joel Anderson. Berkeley: University of California Press, 1993.

Bombaro, John J. *Jonathan Edwards's Vision of Reality: The Relationship of God to the World, Redemption History, and the Reprobate*. Eugene, OR: Pickwick, 2012.

Boyle, Marjorie O'Rourke. "Religion." In *Encyclopedia of Rhetoric*, edited by Thomas O. Sloane, 662-72. Oxford: Oxford University Press, 2001.

Braaten, Carl E., and Robert Jenson, eds. *Union with Christ: The New Finnish Interpretation of Luther*. Grand Rapids: Eerdmans, 1998.

Brümmer, Vincent. *Speaking of a Personal God: An Essay in Philosophical Theology*. Cambridge: Cambridge University Press, 1992.

Bruner, Frederick Dale. *The Gospel of John: A Commentary*. Grand Rapids: Eerdmans, 2012.

Brunner, Emil. *The Christian Doctrine of God*. Translated by Olive Wyon. Vol. 1 of *Dogmatics*. Philadelphia: Westminster, 1949.

Burns, J. Patout. "Delighting the Spirit: Augustine's Practice of Figurative Interpretation." In *De doctrina christiana: A Classic of Western Culture*, edited by Duane W. H. Arnold and Pamela Bright, 182-94. ChJA 9. Notre Dame, IN: University of Notre Dame Press, 1995.

———. *The Development of Augustine's Doctrine of Operative Grace*. Paris: Études Augustiniennes, 1980.

Byrne, Brendan. *Romans*. SP 6. Collegeville, MN: Liturgical Press, 1996.

Caldwell, Robert W., III. *Communion in the Spirit: The Holy Spirit as the Bond of Union in the Theology of Jonathan Edwards*. Studies in Evangelical History and Thought. Eugene, OR: Wipf & Stock, 2006.

Calvin, John. *Antidote to the Council of Trent*. In *Calvin's Tracts*, 3:17-188. Translated by Henry Beveridge. 3 vols. Edinburgh: Calvin Translation Society, 1851.

———. *The Bondage and Liberation of the Will: A Defense of the Orthodox Doctrine of Human Choice Against Pighius*. Edited by A. N. S. Lane. Translated by G. I. Davies. TSRPrT 2. Grand Rapids: Baker Academic, 1996.

———. *Calvin's Commentaries*. 44 vols. Edinburgh: Calvin Translation Society, 1844–1856. Reprinted in 22 vols. Grand Rapids: Baker, 1999.

———. *Institutes of the Christian Religion*. Edited by John T. McNeill. Translated by Ford Lewis Battles. LCC 20-21. Philadelphia: Westminster, 1960.

———. *Ioannis Calvini Opera quae supersunt omnia*. Edited by Guilielmus Baum, Eduardus Cunitz and Eduardus Reuss. CR 30. Halle: Schwetschke, 1864. Reprint, New York: Johnson Reprint, 1964.

Candler, Peter M., Jr. *Theology, Rhetoric, Manuduction, or Reading Scripture Together on the Path to God*. Radical Traditions. Grand Rapids: Eerdmans, 2006.

Carleton, George, John Davenant, Samuel Ward and Thomas Goad. "The Collegiate Suffrage of the British Divines." In *The British Delegation and the Synod of Dort (1618–1619)*, edited by Anthony Milton, 226-93. Church of England Record Society 13. Woodbridge: Boydell, 2005.

Carson, D. A. *The Gospel According to John*. PiNTC. Grand Rapids: Eerdmans, 1991.

Carson, D. A., and Douglas J. Moo. *An Introduction to the New Testament*. 2nd ed. Grand Rapids: Zondervan, 2005.

Cary, Phillip. "Why Luther Is Not Quite Protestant: The Logic of Faith in a Sacramental Promise." *ProEccl* 14 (2005): 447-86.

Catechism of the Catholic Church: Revised in Accordance with the Official Latin Text Promulgated by Pope John Paul II. 2nd ed. Vatican City: Libreria Editrice Vaticana, 1997.

Cavadini, John C. "The Sweetness of the Word: Salvation and Rhetoric in Augustine's *De doctrina christiana*." In De doctrina christiana: *A Classic of Western Culture*, edited by Duane W. H. Arnold and Pamela Bright, 164-81. ChJA 9. Notre Dame, IN: University of Notre Dame Press, 1995.

Charnock, Stephen. *The Doctrine of Regeneration: Selected from the Writings of Stephen Charnock*. Philadelphia: Presbyterian Board of Publication, 1840. Reprint, Grand Rapids: Baker, 1980.

Cherry, Conrad. *The Theology of Jonathan Edwards: A Reappraisal.* Gloucester, MA: Peter Smith, 1974.

Chester, Stephen J. *Conversion at Corinth: Perspectives on Conversion in Paul's Theology and the Corinthian Church.* Studies of the New Testament and Its World. London: T&T Clark, 2003.

Cicero. *Letters to Atticus.* Vol. 3. Translated by D. R. Shackleton Bailey. LCL 97. Cambridge, MA: Harvard University Press, 1999.

———. *Orator.* Translated by H. M. Hubbell. LCL 342. Cambridge, MA: Harvard University Press, 2001.

Clark, David K. "Warfield, Infant Salvation, and the Logic of Calvinism." *JETS* 27 (1984): 459-64.

Clavier, Mark F. M. "Eloquent Wisdom: The Role of Rhetoric and Delight in the Theology of Saint Augustine of Hippo." PhD diss., Durham University, 2010.

Cleveland, Christopher. *Thomism in John Owen.* Farnham, UK: Ashgate, 2013.

Coenen, L. "Call." In *NIDNTT* 1:271-76.

Cohen, Charles. "Two Biblical Models of Conversion: An Example of Puritan Hermeneutics." *CH* 58 (1989): 182-96.

Colijn, Brenda B. *Images of Salvation in the New Testament.* Downers Grove, IL: IVP Academic, 2010.

Collins, Kenneth J. *The Scripture Way of Salvation: The Heart of John Wesley's Theology.* Nashville: Abingdon, 1997.

Collins, Kenneth, and John H. Tyson, eds. *Conversion in the Wesleyan Tradition.* Nashville: Abingdon, 2001.

Compier, Don H. *What Is Rhetorical Theology? Textual Practice and Public Discourse.* Harrisburg, PA: Trinity Press International, 1999.

Cox, Samuel. "Reply of Dr. Cox." *Biblical Repertory and Theological Review* 3 (1831): 483-514.

Cranfield, C. E. B. *A Critical and Exegetical Commentary on the Epistle to the Romans.* ICC. Edinburgh: T&T Clark, 1975.

Crisp, Oliver. "How 'Occasional' Was Edwards's Occasionalism?" In *Jonathan Edwards: Philosophical Theologian,* edited by Paul Helm and Oliver Crisp, 61-77. Aldershot: Ashgate, 2003.

———. *Jonathan Edwards on God and Creation.* Oxford: Oxford University Press, 2012.

———. "Jonathan Edwards's Ontology: A Critique of Sang Hyun Lee's Dispositional Account of Edwardsian Metaphysics." *RelS* 46 (2010): 1-20.

Crisp, Tobias. "The Revealing Evidence of the Spirit of Christ." In *Christ Alone Exalted: Being the Compleat Works of Tobias Crisp, D.D.*, 462-77. London, 1690.

Cullmann, Oscar. *The Christology of the New Testament*. Translated by Shirley C. Guthrie and Charles A. M. Hall. Philadelphia: Fortress, 1959.

Cunningham, David S. *Faithful Persuasion: In Aid of a Rhetoric of Christian Theology*. Notre Dame, IN: University of Notre Dame Press, 1991.

Davidson, Ivor. "Divine Light: Some Reflections After Barth." In *Trinitarian Theology After Barth*, edited by Myk Habets and Phillip Tolliday, 48-69. PTMS 148. Eugene, OR: Pickwick, 2011.

Denney, James. "The Epistles to the Thessalonians." In *Ephesians to Revelation*. Vol. 6 of *The Expositor's Bible*, edited by W. Robertson Nicoll, 315-400. New York: Ketcham, 1895.

DeVries, Dawn. *Jesus Christ in the Preaching of Calvin and Schleiermacher*. CSRT. Louisville, KY: Westminster John Knox, 1996.

Dodd, C. H. *The Interpretation of the Fourth Gospel*. Cambridge: Cambridge University Press, 1953.

Dowey, Edward A., Jr. *The Knowledge of God in Calvin's Theology*. Exp. ed. Grand Rapids: Eerdmans, 1994.

Doyle, William. *Jansenism: Catholic Resistance to Authority from the Reformation to the French Revolution*. Studies in European History. London: Macmillan, 2000.

Dunn, James D. G. *The Epistles to the Colossians and to Philemon: A Commentary on the Greek Text*. NIGTC. Grand Rapids: Eerdmans, 1996.

———. "'A Light to the Gentiles,' or 'The End of the Law'? The Significance of the Damascus Road Christophany for Paul." In *Jesus, Paul, and the Law: Studies in Mark and Galatians*, 89-107. Louisville, KY: Westminster John Knox, 1990

———. *The New Perspective on Paul*. Rev. ed. Grand Rapids: Eerdmans, 2008.

———. "Paul's Conversion—A Light to Twentieth Century Disputes." In *Evangelium, Schriftauslegung, Kirche: Festschrift für Peter Stuhlmacher zum 65. Geburtstag*, edited by Jostein Adna, Scott J. Hafemann and Otfried Hofius, 77-93. Göttingen: Vandenhoeck & Ruprecht, 1997.

———. *Romans 1–8*. WBC 38A. Dallas: Word, 1988.

———. *The Theology of Paul the Apostle*. Grand Rapids: Eerdmans, 1998.

Ebeling, Gerhard. *Luther: An Introduction to His Thought*. Translated by R. A. Wilson. Philadelphia: Fortress, 1970.

Eberhard, Philippe. *The Middle Voice in Gadamer's Hermeneutics: A Basic Interpretation with Some Theological Implications.* Hermeneutische Untersuchungen zur Theologie 45. Tübingen: Mohr Siebeck, 2004.

Eckert, J. "Καλέω, Κλῆσις, Κλητός." In *EDNT* 2:240-44.

Edwards, Jonathan. *The Works of Jonathan Edwards.* 26 vols. New Haven, CT: Yale University Press, 1957–2008.

———. *Works of Jonathan Edwards Online.* Vols. 27-73 of *The Works of Jonathan Edwards.* Jonathan Edwards Center, Yale University, 2008–. http://edwards.yale.edu.

Elliott, Matthew. *Faithful Feelings: Emotion in the New Testament.* Leicester, UK: Inter-Varsity Press, 2005.

Enos, Richard Leo, Roger Thompson, Amy K. Hermanson and Drew M. Loewe, eds. *The Rhetoric of Saint Augustine of Hippo:* De Doctrina Christiana *and the Search for a Distinctly Christian Rhetoric.* Studies in Rhetoric and Religion 7. Waco, TX: Baylor University Press, 2008.

Evans, William B. "Déjà vu All Over Again? The Contemporary Reformed Soteriological Controversy in Historical Perspective." *WTJ* 72 (2010): 135-51.

———. *Imputation and Impartation: Union with Christ in American Reformed Theology.* Studies in Christian History and Thought. Colorado Springs, CO: Paternoster, 2008.

Fatio, Olivier. "Claude Pajon et les mutations de la théologie réformée à l'époque de la Révocation." In *La Révocation de l'Édict de Nantes et le protestantisme français en 1685*, edited by Roger Zuber, 209-27. Paris: Sociéte de l'Historie du Protestantisme français, 1986.

Fee, Gordon D. *The First and Second Letters to the Thessalonians.* NICNT. Grand Rapids: Eerdmans, 2009.

———. *God's Empowering Presence: The Holy Spirit in the Letters of Paul.* Peabody, MA: Hendrickson, 1994.

Ferguson, Sinclair B. *The Holy Spirit.* Contours of Christian Theology. Downers Grove, IL: InterVarsity Press, 1996.

Fesko, John V. *Beyond Calvin: Union with Christ and Justification in Early Modern Reformed Theology (1517–1700).* Reformed Historical Theology 20. Göttingen: Vandenhoeck & Ruprecht, 2012.

———. "The Doctrine of Scripture in Reformed Orthodoxy." In *A Companion to Reformed Orthodoxy*, edited by Herman J. Selderhuis, 429-64. BCCT 40. Leiden: Brill, 2013.

———. "John Owen on Union with Christ and Justification." *Them* 37 (2012): 7-19.

———. "Romans 8.29-30 and the Question of the *Ordo Salutis*." *JRT* 8 (2014): 35-60.

Flavel, John. *The Method of Grace in the Gospel Redemption*. In *The Works of John Flavel*, 2:3-474. 1820. Reprint, Carlisle, PA: Banner of Truth, 1997.

Forde, Gerhard O. *Justification by Faith: A Matter of Death and Life*. Philadelphia: Fortress, 1982.

Fowler, James. *Stages of Faith: The Psychology of Human Development and the Quest for Meaning*. San Francisco: Harper & Row, 1981.

Frame, John. *Systematic Theology: An Introduction to Christian Belief*. Phillipsburg, NJ: P&R, 2013.

Furnish, Victor Paul. *II Corinthians*. AB 32A. Garden City, NY: Doubleday, 1984.

Gaffin, Richard. *"By Faith, Not by Sight": Paul and the Order of Salvation*. Waynesboro, GA: Paternoster, 2006.

———. *Resurrection and Redemption: A Study in Paul's Soteriology*. Phillipsburg, NJ: P&R, 1987. Reprint from *The Centrality of the Resurrection: A Study in Paul's Soteriology*. Grand Rapids: Baker, 1978.

Garrigou-Lagrange, Réginald. *Predestination*. Translated by Bede Rose. St. Louis: Herder, 1939.

Gathercole, Simon J. "Justified by Faith, Justified by His Blood: The Evidence of Romans 3:21–4:25." In *Justification and Variegated Nomism*. Vol. 2, *The Paradoxes of Paul*, edited by D. A. Carson, Peter T. O'Brien and Mark A. Seifrid, 147-84. Grand Rapids: Baker Academic, 2004.

Gaventa, Beverly. *From Darkness to Light: Aspects of Conversion in the New Testament*. Overtures to Biblical Theology 20. Philadelphia: Fortress, 1986.

Gilkey, Langdon. "The Concept of Providence in Contemporary Theology." *JR* 43 (1963): 171.

Gill, John. *A Body of Divinity*. Grand Rapids: Baker, 1951.

———. *The Cause of God and Truth: Being an Examination of the Principal Passages of Scripture Made Use of by the Arminians, in Favour of their Scheme*. 4 vols. London: Aaron Ward, 1737.

Goodwin, Thomas. *The Work of the Holy Ghost in our Salvation*. Vol. 6 of *The Works of Thomas Goodwin*. Edinburgh: J. Nichol, 1863.

Gootjes, Albert. *Claude Pajon (1626–1685) and the Academy of Saumur: The First Controversy over Grace*. BSCH 64. Leiden: Brill, 2014.

———. "Un épisode méconnu de la vie de la communauté réformée au milieu du XVIIe siècle: La première controverse pajoniste sur la gràce." *Bulletin de la Société de l'histoire du protestantisme français* 156 (2010): 211-29.

Green, Joel B. "Conversion in Luke-Acts: God's Prevenience, Human Embodiment." In *The Unrelenting God: God's Action in Scripture*, edited by David J. Downs and Matthew L. Skinner, 15-41. Grand Rapids: Eerdmans, 2013.

———. "'To Turn from Darkness to Light' (Acts 26:18): Conversion in the Narrative of Luke-Acts." In *Conversion in the Wesleyan Tradition*, edited by Kenneth Collins and John H. Tyson, 103-18. Nashville: Abingdon, 2001.

Greene, Lawrence D. "Pathos." In *Encyclopedia of Rhetoric*, edited by Thomas O. Sloane, 554-69. Oxford: Oxford University Press, 2001.

Gu, Yueguo. "The Impasse of Perlocution." *JP* 20 (1993): 405-32.

Gundry, Stanley N. "John Owen on Authority and Scripture." In *Inerrancy and the Church*, edited by John D. Hannah, 189-222. Chicago: Moody Press, 1984.

Gundry Volf, Judith M. *Paul and Perseverance: Staying in and Falling Away*. WUNT 2/37. Tübingen: J.C.B. Mohr, 1990.

Gunton, Colin. *The One, the Three, and the Many: God, Creation, and the Culture of Modernity*. Cambridge: Cambridge University Press, 1993.

Habets, Myk. "'Suffer the Little Children to Come to Me, for Theirs Is the Kingdom of Heaven': Infant Salvation and the Destiny of the Severely Mentally Disabled." In *Evangelical Calvinism: Essays Resourcing the Continuing Reformation of the Church*, edited by Myk Habets and Bobby Grow, 287-328. Eugene, OR: Wipf & Stock, 2012.

Hafemann, Scott J. *2 Corinthians*. NIVAC. Grand Rapids: Zondervan, 2000.

Hamilton, James. *God's Indwelling Presence: The Holy Spirit in the Old and New Testaments*. NAC Studies in Bible and Theology. Nashville: Broadman & Holman, 2006.

Harris, Murray J. *The Second Epistle to the Corinthians: A Commentary on the Greek Text*. NIGTC. Grand Rapids: Eerdmans, 2005.

Harrison, Carol. "Delectatio Victrix: Grace and Freedom in Saint Augustine." *SP* 28 (1993): 298-302.

Hart, David Bentley. "Providence and Causality: On Divine Innocence." In *The Providence of God: Deus Habet Consilium*, edited by Francesca Aran Murphy and Philip G. Ziegler, 34-56. London: T&T Clark, 2009.

Hastings, W. Ross. *Jonathan Edwards and the Life of God: Toward and Evangelical Theology of Participation*. Minneapolis: Fortress, 2015.

Hay, David M. "Paul's Understanding of Faith as Participation." In *Paul and His Theology*, edited by Stanley Porter, 45-76. Pauline Studies 3. Leiden: Brill, 2006.

Hector, Kevin. "The Mediation of Christ's Normative Spirit: A Constructive Reading of Schleiermacher's Pneumatology." *ModTheo* 24 (2008): 1-22.

———. *Theology Without Metaphysics: God, Language, and the Spirit of Recognition.* Current Issues in Theology. Cambridge: Cambridge University Press, 2011.

Helm, Paul. *The Beginnings: Word and Spirit in Conversion.* Carlisle, PA: Banner of Truth, 1986.

———. "Calvin (and Zwingli) on Divine Providence." *CTJ* 29 (1994): 388-405.

———. *Faith, Form, and Fashion: Classical Reformed Theology and Its Postmodern Critics.* Eugene, OR: Cascade, 2014.

———. "Vanhoozer IV—The Personal and the Mechanical." *Helm's Deep.* August 1, 2010. http://paulhelmsdeep.blogspot.com/2010/08/vanhoozer-iv-personal-and-mechanical.html.

Helm, Paul, and Terrance Tiessen. "Does Calvinism Have Room for Middle Knowledge? A Conversation." *WTJ* 71 (2009): 437-54.

Heppe, Heinrich. *Reformed Dogmatics.* Edited by Ernst Bizer. Translated by G. Thomson. Grand Rapids: Baker, 1978.

Hobson, Theo. *The Rhetorical Word: Protestant Theology and the Rhetoric of Authority.* Aldershot: Ashgate, 2002.

Hodge, A. A. *Outlines of Theology.* New York: Armstrong, 1897.

Hodge, Charles. *Systematic Theology.* 3 vols. New York: Scribner, 1871. Reprint, Grand Rapids: Eerdmans, 1940.

Hoekema, Anthony. *Saved by Grace.* Grand Rapids: Eerdmans, 1989.

Hofius, Otfried. "Die Auferweckung des Lazarus: Joh 11,1-44 als Zeugnis narrativer Christologie." *ZTK* 102 (2005): 17-34.

Holmes, Michael W., ed. *The Apostolic Fathers: Greek Texts and English Translations.* Translated by J. B. Lightfoot. 2nd rev. ed. Grand Rapids: Baker, 1999.

Holmes, Stephen R. "Does Jonathan Edwards Use a Dispositional Ontology? A Response to Sang Hyun Lee." In *Jonathan Edwards: Philosophical Theologian*, edited by Paul Helm and Oliver Crisp, 99-114. Aldershot: Ashgate, 2003.

Hooker, Thomas. *The Application of Redemption.* London: Peter Cole, 1657. Reprint, New York: Arno, 1972.

Horton, Michael S. "Calvin's Theology of Union with Christ and the Double Grace: Modern Reception and Contemporary Possibilities." In *Calvin's Theology and Its Reception: Disputes, Developments, and New Possibilities*, edited by J. Todd Billings and I. John Hesselink, 72-94. Louisville, KY: Westminster John Knox, 2012.

———. *The Christian Faith: A Systematic Theology for Pilgrims on the Way.* Grand Rapids: Zondervan, 2011.

———. *Covenant and Salvation: Union with Christ*. Louisville, KY: Westminster John Knox, 2007.

———. *Lord and Servant: A Covenant Christology*. Louisville, KY: Westminster John Knox, 2005.

Howson, Barry H. *Erroneous and Schismatical Opinions: The Question of Orthodoxy Regarding the Theology of Hanserd Knollys (c. 1599–1691)*. Studies in the History of Christian Thought 99. Leiden: Brill, 2001.

Huijgen, Arnold. *Divine Accommodation in John Calvin's Theology: Analysis and Assessment*. Reformed Historical Theology 16. Göttingen: Vandenhoeck & Ruprecht, 2011.

Hütter, Reinhard. *Suffering Divine Things: Theology as Church Practice*. Translated by Doug Stott. Grand Rapids: Eerdmans, 2000.

Jarvis, Clive. "The Myth of High-Calvinism?" In *Recycling the Past or Researching History? Studies in Baptist Historiography and Myths*, edited by Philip E. Thompson and Anthony R. Cross, 231-63. Studies in Baptist History and Thought 11. Waynesboro, GA: Paternoster, 2005.

Jasper, David. *Rhetoric, Power and Community: An Exercise in Reserve*. Studies in Literature and Religion. London: Macmillan, 1993.

Jenson, Robert. "Response to Mark Seifrid, Paul Metzger, and Carl Trueman on Finnish Luther Research." *WTJ* 65 (2003): 245-50.

Johnson, Eric. "Rewording the Justification/Sanctification Relation with Some Help from Speech Act Theory." *JETS* 54 (2011): 767-85.

Johnson, Marcus. "The Highest Degree of Importance: Union with Christ and Soteriology." In *Evangelical Calvinism: Essays Resourcing the Continuing Reformation of the Church*, edited by Myk Habets and Bobby Grow, 222-52. Eugene, OR: Pickwick, 2012.

"A Joint Federal Vision Profession." Resources for Understanding the Federal Vision. June 2007. www.federal-vision.com/resources/joint_FV_Statement.pdf.

Jones, Serene. *Calvin and the Rhetoric of Piety*. CSRT. Louisville, KY: Westminster John Knox, 1995.

Jordan, James B. *Thoughts on Sovereign Grace and Regeneration: Some Tentative Explorations*. Biblical Horizons Occasional Paper 32. Niceville, FL: Biblical Horizons, n.d.

Jurieu, Pierre. *Traitté de la nature et de la grace*. 1687. Reprint, Hildesheim: Georg Olms, 1973.

Kapic, Kelly M. "The Spirit as Gift: Explorations in John Owen's Pneumatology." In *The Ashgate Research Companion to John Owen's Theology*, edited by Kelly

M. Kapic and Mark Jones, 113-40. Burlington, VT: Ashgate, 2012.
Keathley, Kenneth. *Salvation and Sovereignty: A Molinist Approach.* Nashville: Broadman & Holman, 2010.
Keener, Craig S. *The Gospel of John: A Commentary.* 2 vols. Peabody, MA: Hendrickson, 2003.
Kennedy, George A. *Classical Rhetoric and Its Christian and Secular Tradition from Ancient to Modern Times.* 2nd ed. Chapel Hill: University of North Carolina Press, 1999.
———. *A New History of Classical Rhetoric.* Princeton, NJ: Princeton University Press, 1994.
———. *New Testament Interpretation Through Rhetorical Criticism.* Chapel Hill: University of North Carolina Press, 1984.
Kim, Seyoon. *The Origin of Paul's Gospel.* Grand Rapids: Eerdmans, 1982.
———. *Paul and the New Perspective: Second Thoughts on The Origin of Paul's Gospel.* Grand Rapids: Eerdmans, 2001.
Kinneavy, James L. *Greek Rhetorical Origins of Christian Faith: An Inquiry.* New York: Oxford University Press, 1987.
Klein, William W. "Paul's Use of *Kalein*: A Proposal." *JETS* 27 (1984): 53-64.
Knapp, Henry M. "Augustine and Owen on Perseverance." *WTJ* 62 (2000): 65-87.
Koch, Dietrich-Alex. "The God-Fearers Between Facts and Fiction." *Studia Theologica* 60 (2006): 62-90.
Koester, Craig R. *The Word of Life: A Theology of John's Gospel.* Grand Rapids: Eerdmans, 2008.
Kolb, Robert. "Contemporary Lutheran Understandings of the Doctrine of Justification: A Selective Glimpse." In *Justification: What's at Stake in the Current Debates*, edited by Mark Husbands and Daniel Treier, 153-76. Downers Grove, IL: IVP Academic, 2004.
Kolb, Robert, and Timothy J. Wengert, eds. *The Book of Concord: The Confessions of the Evangelical Lutheran Church.* Minneapolis: Fortress, 2000.
Köstenberger, Andreas J. *John.* BECNT. Grand Rapids: Baker Academic, 2004.
———. "John." In *CNTUOT* 415-512.
Kraemer, Ross Shepard. *When Aseneth Met Joseph: A Late Antique Tale of the Biblical Patriarch and His Egyptian Wife, Reconsidered.* Oxford: Oxford University Press, 1998.
Krop, Henri A. "Philosophy and the Synod of Dordt: Aristotelianism, Humanism, and the Case Against Arminianism." In *Revisiting the Synod of*

Dordt (1618-1619), edited by Aza Goudriaan and F. A. van Lieburg, 49-79. BSCH 49. Leiden: Brill, 2011.

Kurzon, Dennis. "The Speech Act Status of Incitement: Perlocutionary Acts Revisited." *Journal of Pragmatics* 29 (1998): 571-96.

Kuyper, Abraham. *The Work of the Holy Spirit*. Translated by Henri De Vries. London: Funk & Wagnalls, 1900. Reprint, Grand Rapids: Eerdmans, 1946.

Kuzmič, Rhys. "*Beruf* and *Berufung* in Karl Barth's *Church Dogmatics*: Toward a Subversive Klesiology." *IJST* 7 (2005): 262-78.

Lee, Sang Hyun. *The Philosophical Theology of Jonathan Edwards*. Princeton, NJ: Princeton University Press, 1988.

Lemke, Steve W. "A Biblical and Theological Critique of Irresistible Grace." In *Whosoever Will: A Biblical-Theological Critique of Five-Point Calvinism*, edited by David L. Allen and Steve W. Lemke, 109-62. Nashville: Broadman & Holman Academic, 2010.

Long, Steven A. "Providence, Freedom, and Natural Law." *NV* 4 (2006): 557-606.

Lubac, Henri de. *Augustinianism and Modern Theology*. Translated by Lancelot Sheppard. New York: Herder and Herder, 1969.

Luckensmeyer, David. *The Eschatology of First Thessalonians*. NTOA 71. Göttingen: Vandenhoeck & Ruprecht, 2009.

Lunde, Jonathan M., and John Anthony Dunne. "Paul's Creative and Contextual Use of Isaiah in Ephesians 5:14." *JETS* 55 (2012): 87-110.

Luther, Martin. *Luthers Werke: Kritische Gesamtausgabe*. 97 vols. in 112 parts. Weimar: Böhlau, 1883-1985.

Mailhet, André E. *La théologie protestante au XVIIe siècle: Claude Pajon. Sa vie, son système religieux, ses controverses d'après des documents entièrement inédits*. Paris: Fischbacher, 1883.

Malherbe, Abraham J. *The Letters to the Thessalonians: A New Translation with Introduction and Commentary*. AB 32B. New York: Doubleday, 2000.

Mannermaa, Tuomo. *Christ Present in Faith: Luther's View of Justification*. Translated by Kirsi Stjerna. Minneapolis: Fortress, 2005.

———. "Why Is Luther So Fascinating? Modern Finnish Luther Research." In *Union with Christ: The New Finnish Interpretation of Luther*, edited by Carl E. Braaten and Robert Jenson. Grand Rapids: Eerdmans, 1998.

Marcu, Daniel. "Perlocutions: The Achilles' Heel of Speech Act Theory." *Journal of Pragmatics* 32 (2000): 1719-41.

Marshall, I. Howard. "Election and Calling to Salvation in 1 and 2 Thessalonians." In *The Thessalonian Correspondence*, edited by Raymond F. Collins, 259-76. BETL 87. Leuven: Leuven University Press, 1990.

Martikainen, Eeva. "Baptism." In *Engaging Luther: A (New) Theological Assessment*, edited by Olli-Pekka Vainio, 95-107. Eugene, OR: Cascade, 2010.

Mastricht, Peter van. *A Treatise on Regeneration*. 1699. Morgan, PA: Soli Deo Gloria, 2002.

Matson, David. *Household Conversion Narratives in Acts: Pattern and Interpretation*. Sheffield: Sheffield Academic Press, 1996.

Matthias, Markus. "*Ordo Salutis*—Zur Geschichte eines dogmatischen Begriffs." *ZKG* 115 (2004): 318-46.

Mayer, Cornelius P. "Delectatio (delectare)." In *Augustinus-Lexikon*, edited by Cornelius P. Mayer, 2:267-85. Basel: Schwabe, 1986.

McCormack, Bruce L. "What's at Stake in Current Debates over Justification? The Crisis of Protestantism in the West." In *Justification: What's at Stake in the Current Debates*, edited by Mark Husbands and Daniel Treier, 81-117. Downers Grove, IL: IVP Academic, 2004.

McDonald, Suzanne. "Beholding the Glory of God in the Face of Jesus Christ: John Owen and the 'Reforming' of the Beatific Vision." In *The Ashgate Research Companion to John Owen's Theology*, edited by Kelly M. Kapic and Mark Jones, 141-58. Burlington, VT: Ashgate, 2012.

McGowan, A. T. B. "Justification and the *Ordo Salutis*." In *Justification in Perspective: Historical Developments and Contemporary Challenges*, edited by Bruce L. McCormack, 147-63. Grand Rapids: Baker Academic, 2006.

McKnight, Scot. *Turning to Jesus: The Sociology of Conversion in the Gospels*. Louisville, KY: Westminster John Knox, 2002.

Mihailovic, Alexandar. *Corporeal Words: Mikhail Bakhtin's Theology of Discourse*. Evanston, IL: Northwestern University Press, 1997.

Mihalios, Stefanos. *The Danielic Eschatological Hour in the Johannine Literature*. LNTS. London: T&T Clark, 2011.

Miley, John. *Systematic Theology*. New York: Hunt & Eaton, 1892.

Moltmann, Jurgen. *The Spirit of Life: A Universal Affirmation*. Minneapolis: Fortress, 1992.

Moo, Douglas J. "Creation and New Creation." *Bulletin for Biblical Research* 20 (2010): 39-60.

———. *The Epistle to the Romans*. NICNT. Grand Rapids: Eerdmans, 1996.

———. *The Letters to the Colossians and to Philemon*. PiNTC. Grand Rapids: Eerdmans, 2008.

Morimoto, Anri. *Jonathan Edwards and the Catholic Vision of Salvation*. University Park: Pennsylvania State University Press, 1995.

Moritz, Thorsten. *Profound Mystery: The Use of the Old Testament in Ephesians*. NovTSup 85. Leiden: Brill, 1996.

Morlan, David S. *Conversion in Luke and Paul: An Exegetical and Theological Exploration*. LNTS. Edinburgh: T&T Clark, 2012.
Moxnes, Halvor. *Theology in Conflict: Studies in Paul's Understanding of God in Romans*. NovTSup 53. Leiden: Brill, 1980.
Muller, Richard A. *Calvin and the Reformed Tradition: On the Work of Christ and the Order of Salvation*. Grand Rapids: Baker Academic, 2012.
———. *Dictionary of Latin and Greek Theological Terms: Drawn Principally from Protestant Scholastic Theology*. Grand Rapids: Baker, 1985.
———. "Perkins' *A Golden Chaine*: Predestinarian System or Schematized *Ordo Salutis*?" *Sixteenth Century Journal* 9 (1978): 68-81.
———. *Post-Reformation Reformed Dogmatics: The Rise and Development of Reformed Orthodoxy, ca. 1520 to ca. 1725*. 4 vols. Grand Rapids: Baker Academic, 2003.
Murray, Ian. *Spurgeon v. Hyper-Calvinism: The Battle for Gospel Preaching*. Edinburgh: Banner of Truth, 1995.
Murray, John. *Collected Writings of John Murray*. 4 vols. Carlisle, PA: Banner of Truth, 1977.
———. *Redemption, Accomplished and Applied*. Grand Rapids: Eerdmans, 1955.
Narducci, Emanuele. "*Orator* and the Definition of the Ideal Orator." In *Brill's Companion to Cicero: Oratory and Rhetoric*, edited by James M. May, translated by James M. May, 427-44. Leiden: Brill, 2002.
Nock, Arthur D. *Conversion: The Old and the New in Religion from Alexander the Great to Augustine of Hippo*. Oxford: Clarendon, 1933.
O'Brien, Peter. *The Letter to the Ephesians*. PiNTC. Grand Rapids: Eerdmans, 1999.
O'Connell, Robert J. *Images of Conversion in St. Augustine's Confessions*. New York: Fordham University Press, 1996.
Olson, Roger. *Against Calvinism*. Grand Rapids: Zondervan, 2011.
Ortlund, Dane. "Inaugurated Glorification: Revisiting Romans 8:30." *JETS* 57 (2014): 111-33.
Osborne, Thomas M., Jr. "Thomist Premotion and Contemporary Philosophy of Religion." *NV* 4 (2006): 607-32.
Owen, John. *The Works of John Owen*. Edited by William H. Goold. 16 vols. London: Johnstone & Hunter, 1852. Reprint, Carlisle, PA: Banner of Truth, 1965-1968.
Pajon, Claude. "Sommaire de la Doctrine de M. Pajon, sur le sujet de la Grâce." In *La théologie protestante au XVIIe siècle: Claude Pajon. Sa vie, son système religieux, ses controverses d'après des documents entièrement inédits*, edited by André E. Mailhet, 69-97. Paris: Fischbacher, 1883.

———. "Traité de l'opération de l'Esprit de Dieu en la conversion de l'homme." In *La théologie protestante au XVIIe siècle: Claude Pajon. Sa vie, son système religieux, ses controverses d'après des documents entièrement inédits*, edited by André E. Mailhet, 97-146. Paris: Fischbacher, 1883.

Parnham, David. "The Humbling of High Presumption: Tobias Crisp Dismantles the Puritan *Ordo Salutis*." *JEH* 56 (2005): 50-74.

Peace, Richard. *Conversion in the New Testament: Paul and the Twelve*. Grand Rapids: Eerdmans, 1999.

Pelikan, Jaroslav. *Acts*. Brazos Theological Commentary on the Bible. Grand Rapids: Brazos, 2005.

Pelikan, Jaroslav, and Valerie Hotchkiss, eds. *Creeds and Confessions of Faith in the Christian Tradition*. 4 vols. New Haven, CT: Yale University Press, 2003.

Perelman, Chaim, and L. Olbrechts-Tyteca. *The New Rhetoric: A Treatise on Argumentation*. Translated by John Wilkinson and Purcell Weaver. Notre Dame, IN: University of Notre Dame Press, 1969.

Peura, Simo. "Christ as Favor and Gift (*Donum*): The Challenge of Luther's Understanding of Justification." In *Union with Christ: The New Finnish Interpretation of Luther*, edited by Carl E. Braaten and Robert Jenson, 42-75. Grand Rapids: Eerdmans, 1998.

Pieper, Franz. *Christian Dogmatics*. Translated by Theodore Engelder. 4 vols. St. Louis: Concordia, 1950.

Piper, John. *Finally Alive: What Happens When We Are Born Again*. Minneapolis: Desiring God, 2009.

———. *The Justification of God: An Exegetical and Theological Study of Romans 9:1-23*. 2nd ed. Grand Rapids: Baker, 1993.

Pope, William. *A Compendium of Christian Theology: Being Analytical Outlines of a Course of Theological Study, Biblical, Dogmatic, Historical*. 2nd ed. New York: Hunt & Eaton, 1889.

Poythress, Vern S. "Reforming Ontology and Logic in the Light of the Trinity: An Application of Van Til's Idea of Analogy." *WTJ* 57 (1995): 187-219.

Rambo, Lewis. *Understanding Religious Conversion*. New Haven, CT: Yale University Press, 1993.

Ramm, Bernard. *The Witness of the Spirit*. Grand Rapids: Eerdmans, 1960.

Rex, Walter. *Essays on Pierre Bayle and Religious Controversy*. International Archives of the History of Ideas 8. The Hague: Martinus Nijhoff, 1965.

Ridderbos, Herman N. *The Gospel According to John: A Theological Commentary*. Translated by John Vriend. Grand Rapids: Eerdmans, 1997.

———. *Paul: An Outline of His Theology*. Translated by John Richard De Witt. Grand Rapids: Eerdmans, 1975.

Robbins, Vernon K. *Exploring the Texture of Texts: A Guide to Socio-rhetorical Interpretation*. Valley Forge, PA: Trinity Press International, 1996.

Rollock, Robert. *A Treatise of God's Effectual Calling*. Translated by Henry Holland. Vol. 1 of *Select Works of Robert Rollock*. London: Kyngston, 1603. Reprint, Edinburgh: Wodrow Society, 1849.

Ruler, J. A. van. *The Crisis of Causality: Voetius and Descartes on God, Nature and Change*. Brill's Studies in Intellectual History 66. Leiden: Brill, 1995.

———. "New Philosophy to Old Standards: Voetius' Vindication of Divine Concurrence and Secondary Causality." *Nederlands Archief voor Kerkgeschiedenis* 71 (1991): 58-91.

Schaeffer, Hans. *Createdness and Ethics: The Doctrine of Creation and Theological Ethics in the Theology of Colin E. Gunton and Oswald Bayer*. Theologische Bibliothek Töpelmann 137. Berlin: de Gruyter, 2006.

Schaff, Philip, ed. *The Creeds of Christendom: With a History and Critical Notes*. 3 vols. 6th ed. Harper & Row, 1931. Reprint, Grand Rapids: Baker, 1983.

Schleiermacher, Friedrich. *The Christian Faith*. Edited by H. R. Mackintosh and J. S. Stewart. Edinburgh: T&T Clark, 1928. Reprint, New York: T&T Clark, 1999.

———. *Der christliche Glaube nach den Grundsätzen der evangelischen Kirche im Zusammenhange dargestellt*. Edited by Rolf Schäfer. 2nd ed. KGA 1:13/1-2. Berlin: de Gruyter, 2003.

Schmid, Heinrich. *The Doctrinal Theology of the Evangelical Lutheran Church*. Translated by Charles Hay and Henry Eyster Jacobs. 3rd rev. ed. Philadelphia: Lutheran Publication Society, 1899. Reprint, Minneapolis: Augsburg, 1961.

Schmidt, K. L. "Καλέω κτλ." In *TDNT* 3:487-536.

Schnelle, Udo. *Theology of the New Testament*. Translated by M. Eugene Boring. Grand Rapids: Baker Academic, 2009.

Schreiner, Thomas R. "Corporate and Individual Election in Romans 9: A Response to Brian Abasciano." *JETS* 49 (2006): 373-86.

———. *Paul, Apostle of God's Glory in Christ: A Pauline Theology*. Downers Grove, IL: InterVarsity Press, 2001.

———. *Romans*. BECNT. Grand Rapids: Baker, 1998.

Schreiner, Thomas R., and Ardel B. Caneday. *The Race Set Before Us: A Biblical Theology of Perseverance and Assurance*. Downers Grove, IL: InterVarsity Press, 2001.

Schultz, Walter J. "Jonathan Edwards's Concept of an Original Ultimate End." *JETS* 56 (2013): 107-22.

———. "Jonathan Edwards's *End of Creation*: An Exposition and Defense." *JETS* 49 (2006): 247-71.

Schumacher, Lydia. *Divine Illumination: The History and Future of Augustine's Theory of Knowledge*. Malden, MA: Wiley-Blackwell, 2011.

Schurb, Ken. "The New Finnish School of Luther Research and Philip Melanchthon." *Logia* 12 (2003): 31-36.

Schweitzer, William M. *God Is a Communicative Being: Divine Communicativeness and Harmony in the Theology of Jonathan Edwards*. SST. Edinburgh: T&T Clark, 2012.

Schwöbel, Christoph. "God as Conversation: Reflections on a Theological Ontology of Communicative Relations." In *Theology and Conversation: Towards a Relational Theology*, edited by Jacques Haers and Peter De Mey, 43-67. BETL. Leuven: Peeters, 2003.

Searle, John. "A Classification of Illocutionary Acts." *Language in Society* 5 (1976): 1-23.

Seifrid, Mark A. "Romans." In *CNTUOT* 607-94.

Shedd, William. *Dogmatic Theology*. Edinburgh: T&T Clark, 1889. Reprint, Grand Rapids: Zondervan, 1953.

Shepherd, Norman. *The Call of Grace: How the Covenant Illuminates Salvation and Evangelism*. Phillipsburg, NJ: P&R, 2000.

Sinnema, D. "Reformed Scholasticism and the Synod of Dort (1618–19)." In *John Calvin's Institutes: His Opus Magnum*, edited by B. J. van der Walt, 467-506. Potchefstroom: Institute for Reformational Studies, 1986.

Smith, Craig R. *Rhetoric and Human Consciousness*. 4th ed. Long Grove, IL: Waveland, 2013.

Smith, James K. A. "Between Predication and Silence: Augustine on How (Not) to Speak of God." *HeyJ* 41 (2000): 66-86.

———. *Imagining the Kingdom: How Worship Works*. Cultural Liturgies 2. Grand Rapids: Baker Academic, 2013.

Spence, Alan. *Incarnation and Inspiration: John Owen and the Coherence of Christology*. London: T&T Clark, 2007.

———. *The Promise of Peace: A Unified Theory of Atonement*. London: T&T Clark, 2006.

Springer, Elise. *Communicating Moral Concern: An Ethics of Critical Responsiveness*. Cambridge, MA: MIT Press, 2013.

Stam, Frans P. van. *The Controversy over the Theology of Saumur, 1635–1650:*

Disrupting Debates Among the Huguenots in Complicated Circumstances. Amsterdam: APA-Holland University Press, 1988.

Stanciu, Diana. "The Feelings of the Master as Articles of Faith or Medicine against Heresy? Jansenius' Polemics Against the 'New Pelagians.'" *Ephemerides Theologicae Lovanienses* 87 (2011): 393-418.

Stendahl, Krister. "Paul Among Jews and Gentiles." In *Paul Among Jews and Gentiles: and Other Essays*, 1-77. Philadelphia: Fortress Press, 1976.

Stenschke, Christoph. *Luke's Portrait of the Gentiles Prior to Their Coming to Faith.* WUNT 2/108. Tübingen: Mohr Siebeck, 1999.

Stoever, William K. B. *"A Faire and Easie Way to Heaven": Covenant Theology and Antinomianism in Early Massachusetts.* Middletown, CT: Wesleyan University Press, 1978.

Strauss, David Friedrich. *Die christliche Glaubenslehre in ihrer geschichtlichen Entwicklung und im Kampfe mit der modernen Wissenschaft dargestellt.* 2 vols. Tübingen: C. F. Osiander, 1840.

Strayer, Brian E. *Suffering Saints: Jansenists and* Convulsionnaires *in France, 1640-1799.* Brighton: Sussex Academic Press, 2008.

Strobel, Kyle C. *Jonathan Edwards's Theology: A Reinterpretation.* SST 19. London: Bloomsbury T&T Clark, 2013.

Strong, Augustus Hopkins. *Systematic Theology: A Compendium and Commonplace-Book Designed for the Use of Theological Students.* Philadelphia: Judson, 1907.

Stuhlmacher, Peter. *Biblische Theologie des Neuen Testaments.* Göttingen: Vandenhoeck & Ruprecht, 1999.

Tannehill, Robert C. *The Acts of the Apostles.* Vol. 2 of *The Narrative Unity of Luke-Acts: A Literary Interpretation.* Minneapolis: Fortress, 1990.

Tanner, Kathryn. *Christ the Key.* Current Issues in Theology. Cambridge: Cambridge University Press, 2010.

———. *God and Creation in Christian Theology: Tyranny or Empowerment.* Oxford: Blackwell, 1988.

TeSelle, Eugene. "Exploring the Inner Conflict: Augustine's Sermons on Romans 7 and 8." In *Augustine: Biblical Exegete*, edited by Frederick Van Fleteren and Joseph C. Schnaubelt, 313-45. Augustinian Historical Institute. New York: Peter Lang, 2004.

Thiel, John. Review of David Cunningham, *Faithful Persuasion.* TS 54 (1993): 366-68.

Thiselton, Anthony. *The Hermeneutics of Doctrine.* Grand Rapids: Eerdmans, 2007.

Thompson, Marianne Meye. *The God of the Gospel of John*. Grand Rapids: Eerdmans, 2001.

———. "The Raising of Lazarus in John 11: A Theological Reading." In *The Gospel of John and Christian Theology*, edited by Richard Bauckham and Carl Mosser, 233-44. Grand Rapids: Eerdmans, 2008.

Thrall, Margaret E. *A Critical and Exegetical Commentary on The Second Epistle to the Corinthians*. 2 vols. ICC. Edinburgh: T&T Clark, 1994.

Tiessen, Terrance. "Why Calvinists Should Believe in Divine Middle Knowledge, Although They Reject Molinism." *WTJ* 69 (2006): 345-66.

Toon, Peter. *The Emergence of Hyper-Calvinism in English Nonconformity, 1689-1765*. London: Olive Tree, 1967.

Treier, Daniel J. "Proof Text." In *DTIB* 622-24.

Trueman, Carl. *The Claims of Truth: John Owen's Trinitarian Theology*. Carlisle, UK: Paternoster, 1998.

———. "Is the Finnish Line a New Beginning? A Critical Assessment of the Reading of Luther Offered by the Helsinki Circle." *WTJ* 65 (2003): 231-44.

Turretin, Francis. *Institutio theologiae elencticae, in qua status controversiae perspicuè exponitur, praecipua orthodoxorum argumenta proponuntur & vindicantur, & fontes solutionum aperiuntur*. Geneva: Apud Samuelem De Tournes, 1688.

———. *Institutes of Elenctic Theology*. Edited by James T. Dennison Jr. Translated by George Musgrave Giger. 3 vols. Phillipsburg, NJ: P&R, 1992.

Vainio, Olli-Pekka, ed. *Engaging Luther: A (New) Theological Assessment*. Eugene, OR: Cascade, 2010.

———. *Justification and Participation in Christ: The Development of the Lutheran Doctrine of Justification from Luther to the Formula of Concord (1580)*. SMRT 130. Leiden: Brill, 2008.

Vanhoozer, Kevin J. "Discourse on Matter: Hermeneutics and the 'Miracle' of Understanding." *IJST* 7 (2005): 5-37.

———. *The Drama of Doctrine: A Canonical-Linguistic Approach to Christian Theology*. Louisville, KY: Westminster John Knox, 2005.

———. "Effectual Call or Causal Effect? Summons, Sovereignty and Supervenient Grace." In *First Theology: God, Scripture and Hermeneutics*, 96-124. Downers Grove, IL: InterVarsity Press, 2002.

———. "From Speech Acts to Scripture Acts: The Covenant of Discourse and the Discourse of the Covenant." In *First Theology: God, Scripture and Hermeneutics*, 159-203. Downers Grove, IL: InterVarsity Press, 2002.

———. *Remythologizing Theology: Divine Action, Passion, and Authorship*. CSCD. Cambridge: Cambridge University Press, 2010.

Velde, R. T. te, ed. *Synopsis Purioris Theologiae: Synopsis of a Purer Theology. Latin Text and English Translation*. Vol. 2. Studies in Medieval and Reformation Traditions. Leiden: Brill, forthcoming.

Venema, Cornelis P. "The Election and Salvation of the Children of Believers Who Die in Infancy: A Study of Article I/17 of the Canons of Dort." *MJT* 17 (2006): 57-100.

Walker, Jeffrey. "*Pathos* and *Katharsis* in 'Aristotelian' Rhetoric: Some Implications." In *Rereading Aristotle's "Rhetoric,"* edited by Alan G. Gross and Arthur E. Walzer, 74-92. Carbondale, IL: Southern Illinois University Press, 2000.

———. *Rhetoric and Poetics in Antiquity*. Oxford: Oxford University Press, 2000.

Wanamaker, Charles A. *The Epistles to the Thessalonians: A Commentary on the Greek Text*. NIGTC. Grand Rapids: Eerdmans, 1990.

Warfield, Benjamin B. "The Development of the Doctrine of Infant Salvation." In *Two Studies in the History of Doctrine*, 143-239. New York: Christian Literature Crusade, 1897. Reprint, Eugene, OR: Wipf & Stock, 2001.

Webb, Stephen. *The Divine Voice: Christian Proclamation and the Theology of Sound*. Grand Rapids: Brazos, 2004.

Webster, John. *The Domain of the Word: Scripture and Theological Reasoning*. London: T&T Clark, 2012.

———. *Holy Scripture: A Dogmatic Sketch*. Cambridge: Cambridge University Press, 2003.

———. "Illumination." *JRT* 5 (2011): 325-40.

———. "'It Was the Will of the Lord to Bruise Him': Soteriology and the Doctrine of God." In *God of Salvation: Soteriology in Theological Perspective*, edited by Ivor Davidson and Murray Rae, 15-34. Burlington, VT: Ashgate, 2011.

———. "On the Theology of Providence." In *The Providence of God: Deus Habet Consilium*, edited by Francesca Aran Murphy and Philip G. Ziegler, 158-75. London: T&T Clark, 2009.

———. "Prolegomena to Christology: Four Theses." In *Confessing God: Essays in Christian Dogmatics*, 2:131-49. London: T&T Clark, 2005.

Wenk, Matthias. "Conversion and Initiation: A Pentecostal View of Biblical and Patristic Perspectives." *JPT* 17 (2000): 56-80.

Wesley, John. "The Scripture-Way of Salvation: A Sermon on Ephes. ii. 8." In *Sermons, II, 34-70*, vol. 2 of *The Works of John Wesley*, edited by Albert C. Outler, 153-69. Nashville: Abingdon, 1985.

White, Jonathan Anthony. "A Theological and Historical Examination of John Gill's Soteriology in Relation to Eighteenth-Century Hyper-Calvinism." PhD diss., Southern Baptist Theological Seminary, 2010.

Wiederkehr, Dietrich. *Die Theologie der Berufung in den Paulusbriefen*. Studia Friburgensia 36. Freiburg: Universitätsverlag, 1963.

Wiley, H. Orton. *Christian Theology*. 3 vols. Kansas City, MO: Beacon Hill, 1952.

Willis, E. David. "Rhetoric and Responsibility in Calvin's Theology." In *The Context of Contemporary Theology: Essays in Honor of Paul Lehmann*, edited by Alexander J. McKelway and E. David Willis, 43-63. Atlanta: John Knox, 1974.

Wisse, Jakob. *Ethos and Pathos: From Aristotle to Cicero*. Amsterdam: Adolf M. Hakkert, 1989.

Wisse, Maarten, and Hugo Meijer. "Pneumatology: Tradition and Renewal." In *A Companion to Reformed Orthodoxy*, edited by Herman J. Selderhuis, 466-517. BCCT 40. Leiden: Brill, 2013.

Witherington, Ben, III. *John's Wisdom: A Commentary on the Fourth Gospel*. Louisville, KY: Westminster John Knox, 1995.

———. *New Testament Rhetoric: An Introductory Guide to the Art of Persuasion in and of the New Testament*. Eugene, OR: Cascade, 2009.

———. *The Problem with Evangelical Theology: Testing the Exegetical Foundations of Calvinism, Dispensationalism, and Wesleyanism*. Waco, TX: Baylor University Press, 2005.

Witsius, Herman. *The Economy of the Covenants Between God and Man: Comprehending A Complete Body of Divinity*. Translated by William Crookshank. 2 vols. 1693. Reprint, Edinburgh: Thomas Turnbull, 1803.

Wolterstorff, Nicholas. "Authorial Discourse Interpretation." In *DTIB* 78-80.

———. *Divine Discourse: Philosophical Reflections on the Claim That God Speaks*. Cambridge: Cambridge University Press, 1995.

Wright, David F. "Calvin's Accommodating God." In *Calvinus Sincerioris Religionis Vindex: Calvin as Protector of the Purer Religion*, edited by Wilhelm H. Neuser and Brian G. Armstrong, 3-19. Sixteenth Century Essays and Studies 36. Kirksville, MO: Sixteenth Century Journal, 1997.

———. *Infant Baptism in Historical Perspective: Collected Studies*. Eugene, OR: Wipf & Stock, 2007.

———. "Was John Calvin a 'Rhetorical Theologian'?" In *Calvin Studies IX: Papers Presented at the Ninth Colloquium on Calvin Studies*, edited by John H. Leith and Robert A. Johnson, 46-69. Davidson, NC: Davidson College, 1998.

Wright, N. T. *Paul: In Fresh Perspective*. Minneapolis: Fortress, 2005.

———. *The Resurrection of the Son of God*. Christian Origins and the Question of God 3. Minneapolis: Fortress Press, 2003.

Wright, Scott R. "Regeneration and Redemptive History." PhD diss., Westminster Theological Seminary, 1999.

Young, William. "Historic Calvinism and Neo-Calvinism. Part 1 & 2." *WTJ* 36 (1973): 48-64, 156-73.

Zachman, Randall C. *The Assurance of Faith: Conscience in the Theology of Martin Luther and John Calvin*. Minneapolis: Fortress, 1993.

General Index

Abasciano, Brian J., 42-43, 53-56
Abraham (patriarch), 73
  faith of, 50
  family of, 51-52, 54
absolution, word of, 64, 66-67
Academy of Saumur, 101-2
accommodation
  examples of divine, 181
  participation in communication, 182
Achtemeier, Paul J., 82
Allen, R. Michael, 1, 42
Alston, William, 184
Ambrose, Saint, 93
Ames, William, 13, 41, 139, 216
Andrews, James A., 177, 179
Aquinas, Thomas, 2, 10, 11, 34, 153, 160
  definition of calling in, 10
Aristotle, 170, 190, 196-97, 201
Arminian theology, 2, 3, 52, 100, 126, 163, 206
Arminius, Jacob, 2, 8
Armstrong, Brian, 101, 186
Arnold, Duane W. II., 177
Ascough, Richard, 205
Asselt, W. J. van, 106, 107
assurance of salvation, 7, 57
atonement, doctrine of, 19
attunement, 114-15, 117, 199
Augustine
  on baptismal regeneration, 217
  conversion account, 17-18, 75
  on effectual calling, 2, 6
  on human mutual dependence, 179
  on illumination, 80, 93
  on Lazarus, raising of, 129
  perseverance, doctrine of, 57
  on preaching and divine aid, 176-79
  rhetoric and, 171, 177-79, 190, 201
  on victorious delight, 203-4
Augustinian tradition, 7, 12, 21, 203
Aune, David, 137
Austin, J. L., 184
authorial analogy, 34, 168
Bac, J. Martin, 106-7
Bakhtin, Mikhail, 34-37, 165
Balla, Peter, 90
Balserak, Jon, 180-82
baptism, 64-68, 126, 137, 142
  circumcision and, 144
  controversy in Dutch Reformed Church, 28
  eschatological transition, 138
  illumination as, 93
  regeneration and, 217
Barclay, John M. G., 75
Barnett, Paul, 171
Barrett, C. K., 85
Barrett, Matthew, 69
Barth, Karl
  on effectual calling, 215
  on illumination, 79
  on Jesus Christ as calling, 192-94, 216
  on justification, 72
  on Lazarus, raising of, 131, 136
  on order of salvation, 221-23
  providence, doctrine of, 106, 107, 108
  word of God, doctrine of, 174, 199-200
Barth, Markus, 84
Battles, Ford Lewis, 180
Bavinck, Herman, 12-14, 38, 224
  on effectual calling before regeneration, 28
  on effectual calling, power of, 1, 29
  on God's call as unified, 214-15
  on infant salvation, 218-20
  Jansen and, 203
  Kuyper, disagreement with, 23-25
  on Lydia's conversion, 205
  providence, doctrine of, 109
  on regeneration, 123, 124
  on word as instrument, 27-30, 131-32
Bayer, Oswald, 22, 62-68, 71, 73, 76
Beale, G. K., 46, 85-86, 89, 134
Beasley-Murray, G. R., 137
Beeke, Joel R., 97
Bellarmine, Robert, 35, 38, 176
Belleville, Linda, 136-37
Belt, Henk van den, 2, 28, 202
Berkhof, Louis, 24, 25, 140
Berkouwer, G. C., 10, 25, 222
Bernard, Robert W., 177
Best, Ernest, 140, 142
Beza, Theodore, 8
biblical reasoning, 19

biblical theology, 126, 146, 165
Bieder, Werner, 42
Billings, J. Todd, 181
Blumenberg, H., 80
Bombaro, John J., 152
Boyle, Marjorie O'Rourke, 195
Bright, Pamela, 177
Brümmer, Vincent, 185
Bruner, Frederick Dale, 131
Brunner, Emil, 6
Burns, J. Patout, 177, 203
Byrne, Brendan, 43
Caldwell, Robert W., III, 152
calling
 as invitation, 53
 lifestyle in response to, 59
 New Testament use, 22
 sphere of life, 2
 See also effectual calling; *kalein* (to call)
calling in Paul
 conversion and, 48
 creation from nothing and, 50
 gracious, 44
 historic experience of conversion, 49
 selective, 44
 undeserved, 44
Calvin, John, 138, 140
 on accommodation, 176, 177, 179-82
 on calling in Scripture, 51
 on effectual calling, 6-7, 42
 on illumination, 94
 on ineffectual call, 6, 57-58
 on Lazarus, raising of, 131-32
 on Lydia, conversion of, 205
 new birth in, 136-37
 Osiander and, 73
 on physical agency, 13, 15
 on regeneration, 166
 on regeneration as repentance, 10
 on testimony of the Holy Spirit, 98, 119
 on word and spirit, 23, 24, 163
Cameron, John, 101, 186
Candler, Peter M., Jr., 172

Caneday, Ardel B., 57
Carleton, George, 12, 165, 186
Carson, D. A., 136, 137, 138, 140
Cary, Phillip, 7
Catholic theology, 126, 203
Cavadini, John, 177, 178
Charnock, Stephen, 132
Cherry, Conrad, 152
Chester, Stephen J., 16, 42, 51
Christology, 28
Cicero, Marcus Tullius, 171, 172, 177, 188, 190, 201
circumcision, spiritual, 144
Clark, David K., 220
Clavier, Mark F. M., 177, 178, 179
Cleveland, Christopher, 32, 152
Coenen, L., 42
Cohen, Charles, 205
Colijn, Brenda B., 17, 20
Collins, Kenneth J., 3, 223
coming to life. *See* resurrection
communicative agency, 34
communicative theism, 158-64
Compier, Don H., 170
concursus. *See* providence, doctrine of
contingency, 107
continuous creation, 155
conversion, 57, 58
 human experience of, 16, 17
 interpreted as divine action, 46
 Lydia as example of, 206
 mediated by the Word, 112
 physical action, 12
 Schleiermacher and, 111-14
converting change, 6, 16-17, 21, 22, 39, 80, 81, 87, 109
 definition of, 17
 divine action in, 151
 metaphors in Scripture, 39
 necessity of preached word, 132
 ontology of, 123, 124, 147
 unmediated, 155
Council of Trent, 7
covenantal ontology, 32
Cox, Samuel, 149

Cranfield, C. E. B., 56
creation from nothing, 33, 51, 52, 73, 158, 164, 185
Crisp, Oliver, 150, 155
Crisp, Tobias, 70
Cullmann, Oscar, 195
Cunningham, David, 172, 174, 175, 191
Davidson, Ivor, 80
death, spiritual, 139
declarative (speech-act type), 65, 71, 185
decree of God, 72
delectatio victrix, 203-4
Denney, James, 46
determinism, causal, 106, 108
DeVries, Dawn, 112
dialogical author, 35
dialogism, 173
dialogue, 37, 162, 165
 theology as, 174
directive (speech act type), 76
divine action, interpersonal, 36
divine decree, 163
divine light, 81
 in creation, 90, 96
 power of regeneration, 99
divine rhetoric, 74, 180
 Lydia's conversion and, 206
divine teaching, 204
Dodd, C. H., 133
dogmatic account, 1, 42, 79, 213
Dort, Synod of, 4, 8, 9, 11, 29, 35, 125, 147, 165, 203, 217
 affirmation in Reformed tradition, 23-30
 effectual calling and, 9
 persuasion and, 186
 preaching and regeneration and, 11
double-agency discourse, 45
Dowey, Edward A., Jr., 94, 181
Doyle, William, 203
Dunn, James D. G., 18, 42, 43, 89, 144
Dunne, John A., 83, 84
Ebeling, Gerhard, 64
Eberhard, Philippe, 160
Eckert, J., 42
Edwards, Jonathan, 22, 124, 150-58, 165

General Index

on communicative being,
  God as, 125, 159
on divine and supernatural
  light, 18, 198
on divine speech, 189
on Holy Spirit, presence
  of, 154, 156, 162, 166, 147
on Lazarus, resurrection
  of, 128-29
on new spiritual nature,
  153
on passivity in conversion,
  157, 149
on sense of the heart, 160
effective word, 63-65, 73
effectual calling, 2
  appeal to non-Calvinists,
    2-4
  biblical term, 19
  casting call, 33
  communicative, 4, 31
  content of the call, 61-77,
    62
  creation and, 51, 52
  definition of, 4, 59, 213
  dialogue and, 3, 34-36, 166
  discourse, 161
  divided into two calls, 74
  dogmatic questions for,
    21-22
  Edwards and, 150
  ethos of, 190, 191, 194
  external, 132
  following regeneration,
    24-26
  forensic verdict, 72
  history of, 6-16
  Holy Spirit, work of, 32, 35
  human passivity in, 8
  human proclamation and,
    28, 45, 61, 197
  illumination and, 79, 118,
    120-22
  individualized, 165
  infant salvation and, 219
  mechanistic, accusation
    of, 3, 6
  medium of, 22, 226
  metaphorical, 4, 28
  objections to, 52-58
  objective declaration, 26
  order of salvation, 221, 223

Pauline evidence for, 42-45
  personal encounter, 4, 22
  persuasion and, 215
  power of, 167
  relationship to
    regeneration, 5, 6, 12, 23,
    26, 124, 165-68, 224
  result of election, 7, 9, 57
  resurrection, 202
  speech, 4, 22, 23, 38
  speech, metaphorical, 4, 28
  summons, 26, 43, 45, 53,
    61, 63, 70, 73, 76, 121, 185
  triune rhetoric, 189-90,
    209-11
election, doctrine of, 54, 223
  basis for calling, 7, 9, 57
  warrant for faith, 69
Elliot, Matthew, 204
enlightenment. *See*
  illumination
Enos, Richard Leo, 177
Erasmus of Rotterdam, 101,
  186, 194
eternal justification, 28, 69
Evans, William B., 138, 221
external call, 13, 14, 69
  relation to internal call,
    214
faculty psychology, 104
faith, 123, 215
  as ability and act, 130
  Abraham's, 50
  Christ as the form of, 68
  fiducia, 66
  hearing and, 41
  order of salvation and, 222
  passive, 64, 65
Fatio, Olivier, 101, 104
federal vision, 138
Fee, Gordon, 47, 49, 87
Ferguson, Sinclair B., 222
Fesko, John V., 43, 72, 97, 221
filioque, 202
Finnish interpretation of
  Luther, 67-68
Flavel, John, 101, 140, 204, 209
Forde, Gerhard O., 63, 65
foreknowledge, 43
Fowler, James, 17
Frame, John, 32, 43, 222
Furnish, Victor Paul, 88

Gadamer, Hans-Georg, 160
Gaffin, Richard, 126, 141, 142,
  167, 215
Garrigou-Lagrange, Réginald,
  38
Gaventa, Beverly, 16, 19, 89
Gilkey, Langdon, 106
Gill, John, 62, 69, 70, 74, 129,
  220
God the Father
  agent of the call, 214
  grammar and, 189
  originator of the call, 5, 191
  role in effectual calling,
    190-94
God's glory, 90
God's speech, 4, 28, 30, 32, 38,
  41, 61, 68, 165, 166, 167
  creative word, 50, 71
  effectiveness of, 182
  human words and, 176, 182
  normative stance of, 61
  persuasion and, 188
Goodwin, Thomas, 219
Gootjes, Albert, 75, 101, 102,
  104, 105, 106, 108
gospel, 64, 90
grace
  congruent, 35, 38
  immediate, 103, 109
  irresistible, 205
  universal, 65
Green, Joel, 16, 86
Greene, Lawrence D., 201
Gregory of Nazianzus, 93
Gu, Yueguo, 184
Gundry, Stanley N., 94
Gundry Volf, Judith M., 57
Gunton, Colin, 5, 201
Guyraut, Jacques, 102
Habets, Myk, 217
habitus, 26, 32, 147, 160
Hafemann, Scott J., 87
Hamilton, James, 219
Harris, Murray J., 90, 200
Harrison, Carol, 203
Hart, David Bentley, 3, 31, 106
Hastings, W. Ross, 156
Hay, David M., 169
heart, 216
Hector, Kevin, 111, 113, 114, 115,
  116

Heidelberg Catechism, 144
Helm, Paul, 26, 37, 38, 106, 159
Heppe, Heinrich, 8, 26, 66, 132, 144, 186
hermeneutic of suspicion, 173
high Calvinists. *See* hyper-Calvinism
history of salvation, 141
Hobson, Theo, 172, 173, 174
Hodge, A. A., 26
Hodge, Charles, 15, 132, 149, 167, 186
Hoekema, Anthony, 26, 44, 69
Hofius, Otfried, 135
Hollatz, David, 85, 222
Holmes, Stephen R., 150
Holy Spirit, 48
  agency in calling, 5
  dependence on, 152
  effectual calling and, 32, 35
  eschatological gift, 84, 87
  illumination and, 119
  mediated through word, 101
  "mother of events," 109
  normative judgments and, 111
  pathos, 201-3
  personal presence of, 73, 149, 151, 155-58, 164
  regeneration and, 9
  resurrection and, 125
  as rhetoric, 189
  unmediated work of, 25, 70, 158, 163, 166, 168
  work as mysterious, 13
Horton, Michael, 22, 39
  Bayer, similarity to, 62
  on content of effectual calling, 23, 71-73, 76
  on effectual calling, 23, 31-34, 37
  justification, doctrine of, 67, 74
  on Lazarus, raising of, 131
  on personal agency, 31
  on speech-act theory, 162
  on testimony of the Holy Spirit, 119
Howson, Barry H., 69
Huijgen, Arnold, 180
human beings, dialogical nature of, 23
Hütter, Reinhard, 64
hyper-Calvinism, 62, 68-70, 74, 76, 226

Ignatius of Antioch, 194
illocution, 76, 162, 182, 183, 184
illumination, 22
  conversion as, 80
  effectual calling and, 120-22
  epistemology and, 80
  with God's word as means, 103
  narrative of, 100
  in Owen, 94-100
  personal encounter, 82
  preparatory, 95-96
  scriptural, 97-99
  scriptural evidence for, 80, 82-91
  soteriological, 81, 87
  testimony and, 117
immediate grace, 103, 109
ineffectual call, 57
infant salvation, 22, 217-21
infused habits, 119, 130, 150, 160
  See also *habitus*
infused qualities, 140, 146
internal call, 6, 26, 69
Irenaeus of Lyon, 137
Jansen, Cornelius, 203
Jarvis, Clive, 69
Jasper, David, 173, 188
Jenson, Robert, 67, 68
Jesus Christ
  beauty of, 198
  divine light, 91
  face of, 90
  influence of, 110, 111, 115
  logos of effectual calling, 194-201
  personal encounter with, 81, 88
  rhetoric and, 198-201
Jesus is your saving Lord, 74-76, 198, 214, 216
Johnson, Eric, 71
Johnson, Marcus, 71
Jones, Mark, 97
Jones, Serene, 180

Jordan, James, 138
Jurieu, Pierre, 101, 106
justification, doctrine of, 31, 53, 62, 64, 68, 69, 71, 72
  announcement, 32
  faith, 43
  hearing, 63
  verdict, 74
  works of the law, 54
Justin Martyr, 93, 137
kalein (to call), 42, 44, 46, 48, 50, 53, 74, 82
  definition of, 44
  historic conversion, 58
  naming sense, 53-57, 55
  Old Testament usage, 54
  "the one who calls," 47
  spoken word, 56
  summons, 55, 56
  use in Jewish texts, 51
Kapic, Kelly M., 94
Keathley, Kenneth, 18, 134
Keener, Craig S., 138
Kennedy, George A., 169, 170, 171, 172, 189
Kim, Seyoon, 74, 89, 90
Kinneavy, James L., 169
Klein, William W., 42, 53, 56
Knapp, Henry M., 57
Koch, Dietrich-Alex, 206
Koester, Craig R., 135
Kolb, Robert, 63
Köstenberger, Andreas J., 133, 136
Kraemer, Ross Shepard, 52
Krop, Henri A., 14
Kurzon, Dennis, 184
Kuyper, Abraham, 24, 25, 27, 30, 131, 218
Kuzmič, Rhys, 192
Lazarus, 128-32, 164
Lee, Sang Hyun, 150
Lemke, Steve W., 126
libertarian freedom, 206
light
  Christians as, 83-84
  eschatological epoch, 82-83
  Jesus Christ as, 83
  locution, 183
Long, Steven A., 106
lordship in the New Testament, 75

General Index 257

Lubac, Henri de, 203
Luckensmeyer, David, 48
Lunde, Jonathan, 83, 84
Luther, Martin, 41, 61, 63, 64, 65, 66, 189
  and block of wood, 13
  Finnish interpretation of, 67-68, 73
Lutheran Book of Concord, 64, 65
Lutheran theology, 22, 31, 62, 126, 206, 217
  See also Hollatz, David
Lydia's conversion, 61, 192, 205-9
Maccovius, Johannes, 14, 25
Mailhet, André E., 101, 102
Malherbe, Abraham J., 45, 48, 49
Mannermaa, Tuomo, 62, 67, 68, 73
Marcu, Daniel, 184
Marshall, I. Howard, 53, 57
Martikainen, Eeva, 68
Mastricht, Peter van, 14, 15, 129, 130, 136, 140, 149
Matson, David, 205
Matthias, Markus, 85, 221
Mayer, Cornelius P., 203
McCormack, Bruce, 32, 71, 72
McDonald, Suzanne, 94
McGowan, A. T. B., 221, 222
McKnight, Scott, 16, 17
mechanical causality, 31
Meijer, Hugo, 94
metaphors for converting change, 22
metaphysics, 108
middle voice, 161, 163
Mihailovic, Alexandar, 35
Mihalios, Stefanos, 133, 134, 135
Miley, John, 3
Molinism, 38, 176
Moltmann, Jürgen, 202
Moo, Douglas J., 43, 55, 56, 117, 140, 144, 192
moral agency, 14, 95
  effective, 28
Morimoto, Anri, 152
Moritz, Thorsten, 83
Morlan, David S., 42

Moxnes, Halvor, 51, 56
Muller, Richard A., 8, 38, 107, 125, 130, 221, 222
Murray, Iain, 69
Murray, John, 5, 23, 24, 26-27, 27, 30, 32, 36, 38, 43, 136
Narducci, Emanuele, 201
nature, change of, 153
new birth, 136-39
  regeneration as, 136
new covenant, 139
new creation, 72, 117, 145
Nock, Arthur D., 16
O'Brien, Peter, 83, 84
occasionalism, 155
  Jonathan Edwards and, 154
O'Connell, Robert J., 203
Olbrechts-Tyteca, L., 205
Olson, Roger, 163, 187
operative grace, 26
order of salvation, 22, 31, 71, 125, 146, 221-25
  effectual calling in, 224
  infused habits, 32
  Lutheran, 85
  union with Christ and, 222
Ortlund, Dane, 43
Osborne, Thomas M., Jr., 107
Osiander, Andreas, 73
Owen, John, 149
  filioque in, 202
  on Holy Spirit, work of, 5, 118, 155
  on illumination, 22, 81, 93-100, 110, 191
  on infused qualities, 32, 140, 152, 160
  on Lazarus, raising of, 129
  on persuasion, 186
  on physical agency, 14
  on preparationism, 165
  on regeneration, 15, 24
  on testimony of the Holy Spirit, 99, 119-20
  on union with Christ, 72
Pajon, Claude, 22
  on human proclamation, 93, 100, 102, 109, 118
  on illumination, 101-10
  on immediate grace, 102-3
  on intellectualism, 104-6, 110

  on Lazarus, raising of, 131
  providence, doctrine of, 37, 106-9, 112, 116, 208
panentheism, 36
Parnham, David, 70
passivity, 8, 163
  conversion, 127
  regeneration, 141
pathos, 170, 201-3
  Aristotle and, 171, 190
  emotion and, 189, 201, 204, 210
  Holy Spirit and, 201
  Lydia's conversion and, 208
  objection to, 204-5
Paul (apostle)
  on conversion as calling, 88
  Damascus Road, 85, 88, 89, 193
  metaphors for conversion, 18
  power dynamics in, 173
  raised with Christ in, 139-45
Peace, Richard, 16, 85, 86
Pelikan, Jaroslav, 85
Perelman, Chaim, 205
performative (speech-act type), 71, 185
perlocution, 162, 183-85, 184
  effect, 33
  force, 32
  Holy Spirit and, 183
perseverance, doctrine of, 7, 57-58, 138
personal presence, 216
persuasion, 5
  definition of, 210
  effectual calling as type of, 22, 35-36, 101, 197, 209, 215
  faith and, 169
  God's participation in, 175, 179, 210
  gospel proclamation as, 95-96, 97, 171, 196
  Holy Spirit, work of, 168
  insufficient for conversion, 14, 16, 33
  objection to, 204, 205
  pathos and, 203

rhetoric and, 170, 172, 174, 176
speech-act theory and, 184-85
Synod of Dort and, 186
tender necessity of, 187-88
testimony of the Holy Spirit, 119
theology as, 174
Peura, Simo, 68
physical agency, 14, 16, 158
Pieper, Francis, 207
Pighius, Albert, 163
Piper, John, 54, 131
Polycarp, Saint, 174
Pope, William, 52
Poythress, Vern S., 201
preaching, 29
  as means of conversion, 13
  See also effectual calling: human proclamation and; proclamation
predestination, 7, 43
premotionism, 106, 107, 109
  See also providence, doctrine of
preparationism, 165
presumptive regeneration, 25
prevenient grace, 86, 206
process theology, 36
proclamation
  Christ present in, 67
  means for opening eyes, 87
  means of regeneration, 29
promissio, 62, 63, 66, 73
  perseverance denied, 65
providence, doctrine of, 37, 105, 106-9, 112, 116, 208
  concursus, 108
  middle knowledge, 38
  premotionism and, 107
Rambo, Lewis, 17
Ramm, Bernard, 98, 119
Reformed orthodoxy
  agency, God's, 30, 34, 38, 113
  early modern, 94
  effectual calling, 2
  Enlightenment and, 149
  new life, 140, 146
  persuasion, 211
  Schleiermacher and, 110

Reformed theology, 117
  baptism, 217
  exegesis, 44
  illumination, 121
  regeneration, 124
Reformed tradition
  definition of, 2
  effectual calling, 6, 21, 214, 223
  French, 101
  Holy Spirit, work of, 13
  hyper-Calvinism, 69
  illumination, 93
  infused qualities, 36
  passivity, human, 163
  regeneration, 26
  Schleiermacher and, 81
regeneration, 5
  apart from means, 11, 24, 102
  baptism of infants, 25
  before effectual calling, 24-26
  biblical metaphors for, 150
  causal categories, 6
  definition of, 15
  following effectual calling, 225
  good trees and, 11-12
  Holy Spirit in, 166
  illumination as preparatory, 95-96
  infused qualities, 8-11, 10, 15, 36
  internal call, 26
  narrow sense of, 125
  new life, 6
  New Testament evidence, 127
  Owen and, 94
  passivity in, 37, 158
  physical agency, 31, 96
  prior to faith, 10
  relation to effectual calling, 12, 23, 165-68
  resurrection, 142
  Schleiermacher and, 111
  sense of the heart, 152
  Synod of Dort, 9
Remonstrants, 2, 8, 10, 11, 103, 218
  resistible grace and, 9

remythologizing. *See under* Vanhoozer, Kevin
resurrection, 165
  converting change and, 124
  eschatological transition, 167
  inaugurated, 135
  Old Testament and, 84, 133
  spiritual, 6, 127, 128, 132-35, 139, 140, 145, 168, 215
  substitute for calling, 5
Rex, Walter, 106
rhetoric
  definition of, 170
  divine, 74, 180
  enthymeme, 196-97
  as genre for theology, 172-75
  God's speech as, 177
  logos, 194-201
  New Testament and, 170
  paradigm, 197
  pathos and, 201-3, 204
  radical Christian, 172, 189
rhetorical criticism, 172
Ridderbos, Herman N., 137, 146
righteousness, passive, 63
Robbins, Vernon, 170
Rollock, Robert, 8
Roman Catholic theology, 126, 203
Ruler, J. A. van, 106
salvation, doctrine of, 20
sanctification, doctrine of, 71
Saumur, Academy of, 101-2
saving illumination. *See* soteriological illumination
Schaeffer, Hans, 63
Schleiermacher, Friedrich, 2, 22
  Holy Spirit in, 81, 115
  on illumination, 111
  on influence of Jesus Christ, 93, 110, 113, 114, 120, 216
  on personal presence, 100, 111-12, 199
  providence, doctrine of, 112, 116, 154, 200

General Index 259

on redemption, 113
on regeneration, 117
on word, proclaimed, 111-14, 190
Schmid, Heinrich, 66, 85
Schmidt, K. L., 42
Schnelle, Udo, 140
Schreiner, Thomas, 42, 43, 44, 51, 55, 57, 140, 143
Schultz, Walter J., 156
Schumacher, Lydia, 80, 93
Schurb, Ken, 68
Schweitzer, William, 155
Schwöbel, Christoph, 189, 197
Scripture
　doctrine of, 183
　God's speech in, 191
　illumination of, 97-99
Searle, John, 65
secondary cause, 154
Seifrid, Mark A., 56
Shedd, William, 24, 25
Shepherd, Norman, 226
Sinnema, D., 14
Smith, James K. A., 114, 209
soteriological illumination, 90, 111, 120
　John Owen and, 96-97
special call, 6, 26
speech-act theory, 182-86
　See also illocution; locution; perlocution
Spence, Alan, 94
Springer, Elise, 184, 185
Stam, Frans P. van, 101
Stanciu, Diana, 203
Stendahl, Kirster, 89
Stenschke, Christoph, 206
Stjerna, Kirsi, 67
Stoever, William K. B., 70
Strauss, David Friedrich, 98
Strayer, Brian E., 203
Strobel, Kyle, 156, 168
Strong, Augustus Hopkins, 26
Stuhlmacher, Peter, 142
suasion, 101, 186
Swain, Scott R., 42
Synod of Dort. *See* Dort, Synod of
systematic theology, 20
Tannehill, Robert C., 85
Tanner, Kathryn, 106, 163

TeSelle, Eugene, 203
Testard, Paul, 75, 102
testimony, 80
　God's, 93
　personal, 120
testimony of the Holy Spirit, 81, 97, 98, 119, 120, 121, 122
theodrama, 159
Thiel, John, 174
Thiselton, Anthony, 159, 169
Thompson, Marianne Meye, 131, 135
Thrall, Margaret E., 90
Tiessen, Terrance, 38
Toon, Peter, 69
total depravity, 104, 162
Treier, Daniel J., 42
trinitarian appropriations, 32, 170, 183, 189, 190-203, 210
　Lydia's conversion and, 207
triune God
　communication of, 156
　participation in effectual calling, 168
　union with, 157, 158
triune rhetoric, 4, 5, 22, 42, 169, 225
　effectual calling as, 210
Trueman, Carl, 68, 202
Turretin, Francis
　covenant in, 58
　on Holy Spirit, work of, 150, 155, 204, 205
　on human ability to speak, 13
　on hyperphysical operation, 14, 125
　on Lazarus, raising of, 130-31
　Pajon and, 101
　on persuasion, 105, 175-76, 186-89
　on premotionism, 106, 108, 109
　on providence and conversion, 37-38, 208
　on regeneration, 12
　on salvation of infants, 220
　on victorious delight, 204
union with Christ, 62, 68, 71, 74, 167
　ontological, 67, 76

Vainio, Olli-Pekka, 67
Vanhoozer, Kevin, 23
　on action, communicative, 118, 159
　on authorial analogy, 34, 168
　on communicative theism, 34-36, 150, 158-59, 163, 195
　on effectual calling, communicative, 22, 31, 39, 124, 163
　on God's speech in Scripture, 176
　on Lazarus, raising of, 131
　on Lydia's conversion, 36, 208
　on middle voice, 160-61
　on objections to dialogical call, 36-38
　on persuasion, 162
　on remythologizing, 20-21
　on speech-act theory, 183
Velde, Roelf T. te, 106, 107, 147, 192
Venema, Cornelius P., 218
verbum efficax (effective word), 63-65, 73
victorious delight, 203-4
vocatio efficax, 8
　See also effectual calling
Voetius, Gisbertus, 25, 107, 108
Walker, Jeffrey, 170, 201
Wanamaker, Charles A., 45
Warfield, Benjamin B., 218, 220
Webb, Stephen, 172, 174, 194, 195, 202
Webster, John, 1, 19, 20, 80, 94, 106, 118, 197, 199
Wenk, Matthias, 18
Wesley, John, 3
Wesleyan tradition, 3, 223
Westminster Confession of Faith, 5, 57, 217, 219
Westminster Shorter Catechism, 4, 5, 74, 197, 215
White, Jonathan Anthony, 69
Wiederkehr, Dietrich, 42
Wiley, Morton, 52

Willis, E. David, 180
Wisse, Maarten, 94, 201
Witherington, Ben, III, 43, 57, 136, 170, 196
Witsius, Herman, 15, 186, 187, 188, 189
Wolterstorff, Nicholas, 45, 75

word of God
  doctrine of, 199, 216
  instrument of calling, 61
  Jesus Christ as present, 67, 111
  justifying verdict, 64
  object of faith, 66

Wright, David F., 144, 177, 180, 181
Wright, N. T., 42, 53, 75, 143
Wright, Scott R., 141
Young, William, 25
Zachman, Randall C., 7

Scripture Index

OLD TESTAMENT

Genesis
1:3, *33, 90, 96*
17:5, *50, 51*
21:12, *54, 55*

Deuteronomy
1:39, *217*
10:16, *144*
30:6, *144*

Judges
13:5, *219*
13:7, *219*

2 Samuel
12:23, *217*

2 Kings
4:26, *217*
5:14, *137*

Psalms
19:8, *80*
36:9, *80*
43:3, *80*
119:18, *80*

Isaiah
9:1, *84*
9:2, *90*
11:2, *192*
26:19, *84, 124*
32:15, *137*
41:2, *51*
41:4, *51*
41:9, *51*
42:6, *51*
42:6-7, *85*
42:7, *86*
42:16, *86*
43:1, *51*
43:21, *82*
44:3, *137*
45:3-4, *51*
46:11, *51*
48:12, *51*
48:13, *51*
48:15, *51*
49:1, *51, 219*
49:6, *85*
51:2, *51*
51:17, *84*
52:11, *72*
55:1, *70*
55:1-3, *72*
55:11-13, *72*
59–60, *84, 87*
59:9-10, *84*
59:16, *84*
59:21, *84*
60, *84*
60:1, *84*
60:1-3, *84*
60:3, *84*
60:5, *84*

Jeremiah
1.5, *217, 219*
1:7-8, *85*
4:4, *144*

Ezekiel
2:1-3, *85*
16:6, *124*
16:21, *217*
36, *138*
36–37, *138*
36:25-27, *137, 139*
36:26, *124*
36:27, *48, 138*
37:5, *131*
37:14, *48, 124*

Daniel
7, *133*
7:13, *133*
8:17, *133*
8:19, *133*
11:6, *133*
11:35, *133*
11:40, *133*
11:45, *133*
12:1, *133*
12:2, *124, 133, 134*
12:13, *133*

Hosea
2:1, *55*
2:25 (LXX), *55, 56*

Joel
2:32, *192*
3:5, *192*

APOCRYPHA

2 Maccabees
1:3-4, *207*
7:9, *133*

4 Maccabees
15:3, *133*

NEW TESTAMENT

Matthew
2:18, *217*
10:19-20, *178*
11:28, *200*
12:33, *11, 12*
16:16, *151*
16:28, *137*
19:14, *217*
19:28, *127*
22:14, *53, 57*
23:27, *181*
23:37, *70*
28:18, *200*

Mark
4:39, *27*
5:41, *131*
7:34, *63*
9:1, *137*
9:24, *227*
10:13-16, *217*
11:14, *27*

Luke
1:15, *219*
1:16-17, *85*
1:41-45, *219*
1:44, *217*
1:67-79, *219*
1:77-79, *83*
2:30-32, *83*
9:27, *137*
10:7-8, *206*
24:25, *207*
24:31, *86*
24:31-32, *207*
24:32, *207*

John
1:1, *194*
1:4-14, *83*
3, *136*
3:3, *18, 128, 136, 137*
3:3-5, *124, 136, 139, 167*
3:5, *126, 127, 128, 136, 137, 147*
3:6, *136, 138*
3:8, *5, 205*
3:10, *137*

3:14-16, *194*
3:21, *117*
3:22-24, *137*
3:36, *136, 137*
4:14, *153*
4:50, *135*
5, *132, 135*
5:8, *135*
5:19-29, *133*
5:20-30, *135*
5:21, *133, 135*
5:21-29, *124*
5:24, *133, 134*
5:24-25, *133, 134, 135*
5:25, *128, 129, 132, 133, 134, 135, 139, 163, 199*
5:27, *133*
5:28, *133*
5:28-29, *128, 132, 133, 135*
5:36-38, *120*
6:44, *187*
6:44-45, *194*
6:63, *124, 135, 142*
7:38-39, *137, 153*
11, *131, 135*
11:14, *128*
11:17, *128*
11:21, *128*
11:23-26, *135*
11:25, *135*
11:32, *128*
11:43, *130, 131*
11:43-44, *124, 128*
12:32, *187, 194*
14:9, *137*
19:35, *137*

Acts
2:6, *207*
2:36, *192*
2:39, *192*
5:31, *86*
8:6, *207*
8:26-40, *178*
9:3, *88*
9:20, *193*
10, *178*
10:46, *207*
10:48, *206*
11:18, *86*

11:21, *206*
13:14-43, *196*
13:26, *206*
13:47, *85*
13:48, *7*
13:50, *206*
14:15, *206*
15:3, *206*
15:12, *207*
15:19, *206*
16:13-15, *206*
16:14, *36, 61, 192, 207*
16:15, *192*
17:1-9, *46*
17:4, *171, 206*
17:7, *76*
17:12, *206*
17:15-34, *196*
18:4, *171*
19:8, *171*
22:6, *88*
22:9, *88*
22:11, *88*
22:14, *88*
22:14-15, *193*
22:22, *207*
26:6-7, *193*
26:13, *85, 88*
26:16, *86*
26:16-18, *85*
26:17-18, *222*
26:18, *80, 86, 87*
26:20, *85*
26:22-23, *193*
28:23, *171*

Romans
1–8, *43*
1:1, *44, 58*
1:4, *193*
1:5, *192*
1:6, *44, 58, 192*
1:7, *58*
2:28-29, *144*
3:21–4:25, *50*
4, *73*
4:3, *50*
4:16, *50*
4:16-17, *54*
4:17, *33, 50, 51, 52, 53, 58, 64, 65, 72, 73, 131*

4:18, *50*
4:24, *50*
5:1, *43*
5:5, *203*
5:8, *141*
6:3-4, *142*
6:17, *96*
7, *203*
8, *43, 194, 221*
8:9, *200*
8:16, *70*
8:27, *45*
8:28, *58*
8:28-30, *16, 43, 53, 57, 221, 222*
8:29, *43*
8:29-30, *192*
8:30, *5, 26, 43, 44, 52, 56, 58*
9, *42, 43, 53, 54, 55, 56*
9–10, *42*
9:1-23, *54*
9:2, *54*
9:7, *53, 55, 56*
9:7-8, *55*
9:8, *54, 55*
9:9, *55*
9:11, *45, 54*
9:12, *58*
9:22-26, *55*
9:24, *43, 44, 55, 56*
9:24-25, *53*
9:24-26, *55, 58*
9:25, *55, 56*
9:25-26, *55*
9:26, *55, 56*
10:9, *90*
10:17, *74*
11:2, *43*
11:5, *45*
11:6, *54*
11:7, *45*
11:28, *45*
11:29, *59*
12:2, *96*
13:8, *173*
13:11, *45*
13:11-14, *83*
13:12-13, *75*
15:18-19, *190*

1 Corinthians
1:1, *58*
1:1-2, *44*
1:2, *58, 123*
1:7-9, *57*
1:9, *4, 5, 7, 26, 58, 123, 192, 215, 223*
1:17, *171, 180*
1:18, *126*
1:22-23, *196*
1:22-31, *172*
1:23, *43*
1:23-24, *194*
1:24, *43, 44, 58*
1:24-26, *52*
1:24-28, *44*
1:26, *58, 123*
1:26-28, *53*
1:27-28, *44*
1:30, *222*
2:13-15, *96*
3:5, *49*
6:11, *222*
7:14, *218*
7:15, *58*
7:17, *58, 192*
7:19, *146*
7:20, *52, 58*
8:5-6, *75*
9:1, *89*
12:3, *90*
15:1-8, *64*
15:8, *89*
15:45, *142*

2 Corinthians
3:6, *142*
3:8, *87*
3:13, *89*
3:14, *87*
3:16-17, *87*
3:18, *96, 117*
4:1-6, *87, 88*
4:2, *171*
4:4, *89, 90*
4:4-6, *198*
4:5, *88, 90*
4:6, *18, 80, 87, 88, 89, 90, 91, 96, 99, 116, 117, 121, 200*
4:7, *90*
4:16, *142, 215*

Scripture Index

5:11, *171*
5:17, *117, 167*
5:19, *19*
5:20, *200*

Galatians
1–4, *63*
1:6, *44, 58, 76, 88*
1:10, *171*
1:15, *5, 52, 56, 58, 76, 219*
1:15-16, *43, 44, 88, 89, 121*
3:1, *196*
3:26-29, *54*
5:6, *146*
5:8, *44, 58*
5:13, *58, 123*
6:14-15, *76*
6:15, *145*

Ephesians
1:17, *192*
1:17-18, *5, 192*
1:17-19, *80*
1:18, *59*
1:20-21, *143*
1:20-23, *142*
2, *127, 139, 140, 141, 146, 167*
2:1, *128, 145*
2:1-3, *146*
2:1-10, *124, 139, 143, 146*
2:2, *136, 141*
2:3, *146*
2:4-6, *141*
2:4-10, *146*
2:5, *18, 125, 136, 139, 140, 142, 143, 146, 147, 158*
2:5-6, *141*
2:6, *143*
2:10, *140, 141, 146*
2:11-12, *145*
2:12, *126*
4:1, *44, 58, 59, 123*

4:4, *44, 58, 59, 123*
4:5, *142*
4:17-18, *84*
5, *87*
5:8, *83*
5:9-12, *83*
5:11, *83*
5:13, *83*
5:13-14, *83*
5:14, *83, 84*

Philippians
1:12-19, *215*
1:19, *200*
2:12-13, *101, 186*
3:14, *49, 52, 59, 123*
4:3, *58*

Colossians
1:12, *82*
1:12-13, *80, 82*
1:13, *82*
1:20, *145*
1:22, *144, 145*
2, *127, 139, 143, 144, 167*
2:4, *144*
2:10, *144*
2:11, *144*
2:11-12, *144*
2:11-13, *140, 144*
2:11-14, *124, 143, 144, 145*
2:12, *144*
2:13, *125, 139, 141, 144, 145*
2:13-14, *144*
2:18, *145*
3:15, *58*

1 Thessalonians
1:2-5, *45*
1:4, *57*
1:5, *45, 46*
1:6, *45*
1:9-10, *70, 76*
2:1, *45*

2:1-10, *190*
2:2, *46*
2:8, *46, 49, 115*
2:9, *46*
2:12, *45, 47, 49, 53, 58, 120, 123*
2:12-13, *49*
2:13, *47*
4:5, *48*
4:6, *48*
4:7, *45, 47, 50, 58*
4:7-8, *48, 49*
5:1-10, *83*
5:23-24, *48, 49, 57, 94*
5:24, *45, 58*

2 Thessalonians
1:8, *49*
1:8-10, *49*
1:10, *49*
1:11, *45, 49, 59, 123*
1:11-12, *49, 50*
2, *46*
2:3, *46*
2:12, *46, 47*
2:13-14, *46, 47, 49*
2:13-15, *46*
2:14, *4, 18, 45, 46, 47, 49, 53, 56, 58, 61, 77, 214*

1 Timothy
1:16, *44*
5:17-18, *196*
6:12, *58, 120, 224*
6:16, *80*

2 Timothy
1:8-9, *192*
1:9, *26, 58, 59*
2:24-26, *172*

Titus
3:3, *127*
3:5, *16, 126, 127, 167*

Hebrews
1:2, *194*
3:1, *58*
5:4, *58*
6:4, *58, 80*
9:15, *58*
10:32, *80*
11:8, *58*
11:18, *58*

James
1:18, *103, 124, 139, 224*

1 Peter
1:15, *58, 123*
1:23, *124, 139, 224*
1:23-25, *28*
2:9, *58, 120, 123, 214*
2:9-10, *80, 82*
2:10, *82*
2:21, *58*
3:9, *58, 224*
5:10, *58, 224*

2 Peter
1:3, *58*

1 John
1:5, *80*
2:8, *83*
2:15-17, *76*
2:20, *187*
2:29, *139*
3:9, *139*
4:7, *139*
5:1, *139*
5:4, *139*
5:18, *139*

Jude
1, *58*

Revelation
17:14, *58*

The Studies in Christian Doctrine and Scripture Series

Studies in Christian Doctrine and Scripture promotes evangelical contributions to systematic theology, seeking fresh understanding of Christian doctrine through creatively faithful engagement with Scripture in dialogue with catholic tradition(s).

Thus: We aim to publish **contributions to systematic theology** rather than merely descriptive rehearsals of biblical theology, historical retrievals of classic or contemporary theologians, or hermeneutical reflections on theological method—volumes that are plentifully and expertly published elsewhere.

We aim to promote **evangelical** contributions, neither retreating from broader dialogue into a narrow version of this identity on the one hand, nor running away from the biblical preoccupation of our heritage on the other hand.

We seek fresh understanding of Christian doctrine **through creatively faithful engagement with Scripture.** To some fellow evangelicals and interested others today, we commend the classic evangelical commitment of engaging Scripture. To other fellow evangelicals today, we commend a contemporary aim to engage Scripture with creative fidelity. The church is to be always reforming—but always reforming according to the Word of God.

We seek **fresh understanding of Christian doctrine.** We do not promote a singular method; we welcome proposals appealing to biblical theology, the history of interpretation, theological interpretation of Scripture, or still other approaches. We welcome projects that engage in detailed exegesis as well as those that appropriate broader biblical themes and patterns. Ultimately, we hope to promote relating Scripture to doctrinal understanding in material, not just formal, ways.

We promote scriptural engagement **in dialogue with catholic tradition(s).** A periodic evangelical weakness is relative disinterest in the church's shared creedal heritage, in churches' particular confessions, and more generally in the history of dogmatic reflection. Beyond existing efforts to enhance understanding of themes and corpora in biblical theology, then, we hope to foster engagement with Scripture that bears upon and learns from loci, themes, or crucial questions in classic dogmatics and contemporary systematic theology.

Finding the Textbook You Need

The IVP Academic Textbook Selector
is an online tool for instantly finding the IVP books
suitable for over 250 courses across 24 disciplines.

ivpacademic.com